D1607580

Toronto's Provincial Assembly
October 1994.

Errata

P. 175, photo caption, last line, please add Cybulski
P. 290, photo caption, last line, please add Glavine
P. 294, photo caption, please add Curtin

Redemption and Renewal

Paul Lacerda

Ad memoriam
Anthony (Tony) McBriarty, *CSsR*
(1885–1952)
*whose work as an archivist made this
history so much easier to write*

Redemption and Renewal

The Redemptorists of English Canada, 1834–1994

Paul Laverdure

Dundurn Press
Toronto • Oxford

Editor: Diane Mew
Designer: Sebastian Vasile
Printer: Best Book Manufacturers

Canadian Cataloguing in Publication Data

Main entry under title:

Laverdure, Paul
    Redemption and renewal: the Redemptorists of English Canada

Includes bibliographical references and index.
ISBN 1-55002-272-5

1. Redemptorists — Canada — History.
I. Title.

BX4020.Z5C37 1996   255/.64/00971   C96–990003–1

Publication was assisted by the Canada Council, the Book Publishing Industry Development Program of the Department of Canadian Heritage, and the Ontario Arts Council.

Printed and bound in Canada

Printed on recycled paper.

Dundurn Press
2181 Queen Street East
Suite 301
Toronto, Ontario, Canada
M4E 1E5

Dundurn Press
73 Lime Walk
Headington, Oxford
England
OX3 7AD

Dundurn Press
250 Sonwil Drive
Buffalo, NY
U.S.A. 14225

CONTENTS

ILLUSTRATIONS

CHARTS, 1919–94

MAPS

Preface

The Redemptorists of the Toronto Province (Eastern English Canada) approached me in the spring of 1989 to act as their representative for a team researching and writing a multi-volume history of the Redemptorists in the world. They also hoped that my work for the international project would become a separately published history of the Redemptorists in English Canada. This book is the result of that hope.

Why did the Redemptorists of the Toronto Province want a history? Since the Second Vatican Council, every religious congregation has been turning to its origins in order to renew itself. The Redemptorists of English Canada had long felt the need for a closer look at their own history, because their origins had almost been forgotten. This is not surprising. The history of the Redemptorists in English Canada, born in the aftermath of the fall of Napoleon, is overwhelmingly complex and more ancient than most historians of Canadian Catholicism know. The Toronto Province was founded from the United States, but it included houses founded from Belgium, directed Ukrainian houses in Canada for some years, had missions in Japan, men in the British West Indies, students in England, Ireland, Germany, Poland, and Italy, military chaplains almost everywhere, and was the only province for all of English Canada from 1918 to 1961.

Before the creation of the Toronto Province in 1918, over three hundred Redemptorists, from Europe, the United States, and Canada, had worked in English Canada. Between 1918 and 1994 the Redemptorists attracted another seven hundred men, making this one of the largest congregations in Canada. English-Canadian Redemptorists have long known that their impact was important and their history significantly different from both French-Canadian and American religious histories to deserve separate treatment.

When the Redemptorist General Government in Rome last set up a history project in 1948, Anthony McBriarty of the Toronto Province began to collect materials and organize the archives. Unfortunately, when he died suddenly in 1952 he left his historical work unfinished. There have been many attempts since by other Redemptorists to write parts of their history in Canada. Only short, scattered manuscripts came of their efforts, mainly because all of these men, notably Fathers George Daly, Frederick Coghlan, and Daniel Ehman, turned to history late in life and while they were still busy with other work.

When in 1989 the Toronto Province approached me to write their history, I eagerly accepted the project. The history of the English-Canadian Redemptorists is a church historian's dream: big enough to present a challenge yet well-defined enough to be manageable. I also accepted to write this history because there is an obvious lack of information in English about Roman Catholic religious orders. While several women's congregations and more and more congregations of men in Canada, such as the Jesuits, the Oblates, the Sulpicians, and the Brothers of the Christian Schools are producing dictionaries, encyclopedias, biographies, and histories, little of it is in English.

Why else did I accept? I have had a life-long knowledge of individual Redemptorists. With one uncle a Redemptorist in the French-Canadian Province of Ste-Anne-de-Beaupré, a distant cousin a Redemptoristine, and with parents who grew up in a French-Canadian Redemptorist parish, I have had considerable exposure to the Redemptorists. Over the course of working on this history, I have developed a deep admiration for many individual Redemptorists. I have come to admire their great zeal, to sympathize with their failures, and to contemplate their daily search for holiness. Nonetheless, I am not a Redemptorist and this personal distance from the lives and the choices of the Redemptorists provides, I hope, some objectivity.

The Redemptorists themselves throughout this project have tried to live up to Father Provincial Frank Maloney's plea to the Toronto Chapter in 1975:

The experience of the past includes all of our history and tradition, the good and the not-so-good. Some would like to avoid consideration of some aspects of our past, particularly those things which have not been complimentary or constructive. But avoidance of the facts will not take them away ... But if we are going to improve our state in the future we have to build by using the best of our history and tradition while still acknowledging and accepting the negative facts of that history.

Acknowledgments

In the writing of any history, there are several people who are owed gratitude and recognition. Father Desmond Scanlan deserves credit because it was during his tenure as provincial of the Toronto Province that this project began and the Redemptorist archives were opened to me. The Redemptorists under Father Scanlan made my work possible not only by their financial support but also by their trust. Many of them granted interviews and helped with their advice. Many other Redemptorist communities in Canada and around the world welcomed me and tried to make my work easier by providing space and documents. I was allowed to see everything, except the personnel files of living people and the post-1954 materials in the Redemptorist Archives in Rome that generally deal with people who are still alive. In an attempt to be as inclusive as possible, documentary gaps in the contemporary record were supplemented by oral interviews.

I wish to thank Paul Doucet, CSsR, the archivist of the Toronto Province, for his long-suffering tolerance of my many almost impossible requests and my historical opinions in the making. Redemptorist archivists Hernán Valencia-Arboleda in Rome, Alfred Rush and his successor Carl Hoegerl, of the Baltimore Province in Brooklyn, New York, the late John Flynn and his successor, the late Joseph Bilsley, of the St. Louis Province in Glenview, Illinois, Anton Van Ceulebroeck and his successor Jérôme Van Landeghem, of the North Brussels Province, and Jean Beco in Tournai of the South Brussels Province, gave me access to all of their records. Jean-Claude Bergeron, former provincial of the Ste-Anne-de-Beaupré Province, stepped in to help me personally when his knowledgeable archivist, Gérard Lebel, suffered a heart attack shortly before my arrival. Father Bergeron also sent me manuscript drafts of the Beaupré provincial history for my comments and personal use. Sister Catherine Schmeltzer of the Sisters of Service, Toronto, and former provincial Edward Kennedy of the Edmonton Province were also helpful in allowing me to see their files. Former provincial of the Ukrainian Redemptorist Province of Yorkton, now Metropolitan Archbishop Michael Bzdel of Winnipeg, graciously sent me several typescript theses and histories. His successor, Father Provincial Yaroslaw Dybka, granted me permission to view the historical archives. All of them trusted me enough to give me the keys to their archives.

I would like to thank Karl Hoeppe, CSsR, for volunteering to transcribe many of the Gothic German documents. Mr. Anton Kiesenhofer and Antonio Villeneuve, CSsR, became valuable colleagues respectively in translating German and Japanese documents. Drs. Michael Pettem and Robert MacKenzie and Mr. Robert Gerlich have helped tremendously in the use of computers for statistical compilation. Mr. Shamas Nanji of McGill University helped to prepare the maps. The library staff of McGill University's Faculty of Religious Studies were always available and ingenious in procuring rare books and articles while I was a research associate at McGill.

Walter George, of the St. Louis Province of Redemptorists, the coordinator of the North American Redemptorist historians working on the General History project, and Frank Maloney, CSsR, the treasurer of the Toronto Province, were always available for discussions. Fathers Gerard Pettipas, James Mason, and Paul Curtin agreed to act as a Redemptorist history advisory committee, suggesting themes that the Redemptorists would like to see treated. My wife, Louise Bray, also served as an objective and critical sounding board. They all caught several mistakes and made valuable suggestions.

Over the years, draft sections of the second and third chapters of the present history have appeared in the Redemptorist-sponsored history journal, *Spicilegium Historicum*. I would like to thank Dr. Otto Weiss, the director of the journal, for allowing me access to an international audience of knowledgeable Redemptorist historians. Much of the first chapter has already appeared in the *Catholic*

Historical Review (July 1994) as "Early American Redemptorists in British North America, 1834-1863." Its editor, Robert Trisco, has kindly allowed me to use the article for this book.

The Redemptorists asked for a one-volume manuscript which would be chronological, critical, complete, and accessible to the general public, not just to professional historians. An author cannot squeeze everything into a history, and this volume has had strict limits of time and space placed on it from the beginning. It could not be a biographical compilation of each Redemptorist, since there are too many to do justice to them all. Individuals and places who received more attention were outstanding representatives of a larger group or had an impact on the entire Toronto Province or on Canada itself. Still, I hope that readers will enjoy and learn from this institutional biography something of Canadian Catholicism and of the lives and hopes of all Redemptorists in English Canada.

Paul Laverdure
Hochelaga, Montreal

Introduction

After Napoleon Bonaparte had conquered most of Europe, the Holy Roman Empire finally came to an end on 6 August 1806. The old world had been swept away. On the same day, Father Clement Mary Hofbauer wrote from the church of St. Benno in Warsaw to one of his friends: "Presently my greatest pleasure is to think of the forests of Canada. God sends us by persecution there, where he wants us to go." Hofbauer was no stranger to exile and to persecution. He had fled Austrian anti-clericalism to Prussian-controlled Poland in 1787 and now faced persecution from the anti-clerical French revolutionaries. With some companions in the church of St. Benno's, he tried to recreate in Warsaw the life of a Redemptorist as he had known it in Rome. Restricted from preaching missions in the Polish countryside, he instituted a perpetual German-language mission in the church, where preacher after preacher urged hearers to greater repentance and conversion. When Napoleon finally marched on Prussia Hofbauer again wrote: "I never feel more contented than when I am thinking of the savages of Canada." He hoped to find there "a place where we can peacefully await the dawn of better times, while we are educating and training missionaries for unfortunate Europe."

Hofbauer sent letters to England and to Russia asking permission for his German-language Redemptorists to travel through those countries in order to emigrate to Canada. Although Napoleon's blockade of England was not announced until 21 November 1806, most of Hofbauer's letters had already been intercepted by Napoleonic spies, and there is no evidence anyone except the French secret police read Hofbauer's pleas for sanctuary.[1] While the Redemptorists in Poland vainly waited for an answer to Hofbauer's letters, defeated Prussia ceded all of its lands in Poland to France in 1807 and the hapless Redemptorists found themselves in Napoleon's newly created Duchy of Warsaw. In 1808 Napoleon's agents ordered the Redemptorist community of St. Benno to disperse. Some of the men found their way to neutral Switzerland; Hofbauer himself escaped to Vienna and worked there until his death in 1820.

Did any Redemptorists actually make their way to North America at that time? Some of the men who lived with Hofbauer in Poland disappeared and may have reached North America. It is certain that, just after Hofbauer's death and to compensate those who had suffered under the French Revolution, the Austrian government permitted the Redemptorists to establish themselves in Vienna, to own land, and to be recognized as more than an assembly of individuals. From there, missionaries fanned across Europe, into North America in 1832, and finally into Canada.

At the end of 1993 Canadian Redemptorists constituted the third-largest single group in the Congregation, after Americans and Germans. There were 274 Canadian Redemptorist priests, one permanent deacon, fourteen professed students, forty-seven lay brothers, and four bishops in Canada. They are one of the largest groups of religious priests and brothers working in English-speaking Canada. Who are they? What is their place in the English-Canadian Catholic Church? What has been their contribution to the lives of English Catholic Canadians? Finally, how has Canada affected the Redemptorists?

The Redemptorists, officially known as the Congregation of the Most Holy Redeemer, are an association of priests and brothers bound by vows of poverty, chastity, and obedience, together with a vow and oath to persevere until death as members in the Congregation. Founded in 1732 by St. Alphonsus Maria de Liguori (1696–1787), the Congregation grew slowly until it numbered just over two hundred members by 1800. By 1994, however, there were almost six thousand members, making Redemptorists the seventh-largest institute of men in the Roman Catholic Church.[2] Clearly, the Redemptorists answered a need in the Church of the nineteenth and twentieth centuries and attracted an immense number of men in a short period of time.

Alphonsus Liguori (1696–1787)
Bishop and Doctor of the Church. Founder of the Redemptorists. Patron
saint of confessors. He published over one hundred works during his lifetime, most of which have been translated into almost a hundred languages
in thousands of editions.

Those familiar with the Redemptorists know them as dedicated to the preaching of missions, retreats, and novenas, especially to the poor. Their founder Alphonsus, however, wrote in "The True Redemptorist": "Let him [who] would enter the Congregation principally in order to give missions, to preach, and so on, not think of entering, because this is not the spirit of the Institute." The purpose of the Congregation of the Most Holy Redeemer "is to follow as closely as possible the footsteps and examples of Jesus Christ, whose life in this world was one of detachment and mortification, full of sufferings and contempt." Alphonsus desired only those who wanted to be saints and were willing to suffer anything, even death, for perfect union with God. In the Congregation, Alphonsus wrote, "every subject must live solely for eternity."[3]

Asceticism is the practice of strict self-denial in a regimen of personal and, above all, spiritual discipline. All ascetics see themselves as spiritual athletes engaged in a constant striving after holiness. Alphonsus made the Redemptorist Congregation one of the most ascetic organizations in the Church. He built the Congregation on community life with its vows, and on missionary life with the poor, both patterned after Christ's mission and example. The Redemptorist imitation of Christ included forming the inner man through daily meditations, mass, thanksgiving, spiritual reading, recitation of the rosary, examination of conscience, a short visit to the Blessed Sacrament, and prayer to the Blessed Virgin Mary. One day each month was spent in recollection and ten days annually in a spiritual retreat. The year revolved around twelve virtues, one of which was proposed for special imitation and meditation each month of the year. Periods of fasting alternated with liturgical celebrations.

The many rules of the constitutions and statutes, collectively called the Rule, were all formulated to achieve a perfect and minute observance of the vows: poverty, chastity, and, above all, obedience. Everything from the quality of cloth in the black habit, to the number of shirts, to the pictures in the room, to the width of the bed was regulated. Poverty was real. The Redemptorists lived on donations. Begging was forbidden. Permissions were required for almost everything. Small, self-confessed breaches of the Rule usually meant further fasting, prayer, silence, and self-denial. More serious breaches were followed by canonical warnings and then expulsion. Men accepted the heavy yoke of the Rule to conquer themselves physically and spiritually so as to live in community, preserve the vows, and offer both body and soul to the greater service of others and of God. The difficulty of such a life was further emphasized and recognized by the institution of the fourth vow and oath of perseverance in the Congregation required of all members taking final vows. In return, St. Alphonsus guaranteed that heaven awaited all those who kept the Rule and died in the Congregation.

Toronto's newspaper the *Globe* of 14 January 1881 gave almost the same description of visiting Redemptorists:

> [They were] members of one of the most ascetic, zealous, and active religious Orders in the Roman Catholic Church ... a proselytizing agency second only, if indeed it is second, to the Jesuits themselves ... When they began a mission they were to take it for granted ... that ignorance of ... faith and morals was the rule, and by simple, fervent, declamatory sermons, not unmingled with wonderful stories as to purgatory, hell, and the glories of the Saints, especially of the Blessed Virgin Mary, to draw the people heavenwards or to terrify them into morality. Their chief means of grace was to be the confessional, the skill in whose manipulation the fathers gave nearly the whole of their attention during their time of study ... Its fathers were, therefore, ROUGH AND READY in their mode, rather than polished and refined like the Jesuits, or deeply read like the Benedictines and Dominicans. They were to the religious Congregations what the Franciscans were to the great Orders, impressive preachers depending on their power of moving the multitude by sensationalism, often by vulgarity, rather than by deep, scholarly, and finished theological sermons.
>
> ... Like the Jesuits they insist upon the most absolute obedience from all their subjects, each one

of whom is required to be in the hands of his Superior *perinde ac cadaver*, EXACTLY AS A CORPSE. Unlike the Jesuits their rule is terribly ascetic ... On no day in the year do they eat more than one square meal, and that not of the best. By way of mortifying their passions they use the scourge – the "discipline" – to blood every Friday, and oftener during Lent and Advent. In addition to the regular devotions of the Church they have a special "Office" which they say daily, those in Holy Order having besides their Breviary to read, and, if priests, their Mass to say every day. They rise at about 4:30 a.m., and devote the whole of their time between that hour and 9 o'clock to prayer, meditation, study, assisting at or saying Mass, and during missions to hearing confessions or preaching ...

... what is called "Chapter" is held at regular and frequent intervals, when each member confesses publicly any violations of the rule of which he may have been guilty, kneeling down before the Superior, KISSING THE GROUND as he does so, and receiving a penance to add to the already pretty severe mortifications of the Order ... Every member is treated alike, and they have all things so much in common that they talk of "our coat," "our prayerbook," "our hat," even their very razors and shaving apparatus being kept not in their cells but in a common cupboard. Except by permission of the Superior of the house they have NOT ONE CENT to bless themselves with, nor can they even have a pen or a penknife in their possession without permission asked and obtained ... Theoretically each father gives half his time to the mission work, and spends the balance of the year in STUDY AND RELIGIOUS EXERCISES. In practice, however, so great is the demand for their services that the fathers are considerably more out of their convents than in them.

      … In the houses everything goes with the reg-
ulation of clock work, each member of the community being obliged to drop whatever employment he
may be busy over at the sound of the bell – to him as
"THE VOICE OF GOD" – an obligation which not unfre-
quently [*sic*] acts disastrously on the cooking of the
victuals. Any infraction of the rules, even though not
wilful, is visited with penances more or less severe;
wilful disobedience, if persisted in, entails dismissal
from the Order, a penalty tantamount almost to
excommunication. Hence the more than military
exactness and promptitude with which all the community duties are performed, with the inevitable
result of unlimited facilities for PROPAGANDISM SYS-
TEMATIZED AND FORMIDABLE.

The *Globe*'s description illustrates the tension between the
external and the internal life, between the life of missionary action
and the life of prayerful obedience to the Rule. This tension contin-
ues throughout the history of the Congregation.

     The life of Alphonsus himself epitomized the union of these
tensions. Born a Neapolitan nobleman, he renounced his family heritage and his successful law practice to become a priest. His life
alternated between prolonged prayer and difficult mission work in
the poorest villages around the city of Naples. He insisted that each
activity strengthened the other.

     As part of his missionary activities, Alphonsus turned to
writing. His works run the gamut from pious songs that are still sung
in Italy today, from works of Marian devotion still read by the
Catholic laity, to learned multi-volume treatises still consulted by
theologians. While he was promoting prayer among the poor so that
they too could reach saintly perfection, his scholarly fame grew with
the multiple editions of his immense *Theologia Moralis*.

     Alphonsus's moral theology was dedicated to training con-
fessors who would guide the Christian into the paths of perfection.
His moral theology, called equiprobabilism, became known as a pru-
dent middle way between a lax moral theology – satirized by

Pascal's *Provincial Letters* against the Jesuits – and the rigorous, almost Calvinist, moral theology promoted mainly by the French Jansenists. Laxism always favoured liberty of conscience while Jansenism always favoured the law. Equiprobabilism, as Alphonsus described it, established that a law does not bind consciences if there is sufficient doubt about the law's relevance. Thus, equiprobabilism allowed confessors to steer between the extremes of rigorism and laxism, and to maintain church laws, which laxists rarely did, while allowing sinners forgiveness, which Jansenists hardly ever did.

The Church approved and embraced Alphonsus's moral theology in 1831. It became the norm for all confessors in the mid-nineteenth century and the standard guide in Catholic ethics.[4] Alphonsus was canonized in 1839, proclaimed a Doctor of the Church in 1871, and the patron saint of confessors and moralists in 1959. Especially after 1831, bishops around the world introduced Alphonsus's works to their seminaries, and invited his new Congregation to bring his teachings into their dioceses.[5]

In summary, the Redemptorists combined the public missionary zeal and flexibility of a Jesuit, the personal rigorous asceticism of a Jansenist, while developing their own alphonsian sensitivity to daily moral problems, becoming renowned expert confessors and spiritual guides in their own right.

As a body of Redemptorist writings grew around the traditional themes dear to Alphonsus, a more public Redemptorist spirituality spread throughout the Catholic world. For example, Redemptorist spirituality readily available to all Catholics revolves around devotion to saints who died in the Congregation. The most famous saint is St. Gerard Majella, a lay brother who died in 1755 and who is now honoured as a special patron of mothers and families. The most famous example of a Redemptorist devotion unknown to Alphonsus is the one to the icon of Our Lady of Perpetual Help. In 1866 Pope Pius IX gave the icon to the Redemptorist church of Sant' Alfonso in Rome, directing the Redemptorists to make Mary, Our Lady of Perpetual Help, known to the world. Alphonsus's devotion to Mary is well-known, especially through his popular book, *The Glories of Mary*, so that Redemptorist devotions can be seen as a natural development of alphonsian spirituality.

The Icon of Our Lady of Perpetual Help

Entrusted to the Redemptorists by Pope Pius IX in 1866, the icon was probably brought to Rome from Crete in the fifteenth century. Its style is eleventh century and has elements dated to the early seventh century. On 30 May 1876 a fire in Quebec City destroyed some thousand homes. The chronicles of St. Patrick's state that people holding the picture of our Mother of Perpetual Help faced the flames as they roared near, and their homes were untouched.

After the death of Alphonsus in 1787 came the French Revolution and the anti-clerical policies of the Josephists in the Austrian Empire. Austria refused to allow any new religious congregations to establish themselves on Austrian soil, causing Father Hofbauer to leave for Poland. During the upheavals of the French Revolution, the Redemptorists in northern Europe were almost cut off from the Redemptorist father general in Rome, while the Redemptorists in the Papal States under Napoleonic rule had little contact with those in Sicily and Naples. Hofbauer was named vicar general, subject to the general in Rome, to care for the Redemptorists outside of Italy. Those outside Italy who had heard of Alphonsus and the Redemptorists and who wanted to join now went to Hofbauer in Warsaw.

Joseph Passerat (1772–1858)
A conscript in France's revolutionary army, he escaped to Germany to study theology and eventually joined the Redemptorists in Warsaw, where he was professed in 1796. Most of his life was spent fleeing anti-clerical revolutions but he was responsible for the Redemptorists' extraordinary expansion throughout Europe and into North America. His virtues were declared heroic in 1980. (Photograph courtesy of the Baltimore Province Archives)

In spite of Hofbauer's intention to follow the Redemptorist Rule strictly, the rapidly changing face of Europe forced him to adapt the Neapolitan-made rules so that the Redemptorists could survive in the rest of Europe. Instead of only parish missions, which were intended mainly to bring sinners to the confessional, the Redemptorists accepted parish work, as in St. Benno's in Warsaw. They turned the parishes into permanent mission stations where the missionaries gave their talks and sermons, rested before travelling out to other missions, and used their parish salaries to finance their travels.

On Hofbauer's death, his closest associate, a deserter from Napoleon's army, Joseph Passerat, left Switzerland to take up residence as vicar general in the newly established house of Maria-am-Gestade in Vienna. The Redemptorists numbered only five hundred in 1831, and most of them lived in Italy. Nonetheless, the revolutions were over, Alphonsus's moral theology had been formally approved, and Alphonsus was on his way to canonization. In answer to the pleas of the bishops of America, it was Passerat who sent the first European Redemptorists to work in the North American mission fields in 1832. The romantic desire for a life of self-sacrifice in Canada lived on in Alphonsus's and Hofbauer's followers.

1

Pioneers in British North America, 1834–65

Six Redemptorists left Vienna for America early in 1832.[1] That same year, a young man and admirer of the Viennese Redemptorists, Joseph Reisach, asked if he could join the Redemptorists to study for the priesthood. At the age of twenty-four, he had not yet completed any seminary training. Unsure what to do with a man already past the usual age for such education, the Redemptorists tested Reisach by setting him the task of going to the American missions where formal education was less important than sound health, morals, and doctrine. Reisach travelled from Vienna to Portugal where he took a ship for New York. After learning some English in New York, Reisach made his way to Green Bay, in the present state of Wisconsin, and arrived in July 1833. The Redemptorist superior in America, Simon Saenderl, assigned the hopeful candidate to work with Father Francis-Xavier Haetscher in the area between Sault Sainte Marie and Detroit, just south of present-day Ontario. Later, Haetscher, Reisach, and Saenderl all went to British North America. Reisach's written memoirs of those years constitute the first history of the Redemptorists in what is now Canada.[2]

The Redemptorists at first used French, the international language of the day and the language of most of the Roman Catholics in North America at the beginning of the nineteenth century. Later, they, especially Father Saenderl, began to preach in the Iroquoian dialects of the Ottawa and the Ojibwa people.[3] The Redemptorists also naturally used German and English, since German and Irish Catholic immigration continued to grow. As natives of the large and heterogeneous Austrian Empire, they were well prepared for the polyglot nature of the American frontier.

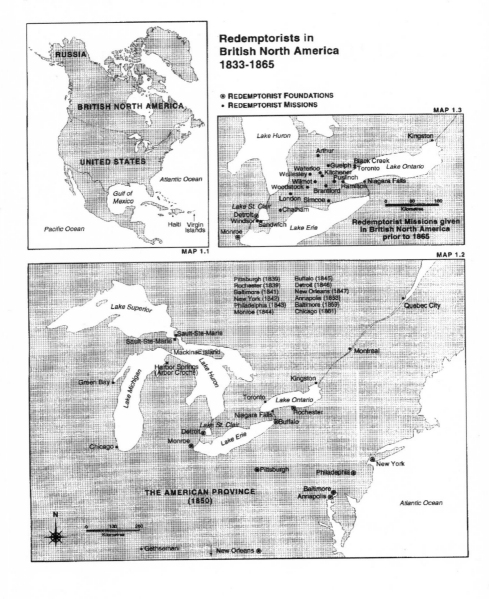

Redemptorists in British North America 1833-1865

⊛ REDEMPTORIST FOUNDATIONS
• REDEMPTORIST MISSIONS

MAP 1.3

Redemptorist Missions given in British North America prior to 1865

MAP 1.1

MAP 1.2

Pittsburgh (1839)   Buffalo (1845)
Rochester (1839)   Detroit (1846)
Baltimore (1841)   New Orleans (1847)
New York (1842)   Annapolis (1853)
Philadelphia (1843)   Baltimore (1859)
Monroe (1844)   Chicago (1861)

THE AMERICAN PROVINCE (1850)

Francis-Xavier Haetscher

Joseph Reisach was soon to learn that Father Francis-Xavier Haetscher was an extraordinary man. Born in 1784, as a young man he had enlisted in the Austrian army. A few years later he deserted and spent some years in Paris. At Napoleon's fall, he made his way back to Vienna where he heard Clement Hofbauer preach. Hofbauer brought Haetscher to repent his previous life to such effect that he joined the young religious congregation in October 1814 at the age of twenty-nine. He had been a Redemptorist barely two months when he was sent as a missionary to the Ottoman Empire where he was ordained. He settled in the Ottoman Province of Wallachia, now in southern Romania, but he and other Catholic priests were later expelled. At forty-nine years of age, he was the eldest of the six missionaries sent to America. Haetscher preached the first eight-day Redemptorist mission in North America, in Tiffin, Ohio. He then fell ill with cholera while helping the plague victims in the Detroit area, survived, and within two weeks was preaching again.[4]

Father Joseph Wissel (1830–1912)
Born in Rabach, Wuerzburg, he was professed in the United States and ordained in 1853. His much used guide *The Redemptorist on the American Missions* first appeared in 1875. (Photograph courtesy of the Baltimore Province Archives)

The Redemptorist Mission

What was the typical American Redemptorist mission that Haetscher tried to preach? From 1875 to 1912 Father Joseph Wissel copied and preserved the English and German sermons given by the oldest Redemptorist missionaries in America and made outlines to be used by new Redemptorist missionaries who underwent a special six-month novitiate for training in preaching parish missions. Wissel's book eventually became the three-volume *The Redemptorist on the American Missions* and remains the best description of the Redemptorist mission for most of the nineteenth and twentieth centuries. Wissel declares:

> A Mission consists of a series of sermons and instructions preached, in connection with administration of the Sacraments, to an organized congregation, for the purpose of making them better Catholics ... A true Mission, therefore, is that which, after restoring the grace of God [through the confessional] to those who have fallen, renews the people in their belief in Christ and Church, teaches sound principles of morality, and re-establishes the pious frequentation of the Sacraments.[5]

In other words, the Redemptorist mission is "an extraordinary work of the apostolate with the purpose of making 'better Catholics' of the people of a parish." Nineteenth-century Redemptorist missions were directed at bringing fallen-away Catholics back to the Church and to the sacraments.

Alphonsus Liguori had fixed the shortest mission at ten days, but longer missions were the norm.[6] By the mid-nineteenth century, North American Redemptorists gave shorter missions in blocks of between eight and ten days overlapping two Sundays. Depending on the size of the church or the parish, a mission could be preached to the entire parish in eight days, or it could be given one week to the women, and then the next week to the men, or it could be divided again into one eight-day mission for the children, eight days for the women and then another mission for the men. Missions could last six weeks or more, if the parish was very large or the church very small.

In a typical mission, there were three sermons each day. These comprised a short instruction in the morning, one longer one in the afternoon, and a very long one (the "great sermon") in the evening. The short morning instructions summarized previous topics, treated prayer, and promoted devotions, such as the rosary. The afternoon instructions were geared to the practical aspects of Christian life and adapted to the people attending that day: marital duties, children, family life, temperance, education, and parish societies. In the great evening sermons, missionaries preached the "Eternal Truths": the "urgency of working out one's salvation, the malice of mortal sin and its punishment, the inevitability and the justice of general judgment, and the pains of hell."[7] Salvation, sin, judgment, and hell were given in the first days of a mission to seize the hearers' attention and gain a larger audience for the rest of the mission. They were also meant to prepare the hearers for confessions that began on Wednesday night. The remaining evening sermons spoke of Christ and conversion. After consulting with the pastor, a special sermon tailored to the audience could be given. For example, a night sermon on temperance would often be preached to Irish Canadians. The Saturday evening sermon on devotion to Mary and the Sunday morning sermon on the means of perseverance summarized the many devotional practices and attitudes developed at length during the week and also closed the mission.

Mission sermons were meant to be logical, popular, simple and, above all, persuasive. To succeed they aimed to move the heart as well as the mind. If length in Wissel's work is any indication, most North American Redemptorists were better trained to preach on hell than heaven, but it also shows that hell was popular. The historians Serge Gagnon, Nive Voisine, and Murray Nicolson state that nineteenth-century preachers whipped their hearers to remorse and drove them tearful to the confessional, terrified by the fear of damnation and begging God's mercy; all of the preachers cited are Redemptorists. When Redemptorist Father Elias Schauer was superior of the American missionaries, he insisted that if the eternal

Remembrance of the Mission

GIVEN BY THE

REDEMPTORIST FATHERS.

TORONTO, 1880.

Look down upon me go d and gentle Jesus, while before Thy face I humbly kneel, and with burning heart pray and beseech Thee to fix' deep in my soul lively sentiments of Faith, Hope and Charity, true contrit.on for my sins, and a firm purpose of amendment; the while I contemplate with great love and tender pity Thy Five Wounds, pondering over them within me whilst I call to mind the words which David Thy Prophet said of Thee, my Jesus, ' They have pierced my hands and feet; they have numbered all my bones.

Plen. Indulg. for the above prayer before the image of Christ Crucified, after Holy Comm'n.

Add five Paters and Aves for the intention of the Sovereign Pontiff.

indulgences
INDULGENCES.

GRANTED BY HIS HOLINESS PIUS IX., TO THOSE WHO PRAY BEFORE THE MISSION CROSSES ERECTED BY THE REDEMPTORIST FATHERS.

1. A Plenary Indulgence, after confession and Communion, on the anniversary of the erection, or on the Sunday following; also on the Feasts of the Finding and Exaltation of Holy Cross, May 3rd and September 14th. (By a Rescript of March 27th, 1852.)

2. An Indulgence of Seven Years and Seven Quarantines, for reciting before the Cross, with a contrite heart, seven Aves in honour of the sorrows of Mary. (By a Rescript of July 15th, 1858.)

3. An Indulgence of Three Hundred Days for reciting before the Cross, with a contrite heart, five Paters, Aves and Glorias in honour of the Sacred Wounds. (By a Rescript of March 27th, 1852.)

With thanks to the Archives of the Archdiocese of Toronto – 1993

DAILY ACTS OF A CHRISTIAN LIFE.

In the Morning.

1. On awaking, give your first thoughts to God. saying: "Oh my God! I give myself entirely to Thee."

2. Getting out of bed, bless yourself, dress modestly, kneel down, say a short morning prayer, adding *three Hail Marys* in honor of the purity of the Blessed Virgin Mary.

During the Day.

1. Whenever you are tempted to any sin, say *Jesus help me! Mary, Mother, pray for me! My Jesus, mercy!*

2. Before you begin your work, say: "*All for Thee, O Lord—O my Jesus, all for Thee.*"

3. Before meals say: "*Bless us, O Lord, and these Thy gifts, which of Thy bounty we are about to receive, through Christ our Lord. Amen.*"

4. After meals say: "*We give Thee thanks, Almighty God, for all Thy benefits, who livest and reignest, world without end. Amen.*" "*May the souls of the faithful departed, through the mercy of God, rest in peace. Amen.*"

At Night.

1. Before going to bed kneel down, bless yourself, recite your night prayers, and then say: "*O my God, give me grace to know wherein I have offended Thee to-day, and grant me a perfect sorrow for my sins.*" Then pause a little to see what sins you may have committed during the day; afterwards ask pardon for the faults you have discovered, by making an act of contrition, as follows:

O my God! I am very sorry for having sinned against Thee, because Thou art so good, and I will not sin again.

2. Then make the acts of Faith, Hope and Charity.

3. Say *three Hail Marys* in honor of the Blessed Virgin Mary.

4. When in bed, fold your arms in the shape of a cross, and say before you sleep: *It is appointed for me once to die, and I know not when, nor where—nor how; but what I do know is that if I die in mortal sin, I am lost.* And then if you are in mortal sin, resolve to go to confession as soon as possible.

Means of Perseverance.

DEAR CHRISTIAN:—If you wish to persevere until death ; 1. Flee from the occasion of sin. 2. Practice holy prayer. 3. Receive the Holy Sacraments frequently. 4. Preserve a tender devotion to the Blessed Virgin Mary. 5. Never allow human respect to interfere with your duties.

An Act of Contrition.

O my God! I am heartily sorry for having offended Thee because Thou art so good, and I firmly purpose, by Thy holy grace, never more to offend Thee.

An Act of Faith.

O my God, I most firmly believe in Thee and all Thou hast revealed to Thy Holy Catholic Church, because thou art truth itself, who neither canst deceive nor be deceived.

An Act of Hope.

O my God, relying on Thy promises, and upon the merits of Jesus Christ, my Saviour, I most firmly hope in thee, and trust that thou wilt grant me grace to observe Thy commandments in this world, and reward me in the next.

An Act of Love or Charity.

O my God, who art worthy of all love, and infinite in every perfection, I love Thee with my whole heart and above all things ; and I love my neighbor as myself for the love of Thee.

Nineteenth-century mission souvenir

The souvenir's printed prayers were meant to help the Catholic laity persevere on the paths of perfection. (Courtesy of the Archives of the Roman Catholic Archdiocese of Toronto) truths were preached, they should not be preached in such a manner that people can say, *"Oh! If hell is not worse than that, then I don't care if I go there."*[8]

Once in the confessional, penitents were not to be denied forgiveness if at all possible. Prior to the arrival of Alphonsus's moral theology, neglect of the sacraments was endemic in Canada owing to clerical shortages and the severe moral theology, usually labelled Jansenism, which dictated that penitents were to be turned away until their constant demand for forgiveness demonstrated their true sorrow.[9] A priest influenced by Jansenism who refused or delayed absolution could cause some penitents to avoid the confessional entirely. Much of the early correspondence and the opening pages of many Redemptorist monasteries' daily chronicles in the northern United States and in Canada witness to the moral severity of the Jansenistic French and French-Canadian clergy towards their penitents.[10] The Redemptorists believed that the missionary needed to highlight God's love and mercy in each of the sermons, to encourage people to go to confession. They also believed that they absolutely had to demonstrate compassion in the confessional in order to reconcile the sinner to such a loving God. So missionaries entered parish after parish, sometimes armed with special diocesan faculties to absolve sins reserved to the bishop and even wielding papal privileges the bishops did not have. The contrast between the thundering sermons and the quiet work of the confessional made the Redemptorists seem like "lions in the pulpit and lambs in the confessional."[11]

Although missions were often measured by the number of confessions, "It should be borne in mind that the end of the mission is not simply to have the confessions of the people heard, but to effect a change in their lives through constant attendance at a series of sermons and instructions which prepare them to receive the sacraments with more than usual care and profit."[12] Above all, the missionaries sought conversion to the ideals of Christian perfection as defined by the Church. Conversion, over a period of time, through personal and communal devotion to the Church and to Christ in the sacraments made the Catholic revival experience in North America's nineteenth century significantly different from the emphasis given by evangelical Protestants to a sudden, personal conversion to Christ alone.

Once relieved of the burden of sin through confession, the renewed Catholic was sent to participate in the sacramental and devotional life of the parish in order to persevere on the paths of conversion, perfection, and salvation. The Redemptorist missionaries moved on, returning to a parish within a year to preach a renewal of the mission. Redemptorists hoped that the renewal would help backsliders and reach those who had not attended the original mission. To help the parishioners further on the path of holiness, the Redemptorists would again teach the practices of the devout life, promote sacramentals, such as scapulars, crucifixes, medals, pictures, candles, rosary, prayer books and, above all, parish devotions. As one Redemptorist wrote, "Among our lower classes especially, [the sacramentals] do more good than all the eloquence which even our greatest preachers could display."[13] Together the mission and the renewal comprised the complete Redemptorist mission and, united with organization, oratory, and solemnity, the complete mission became a powerful experience for thousands.

The Sault Sainte Marie Mission

In early July of 1834 Bishop Frederick Rese of Detroit sent Haetscher to Sault Sainte Marie, Michigan, to establish a permanent mission at this trading post where French Canadians and Winnebago natives lived. Previously, mass had been celebrated by visiting priests in a private house on Water Street; Haetscher and Reisach now built a log chapel. On 31 July Bishop Rese arrived to administer confirmation to the Winnebagos and French Canadians that Haetscher had gathered. The Cincinnati *Catholic Telegraph* of 10 October 1834 reported:

> The Indians flocked together from all directions. They were marshalled in orderly array and fired the guns both at the arrival and departure of the Bishop, so that he could scarcely get through the smoke. The Indians had erected a church of bark, open in front.

The whole time this mission lasted, was spent in the most solemn and religious exercises, preparing them for the reception of the holy sacraments of baptism, confirmation, penance, Eucharist, extreme unction, and matrimony. More than one hundred were confirmed.

Once it was known that the American bishops had sent priests into the western border areas, Canadian bishops requested that these priests visit British territory to help the Catholics scattered there. One such request made its way to Haetscher, inviting him to come to Upper Canada, now Ontario. Haetscher and Reisach went to the American island of Mackinac, located between the two countries, and turned an abandoned armoury into a chapel. Every three weeks they regularly travelled by canoe from the American to the Canadian Sault Sainte Marie. When the river froze, Reisach wrote, they walked across to Canada.

During the late fall and early spring crossing the frozen river was always a matter of mortal danger. Reverend Father Haetscher often crawled on the ice on his hands and knees because the ice was broken and bent in the middle and yet he could not be held back. The winter is extraordinarily cold and one is not in a position to walk with one's face toward the wind. Throughout the winter we used the lower part of our apartment in the newly built church for mass, namely 20 to 40 feet. We had set up a very good stove, about ten feet from the altar; I had heated it very well and yet it was not possible to say Mass. While praying the *confiteor* I could not speak any more but I was completely conscious; the Reverend Father prayed my part as well and went to the altar; during the reading of the Epistle his hands became completely stiff so that he was forced to leave the altar. I saw all of this and was glad that he had to stop; I had already become completely frozen. Only

when I tried to stand up did I collapse. They had to
carry me to bed.[14]

Father Haetscher also suffered from the severe climate.
When he tried to travel to St. Joseph over one hundred kilometres
from the Sault, the natives wrapped him in furs and ran ahead of a
six-dog sleigh to light fires at which Haetscher warmed himself. At
these short stops along the way, he would instruct native families.
After eight days of this kind of travelling, he returned to the Sault,
weakened "because of the extreme cold."

In September 1834 the French-Canadian Catholics of the
Sault asked one of their English-speaking members to draft a petition to the Roman Catholic Bishop of Kingston, Alexander
MacDonell. They wanted money to build a church, now that they
had a pastor of "their own denomination." Forty-five French-
Canadian names were signed over the name of the drafter of the
petition, Dr. William Bell. No help came. MacDonell might have
been more generous if he had had the means or if he had known that
some of the names, such as the entire Cadotte family, were soon to
join the other churches. The petition was renewed in January of
1835 to Lieutenant-Governor Sir John Colborne. It pointed out that a
priest from the American side had to be asked to help out, because
there was no money to attract a priest from the settled areas of the
Canadian colonies. The Anglican Colborne was kind enough to pass
on the letter to MacDonell who, of course, still had no money.[15]

Although the French-Canadian Catholics tried to organize a
parish for the Redemptorists, not everyone in the Sault eagerly welcomed them. The earliest records of the Redemptorists' work with
the French Canadians in the United States and in Canada, compiled
by Reisach and others, were descriptions of the immorality that had
crept into life on the frontier. The Redemptorists chronicled drunk-
enness, adultery, polygamy, and murder. Father Saenderl affirmed:

If the reception of the Sacraments was turning savages
into seraphs, all too many Catholic French-Canadians
were bent upon degeneration. Most of these half-breed
trappers were little more than pagans. For some it had

been anywhere from twenty to forty years since they had last seen a priest. One old man remembered vaguely that some sixty years before he had gone to Communion in Montreal for the last time. In every family there were youngsters who had to be baptized … Polygamy was a common affair and the trading of wives for a load of hay or a cow was not unheard of … many of the Canadian trappers were drunken sots.[16]

In the Sault, the missionaries faced the opposition with vigour.

Once when working in a Canadian village Haetscher reprimanded a local rake for an illicit love affair. The hot-headed Canadian stalked up to the missionary full of threats. Haetscher grabbed him by his shirt front and held him suspended in the air with his right hand. In his left he held a crucifix that he practically pushed into the fellow's enraged face. The Canadian cried out his threats and struggled to get away. This time Haetscher, who had command of the situation, threatened his victim in turn, brandishing his crucifix before him. The rake did not set his feet on *terra firma* until he had cooled off and had come to a better state of mind.[17]

Reisach added:

One day, we – the priest and I – were together. (We still lived in the old block-house.) The priest was praying the breviary and I was working on the windows of the new church, then all at once the door sprang open and [a] wild man jumped at the priest with clenched fists. I did not hesitate very long. I took my axe and placed myself in front of him saying that he had better get out immediately or I would crack open his head, whereupon he left the room with threats to shoot us to death. Through many nights I kept an axe by my bed. The priest awoke me at the slightest noise.[18]

Trouble came not only from lapsed Catholics but from Protestants. Abel Bingham of the American Baptist Union had been working in the Sault since 1828. On the British side, James D. Cameron, a poorly paid, half-native working for the Anglican Missionary Society, led his followers out of the Church of England and into the vigorous American Baptist Church. The Wesleyan Methodist Church in Canada sent William Case and another half-native, Peter Jones, to the area and they brought in the circuit riders James Evans, Jonathan Scott, and Gilbert Miller. Although the Church of England appointed William McMurray to replace Cameron, and the Wesleyan Methodist Church in Canada built a church in the Sault, the natives preferred the Catholic priest, "a *true* Blackrobe."[19] With their long black cassocks, the Redemptorists had awakened memories of the Jesuits of New France.

The American Baptist minister observed: "Since the Catholick priest came here last, our school has till, lately, been reduced to our boarding schollars ... when the Romish priest came, the children from Catholick families were prevented from coming." He added: "I am told by those who saw it, that in the midst of his discourse, he tore a protestant Bible to pieces, & threw it into the fire place, to show his kind intentions to burn it. I believe there was no fire in it, the room being heated by a stove. But he publicly declared it to be a great sin for his people to read it."[20]

Perhaps in response to Haetscher's preaching and his success in winning back several lapsed Catholics, or perhaps to forestall any conversions to Roman Catholicism among the natives, the Methodist preachers began a fiery preaching campaign against the Roman Catholic Church and against Haetscher in particular. The Anglicans exhorted their brethren to "overcome the *black bird*, which had been singing about their ears for some time past, even as the Great God hath overcome the evil spirit."[21] Bishop Rese reported the results:

I can only mention with tears the contemptible vandalism perpetrated on our little chapel at Sault Ste. Marie. The windows were smashed, then the sacred vessels thrown out, crushed and destroyed, the missal torn into a thousand fragments, and after the good Father Haetscher, without a word of complaint, on the eve of All Saints, repaired the damage as best as he could, the whole building was set ablaze by throwing fire into it. The loss is incalculable for us, inasmuch as it is very difficult to obtain here the articles which are indispensable. Yet the affair has turned out unexpectedly in our favor, for the Baptist and Methodist preachers were compelled to seek safety in flight [to Canada] to escape the vengeance of an angry people who now all sympathize with us. Thus a temporal loss and a persecution have brought us much spiritual benefit. Yet it is hard for us to bear it nonetheless.[22]

Asked to report on the cross-border incident for the British authorities, Captain Thomas G. Anderson justified the destruction of the American chapel:

a Roman Catholic Priest, a foreigner, living on the American side, visited the Canadians & almost daily, that he had actually burnt an English Bible on that side [of] the water, and that he had tried to get some on our side for the same purpose, that Mr. McMurray [the Anglican missionary] had been compelled to turn him out of his enclosures when he had made his way to Mr. McMurray's Indians and that he had actually caused a Bark Chapel to be built adjoining this [native] enclosure, much to the annoyance of Mr. McMurray and his adherents.[23]

Captain Anderson and the Anglican Reverend A. Elliot recommended to the authorities the removal of the French-Canadian "squatters" from the banks of the Sault, because, the captain claimed, they misled and corrupted the natives by vicious example and "seriously and even violently obstruct[ed] the Missionary in the performance of his duty."

After the fire, Haetscher spent much of the winter at Mackinac. In the spring of 1835 Bishop Rese ordered him to build a new church in the American Sault. On arrival at the Sault, he and Reisach lodged with an English officer who had deserted from the British army, married a Catholic, and now lived on the American side of the border. But dances – seen as occasions of sin – were held at the house, so the Redemptorists left for a hut in the forest.

The hut was over a kilometre away from the chapel and young Joseph Reisach carried the altar materials back and forth for each mass. The hut itself soon became a confessional of sorts. Reisach, who had to get up at four in the morning to get the chapel ready, now also found himself saying his prayers in the night air while penitents and visitors went to the hut. However, Haetscher rewarded Reisach for his devotion by clothing him in the Redemptorist habit in October 1835. Reisach's formal religious training as a Redemptorist novice had begun.

The next spring, in May of 1836, after rebuilding the chapel in the Sault, Haetscher was called back to Green Bay. The Sault's population had declined and Haetscher was needed more elsewhere. The constant travel, first by order of the bishop and then by Redemptorist superiors, and now his declining health, convinced Haetscher that he could not establish a permanent Redemptorist house in America. The American economy was in a shambles after the crash of 1837; there had been nothing but poor crops from the moment he arrived. Canada and the United States were becoming estranged over border disputes; the British Empire had prohibited slavery since 1834 and American slaves appeared more and more often in Upper Canada. The Canadas were experiencing financial and agricultural troubles that would lead to their Rebellions of 1837 and 1838. Joseph Reisach entered a six-month novitiate in Green Bay and at the end he and an exhausted Haetscher left for Vienna. One might imagine Haetscher's pessimistic report, for the Viennese Redemptorists were ready to recall all of the missionaries, but "Brother Joseph by his earnest pleading succeeded in having the decree suspended, and obtained new laborers for the Mission."[24]

Joseph Reisach

Joseph Reisach had used whatever spare time he had in the woods to study Latin and had asked permission to study for ordination. Although a short, slight man, seemingly less fit for manual work than for study, the immediate need for lay brothers induced his superiors to ask him to consider life as a Redemptorist lay brother. An ideal Redemptorist monastery held twelve priests and six lay brothers. In America, as in post-revolutionary Europe, everything – church, rectory, school, and hall – had to be built from scratch and maintained at little or no cost, so the need for skilled brothers often equalled the need for priests.

Reisach began his second six-month novitiate in Vienna. A lay brother's first or second novitiate differed little from that of choir novices going for ordination or from either brothers' or priests' retreat days. Unlike choir novices, the lay brothers' two novitiates could be joined into one two-year novitiate or be split, as was the choir novice's training, into a period of one year followed by several years of work and then completed by a second novitiate. All Redemptorists prior to the Second Vatican Council were expected to complete a second novitiate – a period of six months of recollection and further preparation for the missions – by a renewal of their religious spirit through prayer, study, and conferences. Those who had chosen not to go on to ordination spent part of their second novitiate in technical training. Those who became priests entered the second novitiate, usually after some years in pastoral work, to receive further training, particularly in preaching and confessional practice.

Redemptorist daily life was strictly prescribed by Rule and changed little from St. Alphonsus's time to the Second Vatican Council.[25] Joseph Reisach's novitiate was virtually identical to that of any other novice, except that the student for ordination and the brother did manual or other work during the times priests worked on their mission sermons or studied St. Alphonsus's moral theology. Reisach's retreat schedule would have been typical for the period.[26]

4:30   rise
5:00   community meditation
5:30   preparation for holy communion, mass, and thanksgiving
7:30   spiritual reading and meditation
8:00   manual work
9:30   visit to the Blessed Sacrament and to our Blessed Lady
10:00   first part of the rosary, personal meditation and examination of conscience
10:30   lives of the saints
11:00   listing blessings
11:30   examination of conscience
11:45   particular examination on the virtue of the month
12:00   meal then help in the kitchen or refectory until 1:30, with community recreation
1:30   visitation (visit to or from Superior or retreat master), way of the cross, second part of the rosary
3:00   spiritual reading
3:30   meditation
4:00   manual work
5:30   unstructured worship and recreation
6:00   private devotions and spiritual reading if desired
6:30   meditation
7:00   meal, help in the kitchen or refectory, then the third part of the rosary
8:30   evening prayer, worship
9:30   retire

The brothers and the novices enjoyed short recreational periods of conversation or walks in the garden after lunch and supper. Novices and, occasionally, professed brothers would receive one or more daily talks or conferences from the novice master or other lecturer chosen by him to deepen their piety and their knowledge of some aspect of Catholicism, spirituality, or of Redemptorist life. In the novitiate as in the monasteries, the Church's feast days as well as the Congregation's holidays provided variety in the intense routine of work and prayer. For example, Redemptorists would celebrate a "little Christmas" on the twenty-fifth of every month. The father superior might arrange for special foods, or a community outing, while the novices wrote letters to the infant Jesus.

In the theology of the day, the status of a lay brother was considered superior to that of a Christian labourer in the world, because the lay brother spreads "the kingdom of God on earth. He accomplishes this not only by his prayers and edifying life, but also by his labor, be it ever so humble or menial; so that even by washing the dishes and sweeping the floor, he can help to save souls," by freeing a priest for other work or by teaching lay people about the devotion with which a person can do even menial work. A brother "seeks no earthly reward, he labors only for God." In fact, a brother had fewer spiritual responsibilities than a priest, since he did not have to care for people through the confessional and could avoid contact with the sin of the world. Only priests could be in a position of authority as superiors or as consultors to superiors and could deal with the public as pastors, chaplains, and as confessors or missionaries. Brothers, however, dealt with the public in the physical maintenance of the monasteries or lands owned by the Congregation, as buyers and sellers of produce from farms, as musicians or sacristans in the churches, or as organizers of altar boys. A brother with special training was commonly appointed as nurse and would have authority over one or more sick or dying Redemptorist priests, students, or other brothers. Together, professed students, priests, and lay brothers were to form a family working together to help each other in holiness and in ministry or, as was commonly said, to save one's own soul and the souls of others. Whether as a priest or as a lay brother, dying in the Congregation, wrote St. Alphonsus, guarantees salvation.[27] At the end of his novitiate, Reisach pronounced his final vows as a lay brother on the 19 March 1838. As Brother Joseph he immediately volunteered for America. Instead, he was assigned to the house in Vienna to deepen his training in religious life.

Simon Saenderl

During the years Reisach lived in Vienna, the American mission underwent profound changes, as the Redemptorists worked more and more with the German immigrants. From 1837 to 1840 Redemptorist missionaries did not travel to British North America, since the Rebellions of 1837 made travel there even more difficult. There was work enough in the United States, where German immigration had swelled. In 1834 there were already 40,000 Germans making their way to the United States. That number increased to 86,000 in 1839 and reached 654,000 in 1854; in fact, it never dipped below 200,000 from 1854 to 1874. After 1870 it leapt even higher as many young men fled the military draft imposed on the newly united German nation.[28] Shortly before Reisach left the United States in 1837, the father superior, Joseph Prost, decided to concentrate on the urban Catholic immigrants, especially the Germans who had almost no German-speaking priests working for them. Later, in 1841, a new superior from Vienna, Alexander Czvitkovicz, decided to dedicate the Redemptorists henceforth solely to the German immigrants. In contrast to the many French-speaking religious communities fleeing France's anti-clerical crises, or to the Irish secular priests following their flocks, most of the Redemptorists spoke German and became known as the German Fathers.[29] As a consequence, Simon Saenderl, the former superior, saw most of his efforts with natives overturned by this change in direction.

When the Redemptorists finally abandoned their attempts at applying the structured Redemptorist life and Rule to the itinerant natives on the frontier and concentrated on immigrant urban Roman Catholics, success crowned their search for stability and regular community life. Redemptorist houses were established in Pittsburgh and then Rochester in 1839. Monasteries began to multiply on the east coast and along the transportation routes of the immigrants: Baltimore (1841), New York (1842), Philadelphia (1843), Buffalo (1845), and Detroit (1846) were all built while Brother Joseph lived in Vienna. Each foundation, an almost complete copy of every other, borrowed each other's blueprints and built bigger and bigger churches, schools, halls, and rectories.

Redemptorists who found it hard to adapt to the new situation in the United States were sent to British North America. Simon Saenderl was sent to the diocese of Toronto in 1843. He had displeased an American bishop with some newspaper articles about American politics and his superiors thought it better to send him elsewhere.[30] Bishop Michael Power of Toronto, worried about a similar newspaper controversy in Canada, controlled every word Saenderl wrote. He even went so far as to forbid Saenderl to establish a printing press in the diocese unless he submitted everything, except his German writings, for Power's approval. Power probably could not read German.

Bishop Power also insisted that Saenderl make sure that all property bought by lay people for church use be deeded to the bishop.[31] Furthermore, Power advised Saenderl that lay people who had not paid their dues to the church were to be denied Christian burial, causing a scandal when Saenderl refused to bury a debtor's daughter in consecrated ground. It is reported that Saenderl attempted to enforce the bishop's will by threatening to disinter anyone buried without his knowledge and by handing the body over to a medical school which, according to Redemptorist tradition, he did. This caused him even more trouble among his parishioners. Pleased with Saenderl's obedience, in 1845 Power formally invited the Redemptorists to found a monastery in his diocese. Unfortunately, there were not enough Redemptorists to accept.

Saenderl returned to the United States in 1846, but not before a long series of misunderstandings cut him off from the Congregation. Working alone in the Toronto diocese, he deposited his income in the Toronto parish of St. Paul. Ordered to report to the house in Monroe, Michigan, Saenderl suffered a fall from his horse during the trip and broke his leg. He was found by a passing traveller and nursed back to health, but it was some time before he could walk, and more time before he could send word of his delay. When he did not appear at the appointed day, a dispensation from his vows was sent to Monroe. Saenderl was accused of breaking his vow of poverty by saving money for personal use; his failure to return to his monastery in the United States when ordered to do so convinced the American superior, Peter Czackert, of Saenderl's disobedience.[32] The dispensation was not immediately served on him, because the bishop of Toronto had written telling of the accident. When Saenderl did learn of it, he was shocked to learn that his superiors thought so badly of him that they were ready at a moment's notice to expel him. He decided to leave the Congregation and was then immediately accepted into the diocese of Toronto in September of 1847.

Saenderl was sent to work in St. Agatha's parish, Waterloo County, which later became part of the diocese of Hamilton. He also worked in Guelph, Arthur, and Hamilton, and in 1850 he began a hermitage on Puslinch Island in southwestern Ontario. During the building of the hermitage, he left on a pilgrimage to Jerusalem. On his return in 1852, his desire for solitude and quiet gained the upper hand, and Saenderl, like so many other early Redemptorists, decided to join a contemplative order. The first superior of the Redemptorists in North America, called the founder of the Redemptorists in America, ended his days in 1879 as a Trappist in the monastery of Gethsemani, Kentucky.[33]

Frederick de Held

Saenderl's departure came partly in reaction to a growing rigid conformity to regular discipline within the Redemptorist Congregation in North America. The new superior entrusted with the American missions, Frederick de Held, visited North America in 1845 and left copious recommendations for stricter adherence to the Rule. Although de Held had been a disciple of Clement Hofbauer, he now lived under Joseph Passerat during the period that tried to undo the work of the revolutions. Hofbauer had adapted the Rule during Europe's revolutionary period, but Passerat and de Held moved from living the spirit of the Rule in revolutionary times to living the letter of the Rule in a time of restoration.

Passerat and de Held also saw the restructuring of the Congregation as an attempt to reflect its original emphasis on strict hierarchy and obedience. The vicar-generalate for the Redemptorists outside Italy was abolished. To improve administration, the Redemptorists were reorganized in 1841 into ecclesiastical provinces, each headed by a provincial answering to a superior general in Rome. Rome, Naples, Sicily, Switzerland, Austria, and Belgium became the first six provinces in the Congregation. North America remained a region with a superior, called a visitor, under Belgium's authority. De Held was the provincial of the Belgian Province and an extraordinary visitor whose decisions for the American missions were subject only to the superior general in Rome.

The Redemptorists credited their successes neither to the population explosion in Catholic America, nor to the fundamental shift from frontier native missions to missions among the urban Catholic immigrants. De Held and others firmly believed that regular order was blessed by God and was responsible for success.[34] The stricter mood in America helped to drive Saenderl and others out of the Congregation. In contrast, others joined the Congregation because they were attracted by the zeal Redemptorists displayed in caring for their immigrant flocks. These same newcomers might have wished to flee the chaos of American life.

The anti-clerical persecutions building in Austria convinced more German-speaking Redemptorists to flee to North America. Although Haetscher went to England, Brother Joseph Reisach was sent to America in 1847. The revolutions that broke out across almost all of Europe in 1848 scattered the remaining Redemptorists of Vienna as well as many other religious communities and, by swelling the American Redemptorist ranks, forced North America to become a separate religious province independent of any European provincial. The arrival of German-speaking Redemptorists again cemented the fundamental orientation in Redemptorist priorities to immigrant Catholics. Brother Joseph was stationed in Rochester as a carpenter. There, he witnessed the growth of the Congregation, the growing discipline of the Redemptorist community, and the occasional mission into British North America. In the United States, monasteries were founded in New Orleans in 1847, in Annapolis, Maryland in 1853, another in Baltimore in 1859, and in Chicago in 1861, all within Brother Joseph's lifetime. By 1859 there were fifty-six priests, forty-six brothers, twenty-eight novice brothers, and sixty students in eleven houses.

De Held's visit to the United States in 1845 also illustrated another truth about the development of the Congregation. De Held and Redemptorists fleeing European persecution travelled from Belgium via England and through British North America. Cheaper transatlantic and transcontinental water routes made British North America the best way to travel from Europe to the United States. Even in America, the shortest distance between Detroit and Buffalo was along the water routes through Canada. The Redemptorists of the American Northwest often travelled from their new monasteries in Monroe, Rochester, and Buffalo into the Windsor and Niagara Falls regions of Canada. Missionaries such as Francis-Xavier Tschenhens, Anton Schmid, Lawrence Holzer, Karl (Charles) Kannamueller, Benedict Bayer, Jacob (James) Keitz, and Joseph Wissel became known throughout southwestern Ontario. They ministered mainly to Germans along the international border and railway lines who had not seen a priest since the New York diocesan priest, John Neumann, left the area to join the Redemptorists.[35]

St. John Neumann (1811–60)
Born in Bohemia, he volunteered for the American missions where he was accepted into the diocese of New York and sent to work around Buffalo. In 1842 he became the first priest in North America to join the Redemptorists.

Canadian Invitations

In 1852 Power's successor in Toronto, Bishop Armand de Charbonnel, impressed with the mission preaching of the Redemptorists in Cincinnati and continually looking to alleviate the chronic shortage of clergy in his diocese, urged the Redemptorists to accept the care of all of the Catholics in Brantford or in Hamilton. When refused, he offered Niagara Falls. "Would to God," de Charbonnel exclaimed, "I would be soon so happy as to possess some of St. Liguori's Children!"[36] The bishop travelled to Europe to see the Redemptorist superiors, but there was also a shortage of clergy in Europe. In 1854 the bishop of Toronto offered a central mission on the Canadian rail line between Buffalo and Detroit, but the answer was the same. More disappointing, Provincial Ruland informed Bishop de Charbonnel that he was considering closing one or more of the monasteries that were near Canada. Steps were taken to close both Monroe and Detroit, Michigan, but fortunately only Monroe was closed for lack of men to maintain regular order.[37] With eleven foundations in the United States in 1854, and just over fifty priests and under fifty brothers, the Redemptorists were spread too thinly to have much community life together. It seemed as if every single priest in a foundation was out on missions, leaving the parish shorthanded and the religious exercises undone. When the nativist, anti-Catholic political Know-Nothing movement reached its height in the United States in 1855, the bishop of Toronto again seized his chance and approached Father Ruland to recommend a Canadian house of refuge from American Protestant bigotry. He offered any of Simon Saenderl's former parishes, such as St. Agatha's in Wilmot, a church in New Germany, or St. Clement's in Wellesley. Lack of men again brought the hard-pressed Redemptorist provincial in Baltimore to decline de Charbonnel's offer.

Only one Canadian was attracted to the Redemptorists between 1834 and 1874. François-Xavier Bricôt (1827–58), of Pointe-aux-Trembles on the eastern tip of the island of Montreal, left the Grand Séminaire of Montreal and his alphonsian moral theology textbooks. After a two-year stint of teaching school for the Redemptorists in Monroe, he joined the Rochester monastery in

1852. Father Bricôt left the reputation of a silent man who dedicated himself to prayer, mortifications, and to the French-Canadian parishioners given to his care. He attended the recreation periods with Brother Reisach, but he spoke little other than French, while Brother Joseph spoke only German and some English. Bricôt died in Baltimore on 23 April 1858. No other Canadian joined in this early period.

Shortly before Bricôt died, Bishop Charles-François Baillargeon, administrator of the archdiocese of Quebec, approached the Redemptorists for a foundation in his archdiocese. Father Provincial Ruland gave the same polite answer; he would be delighted to have a house in Canada, but lack of men prevented him from thinking of it for at least another two years. Baillargeon immediately informed the Redemptorists that he expected them to establish a house in the Quebec archdiocese in 1858 and he offered the English-language church of St. Patrick's in Quebec City itself.[38] The Redemptorists reluctantly sent Father Joseph Helmpraecht to investigate the proposed foundation.

The rumour of an English house in French Canada upset several of the English-speaking Redemptorists, notably Isaac Hecker, who left for Rome to plead for an English house in the United States instead of Canada. These young, second-generation American Redemptorists wanted an English-language mission house in the United States in order to move the Redemptorists from German to English parochial work and missions.[39] Hecker was expelled by the superior general for disobeying a directive against travelling to Rome, but he gained permission from the pope to found the Paulist Fathers for missions to non-Catholic Americans, who were mainly English-speaking.

Isaac Hecker need not have worried that the Redemptorists were about to go to Quebec. Helmpraecht reported that the Jesuits and the Oblates were already giving French-language missions in the Quebec City area. There were several territorial parishes that gave services to the English community. There was little work outside of the parish so that Redemptorists would not be called on for missions and would work only as parish priests. There was little work for more than a few priests and a brother so that a regular foundation with a full complement of Redemptorists would be unnecessary. Finally, the administration of the church was in the hands of lay people so that the Redemptorists would not be in control of the temporal management of the proposed parish. Claiming a lack of men, Ruland informed Bishop Baillargeon that the Redemptorists could not possibly accept the foundation even in two years and the bishop, in spite of impassioned pleas for help, was forced to accept this decision.

The same story was repeated in the dioceses of London and Toronto. The need for priests increased with the Catholic immigrant population. From 1856 to 1857 Francis Krutil, a brilliant polyglot who preached in eleven languages and could hear confessions in thirteen, travelled from Detroit into the Sandwich-London diocese to give missions to the Polish and to the Bohemians in Hamilton, Port Stanley, Simcoe, Windham (soon to become a township), Paris, London, and other towns of southwestern Ontario.[40] The bishop of London then offered to the Redemptorists the care of Chatham, Ontario, and the surrounding area where six thousand Catholics of various nationalities lived. Bishop Lynch renewed Toronto's request for the Redemptorists in 1861 and offered Niagara Falls as a pilgrimage site. Although the American Civil War broke out and a foundation outside of the United States would have been desirable, the offer was again rejected. The war absorbed all of the Redemptorists' attention and there were too few Redemptorists available for the places offered in Canada.

Centralization and uniformity became the rule in the Congregation under Superior General Nicholas Mauron as it was in the Roman Catholic Church in the nineteenth century under Pope Pius IX. Redemptorists had always been stout ultramontanists looking to Rome for their direction. They republished St. Alphonsus's dissertations in favour of the Immaculate Conception of the Virgin Mary, which was dogmatically defined by Pope Pius IX in 1854, and turned their mission centres around the world into rallying places for those promoting the dogma of the infallibility of the pope. Those who could not or would not adapt to the German-American urban parish missions were out of place in the United States. Those who differed left, as did Simon Saenderl and Isaac Hecker and the later members of Hecker's Missionary Society of Saint Paul, the Paulists.[41]

Unlike the Redemptorists, the early Paulists seemed to have adapted to the North American religious and cultural context and were skilled in English oratory aimed at both Roman Catholics and Protestants. They had inspired Bishop de Charbonnel to invite the Redemptorists to English-speaking and Protestant Toronto, but the departures to the Paulists meant that new foundations in the United States and in Canada were regularly refused for lack of men. Although there were now twelve hundred members worldwide by 1855, in America the Congregation numbered just over one hundred, less than 10 per cent of the total, and most of them were immigrant German-speaking Redemptorists. The German nature of the Congregation and the small number of its English orators further hampered the Redemptorists from going into Canada.

Father Christian Kauder, a Luxembourg Redemptorist recently professed in Belgium, arrived in the United States in 1845. He became quickly disenchanted with his work among the German immigrants in the United States and requested his dispensation in the same year. After spending some time in retreat with the Trappists of Gethsemani, Kentucky, he was dispensed from his Redemptorist vows in 1852. He travelled to the Trappist monastery in Tracadie near Antigonish, Nova Scotia, and worked extensively with the Micmac natives in the Maritimes. While in Tracadie, he requested permission to rejoin the Redemptorists. Father General Mauron refused but conferred on Kauder the honorary title of Oblate of the Most Holy Redeemer. Kauder produced a Micmac grammar, a prayer book, and a catechism published in Europe for the use of German-language missionaries. He became well-known in continental Europe but there is no evidence that his fame as a Micmac missionary and his status as an oblate of the Congregation became known to any Redemptorist working in North America. By its German nature and its preoccupation with immigrant Catholics in the United States, the Congregation overlooked both the native populations and British North America. Individuals, however, such as Saenderl and Kauder, began to spread St. Alphonsus's missionary ideals far beyond the Congregation itself.

From Brother Joseph Reisach's perspective, much had changed since he had arrived in North America. Besides wearing slightly different clothing, brothers were now given religious names. The new foundations and their many new members allowed the brothers and the fathers to separate to do their own work. After meals, the priests now read the newspapers and had recreation together, while the brothers cleaned the dishes and had their own recreation. How different it was with Father Haetscher! When there was work to be done, both priest and brother did the work together. When there were a few moments free, they read or spoke to each other.

Early on 8 November 1862, during breakfast, Brother Joseph suddenly felt chest pains so fierce that he could not rise from his chair. He stayed in the common room, sometimes sitting and sometimes walking around, but the pain never left him. Father Wissel rushed over to hear his gasping confession at half-past ten and gave him absolution and extreme unction. The other members of the community, shocked at the speed with which death was overcoming Brother Joseph, rushed in to say the prayers for the dying. He had been sitting with them at breakfast; by lunchtime he was dead.

The week before, Father Haetscher travelled to Vienna from Puchheim in Austria. He brought Clement Hofbauer's remains to be reburied in the church of Maria-am-Gestade where Hofbauer had preached. From across Germany and Austria, Redemptorists came to celebrate Hofbauer's return to Vienna and the end of the liberal revolutions that had forced the dispersals of Roman Catholic religious identified with the forces of hierarchy and reaction. Just before Christmas of 1862, Haetscher, now seventy-eight years old, suffered a stroke and died shortly after. So passed the first Redemptorist to work in Canada.

Between 10 December 1865 and 2 January 1866 in Montreal's St. Patrick's church, ten Redemptorist missionaries from the United States heard over fifteen thousand confessions, helped with almost one thousand confirmations administered by the bishops of Toronto and Montreal, converted twenty-five Protestants, administered the temperance pledge to two thousand, and vigorously denounced secret societies. The Montreal church was sometimes full to overflowing. The bishop of Toronto, John Lynch, seized the occasion to invite the Redemptorists to give missions in his own diocese. Missionaries stationed in Detroit began to travel even more regularly in southwestern Ontario. The Montreal mission effectively opened Canada to the Redemptorists.[42]

This Montreal mission became known in Redemptorist circles in Rome and throughout North America as the classic example of a North American Redemptorist English mission and was often cited as the first real mission given in Canada. It was so successful that the mission itself became a part of English Catholic culture and froze into a form that hardly changed until the Second Vatican Council. Wissel's reminder that his sermon and mission outlines were guides and that each missionary had to develop his own style and adapt to different audiences to be most effective became lost in the drive for further uniform success. Besides, most Redemptorists realized that the Irish Catholic audiences throughout North America were generally homogeneous. Wissel's book of sermon outlines was reprinted, minus the German sermons, in 1920. It was studied, memorized, and used by Canadians, Americans, and some Europeans up until the Second Vatican Council.[43]

The year 1866 also saw Pope Pius IX entrust the icon of Our Lady of Perpetual Help to the Redemptorists. Devotion to Mary was already very much part of Redemptorist life; now it had a face. Copies of the icon became an important element in many Redemptorist missions. By 1870 the nineteenth-century Redemptorist mission had stabilized into its classic form.

The main patterns of Redemptorist work in Canada had been established. Canadian clergy were eager to have Redemptorists expert in St. Alphonsus's thought. Clergy shortages and a growing immigrant population made the need for a polyglot religious clergy even more acute. The American Redemptorists now worked in several languages: French first, then German, and lastly but more and more in English, the language of North America and the British Empire. The short-term, intense Redemptorist missions were immensely successful. As a consequence, the Redemptorists once again received offers to establish themselves in Toronto and in Quebec City, two of the most important dioceses of Canada. As Alphonsus Liguori's theology swept the Catholic world, men joined the Redemptorists, the Redemptorist missions increased, and American Redemptorist missionaries moved into Canada.

Foundations in Canada could not be far behind.

2

The First Foundations
in Canada, 1865–93

After the American Civil War ended in 1865 the number of Irish and second-generation Irish-Americans joining the American Redemptorists jumped. English missions increased and English- rather than German-language foundations became more attractive. The Redemptorists were now better prepared to work among English-speaking Catholics in Canada.

Meanwhile, the reputation of their founder continued to grow. In 1871 the Holy See named Alphonsus *Doctor Zelantissimus*, Most Zealous Doctor of the Church, and declared that any penitent who visited, confessed, and took communion in a Redemptorist church gained a plenary indulgence from the pains of purgatory. Bishops around the world, interested in getting their people into the churches, found the Redemptorists more and more attractive as a congregation.

St. Patrick's, Quebec City (1874)

Prompted by St. Alphonsus's growing fame, in 1873 the new archbishop of Quebec, Elzear-Alexandre Taschereau, invited the American Redemptorist Provincial Joseph Helmpraecht to take over St. Patrick's church in Quebec City. Unlike the offers made in the 1850s, when the church had been first offered to the Redemptorists,

the archbishop this time promised to have the management transferred to the Redemptorists.[1]

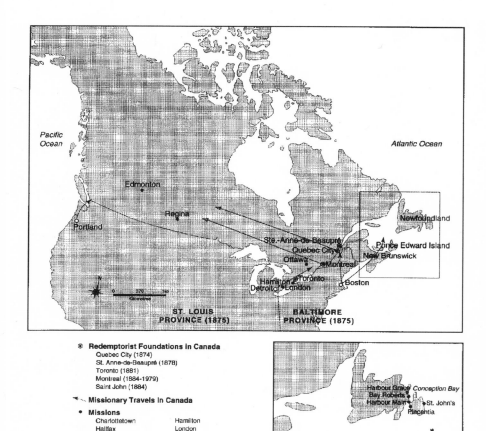

Early Redemptorist Foundations and Missions in Canada, 1874–88

At that time, St. Patrick's was not a parish, merely a church which the English-speaking members of the archdiocese had built themselves. The administration of parishes was against the Redemptorist Rule as they were seen to be a hindrance to the missions. The Redemptorist General Chapter of 1855 in Rome, at which Redemptorists from the United States participated, grudgingly allowed parishes in North America only if they were also mission stations. Not until after the Second Vatican Council would the Rule be changed to accept parishes as an authentic Redemptorist apostolate. Furthermore, the Rule forbade begging, or being paid for the missions; it merely allowed the missionaries to accept donations. The American Redemptorists found, however, that donations rarely covered costs. Unlike the situation in Europe, in North America there were no government and few private subsidies for works of religion. When donations and the sale of devotional books and other items at the missions were poor, the American Redemptorists could pay for their own keep only by taking salaries in parishes.[2] As a result, all of the Redemptorist foundations in the United States were attached to parishes so that many priests were paid out of parish funds for their work overseeing churches and schools while the brothers were paid to maintain parish schools, churches, and cemeteries.

When the American Redemptorists proposed St. Patrick's church to their superior, Father General Nicholas Mauron in Rome, the offer immediately attracted his attention as one that would begin to bring the American Redemptorists into line with the Rule that forbade parishes. He had one reservation: were not most of the Catholics in Canada French-speaking and did this not mean that the Redemptorists should be looking to establish a French mission house?[3]

Father Helmpraecht wrote several letters to convince Mauron that Quebec City was an excellent place for the Redemptorists. The archbishop was interested in a mission house, French or English. Mauron could transfer some French-speaking Europeans to America. Quebec's English-speaking Canadians were abandoned in a sea of French speakers, and there were few English priests. Although the Jesuits and the Oblates of Mary Immaculate had promised to preach missions, the archbishop said that they never gave any. The Redemptorists would have the mission field all to themselves. The archbishop promised even to have the trustees give up not only the management but even the deeds of the property to the Redemptorists. Finally, Helmpraecht declared, the anti-Catholic Know-Nothing party was again making its presence felt in the United States, threatening another round of persecutions. The American Redemptorists needed a place of safety outside of the United States.

The threat of persecution in the United States convinced Mauron to approve the Quebec City foundation. Enemies, it seemed to him, surrounded the Redemptorists on every side. The German Redemptorists were suffering under Bismarck's anti-Catholic Kulturkampf. The Papal States had been annexed by Italy under Victor Emmanuel and Bismarck's example inspired the Italian government to pass similar anti-clerical laws. France was in continual revolution. Redemptorists were fleeing persecution in southern and eastern Europe and were going to England, Austria, Belgium, and Holland. If the United States became hostile to Catholics, Canada could become a place of safety, as Hofbauer had once hoped. Since Mauron could not send French-speaking fathers right away, he ordered Helmpraecht to give up the French parish in New Orleans and send some of the French-speaking American Redemptorists to Canada. He decided that "the transplantation of the Congregation to Canada corresponds to the will of God. Since the Congregation is in danger everywhere, it is good to be established in a great many countries in order to find refuge in an emergency. *One* foundation in Canada will suffice at first and when it is completed, one could contemplate a second."[4]

Archbishop Taschereau signed the articles of agreement on 10 November 1873. In summary, it invited the Redemptorists to establish a missionary house and church. From the mission house Redemptorists would give spiritual exercises to the clergy and to the laity and would give missions throughout the archdiocese. The archbishop bound himself to try to transfer St. Patrick's property to the Congregation of the Most Holy Redeemer as soon as possible. Should St. Patrick's congregation ever need to move into a larger church, the Redemptorists would not be obliged to build the church or move with the congregation. They were to be missionaries working out of St. Patrick's church on McMahon Street, not parish priests.

Father Michael Burke (1837–91)
A poet and writer, he was born in the United States of Irish parents, and joined the Redemptorists in 1857. (Courtesy of the Baltimore Province Archives)

Although he had promised to help transfer the deeds, the archbishop soon became nervous about how the trustees at St. Patrick's would react. He begged that the superior and, if at all possible, one other Redemptorist to be sent to Quebec City be Irish – not German and certainly not French – to avoid any suspicion that French Canadians were taking over the church.[5] In spite of these last-minute changes, which dashed Mauron's hope for a French mission house, the Redemptorists refused two other tempting offers of parish foundations, one in London, Ontario and one in Saint John, New Brunswick, and accepted the Quebec City mission house.

Four priests and two lay brothers were sent from the United States to Quebec City at the end of September 1874. Father Superior Michael Burke, Fathers Michael Oates, William O'Connor, Andrew Wynn, Brothers George Meyer and Patrick Donlan took possession of the McMahon Street house and church on 3 October 1874. Except for the German-speaking Brother George, the American Redemptorists could hardly have brought together a more English-speaking, Irish-looking community. All were experienced in missions; none spoke French.

Trusteeism

Trusteeism – the organization and administration of the parish by the laity – had served Christianity in North America when no clergy had been available. In Quebec trusteeism was tempered by the fact that in civil law the clergy were automatically members of any parish administration. St. Patrick's church in Quebec City did not come under the law, because it had never been incorporated as a parish and so was run only by lay people. Therefore it was outside the archbishop's control. He could only appoint or remove clergy who then worked for the trustees. For nineteenth-century clergy, especially bishops, lay trusteeism seemed like Protestantism and heresy.

A mission began on 25 October 1874 with five visiting missionaries and the four priests of the community. The sermons were well attended, and out of a possible English Catholic population of ten thousand, nine thousand went to communion, while six thousand went to confession.[6]

As they had done in all of their parishes since their arrival in the United States in 1832, the Redemptorists proceeded to dismantle the trustee system. They demanded the ownership of the entire plant: land, church, cemetery, schools, and St. Brigid's asylum for orphans and elderly people, all of it worth over $25,000 and bringing in the considerable revenues of $13,000 a year. The Redemptorists argued that a part-time committee could not do the property and the church the same justice as full-time professional managers such as the Redemptorists were.

The church committee, composed of the leading English-speaking Catholic men of the city, had bought or donated the land and buildings for the use of the English-language Catholic community. They were at first inclined to trust the Redemptorists and merely requested that the trustees be allowed at least to audit the financial accounts and inherit the property should the Redemptorists leave St. Patrick's. The Redemptorists refused. Such a refusal brought some people to suspect that the Redemptorists were in Quebec City only to get their hands on the property. Accordingly, the trustees hardened their position and refused to hand the property over.

The controversy spilled over into the newspapers. On one side, a newspaper article stated: "The Irish can trust our revenues to the Sacred Orders, who laid the foundations of civilization, before committees were invented – long, long before Henry and Anne, and Luther and Calvin, put their heads together to regenerate the world." On the other side of the debate, another newspaper article called the whole business "an ugly skeleton of ecclesiastical greed and Jesuitical double-dealing. Never has the grasping disposition of religious communities been more dangerously shown than in the present attempt to dispossess us, unfortunate Irish people of Quebec, of the few privileges yet remaining to us."[7]

"The war has already begun," wrote Father Michael Burke.[8] The committee decided to visit the archbishop on Sunday morning to verify if he had indeed promised the deeds to the Redemptorists. Fathers Michael Oates and Andrew Wynn with Judge Matthew Hearn, a sympathetic committee member, reached the archbishop first, late Saturday night. The committee received a cold reception from the archbishop the next morning. The archbishop visited the church that same Sunday afternoon and whipped up the crowd against the committee, bringing his speech to a thundering end by shouting the question three times: "The Fathers or the Committee?" and getting louder and louder cries for "the Fathers!" Quebec's more numerous poor sided with the Redemptorists against the richer individuals who had long controlled the purse strings of the charitable organizations. Two thousand votes were cast for the Redemptorists and nineteen, all committee members, voted for the committee. However, legally this changed nothing and the committee still refused to give up the properties.

The meetings chaired by Father Michael Oates declared that the committee was a self-perpetuating elite, an undemocratic and anti-clerical oligarchy, and "a nest of corruption." Lawyers, headed by Judge Matthew Hearn, drafted a petition denouncing the committee and asking for an amendment to the Act of Incorporation for the Roman Catholics of Quebec speaking the English language. The bill proposed the dissolution of the unrepresentative, self-appointed committee and its reconstitution through elections from pewholders, whom the Redemptorists believed they could control. To pressure the government and to overawe any opposition, the Redemptorists organized huge meetings at the foot of the legislature.

In the background to the trustee struggle, the Redemptorists carried out their ministry. For example, the practice of raising the boys in the father's religion and the girls in the mother's had crept into Quebec's English Catholic families as a working compromise with the Protestants. The Redemptorists denounced mixed marriages and placed pressure on the Catholic spouse to renounce a Protestant marriage or raise all of the children as Catholics, causing an uproar among the Quebec City Protestants. Dances, considered dangerous occasions of sin, were also vigorously put down. In February of 1875 Father Andrew Wynn, accompanied by Brother Patrick armed with a shillalah (a short, hard-wood walking stick sometimes used as a club) raided a private dance in Diamond Harbour near Quebec City. "At their appearance," the chronicles state, "the delinquents skedaddled." The annual lieutenant-governor's ball was cancelled at the Redemptorists' insistence and the money that would have gone on the dance was donated to the poor of St. Patrick's. That same month, a house perched on the cliff fell into Diamond Harbour, crushing several of the houses in the poor, Irish Lower Town. Father Michael Oates reaped much admiration and support when he went among the ruins to minister to the dead and the dying.

In the trustee struggle, meanwhile, Father Oates organized another meeting against the committee, just before third reading of the bill. Two days later, with Fathers O'Connor and Wynn, he organized a Tuesday mass and rosary for the bill's success. About a thousand of the congregation marched four abreast to Parliament and six hundred, mainly women, entered to hear the debates. Those who spoke against the bill were later harassed and jostled by the female crowd. One member of Parliament was almost trampled until the crowd was restrained by shouts from Oates and Wynn. The bill quickly passed the very next day with little debate.[9] It now needed only royal assent to become law.

The committee members organized the annual St. Patrick's Day parade, but they were denied attendance on the archbishop and were snubbed by the Redemptorists and their fellow parishioners. The parade dissolved in bickering and heckling as the committee was bypassed by more populist and clerical visions of the role of the church.

Unfortunately for the Redemptorists, the bill transferred only the management, not the ownership of the property to the Redemptorists. The trustees still held the deeds and had the right to audit the accounts at the end of each year. In this way, the committee had a guarantee that the English-speaking Catholics of Quebec City had not handed their properties to a group who might sell them for money to be used in another Redemptorist parish. Although it was an unexpected defeat, the Redemptorists reasoned that the deeds might be obtained later. At least they would not be mere employees who could be hired and fired at the will of the committee. And, as managers, the Redemptorists had control of the nominating list of twenty-five names from which the trustees were to be elected. Five pro-Redemptorist trustees were duly elected, "all good & staunch 'Redemptorists'," Father Joseph Henning declared. "As the law gives the management of the election into my hands I took good care not to have any of the enemies on the list."[10] Matthew Hearn, the Quebec City judge who had helped the Redemptorists in all of their legal dealings to gain control of the property, was made an oblate of the Congregation, the first Canadian made an honorary member of the Redemptorists.

With the support of most of the parishioners, the Redemptorists had succeeded in bringing every aspect of Catholic life under clerical control. Every element in English-Catholic life was to revolve around the church, its sacraments, and its clergy. The Redemptorists reorganized the Ladies Christian Doctrine and Charitable Society, which ran St. Brigid's, and took it over themselves under the name of the St. Patrick's Catholic Benevolent Society of Quebec. The Redemptorists then invited the Sisters of Charity of Halifax (popularly called the Grey Nuns) to take over the work of the old age and orphan asylum under Redemptorist control. An agreement with the sisters was signed on 12 February 1877. Lay people were excluded from the management of the asylum.

The process of clericalization seemed endless. The lay committees dedicated to raising money for the parish were pushed aside and the Archconfraternity for the Benefit of the Souls in Purgatory, also called the Purgatorian Society, for prayer and fund-raising was established for the laity. A new Catholic high school was established in abandoned military barracks and the Christian Brothers were invited to take the place of lay teachers. The brothers too were kept under close supervision, because the Redemptorists owned the land and the buildings. The Diamond Harbour Chapel was built inside an old school bought from the archdiocese and outfitted with funds raised by the Society of Our Lady of Perpetual Help. The picture of Our Lady of Perpetual Help was installed. Calixa Lavallée, the famous organist, composed what became Canada's national anthem, one shot with religious imagery, while he worked at St. Patrick's church. Brother Anselm established a self-improvement library. In 1876, when the St. Patrick's Day parade again disintegrated, as the lay-controlled societies such as the Hibernian Society and several benevolent societies withdrew in protest at Burke's authoritarianism, Burke then established the Catholic-only St. Patrick's National and Beneficial Union with himself as president to help bury poor parishioners and to manage the parade in following years.

The Redemptorists themselves took care of everything, to such an extent that Provincial Schauer worried about the time given over to fairs, picnics, excursions, concerts, and schools instead of to regular observance in the monastery itself. One Redemptorist wrote into the annals on 5 August 1877 that St. Patrick's had become a perpetual mission. Everyone had been organized just as the Redemptorist mission was organized, because perfection and sanctity lay in a regular Catholic life under clerical guidance and hierarchical obedience. All of these devotions and activities needed Redemptorist chaplains, as did the regular work in a church with twelve thousand people needing baptisms, marriages, funerals, charities, religious instructions, daily masses, and masses several times on Sunday.[11]

The overwhelming presence of women in the mobs pressing the government for the transfer of the properties to the Redemptorists illustrates another important element in the Redemptorist campaign. Women were generally present in greater numbers at Redemptorist missions. Later they outnumbered the men almost two to one at the parish activities, devotions, and societies that the Redemptorists organized. A thousand women enrolled in the Redemptorist-sponsored Holy Family, but only two hundred men joined. The Holy Family had had a history of being a woman's society before the Redemptorists took it up for the whole family, and this partly explained women's greater readiness to join it, although there were sections for men, women, boys and girls. Men were more likely to join self-improvement organizations such as the Total Abstinence Society or the St. Patrick's Catholic Literary Institute. Overall, however, there were many fewer men than women who participated in parish activities.

The Rule discouraged Redemptorists from anything more than distant relations with members of the opposite sex, but in spite of this, some Redemptorists took over the spiritual direction of several women. They believed that women, not men, were the key to improving an entire family. A pious mother could regenerate a Catholic home and a converted mother could convert a Protestant home. On the missions, if women and men were separated into two groups, as they usually were, the women heard the sermons first on the grounds that they would go home and convince the men to attend. During the trustee battle of Quebec City, the newspapers declared, on the one hand, how shameful it was that the archbishop wanted to destroy the laity and, on the other hand, how the priests got at the women to pressure the men into accepting the Redemptorists.

Redemptorists, through devotions and societies, such as the Holy Family, created a close relationship between the laity and various religious figures. Women were especially comfortable with the family-centred feminizing of religion because dependence, obedience, and devotion corresponded to the role which nineteenth-century women were expected to assume in marriage. Men, however, who more and more worked outside of the home, felt less comfortable in the devotional, mainly feminine activities. The Redemptorists countered by establishing athletic, literary, and social activities for men in all of their parishes. By the end of the nineteenth century the Redemptorists consciously worked very hard at "saving the male portion of our congregations," since this aspect of the Redemptorist mission, as seen in the St. Patrick's trustee battle, had been much less successful.[12]

Besides standardizing practices within the church, and placing devotion in the parish church under the control of the priest, the story of St. Patrick's in Quebec City demonstrates a third element in the Redemptorist campaign to rally the resources of the church against the dangers of assimilation, through mixed marriages, for example, of English Catholics into the dominant English-Protestant culture.

When the St. Patrick's Catholic Literary Institute dropped the word "Catholic" from its title to attract Protestant members, Father Burke objected and took over the institute as honorary president. The uproar over Burke's unilateral takeover split the institute into two competing factions, each claiming the property and the books. The Redemptorists and their supporters labelled the members of the older institute "anti-clericals," "heretics," and names still less flattering.[13] A majority of former members, however, joined the Catholic institute headed by Burke and the lay institute, composed partly of disgruntled former committee members, disintegrated.

In September of 1875 a mission renewal was preached and the former trustees were given a chance to rejoin the congregation. The newspapers noted the presence of the prominent citizens who had been ousted from the committee. With the parish pacified and thoroughly under Redemptorist control, Father Provincial Helmpraecht began to transfer the English-speaking Redemptorists to other foundations and to send German-speaking Redemptorist fathers and brothers to Quebec. Fathers William Loewekamp, Matthew Bohn, Stephen Krein, and Brothers Anselm Knecht, Cajetan Schwalb, Joachim Kutter, Luke Zenkant and others were gradually sent, one by one, to fill out the community. A German-American superior, Joseph Henning, replaced Burke who had recommended a non-Irish superior so that the Irish nationalists would learn that Catholicism was not tied to any one nation. Burke had also contracted a debt of over $3,000. A strong financial man, William Loewekamp, was needed to clear the debt before the trustees realized the loss.[14]

To sustain these whirlwind activities required superhuman efforts. A visitor in 1878 had nothing but praise for Burke, while the new superior, Joseph Henning, was simply "extraordinary." Father William O'Connor had the reputation of a miracle worker, since "strange things have occurred through his prayers." Andrew Wynn was a vigorous worker, who did not hesitate to take a whip to beat drunkards into sobriety. Stephen Krein, Eugene Walsh, the brothers, were all characterized as strong, steady, excellent workers. In 1880 the superior was given the title of Father Rector in recognition of the size of the community. In 1889, to set the community on firmer ground in its relations with the English Catholics of Quebec City, Father John Hayden petitioned the archbishop to have St. Patrick's mission church erected into a canonical parish, since it was one in all but name. Father Mauron's plans for a French mission house in Canada had gradually taken shape as a German-American Redemptorist parish foundation.

Ste-Anne-de-Beaupré (1878)

Mauron removed Helmpraecht and named Elias Frederik Schauer provincial in July of 1877. In spite of Mauron's displeasure with Helmpraecht's inability to gain the Quebec City deeds and Mauron's warnings against the dangers to religious life in over-expansion, Schauer felt the Baltimore Province strong enough to expand further into Canada. In 1875 there were roughly three times more American Redemptorists than in 1850. The provincial directed one hundred and thirty priests, thirty-five students, and eighty-two brothers. In 1875 Mauron had divided the growing American Province in two, establishing the St. Louis Province west of the Mississippi, and renaming the eastern section the Baltimore Province. Ontario and eastern Canada became officially part of the Baltimore Province. Helmpraecht and Mauron had intended to give the Canadian west to the St. Louis Province. The Latin document, however, left some doubts in the minds of later interpreters as to which province should care for the Canadian west.[15] In any case, the Canadian west was relatively empty of immigrants in 1875, and the St. Louis Province had too few members to pay much attention to it.

In these circumstances, Baltimore effectively took control of all of Canada. Missionaries travelled from Baltimore's houses in the United States to give missions in Canada. Quebec City sent Burke to give an English-language mission in Winnipeg, Manitoba, in 1881. Only in 1887 did the St. Louis Province send men into western Canada to preach missions.[16] Even then, the missionaries restricted themselves to the diocese of Vancouver, which at that time straddled the international border and was practically considered an American diocese. Mountainous British Columbia was closer to the United States than to Canada, because the unorganized western territories of Canada lay between it and Ontario. The north-south continental pull was such that Rome's Propaganda Fide, under which mission territories were administered, planned as late as 1897 to have one of the western American Redemptorists named to the See of Vancouver Island.[17]

A successful French-language mission in Montreal's Notre Dame and Ste-Brigide churches in early 1877 gathered over fourteen thousand confessions, five hundred confirmations, and forty-eight converts. During the renewal, the papal delegate, Bishop George Conroy, was delighted to see over four thousand men with lighted tapers in their hands renewing their baptismal vows. The next year another French mission in Notre Dame brought forty thousand visitors daily and from nineteen to twenty-four thousand confessions. The superior of the twelve-man French mission band from the Baltimore Province was Anton Konings, an experienced Dutch moral theologian and perhaps the best-known moral theologian working in North America. The Swiss Frederick Brandstaetter and the Belgian Louis Dold were the outstanding preachers. Such a triumph had not been seen since the visit of the French Bishop Forbin-Janson of Nancy in 1840-41 who had introduced missions modelled on those of the Italian Redemptorists. Provincial Schauer immediately booked two more Montreal-area missions and a renewal of the Notre Dame mission for the following year.

When the archbishop of Quebec offered the Ste-Anne-de-Beaupré pilgrimage shrine to the Redemptorists, Mauron immediately took notice. The American Redemptorists could not give many English missions in Quebec, for lack of English-Catholic parishes. They were also generally unable to give missions in French for lack of practice in the French language since they were almost entirely taken up with English parish work. The shrine had a long history. Thousands of pilgrims visited it each year and a new and larger church and rectory were being built. The shrine had only one priest at the time. It needed more but Archbishop Taschereau had none to send. Mauron rejoiced: here was the French mission house he wanted. The Beaupré offer, he wrote to Schauer,

> corresponds to the will of God. This way we gain a solid foothold in Canada and a greater, more fruitful area of activity could hardly be found. The pilgrimages will increase greatly due to our efforts. Thus the Congregation will be known everywhere. In addition, a pilgrimage to Ste. Anne holds great attraction, because she is the grandmother of Jesus Christ and certainly very influential with her daughter, the heavenly mother. Therefore I hope for a special protection and blessing from heaven for this foundation.[18]

Four American Redemptorist fathers and two brothers took over the shrine for one cold winter. Their lack of fluency in French and the impossibility of travelling in winter to preach missions made them even more miserable than the cold and they begged to return to the United States.[19] A later Redemptorist described the place in the following terms:

> I am in the new foundation of Ste. Anne, if not completely beyond the world then at least at the end; only a few small, scattered villages past the new foundation and then there are no more human inhabitants.

There are, indeed, more wild animals with whose furs we protect ourselves against the icy cold. In the winter, Ste. Anne looks more like an isolated, frightening desert than a lovely, and pleasant little foundation. The house and church lie in a small, narrow gorge which is bordered by a mountain range on one side and the mighty St. Lawrence River on the other. In this repelling desert ... lies the famous place of grace where for nearly 200 years Ste. Anne has ... proven her great power and force from heaven through the most remarkable intercessions and miracles of all kind ...

The area around Ste. Anne is completely Catholic – there are no other faiths: only one language, only one Faith, one Religion is found here. The people in general are shockingly ignorant – by far the largest group cannot read or write. But still greater than the ignorance is the poverty of the people here.[20]

In response to the complaints by the American Redemptorists in Ste-Anne-de-Beaupré, Mauron and Schauer then devised the "French Plan." In order to prepare a refuge for the Redemptorists in France who could be expelled at any time, Mauron decided to ask the Belgians to take over all of Canada. Schauer also agreed to give the Belgians the French-language parish missions in the United States. The Belgians, overjoyed at the prospect of a new mission territory and one that was French-speaking, accepted on the understanding that they would immediately staff Beaupré and gradually take over the rest of Canada. The Belgians would henceforth be in charge of French Canada, and the Americans would remain in charge of English Canada until the Belgians took over St. Patrick's in Quebec City. The Americans at Beaupré happily made way for the Belgian Redemptorists in 1879.

Proficient in Flemish, a dialect linguistically placed between English and German, and educated in French, the Belgians sent to Canada were well prepared to work in French Canada and to learn

English. Many of them were from wealthy families. The arrival of the first six Belgian missionaries and the donations of significant amounts of money from their families helped to beautify and attract more attention to the shrine. Pilgrims both English and French, Canadian and American, increased from an average of between 20,000 and 40,000 to over 115,000 annually by the end of the century.[21] Beaupré became the scene of huge French-Canadian Catholic assemblies and a showcase for Roman and Flemish religious art and relics imported by the Redemptorists. By 1883 eight French Canadians, some related to the best-known families of Quebec, were sent to the novitiate in Belgium. The Belgians, meanwhile, sent English-language students to the Americans, expecting them to return to work with the Belgians in Canada. In 1887 Beaupré became a minor basilica. St. Anne was declared a patroness of Quebec and the Belgians crowned the statue of St. Anne in Beaupré. French Belgian publications poured into Canada and the Belgians took over the publication of the *Annals of St. Anne-de-Beaupré*, a popular monthly family magazine published in both French (begun by the diocese in 1873) and in English (since 1887) and sent to hundreds of thousands of subscribers from the end of the nineteenth century and throughout the twentieth. The sodality of St. Anne spread throughout French North America. Belgian French-language missions, except for a greater emphasis on conversion, were almost identical to the American English-language missions. They began to cover French Canada systematically and were invited to preach the French parish missions in the United States.

St. Patrick's, Toronto (1881)

During these years there had been continual requests for missions and offers of foundations in English Canada. Father Michael Burke, the superior in Quebec City, gave solo missions and clergy retreats throughout the Hamilton, London, and Toronto dioceses, as did his successor, Joseph Henning. After the English-language foundation in Quebec City, the offers became more insistent. John Joseph Lynch, archbishop of Toronto since 1870, offered Niagara Falls in 1874 and in 1875. At the end of the 1880 mission in his cathedral,

Lynch asked the people to pray that the Redemptorists would remain in Toronto to "do a world of good as city missionaries and as a centre of missionary action for the whole Province, and even the whole Dominion." He offered St. Patrick's parish, with its new yellow-brick church, residence, and school in downtown Toronto.[22]

Interested in a foundation outside Quebec, Schauer hurried from Baltimore to see the place and wrote Father Mauron for permission to accept. Schauer called St. Patrick's physically the best parish in the city, but spiritually made up of mostly poor and abandoned people, corrupted by indifference and mixed marriages with Protestants: in other words, just the kind of parish for Redemptorists. Schauer capped his argument with the statement that the archbishop promised to transfer all of the land and the buildings to the Redemptorists if they would take over the large parish debt to the archbishop of $16,000. "We have never been made a better offer in America." Mauron trusted Schauer's judgment and accepted the parish, advising Schauer to make sure that the property was properly transferred in order to avoid adding to Baltimore's debt and to any problems with the elderly archbishop's successors.[23]

The negotiations dragged on because, as Schauer complained, "The Archbishop ... is getting on in years and is a real Canadian, i.e., a real fusspot, ... he has not yet signed ... because he thinks that much more should be spelled out in detail."[24] Lynch also asked the Redemptorists to provide someone to look after the forty or so German families in the city. After lengthy negotiations, and over the protest of the parishioners at the loss of their beloved pastor, Joseph Laurent, the agreement was signed in January 1881. It bound the Redemptorists to pay the parish debt to the archbishop and handed over the church, rectory, and parish to the Redemptorists.

Unfortunately, Archbishop Lynch refused to transfer the land on the grounds that the Redemptorists were not incorporated in Ontario. Even when the Redemptorists were incorporated in 1881, he still refused. Advised by lawyers that this meant the Redemptorists could never get a mortgage or sell without the archbishop's permission, Father Eugene Grimm, the local superior, negotiated a final clause requiring the archdiocese to compensate the Redemptorists for any improvements or buildings not entirely built from parish funds. Later still, the aging archbishop initiated several squabbles about other monies owing to him, and the Redemptorists paid every request. At his death in 1888, the former pastor of St. Patrick's stated to the Redemptorists that there had never been any debts owed to the archbishop. Henning begged Schauer to tell him what to do. Were the Redemptorists obliged to seek restitution? Were they guilty of simony, of buying their way into a spiritual office? Were the parishioners obliged to help pay a debt they had never owed? Henning sadly declared, "There are other crooked transactions like this before the people of Toronto and they will not add to the faith and confidence catholics ought to have in their priests and bishops."[25] In effect, Archbishop Lynch had gained priests for a burgeoning Catholic immigrant population without bankrupting the archdiocese or relinquishing control over the parish.

St. Patrick's began as a canonical Redemptorist foundation on 17 January 1881. The best-known American missionaries, Fathers Eugene Grimm, John Hayden, Augustine J. McInerney, and Francis Xavier Miller, with Brothers George Meyer and Alexander O'Neill, were appointed to St. Patrick's. Father Stephen Krein arrived shortly after to care for the Germans.[26] Father Miller wrote of their introductory mission in St. Patrick's:

> Our two week's mission has come to a happy conclusion. God blessed our work. St. Alphonsus prayed for his warriors. We had over a thousand confessions. What was lacking in number was more than amply supplied by the dispositions of the penitents, and by the bringing back to the faith men and women who for 10, 15, 25, 30 years strayed away bearly [*sic*] remembering that they were baptised in the one saving faith. Deo Gratias! Toronto is a city of apostates, owing especially to mixed marriages that were encouraged by many of the clergy. The people call the Redemptorists "Reformers of Catholicity."[27]

The number of missions multiplied. Even as early as 1881 fourteen weeks of missions were given and nine weeks of renewals in the archdiocese of Toronto and surrounding dioceses. In one year alone, from 1882 to 1883, thirty-two missions and several renewals were preached, two of them in French. Missionaries from the Toronto house also gave nine retreats to clergy and religious in the archdiocese. German missions increased, because the German-American Redemptorists from Detroit could now stop in Toronto during their trips through Ontario. In 1884 Archbishop Lynch gave the Redemptorists faculties for all of the Germans in the archdiocese. Schauer rejoiced: "Our missions in Canada have increased so much since we acquired the house in Toronto, ... It has thus opened a brand new field for us."[28] More invitations for foundations came in. The Redemptorists transferred several of their men from Quebec City to Toronto to make it the centre for Redemptorist English-language missions in Canada, while the Quebec City foundation became mainly parish-oriented.

St. Patrick's rectory, Toronto

In Toronto the Redemptorists bought property to enlarge the house as far as McCaul Street and moved into their new home in 1882. Then the parish work began in earnest. The picture of Our Lady of Perpetual Help replaced the picture of Our Lady of Lourdes in the parish church. During the 1880s around four hundred women and one hundred men belonged to the Archconfraternity of the Holy Family. The Archconfraternity of Our Lady of Perpetual Help and of St. Alphonsus was also established. Devotional organizations, the Angels of the Sacred Hearts of Jesus and Mary for young girls and the Society of the Sacred Heart of Jesus for older boys, were established. St. Catherine's Young Ladies Literary and Scientific Association attracted forty members in its first year. The Purgatorian Society soon reached a thousand members. In 1894 the St. Alphonsus Catholic Association for young men built a new club house on William Street (now St. Patrick's Street), which was to become a focus for many parish activities for young men over the next fifty years.

In 1886 Archbishop Lynch laid the cornerstone for a new monastery to house the full complement of eighteen Redemptorists. For $17,000 and the donated time of an architect living in the parish, a large yellow-brick rectory was built and still stands. The community moved in on 7 February 1887 and shortly afterwards the superior was given the title of rector to indicate the permanency of the Toronto foundation.

St. Peter's in Saint John, New Brunswick (1884)

The missions in the Maritimes were also growing in importance. Archbishop Michael Hannon of Halifax, who had heard of their work in Ireland, invited the Redemptorists for a series of missions. Fathers F.X. Miller and A.J. McInerney left Toronto in February of 1882 to join the mission band from Boston under Father Joseph Wissel. Together they went into the Halifax and Harbour Grace dioceses of Nova Scotia and Newfoundland to give perhaps the first Redemptorist mission in the Atlantic region. Missions were given at St. Patrick's in St. John's, St. Patrick's in Carbonear, and the cathedral and St. Joseph's in Halifax.[29]

The Redemptorists, mostly German-Americans, hammered away at the Irish nationalism of the local people and upheld the universal nature of the Church. Their successes were astounding. After long-standing squabbles amongst themselves, Bishop Thomas Power of St. John's, Bishop Reginald MacDonald of Harbour Grace, their priests and people were all reconciled. There were several thousand confessions in the cathedral of St. John the Baptist in St. John's, Newfoundland. The dangerous travel by boat around the coast only inspired the missionaries to greater efforts. Maurice Bonia of Greater Placentia had long wanted to be a priest but was teaching in River Head to pay his debts to the government for his education. After attending the Harbour Grace mission, he applied to join the Redemptorists and became the first Redemptorist priest from Newfoundland. A new archbishop of Halifax, Cornelius O'Brien, offered the Redemptorists a foundation in Bermuda to keep them in his diocese. The missionaries travelled to Prince Edward Island in 1883 and 1884 to give more missions.

The most memorable mission preached by the Boston missionaries caused an international incident and was reported in newspapers around the world. It happened in Bay Roberts on Conception Bay, fifty kilometres west of St. John's, Newfoundland. Early in November 1884 Fathers Patrick M'Givern, John O'Brien, and Francis Delargy started out from Boston to give missions in Newfoundland, and everywhere the Catholics turned out in full force. Individuals converted from Protestantism. During the mission, one of the American Redemptorists said what he thought of the chances of Protestant heretics, such as Queen Victoria, going to hell. Word of these statements quickly spread. Unknown to the visiting Redemptorists, in the previous year, just after the missions of 1883, at the height of the Orange Order's power, five men died as a result of a St. Stephen's Day Parade riot. During the inquiry, several witnesses pointed at Redemptorist preaching as one of the causes of the tensions between Catholics and Protestants. Five residents swore before a magistrate that they heard one Redemptorist say that "the Protestant religion was established by Queen Elizabeth who was an illegitimate child – that is a bastard." Another five stated that they heard the Redemptorists "preach to the effect, '... put a collar on a

,4 of 414

monkey's neck and he would make a first class Wesleyan preacher.'
[They] further stated that the priests asked, 'What can you think of
the Church of England when it sprang from a bastard? ... From
Elizabeth down, we may call the Protestants a set of whores and bas-
tards'."[30] There was no denial in the statements recorded.

Inevitably, the Orange Order was waiting for the
Redemptorists when they returned in 1884. Hecklers harassed the
missionaries in the streets during the day and gathered outside their
windows at night. A group of Orangemen built an arch flying
Orange flags under which the missionaries and the Catholics had to
pass on their way to and from the church. When this did not satisfy
the more militant Protestants of the place and violence was threatened, the Redemptorists broke off the mission and went on to North
River and Harbour Main. They later returned with Bishop
MacDonald of Harbour Grace who refused to go under the Orange
arch. The Redemptorists demanded protection, but the Bay Roberts
magistrate refused to admit that the priests were in danger. As
American citizens, the missionaries then called on the American
consul in St. John's who managed to get the gunboat *Tenedos* stationed just outside St. John's harbour. The "Fathers said that they
had completed their mission at the Bay at the point of the bayonet
and at the muzzle of the Gatling guns."[31]

The fame of the Redemptorists continued to grow throughout
the Maritimes. Bishop John Sweeney of Saint John, New Brunswick,
who had begged Helmpraecht in 1876 for a foundation in his city, now
approached the missionary Joseph Wissel for a foundation in the town
of Portland on the outskirts of Saint John. Wissel praised Portland:

> A house at S. John's [*sic*] would be a very great
> advantage. The North East of the country is now open
> to us. From S. John's we have easy RR [railroad]
> accommodations into the North of Maine, into all
> New Brunswick which comprises two dioceses
> whose Bishops are favorably disposed towards us,
> into Nova Scotia, Prince Edwards Island, even into
> New Foundland. We have to locate ourselves in this
> direction sooner or later.[32]

Community hall, church and rectory, St. Peter's, Saint John, New Brunswick.

On the debit side, Portland's frame church on Elm Street was too small for its four thousand parishioners. The new church site, with a church half-built and encumbered with $4,000 of debt, was an old graveyard next to a swamp that could not be sold or used for anything but a church. To its credit, the town of Portland would soon be incorporated into Saint John and the Redemptorist priests who had been working in the Maritimes for the previous two years needed a mission house. The Redemptorists took possession of the parish on the feast of St. Peter-in-Chains, 1 August 1884. But again, they did not own the land. The Annals state that after blessing the makeshift monastery, Schauer left saying, "Now you have everything." In fact, "everything" consisted of borrowed vestments, a stove, and a temporary altar.[33]

The missions out of the Saint John house, however, were spectacular. In 1887 missionaries from there gave fourteen missions and seven renewals, almost all of them in the province of New Brunswick. This equalled the number of missions given by the specially named Boston "Mission" house in all of New England that year. The Redemptorists quickly organized St. Peter's into a typical Redemptorist parish. The parishioners drained the swamp and the land became a beautiful field for picnics and games. The Redemptorists took over the pastoral care of Chapel Grove on the Kennebecasis River, finished the building of St. Peter's church, at a cost of over $21,000, and arranged to build a convent for the Sisters of Charity and a new rectory for themselves. A resident Belgian nobleman donated money and stained glass windows. Saint John's superior became rector of a well-staffed foundation in 1890.

Chapel Grove, New Brunswick
A favourite vacation spot for the Redemptorists, novices, and parishioners of St. Peter's in Saint John.

St. Ann's, Montreal (1884)

It was not until 1884 that the Redemptorists received an invitation to take over a foundation in Montreal. When Bishop Edouard-Charles Fabre of Montreal considered bringing in a religious Congregation to care for the Irish parish of St. Ann, then under the care of an

elderly priest and four assistants, he consulted Bishop Thomas
Duhamel of Ottawa and Quebec City's vicar general, Cyrille Marois.
Both recommended the Redemptorists; Duhamel enthused, "In any
case take the Redemptorists, because they are the people for our
times!" So Fabre wrote to Schauer in Baltimore:

> I have in my episcopal city, five parishes where only
> English is spoken. One of them is in the care of the
> Gentlemen of St. Sulpice and the four others are in
> the care of secular priests. I had the intention of con-
> fiding one, St. Ann's, to a religious community. It is
> the most populous of the four; the last census shows
> almost 1300 families. I just removed between 5 and
> 600 to form a neighboring parish. It had had 1800
> families. There is a good church and rectory. The
> church is managed by church trustees with the pastor
> as president.[34]

St. Ann's church, Montreal.

St. Ann's pastor, James Hogan, was ill and would soon retire. Schauer also heard that Hogan had, in fact, opposed the bishop in the division of the parish. It appeared either that he was retiring in protest or that the bishop was forcing him out because of his drinking. Whatever the case, the bishop was short of good English-speaking priests and Hogan's retirement would cause Montreal some difficulty.

The Quebec City house of St. Patrick's had never fulfilled its promise as a mission house, since there were too few English-speaking Catholics in the area. Moreover, the English-language population of Quebec City had begun to move to Montreal, which was increasingly seen as the transportation centre for Canada. While the Toronto house of St. Patrick's cared for Ontario and the Saint John house of St. Peter's was planned to care for the Maritimes, there was still a need for an English mission house in Quebec.

Although Schauer had just accepted the house in Saint John, New Brunswick, it was still anticipated that all of the American Redemptorists would be recalled to the United States as the Belgians gradually took over the Canadian mission field. So Schauer invited the Belgians to take over Montreal. On the morning of 19 July 1884 he met with Jean Kockerols, the Belgian provincial visiting Canada. He repeated what had already been decided when Beaupré was turned over to the Belgians: Baltimore would give up all of the other houses in Canada as soon as the Belgians wished to take them. Furthermore, Baltimore would lend an English-speaking father to teach English to the Belgians. "It appears to me," Schauer wrote to Rome, "the best thing for the church in Canada and for the salvation of legions of immortal souls."[35]

So eager were they for a foothold in Montreal that the Belgians immediately agreed to the offer. Kockerols named his travelling companion, Jean Catulle, the new superior of the Montreal foundation and transferred William Godts from Beaupré to Montreal. The contract was signed on 15 August, and the Belgian Redemptorists were officially installed in the parish on 30 September 1884. Thus the Belgians gained a second foothold in Canada and could begin expansion into English Canada. They would be forever grateful for the Baltimore Province's generosity. Nevertheless, the land of St. Ann's foundation still belonged to the Sulpicians, the original owners of the island of Montreal. The trustee system also remained in place.

Jean Catulle (1835–99)
After almost twenty years as a diocesan priest in Belgium, he joined the Redemptorists in 1879 and spent the rest of his life in Montreal establishing the Redemptorists in Canada.

The Belgians launched French and English missions within a year. In order to learn English and understand the slight differences between a North American and a Belgian mission, the Belgians invited Wissel and his mission band to give an English mission in St. Ann's, and participated in Wissel's later missions in Charlottetown, Prince Edward Island. In 1892 Father Jean Catulle visited the Canadian Northwest on the invitation of Albert Lacombe, OMI, and in the next two years he sent William Godts to preach missions in English, French, Flemish, and German to Regina and Edmonton, and to prepare for the foundation of a Belgian Redemptorist house in western Canada.[36]

Meanwhile, in Montreal, St. Ann's parish quickly established Redemptorist devotions, processions, and societies, bringing in other religious congregations for schools, orphanages, and old age homes similar to every other Redemptorist parish. The relic collection at St. Ann's, begun by the Vicomtesse Mathilde Vilain of Brussels in 1884, became an important devotional attraction.[37] The Belgians raised and spent more than $100,000 for the institutions and the church. St. Ann's superior became rector in 1887.

Although the Montreal Irish diocesan priests at first resented the loss of an important English parish to a religious congregation – and a Belgian one at that – zealous work, especially against alcoholism, among the poorer Irish won the respect of neighbouring Irish pastors. To be accepted by the local community, the Belgian Redemptorists naturally adapted quickly to the Irish-Canadian culture. At the inauguration of the St. Ann's Young Men's Society hall to house choirs, dramatics, a gymnasium, and literary circles, Father Edward Strubbe stated, not without some irony,

> It did not please Divine Providence to make us Irish by birth; that is none of our faults; and as for me, if my parents could have taken my advice on that occasion, I assure you, I would not have been born elsewhere than on the soil of green old Erin. But Irish we are by the grace of our sacred priesthood, Irish we are by heart, by sympathy and love; Irish we are like the first Redemptorist Fathers that labored in that old country of yours. Nay, Irish we are as thoroughly as St. Patrick himself; Irish we are, Irish we will live, and Irish we will die.[38]

Schauer rejoiced when Montreal was established by the Belgians. Every major Canadian city then in existence – Saint John, Quebec City, Montreal, and Toronto – now had a Redemptorist house. "I am glad of it, because thereby our outposts in Canada are now at the strongholds of the Evil One, and our Mission campaigns in Canada will be a few years hence along the whole line of inhabited Canada. Deo gratias."[39] Whether the property belonged to the Redemptorists or not, whether the language of the people was the same as the Redemptorists or not, and whether the foundation was a parish or not, it did not matter as long as Redemptorists could give missions. Yet the Redemptorist experience in Canada was significantly different from that in the United States. The Redemptorists in Canada were less stable financially, since they rarely owned property, and were much more dependent on parish salaries and donations than even the parish-oriented Americans.

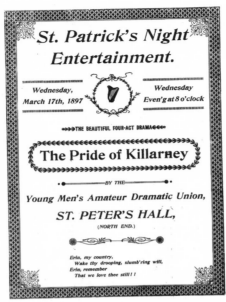

St. Patrick's Day Broadsheets

Parish entertainments in St. Peter's, Saint John, New Brunswick, and St. Ann's, Montreal at the turn of the century show that whether the parish priests were German-Americans as in St. Peter's or Belgians as in St. Ann's, the Irish-Canadian laity set the tone for the parish and the English-language Church of Canada.

The North American Redemptorist parish missions, however, were identical to the European missions, with both Belgian French and Baltimore English missions being interchangeable. The Redemptorist missions, under Wissel and his followers, were immensely popular. Schauer imposed Wissel's *The Redemptorist on the American Missions* as the mission handbook for all of the missionaries in the American Province.[40] In turn, the Belgians learned from Wissel the finer points of English-language missions in North America. More missions and more offers of foundations came in each year as the Redemptorists' reputation as missionaries and as parish leaders continued to grow.

As for the message of the missions, it too received wide support and publicity. Quebec's Archbishop Taschereau named Jean Tielen of Ste-Anne-de-Beaupré as a theologian to the Ecclesiastical Provincial Council of Quebec. The same council decreed that all Canadian seminarians should study St. Alphonsus's moral theology and recommended a summary volume adapted for North America written by the renowned Dutch Redemptorist theologian and recent Montreal missionary, Anton Konings. Father Eugene Grimm in Toronto translated St. Alphonsus's writings for English readers. As the bishops accepted Rome's favourable pronouncements about Alphonsus, taught him to their seminarians, and brought in Redemptorists for their people, the Redemptorists combined their missions with parishes. Their aim was nothing less than a moral revolution whereby nominal Roman Catholics would come to confession and communion regularly.

The path of Christian perfection in the parish came after reconciliation in the confessional, not before. Devotions to St. Alphonsus, Our Lady of Perpetual Help, and the many sodalities and societies, especially the Holy Family – all promoted during the mission – were firmly entrenched in the Redemptorist parish and in the Catholic mind as part of the perfect life. The societies the Redemptorists founded and refounded might have had brief lifespans, but the devotions remained constant. The names people began to give their children show their influence: Alphonsus, Clement, and, more and more as the century wore on, Gerard, the name of a brother famed for his miracles on behalf of expectant mothers. The

Redemptorists succeeded in uniting the formal and liturgical traditions of an institutional church to personal devotion and domestic
piety.[41]
          Consolidation in all of the Redemptorist parishes proceeded
apace with important donations and buildings. At the end of 1877
extensive property in Quebec City was purchased for a new cemetery. Looking far into the future, Father Joseph Henning stated to the
provincial, "any time you wish to build a Mission house –
Studendate [a seminary] – Novitiate etc, you have a place which is
the admiration of everybody."[42] In 1887 the Redemptorists in
Canada celebrated the centenary of the death of St. Alphonsus with
great solemnity and the following year a triduum in honour of the
newly-canonized saint Clement Hofbauer. It seemed as if the
Redemptorist saints were promoting the Congregation in the
Canadian missions and around the world. Occasional missionaries
travelled through Canada in the first part of the nineteenth century.
By the end of the century the Redemptorists were established in
Canadian parishes, the better to travel even farther in giving their
missions.

3

The First Vice-province of Toronto, 1893–1904

Beyond the prosperous parish foundations in Canada lay the hardships of the Canadian missions. "The work is harder than elsewhere," one of the American missionaries explained, "not only because of the incomprehensible ignorance of the majority, but because of the incessant preaching, the rough travelling, the poor diet, & the miserable lodgings."

> On one occasion, after closing a mission I had to drive 21 miles in a heavy rainstorm, put up for the night, & next morning drive 18 miles again in a blinding snowstorm. Then, too, not infrequently but one of us can give the mission & then imagine how pleasant it is to say mass everyday at 9 1/2 or 10 a.m., preach for an hour after it, bless articles of devotion, settle little difficulties, & drive a few miles before getting a bite to eat, hurry back again … hear confessions until service-time, then give a short instruction, say the beads, preach an hour's sermon, and sing the Benediction, – bless articles & go back to the confessional to remain till 8 or 9 o'clock at times before getting a supper. At the same time, we have to be carpenters, painters, locksmiths, & tailors, we have to

> make the cross & paint it, make grates for hearing
> confessions, & put up a store for the mission-goods.[1]

Most of the missionaries tried to keep up a regular life of prayer when on the road; others simply gave up trying.

The small parishes, the frontier nature of rural Canadian Catholicism, and the difficulties in travel and in scheduling missions around the farming seasons changed the Redemptorist mission. In spite of tradition and training, the typical Canadian parish mission given by American and Belgian Redemptorists slowly declined from one month to eight or even five days by the end of the nineteenth century. Instead of using a large team of missionaries for the small parishes, mission house superiors regularly sent solo and two-man mission teams.

The missionaries were sometimes forced to call on neighbouring parish priests to supply extra confessors. This removed two reasons for a Redemptorist mission: to offer penitents the chance to experience God's forgiveness in a new way, and the chance to seek divine forgiveness without having to face and be recognized by a familiar priest. With fewer preachers on a mission, there were fewer good preachers, fewer ways to present the doctrines of the Church, and fewer chances to move hearts to repentance.

Redemptorists in Canada also postponed the second part, or the renewal mission. St. Alphonsus had recommended the renewal six months after the original mission to strengthen the moral teachings and to emphasize God's mercy and love. By the end of the nineteenth century, distant Canadian parishes saw the renewal only a year later if at all. Some parish priests, in fact, preferred the yearly renewal so that they could take their annual holiday. Thus the mission for most people became a truncated experience, remembered more for the terrifying sermons on sin, judgment, and hell than for the sermons on the love of God. Since the Redemptorists had visited most of the parishes of English Canada with these shorter missions, the popularity and the demand for missions declined in Canada.[2]

Between 1876 and 1894 the total Canadian population was under five million people. At the end of the century Canadian Catholics constituted fewer than two million people, of whom roughly four-fifths were French Canadians. Besides the growing rivalry between the American and the Belgian Redemptorists for the few English-Canadian missions available, other congregations such as the Oblates of Mary Immaculate and the Jesuits also competed for the same parish missions. Until a new generation of English-Canadian Catholics in need of renewal came forward, the Redemptorist parish mission as practised in North America since 1832 could do nothing but slow to a stop.

Americans and Belgians in Canada by 1897

With declining Canadian missions and growing responsibilities in the United States, parishes became the American Redemptorists' main focus in Canada. The Canadian houses differed from each other only in that St. Patrick's in Toronto and St. Patrick's in Quebec City were known as English-language or, rather, Irish foundations, while St. Peter's in New Brunswick was often staffed with German-American priests. The Irish Catholics in Saint John, New Brunswick, were not overwhelmed by a French majority as in Quebec or a Protestant one as in Toronto and were therefore perhaps less insistent on having Irish priests. In everything – architecture, decorations, and parish organization – the houses were indistinguishable from any American house. Up to the First World War, English-speaking Catholics, usually recent immigrants, identified more strongly with the British Empire, or even with the United States, than with Canada and the French-speaking Canadians. There was little difference between an Irish immigrant to a Redemptorist parish in the United States and one that arrived in a Redemptorist parish in Canada. So, year after year, American Redemptorist missionaries, priests, and brothers came and went, treating Canadians as if they were Americans.

Expecting the Belgians to expand and needing his men in the United States, Provincial Schauer gradually withdrew his missionaries from Canada. Some of the Americans disliked the cold, sparsely populated wastes of Canada, the lack of missions, the different flag, government, and customs, and begged to return to the United States.[3] With the Belgians so near to Quebec City in Ste-Anne-de-

Beaupré, Schauer planned to abandon St. Patrick's in Quebec City. In any case, as industry increasingly moved to Montreal, the parish had shrunk from fifteen thousand to just over seventy-five hundred by the end of the century.[4] Schauer was also prepared to give Toronto and Saint John to the Belgians whenever they were ready. By 1894, therefore, the American foundations in Canada were no longer treated as mission houses but merely as parishes. All were staffed by older, semi-retired American Redemptorists. If any Americans gave English-language missions in Canada, they were usually given from the houses in the United States.

To overcome the distance between Belgium and Canada and to encourage more Canadian vocations, Father General Mauron had considered founding a separate Canadian Redemptorist province as early as 1884 to administer all of the Redemptorist houses in Canada. But with Ste-Anne-de-Beaupré sending missionaries farther afield in search of missions throughout Quebec, New Brunswick, Maine, or wherever there were French Canadians, and with St. Ann's parish in Montreal giving missions in whatever English parish the Americans or other congregations overlooked, the Belgian Redemptorists saw no need to expand. There were too few missions to warrant establishing a separate provincial administration in Canada. The novices would continue to go to Belgium for their training.

Nor did the Belgians want to expand into the American parish foundations of Canada. Having left home, country, and continent to go on the missions, few Belgians wanted to work in parishes. Living mainly in French Canada, few Belgians actually learned English, so English-language parish foundations were regularly refused. The Redemptorist Rule, the Belgians constantly reasoned, forbade parishes in order to keep good missionaries on the missions. Indeed, the Belgian Provincial Ernest Dubois traced the decline in the American missions in Canada to the fact that the parishes were using up good missionaries. Since the Belgians had only two parishes in Canada, this could hardly be true for the Belgian foundations. The causes for their decline were more likely to be found in the shorter length of the mission, the fewer men preaching the mission, or the practice of inviting secular clergy as confessors. Nonetheless,

Provincial Dubois repeated to Father Mauron that Belgians were missionaries, not parish priests like the American Redemptorists.

The rivalry between the American and Belgian missionaries on the shrinking mission field came to symbolize more than the missions themselves. At stake for the Americans was the principle of parishes as an authentic Redemptorist apostolate. American and Canadian bishops demanded that religious take care of parishes where diocesan clergy were scarce. The Americans believed parishes should therefore become part of their apostolate in obedience to the needs and wishes of the bishops. The parishes might become perpetual missions, or centres where missionaries could rest and work when not on the missions, and were excellent sources of vocations. The Belgians refused parishes and insisted on the European model of mission houses without the care of parishioners. Some Belgians openly criticized the American missionaries as mere secular clergy, an insult among religious missionaries who saw themselves, if not superior, at least in a higher state of heavenly grace than diocesan priests. The Belgians backed up the insult by stating that missionaries were not supposed to smoke, drink, or eat meat three times a day, all of which Americans had been seen to do in Canada. The complaints, sent to Rome, soon made their way to the United States, souring relations between the Belgians and the Americans. The Americans were shocked at the Belgians for throwing doubt on their loyalty to the Rule and to the traditions of the Redemptorist mission, especially since they had opened the Canadian field to the Belgians. Rumours circulated about which province would win the Canadian field.[5]

The monasteries in Belgium were full, causing the Belgians to become the great Redemptorist foreign missionaries of the nineteenth century. The Belgians were therefore less than eager for Canadian candidates and screened them strictly, almost harshly, on two counts: education and nationalism. First, Belgians declared Canadian education to be inferior by European standards. If one looked at the private Catholic schools or the government-sponsored schools in Belgium and compared them to the poverty-stricken parish schools and classical colleges making their appearance amongst Canadian Catholics, the Belgians had a point. As for the

English Canadians, the Belgians noted that public schools in Ontario were sound in mathematics, but sorely deficient in the humanities, French, and Latin.

Second, Belgians declared that French Canadians were nationalistic, emotionally attached to their country and hardly tolerated any criticisms of it. The Belgians saw how French Canadians looked down on the Irish as recent arrivals who had more in common with the English Protestants than with the French Catholics. The Irish simply repaid the hostility in kind. As a missionary Congregation, with men from several backgrounds working together in different countries, the Redemptorists could not afford nationalism. The Belgian superiors forbade all discussions of nationality. While they recognized that English was necessary in Canada, the Belgians could not decide which group to promote within the Congregation. The English were characterized as "expansive, insincere, inconstant, and tending to alcohol." Those knowing neither French nor Latin could be sent to the St. Louis Province in the western United States. The French Canadians were "light, vain, argumentative, yet weak in humanities." To improve their education and to stamp out their nationalism, the Belgians insisted that all French-Canadian candidates and only those English Canadians who knew enough French or Latin could study in Belgium.[6]

Between 1881 and 1896 the Belgians accepted forty-seven novices, most of them French Canadians. Unfortunately, few of these men survived the challenge of having to give up both family and country. The ones who persevered in their vocation were old enough to withstand the shock of going overseas for the novitiate and many came from the ranks of the diocesan priesthood or from the classical colleges. Even when the Canadians arrived in Belgium, there were other problems. It may be amusing today to consider how central heating could make or break a priestly vocation, but even in 1897 a Canadian was totally unprepared for the lack of central heating in the Belgian houses and ran a severe health risk. The Belgians could not understand how Canadians, after surviving the Canadian winter, could suffer in Belgium. More than one Canadian Redemptorist suffered an early death. The French-Canadian Alfred Pampalon died of tuberculosis at the age of twenty-nine. The

English-Canadian Francis Scanlan of Montreal suffered constantly in Belgium. Although he worked in St. Ann's after his ordination in 1896, in 1900 he was transferred to the easier work of editing the English *Annals* of Ste-Anne-de-Beaupré until his early death at the age of thirty-four in 1902. He had left Montreal for Belgium in perfect health and he returned a dying man. His example, of course, discouraged others. Young men sent back to Canada as unprepared, unsuitable, or broken in health prejudiced parents of several other young men against the Redemptorists.

When the Belgians further complained about the lack of good candidates, the French Canadians countered that the Belgians in Canada were not always perfect themselves. Some were sent to Canada because they had become undesirable in Europe and were equally undesirable in Canada; others were arrogant in their assumption of European superiority and French-Canadian inferiority.[7] The Belgians themselves were not immune to nationalism. Flemish Belgians were more apt to learn English, notice the number of English-speaking Catholics needing missions, and encourage English-Canadian vocations. Walloon Belgians were more likely to see the majority of French-speaking Roman Catholics and promote French-speaking vocations.

The Canadian Redemptorists also pointed out that the Belgians had been in Canada since 1878, yet nothing had been done to anchor the Redemptorists permanently in Canada. No novitiate, no minor seminary, and certainly no major seminary had been established. After spending huge amounts of money in Beaupré and in St. Ann's, Montreal, the Belgians were then content to tax the Canadian houses of any surplus revenues for projects elsewhere. The Belgians declared that any money made on the Canadian missions would not remain in Canada to pay for any educational institutions but would go to Belgium to pay for the Canadian students there. Furthermore, they declared that no expansion into the American foundations would be allowed until the Belgian-Canadian houses were full. Yet Canadians were being sent to the Antilles, if they did not remain in Belgium.[8]

English Canadians hesitated to undergo Belgian training. It seemed easier to join other religious congregations or the American provinces where fluent French, excellent Latin, a long sea voyage, meagre meals, and unheated houses were not prerequisites for entry. Records show that prior to 1898 at least fifty Canadian-born candidates to the priesthood, most of them trained in American Redemptorist minor seminaries, and ten candidates to the brotherhood presented themselves to the novitiates of the American provinces. Many of these candidates came from the American foundations of Toronto, Quebec, and Saint John, but a dozen Montreal English Catholics also went to the Baltimore and the St. Louis provinces. Prior to 1898 only three English Canadians – Francis Scanlan, John McPhail, and Daniel Holland – were ordained in Belgium. Significantly, neither McPhail nor Holland were from the parish of St. Ann's.

John McPhail was born in Alexandria, Ontario, in 1864. He was teaching school in Kingston and thinking about the priesthood when visiting Redemptorist missionaries seized his attention. He left for Belgium in 1889 at the age of twenty-five and was ordained in 1893. The Belgians categorized him as a typically cold, stiff Scot more interested in reading the works of Cardinals Manning or Newman and improving his English oratory than in learning more French. Several times on the verge of being dismissed for poor marks and for his lack of personal warmth, he was passed on the strength of his unshakable virtue and orthodoxy. He was declared unfit for Belgium but acceptable possibly in America. He went on to an extraordinary missionary preaching career, using English, French, and Gaelic, throughout Canada and the United States until his death in 1932.[9]

Daniel Holland was born in 1858 in Placentia, Newfoundland. He also was attracted by the missionaries and he left Newfoundland in 1889 for Montreal at the age of thirty-one. Although Rector Jean Catulle suggested he join as a lay brother because of his age, Holland insisted on going for ordination and left for Belgium immediately. Belgian Redemptorists doubted he had any priestly vocation and declared that, although he seemed intelligent enough to learn Latin, "he is Irish, and *a character to excess*, so much so that one may ask whether he has any judgement." Big, bluff, loud, and musical, all of which was frowned upon in crowded monasteries dedicated to silence, the Belgians delayed his profession until he had completed some make-up education and proven that he could succeed at his theological studies. Although his lack of French also hampered his studies, his goodness, his prior experience as a store clerk which gave him a large fund of common sense and knowledge and, above all, his excellent health and physical strength recommended him for the missionary life. He was ordained in 1895 and spent the early part of his Redemptorist life on missions in the Antilles and then in Canada until his health failed. He then worked in the Montreal and Quebec City parishes until his death at the age of sixty-three in 1922.[10]

Two other Montreal Catholics, George Daly and Edmund Flynn, are often thought to be English-Canadian Redemptorists, but they grew up speaking French because their mothers were French Canadians. The Belgians did not consider them English until Daly's and Flynn's knowledge of English made them valuable in the parish of St. Ann's. When it came time to choose between an English or a French province, Edmund Flynn chose to work in French. Furthermore, Daly returned only in 1900 to Canada from Belgium, where he had been since 1887.

Complaints from Canada flowed to Rome as English-Canadian candidates continued to leave Canada for the American provinces and as French-Canadian candidates for Belgium were being turned away, discouraged or, worse, were being accepted only to ruin their health in Belgium or in mission fields far from Canada.[11]

The Vice-province of Canada (1893)

To stop the rivalry between the Americans and the Belgians, to reverse the decline in the Canadian missions and to increase Canadian vocations, in 1893 Father Mauron set up the Belgian Vice-province of Canada, which included the two Belgian houses of Canada and the Belgian Redemptorist houses in the West Indies. He established the vice-provincial headquarters in St. Ann's, Montreal, intending it to become the centre of a bilingual Redemptorist province for all of Canada. As for the "American settlements in

Canada," Mauron wrote to the Baltimore provincial, "a decision will be made later whether and how and which one of them can be transferred to the Belgian province."[12] Mauron then named the most active critic of the American parish and the most active proponent of Belgian expansion into English Canada, Jean Catulle, to head the Vice-province of Canada. Rome had spoken, and it seemed that the Redemptorists would live in English Canada according to the Belgian model of Redemptorist life and missions.

Catulle insisted that Belgium immediately take over the other English houses of Canada. The Redemptorists, he said, absolutely needed the English language, English houses, and English priests to succeed on the English-Canadian missions. This English-only policy further alienated the French Canadians. As one stated, "The Belgians do not want French Canadians who want to join, but they want the Irish who do not want to join and who go to the Baltimore Province … French Canadians form four-fifths of the Catholics in the country and the three houses the Baltimore Province has in Canada could easily suffice for the English language Catholics."[13]

In the face of this opposition, Catulle proposed to begin by taking over the house in Quebec City to turn it into a foundation similar to St. Ann's, Montreal where the community spoke French inside the monastery but English inside the church. If the English parish died, as the Americans had often predicted, then the Belgian and Canadian Redemptorists could easily switch to French in the church or turn it into a mission church with no parish responsibilities.[14] In the best of all possible worlds, the Belgians would spread into English Canada with Flemish Belgians and Irish Canadians while growing in Quebec with French Canadians and Walloon Belgians. Catulle naturally assumed that Baltimore would willingly withdraw from Toronto, Quebec City, and Saint John as they had long said they would. Unfortunately for Catulle, Father Mauron never followed through with a decision about the American houses. He died in July of 1893 shortly after establishing the vice-province. Schauer was no longer provincial. Forgotten were the old agreements between Baltimore, Belgium, and Father Mauron to turn over the American houses in Canada to the Belgians.[15]

Baltimore refused to give up St. Patrick's parish in Quebec City. The Americans pointed out that the Belgians had few English-speaking fathers. There were not enough English Canadians amongst the Belgians to replace even the few semi-retired Americans the parish foundations employed. When bilingual French Canadians who had studied in England or had worked in the Antilles were found, the Americans insisted that the parishioners would revolt under French-Canadian priests. The Irish parishioners of St. Patrick's wanted only Irish priests, which only the Americans could provide.[16] The Belgians working in St. Ann's, Montreal, thought otherwise. Irish parishioners did accept other priests if the priests were totally dedicated to the parishioners and did not cause rivalries by splitting their attention between the French and the English or by assimilating the English parishioners into the French majority.

Why did the Americans keep a parish that had never lived up to missionary expectations, that had been visibly declining in population for years, and which they had been willing to let go a few years earlier? The Belgians in Canada were a constant reminder to the Americans of how far they had moved from the Redemptorist Rule, which caused them to insist all the more strongly on the value of their parishes. Besides, if the European authorities ever became convinced that the Belgians had successfully introduced the European model of Redemptorist life into North America, then the American Redemptorists could be asked to withdraw from most of their parishes. The Americans, relying on fifty years of success with the North American parish model, refused to withdraw from their Canadian parishes.

The American evidence is clear; since 1832 the German Americans had established on average one parish foundation every two and a half years. The Belgians had founded only two houses in twenty years. In 1897 the American Baltimore Province had over three hundred and twenty professed Redemptorists, not counting novices or students. Over half of the ordained men of the Baltimore Province were American-born while the new Vice-province of Canada still contained a majority of Belgians and relied almost entirely on Belgians for its work in English Canada. In 1897 there were only twenty-six French-Canadian Redemptorists; ten of them

had been diocesan priests before going to Belgium for their novitiate, while over thirty-five Belgians worked in Canada.[17] The
Americans had been in Canada only four years longer than the
Belgians and had received over sixty English-Canadian novices
from the Redemptorist parishes in Canada by 1898. American successes must be traced partly to their parish foundations.

Although the Belgians had attracted French-Canadian vocations, which brought the Roman authorities to think that the future
of the Congregation in Canada lay with the Belgians, their French-
Canadian candidates generally came through the missions. French
parishes were already well established and the Belgian
Redemptorists were able to work very much as they had in Europe
as a missionary auxiliary to the parish clergy. By restricting themselves to parish missions, when many North American parishes were
not yet established, the Belgian Redemptorists could not expect to
expand. If the Redemptorists were to have a future in North
America, the Americans had realized, the parish itself had to become
a perpetual mission and an example to surrounding areas. Baltimore
Provincial Litz wrote: "I know that though we are in far away
America – we can compare favorably with those who are nearer the
cradle of the Congregation ... when it comes to *practising* the spirit
of St. Alphonsus – we do as well as the *'preachers'*."[18] In summary,
the Americans came to believe that the Belgians would never accept
or adapt to parishes and they feared that the Belgian model of
Redemptorist life would be imposed and eventually choke off the
Redemptorist Congregation in North America.

The Vice-province of Canada did make one attempt to attract
more vocations. To overcome youthful and parental fears about the
sea trip and the stay in Belgium, it established the first Canadian
Redemptorist minor seminary in 1896. In two years twenty-one
French and thirteen English students graduated, but a mere five lasted the major seminary course in Belgium, only one of them English-
speaking. The Belgians still refused to go beyond the minor seminary to allow a novitiate in Canada, because they did not trust the
Canadians to form their candidates properly in the true Redemptorist
spirit. Besides, the professed novices would have to go to Belgium
in any case for their theological training, because Canada had no

major Redemptorist seminary. Since Canadians would have to work elsewhere than in Canada, because the Canadian parish mission field was so small, why bother with a novitiate in Canada? English-Canadian students continued to trickle to the American provinces. Not until 1898 would a Canadian, Alphonse Lemieux, become vice-provincial. Only then would the French-Canadian Redemptorists begin a novitiate, but it was too late; the Americans had decided to stay.

A growing sense of continental "manifest destiny" also accounts for the American Redemptorists' refusal to leave Canada. Americans, English Canadians, and even many of the Belgians believed that Canada was destined to become an English-speaking country. As the French Canadians assimilated and disappeared, so the thinking went, the future of the Congregation in Canada lay with the English Catholics. From the Americans' viewpoint, Canada naturally belonged to a North America dominated by the United States.

The American refusal to give up St. Patrick's parish in Quebec City brought the Vice-province of Canada to consider accepting a French parish in Quebec City, but the possible problems of having two Redemptorist houses close to each other, causing comparisons, convinced the Belgians to look elsewhere. In 1895 they purchased the Carmelite nuns' monastery, Our Lady of the Sacred Heart, in Hochelaga, in the east end of Montreal. Close to the port of Montreal, surrounded by the working class and the poor, Sacred Heart was a French-Canadian equivalent of St. Ann's in the west.

Hochelaga became the only North American foundation that truly duplicated the European model of a Redemptorist mission house without a parish attached. Several of the men at St. Ann's were transferred to Hochelaga. Embodying the ideals of Redemptorist community life as lived in Belgium and Naples, it also naturally became the vice-provincial novitiate to form young men in the proper spirit of the Congregation. Hochelaga, however, like most monasteries in the United States, soon embroiled itself in jurisdictional disputes with the surrounding territorial parishes and, to solve the problem, petitioned to become a territorial English or French parish as early as 1897. The European authorities refused, insisting on the European missionary house model. The mission house monastery chapel later became the nucleus of a new French parish under secular priests, the parish of Très-Saint-Rédempteur established in 1913, while the mission house was eventually demolished, demonstrating yet again the importance of parishes in North American life.[19]

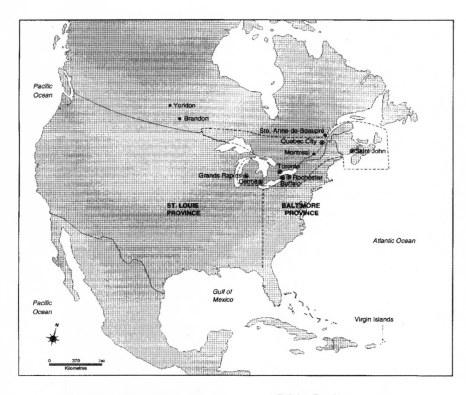

® **The Great Lakes Vice-Province of Toronto**
     (Baltimore Province)

Canada:
    St. Patrick's, Quebec City
    St. Patrick's, Toronto
    St. Peter's, Saint John

United States:
    Grand Rapids, Michigan
    Detroit, Michigan
    Rochester, New York
    Buffalo, New York

• **Belgian Province:**

French language:
    St. Anne-de-Beaupré
    Our Lady of the Sacred Heart, Hochelaga,
    Montreal

English language:
    St. Ann's, Montreal
    St. Augustine's, Brandon, Manitoba
    St. Gerard's, Yorkton, Saskatchewan
    and the Virgin Islands

The Great Lakes Vice-province of Toronto, 1898–1901.

The Vice-province of Toronto (1898–1901)

The new father general, Matthias Raus, ordered an official visit of North America to examine the American parish foundations, to end the continuing conflicts on the mission field, and to find solutions to the Belgians' inability to attract English-Canadian vocations or to expand into English Canada. Father John Bennett, born in Newfoundland and a former provincial of the English province, accompanied the American Consultor General Joseph Schwarz on the visit.[20] Although he fell ill during the visitation and resigned without finishing, Bennett left notes condemning the Baltimore Province for bad administration, large debts and, above all, too many parishes that had caused the debts and the strain on the administration. Baltimore, he wrote, had abandoned Redemptorist tradition and had created a division between Redemptorists who were missionaries and those who were parish priests. The parishes, he suggested, could be turned over to the dioceses and the houses closed. Other houses could be taken from Baltimore to form another, separate Redemptorist province.[21]

When Bennett resigned, Raus named Father Daniel Mullane of the St. Louis Province to accompany Schwarz on the rest of the visitation. Armed with Bennett's notes, the visitors rapidly, perhaps superficially, completed the visitation.[22] Together they discussed the possibility of taking a section of the densely populated Baltimore Province for a semi-independent vice-province. Significantly, neither American raised the issue of closing any parish houses.

Daniel Mullane, who had worked in the Great Lakes region, suggested that the three American houses in Canada be joined to the American houses near the Great Lakes, which all had mixed populations of French-Canadian, Irish, and German immigrants, to form a Great Lakes vice-province.[23] St. Louis held Grand Rapids and Detroit in the state of Michigan, while Baltimore held Rochester and Buffalo in New York State near Canada. Logically, the proposal had merit. The Baltimore Province already covered eight dioceses in the United States, St. Louis held ten, while Canada had twelve. Geographically, Canada should have had a separate province. The American houses were relatively close together and had been sending missionaries into Canada and attracting Canadian-born novices.

Other less geographic and more Redemptorist considerations supported a Great Lakes vice-province. The provincial of St. Louis, Ferreol Girardey, agreed readily to the proposal. By giving two houses to a Baltimore-controlled vice-province, St. Louis could take its own men to fill other western houses. Both Detroit and Grand Rapids were in debt, while Grand Rapids, with six men, no church, and close to Detroit, was the smallest house in the St. Louis Province and had been threatened repeatedly with suppression. Girardey assured the father general that the debts on Detroit and Grand Rapids were small and that both foundations were financially healthy and would help establish the new vice-province. When Daniel Mullane learned that the small debt in Detroit was offset by great revenues and that Detroit was the most fruitful in vocations of the entire province, he begged Schwarz to leave Detroit in the St. Louis Province.[24] Grand Rapids, however, was farther in St. Louis's territory than Detroit, and it was illogical to give Grand Rapids to the vice-province without giving Detroit, which was on the international border between the United States and Canada.

International political reasons also came into play. Joseph Schwarz noted that the large American provinces were under-represented in the Congregation. This had come about with the continual subdivisions of the European provinces and was about to get worse. Schwarz had just finished visiting the British Isles to recommend that the conflicts between the English and the Irish be solved by dividing them into separate provinces. Ireland, if it were established as a separate province with only two houses, would have as many representatives at the next chapter as Baltimore with twenty-four houses. Dividing Baltimore would give the Americans greater representation in Rome to counter European criticisms of the parish foundations in North America. If the Vice-province of Canada thought of expanding its European system into western Canada, it would find the new American Great Lakes Vice-province and its parishes blocking the way. Moreover, Father General Raus received letters from other Redemptorists, notably Cyril Dodsworth working in Toronto, urging a division in the Baltimore Province, because it was becoming too large for any one man to administer. When Provincial Litz spoke of his doubts about the division, Schwarz merely reported to Litz how much criticism there had been of the over-large Baltimore Province.[25]

After the visitation, Schwarz secretly proposed a vice-province for all of the Canadian houses, both American and Belgian. Jean Catulle made the same suggestion, but while Catulle suggested a Belgian vice-province, Schwarz asked that all of the houses be given to Baltimore. He gave several reasons. English houses, such as St. Patrick's house in Quebec City, were necessary for the growing number of Baltimore's English-speaking Americans. Since the Belgians did not have enough English-Canadian priests to take over the parish foundations, Schwarz objected to houses with American subjects and Belgian or French-Canadian superiors who held different ideas about living the Redemptorist Rule. Schwarz also admitted to the provincial of Baltimore that he did not want the Belgians to expand into what had been his and American jurisdiction.[26]

Schwarz's hopes for a Baltimore vice-province of Canada including the French houses was rejected. If the Americans did not want to join the Belgian Vice-province of Canada, the French Canadians and the Belgians in Canada did not want to join the Baltimore Province. So on 1 April 1898 Father Raus accepted Mullane's original Great Lakes plan in its entirety. He created a Great Lakes Vice-province consisting of American houses on both sides of the international border and from both the St. Louis and Baltimore provinces. Toronto, Quebec City, and Saint John in Canada were lumped with St. Joseph in Rochester, Immaculate Conception in Buffalo, Holy Redeemer in Detroit, and St. Alphonsus in Grand Rapids. John Loewekamp, who had been suggested as the next Baltimore provincial, became vice-provincial. The Baltimore Province proceeded to make a success of the vice-province by staffing the English-Canadian houses with younger, more active missionaries and administrators.[27] With headquarters in St. Patrick's, Toronto, the new Great Lakes vice-province was to be called the Toronto Vice-province. Mullane was named provincial of St. Louis; a new provincial, William Luecking, was named to Baltimore. The French-Canadian Alphonse Lemieux was named vice-provincial of Canada and began the novitiate in Hochelaga. These exciting changes, along with many others in the Congregation around the world, reorganized the Congregation for the twentieth century.

The Collapse of the Vice-province of Toronto

While Schwarz confidently predicted that the vice-province would be for the best and even St. Louis, which had lost Detroit, would get used to it, the new provincial of Baltimore privately predicted that it would not last long. Both Litz, the former provincial, and Luecking, the new provincial, wrote to Schauer that everything was a mess.[28] Although there had been unanimity before its creation, it was fleeting. The Toronto Vice-province appeared in a context vastly different from the one that created it. The new context was definitely hostile.

The first factor was the new St. Louis provincial, Daniel Mullane. He regularly visited Detroit as if it were still part of the St. Louis Province, spreading news, rumours, and doubt about the permanency of the changes. He incited several St. Louis members to write directly to Schwarz to protest the changes. He refused to negotiate with Baltimore about the transfer of the property and convinced the Baltimore provincial that no peace could be had until Detroit was returned. Finally, Father Raus decided to reopen the question and in December asked whether and when the houses of Detroit and Grand Rapids should be returned to St. Louis. Schwarz wrote an accompanying letter asking that if the answer was in the affirmative then the transfer would be held at the end of the triennial appointments to avoid the appearance of a mistake or haste. Immediately on receiving Father General Raus's letter, the St. Louis provincial convened his consultors and ordered them to write their answers that very day, naturally in the affirmative. One of them did not bother to state his reasons, saying only that Provincial Mullane had surely written all of the reasons out in full. Mullane had developed a mania for writing letters, sometimes several to Schwarz in a single day. Mullane's other consultor, Terence Clarke, wrote that Detroit was one of the best houses, as far as money and vocations to the Redemptorists, and its loss was a serious blow to the health of the St. Louis Province. Not content with asking for the return of the houses at the end of the triennium, he further argued that the houses be transferred immediately.

More calmly, Vice-provincial John Loewekamp argued that since the vice-province was created in order to reduce the burden on the Baltimore provincial, the western houses of Grand Rapids and Detroit should be given back to the St. Louis Province. Loewekamp's consultors, Peter Ward and F.-X. Miller, gave fuller explanations. The Detroit and Grand Rapids houses were truly western houses closer to the St. Louis Province than to Baltimore. Furthermore, American bishops did not want Canadian control of American houses and Canadian bishops did not like American control of Canadian houses. So it was best to transfer the houses back, but not immediately, because it would leave an impression of haste among the bishops, priests, and people and would be an embarrassment to those, especially Schwarz, who had planned the vice-province.[29]

The French Canadians were unhappy with these developments. They declared that no Belgians or French Canadians should be allowed to join the Vice-province of Toronto for fear that the Vice-province of Canada would be bled of bilingual or English-speaking Redemptorists. Their hope was for a united pan-Canadian province, because the French Canadians were ready to expand into the rest of Canada. Jean Catulle had already visited the Canadian west in 1892 on the invitation of Albert Lacombe. He then sent Guillaume Godts to negotiate a Redemptorist foundation with Archbishop Taché of St. Boniface, but the archbishop died during the negotiations. Taché's successor, Adelard Langevin, reopened the negotiations while visiting Father Raus in 1898. The Belgians agreed that the Canadians had to move into the Canadian west in order to expand their missions and avoid being hemmed in or absorbed by the parish-based American Vice-province of Toronto. Now that the American houses were part of the Toronto Vice-province and out of the Canadian Vice-province's reach, other means were needed to attract English and bilingual vocations.

Still believing that the future of the Congregation lay with the European-style mission houses favoured by the Belgians, Raus opened the western Canadian field to the Vice-province of Canada. It established a house on 15 August 1898 in the mainly English parish of St. Augustine of Canterbury in Brandon, Manitoba. Alphonse Lemieux launched the drive to a bilingual Canadian province and decreed that all of the Redemptorists in Brandon had to speak and

St. Augustine of Canterbury, Brandon, Manitoba.

even pray in English.[30] Within a short time the Redemptorists organized the parish and Godts embarked on an ambitious building program, financed mainly by his family. Ironically, Lemieux had adopted the American model of parish houses and had dropped the
Belgian insistence on mission houses without parishes.

The rumours and the comings and goings of so many superiors brought the Toronto chronicler to exclaim that "Curiosity is on
tip-toe."[31] The Baltimore superiors then stopped all building projects. Underlying the restraint was the suspicion that Baltimore
money might go to buildings which would soon belong to St. Louis
or to the French-Canadian vice-province.[32] The best the young
Americans in Canada could do was to organize the parish societies,
such as the St. Peter's Young Men's Association, which launched
sports and theatre among the Catholic population of Saint John, New
Brunswick.

By the beginning of 1899, a mere seven months after the creation of the Toronto Vice-province, Schwarz bowed to the pressures

successfully stage-managed by Daniel Mullane. He informed John Loewekamp that at the next triennial appointments in 1901, Grand Rapids and Detroit would be given back to the St. Louis Province.[33] Daniel Mullane immediately visited Detroit and Grand Rapids, dropping hints about the imminent transfer and effectively stopping any other activities by the Baltimore men. Meanwhile he began plans to expand the St. Louis Province farther west and establish a Rocky Mountain vice-province.[34]

Whether the American houses in Canada would be given to the Vice-province of Canada, however, was another matter. Although the Quebec parishioners might revolt, Schwarz thought it a more important consideration that the Baltimore Province would not have enough purely English-language houses for its own men, more and more of whom spoke only English. Second-generation Irish, and German Americans who barely knew any German, had begun to overwhelm the German nature of the American Redemptorists.

Provincial Luecking of Baltimore had once suggested that the transfer of his Canadian houses to the Vice-province of Canada might be a logical solution to Baltimore's administration problems, but he rapidly learned that what was logical was emotionally impossible. His consultors refused to give up the houses and convinced him to hang on to every one of them. They were so close to the United States as to be considered American, especially Toronto, which was described as "the most Americanized city in Canada."[35]

American correspondence from 1898 to 1900 also showed a growing distrust of the French Canadians. Every time the French Canadians asked for permission to give a French mission in the United States, Luecking and Mullane fought against any help for the French Canadians and against the possibility that Canada would be lost to the Americans.[36] Were the American Redemptorists being swept away in the continental current of American manifest destiny? The Spanish-American War had just ended in Spain's utter defeat and gave Puerto Rico, Guam, the Philippines and some control over Cuba to the United States, effectively establishing it as a new world empire.

By the beginning of 1899 many Belgians who would have gone to help in the expansion of the Vice-province of Canada and some already in Canada were sent to the Congo missions. The Vice-province of Canada could no longer take over the English-Canadian Redemptorist parishes of Toronto, Saint John, and Quebec City with Flemish Belgians. Once the Belgians moved their missionary fervour from North America into the Congo, competition for the Canadian west disappeared.

The triennial appointments came in May of 1901. Not only were the Detroit and Grand Rapids houses returned to St. Louis, but the Great Lakes Vice-province of Toronto itself disappeared. When Elias Schauer heard that the vice-province was suppressed, he and many others gave thanks to God.[37] It had been three years of bewildering rumours, tensions, secret negotiations, and half-understood competition and it had paralysed all inter-provincial cooperation on the missions and in the parishes of Canada.

The status quo was restored. Typically, the Americans in Canada returned to their parish work, while the Canadians in the Belgian province prepared for the missions. For example, the Americans approved a new clubhouse for the young men on St. Peter's property in Saint John, bought a new organ, and built a new church for St. Patrick's, Toronto. The Belgians, however, sent the English Canadians Scanlan, McPhail, and Holland to a second novitiate in St. Ann's, Montreal, to study mission techniques. The Americans launched missions in Puerto Rico and encouraged everyone, even the English Canadians, to study Spanish for the American Redemptorists' first "foreign" mission.[38] Canada, of course, was never considered foreign territory. The Belgians turned their attention more and more to the Congo.

Meanwhile, Consultor General Schwarz continued to argue that an English-Canadian vice-province was needed for the neglected souls of English Canada.

4

The Second Vice-province of Toronto, 1904–14

In the years leading up to the First World War, English-Canadian nationalism and immigration to western Canada brought the English-Canadian Redemptorists to direct their missions almost exclusively to English-speaking Canadians. In 1912 they then successfully created educational and administrative structures – a minor seminary and an English-Canadian vice-province – separate from the Belgians and the French Canadians to anchor the English-Canadian mission permanently in Canadian and in Redemptorist life. Attached to the American Province of Baltimore, the new Vice-province of Toronto became the first within the Redemptorist Congregation to be defined by language instead of by geography. Other Canadian congregations fought to preserve the public fiction that their English and French members could work together in territorial divisions modelled on Canada's dioceses; the Canadian Redemptorists discarded the territorial model and were the first to divide themselves openly along linguistic lines in order to work more effectively in all of Canada. The second Vice-province of Toronto might have been original, but it was hardly easy. The Baltimore Province's wider North American view came into constant conflict with English Canada's particular vision.

The Minor Seminary Crisis

The Belgians and the French Canadians could not educate English Canadians in the English language. Students were therefore slipping away to the American provinces or to other congregations if they were not being lost to the church entirely. English-Canadian students were regularly delayed entrance to the novitiate since they had to study more French in the minor seminary at Ste-Anne-de-Beaupré for one or more years. Between 1890 and 1909, only four English-speaking students were professed.[1] The rest went to the Americans or quit in discouragement.

The failure to hold on to English students brought two unlikely allies together: George Daly and John McPhail. From the time of their own education together in Belgium they were rivals in their visions of the future of the Congregation in Canada. Daly wanted one large bilingual province; McPhail wanted an English-Canadian province separate from the French Canadians. These different visions affected their approaches to education.

John McPhail had constantly urged the establishment of a separate English-Canadian province. He gave statistics showing that there were twelve English Canadians in the Baltimore Province, nine in the St. Louis Province, and six in the Vice-province of Canada: twenty-seven Redemptorists in all. He insisted that if the French Canadians had their own vice-province with twenty-five of their own men and over thirty Belgians, English Canada certainly could have one, too, with the help of the Americans.[2]

True, there were fewer Roman Catholics in English Canada to produce students, but by the end of the century Irish and other English-speaking Catholics, according to some estimates, formed over 30 per cent of the Canadian Catholic population. A growing network of parish and private schools, such as the Jesuit-run Loyola College in Montreal, also made higher education and seminary studies possible for an entire generation of Catholic boys. Redemptorist brothers when they trained altar boys and Redemptorist priests when they worked as missionaries, chaplains, and spiritual directors all encouraged vocations. Boys from the Redemptorist parishes of Quebec, Toronto, and Saint John appeared more and more often on the rolls of the Redemptorist minor and major seminaries in the Baltimore Province, while boys from St. Ann's parish in Montreal appeared in the St. Louis and Beaupré minor seminaries. Older boys or men without a classical education or a priestly vocation but with a decided vocation for the religious life were joining the Redemptorist brotherhood. The numbers were there, McPhail insisted; they only needed organization in a separate English-language province. Above all, the province had to begin with a minor seminary to keep these boys in Canada.

McPhail hoped that the minor seminary would be in Ottawa. Since the turn of the century, the archbishop of Ottawa, Thomas Duhamel, had offered the Redemptorists the privilege of establishing a house in the archdiocese. As a first step in the creation of an English-language province, McPhail urged that the Redemptorists take over a mission of Ottawa's St. Patrick's parish, called St. Mary's, in nearby Bayswater. An English foundation in Canada's capital would attract attention and more students among English Canadians. They could all go to the Oblates' bilingual college in Ottawa (the University of Ottawa) instead of the Redemptorists' French minor seminary in Beaupré. McPhail insisted that Redemptorists were not high school teachers; it would be best to leave teaching to others. This would free several Redemptorist minor seminary teachers for the missions. Finally, a house in Ottawa's archdiocese would mean that Redemptorist missionaries could easily visit parts of Ontario north and west of Ottawa.[3]

With their minor seminary in Beaupré, the French-Canadian Redemptorists saw no need to send their students to Ottawa, and while they hesitated, the parish was given to the secular clergy. Ironically, the force of McPhail's arguments swayed Roman authorities to instruct the Vice-province of Canada to establish a foundation in Ottawa, but the parish was already gone. The vice-province reluctantly bought land neighbouring St. Mary's parish, in the hope of again being offered the parish in the future.

George Daly was director of the Beaupré minor seminary. Having come from a bilingual Montreal home with a French-Canadian mother and an Irish father, his intelligence and his command of both English and French had so impressed his teachers in

George Daly (1872–1956)
One of the founders of the Sisters of Service and a much published writer.
His travels were legendary. When he once suffered a broken leg,
Redemptorists were surprised to learn that he had fallen down a few stairs
and not out of a plane. (Photograph courtesy of the Archives of the Sisters
of Service)

Belgium that they predicted to Father General Raus that he would
later do great things for the Congregation in Canada. An eye problem brought his superiors to suspend his studies after ordination, but
corrective glasses in Canada and a reputation for sound judgment
brought him back into education at the minor seminary level.

Both English and French-Canadian Redemptorists eventually
saw Daly as the embodiment of the minor seminary and of the best
Redemptorist ideals. They admired him because he had succeeded in
adapting his Belgian training to North America. Small concessions
to North American sensibilities, after great battles with his superiors
over heating, food, and entertainments, endeared him to his students.
While McPhail and a few supporters, such as Donald MacDougal,
promoted a mature internal commitment to the Redemptorist life
and mission, their insistence on strict obedience to the letter of the
Redemptorist Rule lost them support among many of their colleagues and the students. Most Redemptorists believed McPhail was

wrong in insisting on recruiting mature men, when they knew that a thorough Redemptorist formation in a minor seminary, in the novitiate, and then in a major seminary would nurture Redemptorist vocations more surely than a Jesuit or an Oblate high school.

Daly himself relied heavily on the continuous internal formation of young, immature consciences.[4] His vision of a bilingual Canadian Congregation and his emphasis on a lengthy interior formation reflected his own long preparation in the minor and major seminaries in Belgium. Deep knowledge of the Rule would produce mature interpretations and adaptations of the Rule to new conditions, not slavish obedience.

Daly's experience of men and missions, however, was not so great and his preaching was not so impressive as McPhail's. He was given to preaching the quieter, more private spiritual retreats to clergy and nuns, who appreciated his ability to interpret religious life in the light of the signs of the time. McPhail preached the large public parish missions and emphasized the conversion of individuals to the laws of God. McPhail and Daly seemed to symbolize the paths the Redemptorists were asked to take in Canada, one as publicly English as Protestant Canada appeared, the other as privately bilingual as many Canadian Catholics might have been.

To his Belgian and French Canadian superiors, George Daly, with his bilingualism and his following among the students, seemed a man sent by providence to solve the Canadian language and educational problems. His superiors in Belgium and in Ste-Anne-de-Beaupré turned to him for advice on English-Canadian affairs. He proposed a new and larger school to accommodate a full bilingual program. Although most Catholics were French-speaking, because Canada was a British colony and officially English, his superiors agreed that the bilingual approach was the right solution.[5]

In the years before the First World War, the Eastern Townships in Quebec's south shore contained more or less equal French and English communities. Bishop's College, an Anglican institution in Lennoxville near Sherbrooke, was deeply in debt. Daly strongly urged establishing the Congregation in or near Sherbrooke for the good of the English Catholic population, for the missions in the Eastern Townships, and to attract English students. Daly's cousin, a priest in Sherbrooke, scouted the terrain and reported in 1904 that it was impossible to get the Anglicans to sell Bishop's College to Catholics, but there was a strong possibility that a competing bilingual college by the Redemptorists would be successful. Daly's superiors decided instead to build a bilingual minor seminary nearer to English Canada and chose the land neighbouring St. Mary's church in Bayswater, Ottawa.

Our Lady of Good Counsel, Bayswater, opened with a few students in 1907, but it rapidly became mainly French in its staff and its courses, because the Vice-province of Canada had too few people who could teach in English. The English students were overwhelmed by the large numbers of French students. Nationalism and quick tempers flared occasionally into fist-fights between the two groups of students.[6]

In spite of their mutual dislike and their different approaches, Daly and McPhail came to the same conclusion: English vocations that the Congregation needed to expand in Canada were being lost. Beaupré's educational system had to change or the Congregation would not grow at all in English Canada. They still disagreed as to the end – a separate English or a bilingual province – but they both claimed that Redemptorist education was insufficiently English. Unknown to each other, McPhail's and Daly's many letters to their superiors in Beaupré, Brussels, and Rome worried their French-Canadian and Belgian superiors and drove them to search for solutions.

Everything was frozen, however, because Father General Matthias Raus was too old and feeble to push through any decisions which did not have unanimity. As a stopgap measure, it was decreed in 1903 that until their French was good enough to go to Beaupré, English students would study at Loyola, the Jesuit college in Montreal. They lived at St. Ann's under John McPhail's supervision. And the educational problems might have ended there if it had not been for western Canada.

Belgian Redemptorists in the Canadian West

Between 1897 and 1913 the prairie population tripled to almost a million and a half people. Two new provinces, Saskatchewan and

Alberta, were carved out of the Northwest Territories in 1905. In 1912 Manitoba and Ontario extended their borders northwards and assumed the shape they would have for the rest of the twentieth century. Against this background of fantastic growth, the Catholic Church scrambled to provide services as hundreds of thousands of immigrants followed railways into areas where the Church had no institutions and only a few missionary Oblates of Mary Immaculate. Although hardly a third of the immigrants were of British background, the influx of Ontario farmers made the prairies a colony of Ontario in politics and in language. Surrounded on three sides by English populations in Ontario, British Columbia, and the United States, with government services available usually only in English, immigrants from different parts of the world soon spoke English. Catholic authorities feared that the immigrants would also become Protestant.

The Belgian Fathers in Brandon had participated in the growing anglicization of their parishioners, whether Polish, German, or French, in the knowledge that there was little French immigration and the Canadian west was becoming English naturally, but the rush of immigrants who spoke neither English nor French overwhelmed the Brandon Redemptorists.[7] The Belgians, many of whom knew German as well as Flemish, French, and English, by default found themselves caring for the eastern European immigrants.

The one man who symbolized the Belgian Redemptorist approach to the prairies was Father Achille Delaere. Born in Flanders in 1868 and ordained in 1896, Delaere had been sent to Brandon in 1899 specifically for the Polish Catholics. He quickly learned that many Catholics who had been classified either as Polish or as Orthodox were, in fact, Eastern-rite Catholics, usually speaking Ukrainian. Eastern European languages, such as Russian, Polish, Bulgarian, and Ukrainian, are similar enough to each other that they are generally understood by many eastern Europeans; boundary changes and migrations meant that Ukrainians, for example, could be found with Russian, Austrian, or Polish citizenship. The Roman Catholic hierarchy wanted the immigrants to assimilate to the Latin rite and did not allow married Eastern-rite clergy into Canada, but Ukrainians associated the Latin rite with their traditional oppressors

Achille Delaere (1868–1939)
Called the Apostle to the Ukrainians of Canada. He arrived in Brandon, Manitoba, in 1899 and worked on the prairies for forty years.

and refused to assimilate. Many Ukrainians turned to Russian and Greek Orthodox services, Methodist and Presbyterian missionaries, religious impostors, or they abandoned religion entirely.

Western Canada's needs changed the Canadian Redemptorist way of life by dividing the Redemptorists into smaller communities. Although Father Provincial Jerome Van Aertselaer of Belgium insisted that no monastery be founded in western Canada until at least six men could be put in it, Redemptorists in the field with Delaere at their head, some bishops, and the apostolic delegate to Canada pressured Redemptorist superiors in Rome and Belgium to answer the needs of western Canada's immigrant populations.[8] The Belgian Redemptorists sent Achille Delaere in early 1904 to Yorkton, Saskatchewan, to found the English parish and monastery of St. Gerard in a heavily Ukrainian settlement. In effect, this split the Belgians into two smaller communities, one in Brandon and one in Yorkton.

St. Gerard's, Yorkton, Saskatchewan.

**Brother Idesbald (Louis Monstrey, 1854–1934)
and Yorkton's St. Gerard Brass Band**
Brother Idesbald composed the music for the *Redemptorist Rosary* and
other prayers. (Photograph courtesy of the Yorkton Province)

The European Redemptorist tradition of large, well-staffed monasteries so evident in French Canada was abandoned in favour of small communities. With the foundation of Yorkton, both Brandon and Yorkton now each had, on average, three priests and one or two brothers. There sometimes would be one priest working for the Ukrainians, another in charge of Hungarians or Poles, and a third helping with the English parish, which would often hold every other language, including dialects of Chinese. Then the brother had everything else to do; he acted as porter, janitor, cook, groundskeeper, sacristan, carpenter, and plumber, as well as organizing the altar boys and some of the parish activities. All this left very little time for the community's spiritual exercises, and more than once did Delaere rush in from some outlying mission church to sit down and snore through a community meditation.[9]

Delaere had requested the privilege of passing over to the Ukrainian rite. When he succeeded in gaining the privilege in 1906, bishops requested that others do so as well. Because the western Canadian houses were severely understaffed, the question continually arose: How were Redemptorists to spend their scarce time and energies? Who were the really poor and the truly abandoned – the Polish or the Ukrainians, this village or that town? The debates raged on and on. With some of the Redemptorists also working in the Eastern rite, using a different liturgical calendar, life in common with their Latin-rite confreres was reduced even further to meditation twice a day and meals, if work permitted even these times together. Prevented from praying or worshipping together, subjected to tremendous stresses over language and ritual issues, the Redemptorist communities in western Canada were threatened with complete fragmentation.

Instead of retreating, the crushing load of work spurred Delaere and his colleagues to protest that Redemptorists were needed in western Canada. Although the west's population was too poor, too diverse, and too spread out to allow large centralized monasteries, there were souls to be saved and Redemptorist work to be done among the poor and abandoned. Because of western Canada's special needs, Delaere called for the Redemptorists to establish a separate western Canadian vice-province under Belgium to adapt to western immigrant conditions. Failing that, he and others boldly called for the Redemptorists to establish an Eastern-rite province.[10]

The Ste-Anne-de-Beaupré Province (1911)

In 1909 the election of a new superior general, Patrick Murray, signalled many changes in the Congregation. The election of an English-speaking Irishman seemed appropriate just as the British Empire reached its zenith before the First World War and as the American provinces began to exercise greater influence in Rome. Patrick Murray had experienced the divisive Scottish, Irish, and English nationalisms in Great Britain at first hand. He had lived through the division of the English province into English and Irish provinces in order to avoid the quarrels and irritations that came from close contact between different cultures.

French-Canadian Redemptorists had long wanted a separate province, convinced that the Belgian superiors, busy in other parts of the world and far from events in Canada, were hindering the Canadian Redemptorists from becoming fully responsible, autonomous, and effective. With English-Canadian Redemptorists clamouring for an English-Canadian province, Redemptorists in the west asking for their own western province, and Eastern-rite Redemptorists predicting a province of their own, the pressures mounted on Rome to organize the Canadian Redemptorists into more sophisticated structures.

One Belgian visitor reported that the French Canadians alone could form their own province, because they were well-organized and had a compact French mission field in Canada where about four-fifths of the Catholics still spoke French. He recommended that the small mission field comprising the few English-Canadian Catholics be given into the care of the American Redemptorists. Still, the Belgian Redemptorists hesitated to divide the Canadians, because such a division would weaken the numbers and the institutions required for a self-sufficient province. The Belgian provincial, many French-Canadian and Belgian Redemptorists, as well as George Daly, who supposedly spoke for the English Canadians, were all convinced that only a united, bilingual Canadian province could stand on its own.[11]

Therefore, when the Belgian provincial and Father General Patrick Murray met at the International Eucharistic Congress of

1910 in Montreal, the alternatives were clear. The superiors of the Canadian Vice-province met together in Hochelaga. They came from Beaupré, St. Ann's, Hochelaga, Brandon, Yorkton, Bayswater, and the most recent foundation of St-Alphonse-d'Youville near the north shore on the island of Montreal. They were eight French Canadians, one English Canadian, Father Daly, and one Belgian, Father Delaere from Yorkton. The Belgian provincial formally proposed three alternatives to the superiors: a bilingual province; two vice-provinces under Belgium, one English and one French; and McPhail's solution of two provinces, one French, the other English uniting the American and the Belgian-educated English Canadians. The second and third options were immediately rejected as a division of scarce Canadian resources. McPhail's and Delaere's hopes for separate vice-provinces were momentarily dashed; the bilingual province was accepted. Murray immediately endorsed the recommendation, but he consoled McPhail and Delaere by stating that there was room enough in Canada for four provinces eventually, French, English in the east, English in the west, and Ukrainian.[12]

The bilingual Ste-Anne-de-Beaupré Province was established on 26 July 1911, the feast of St. Ann. The former vice-provincial, Alphonse Lemieux, was made provincial. There were seven houses: three in Montreal – St. Ann's, Hochelaga, and St-Alphonse-d'Youville – and one each in Ottawa, Brandon, Yorkton, and Beaupré. Three – St. Ann, Brandon, and Yorkton – were officially English. There were one hundred and thirty-eight Redemptorists, but nineteen Belgians immediately went home, leaving seventeen Belgians and ninety French Canadians. There were twelve English Canadians, only five of them ordained. For the most part, the Belgians cared for the two western houses while the English Canadians lived at St. Ann's, Montreal. Daly's dream of a bilingual Canadian province had seemingly come to pass.

The Creation of the Second Vice-province of Toronto (1912)

In spite of the establishment of a bilingual province, English Canadians were still denied entry into the novitiate because they knew insufficient French and consequently were failing their courses in the seminary. Should they persevere they were kept from the English mission fields since the Beaupré Redemptorists concentrated on the French mission fields and left most of English Canada to the American Redemptorists in Toronto, Quebec City, and Saint John. In their discussions to establish a Canadian province, the French Canadians had expressed themselves willing to take over all of the American houses in order to expand into English Canada, but this was unrealistic; the Vice-province of Canada had too few English speakers.

Long after the event, George Daly wrote that the entire problem of English candidates came to a head when two students sponsored by McPhail were refused entry to the novitiate because of their poor knowledge of French.[13] This was the last step in Daly's conversion to McPhail's view that only a separate English-Canadian province with its own English institutions would attract and keep English-Canadian students. The fragile compromise which was the bilingual Ste-Anne-de-Beaupré Province shattered, because Daly, the only English Canadian consulted by both the Belgians and the French Canadians and the only one who had believed in bilingualism, no longer did. There were missions to be had in English Canada, the west was becoming English, and English-Canadian students were not joining the Canadian Redemptorists in the same numbers as they were joining other congregations, or even the American Redemptorists. Canada had been divided between the Americans and the French Canadians; a new generation of English-Canadian Catholics was waiting to hear from the Redemptorists.

With Daly and McPhail joining forces and with every English Canadian in the Ste-Anne-de-Beaupré Province now clamouring for separation, Father General Murray ordered Beaupré to double track all of the courses so that the English students could study entirely in English, while the French students studied in French. There were still too few English teachers, and Beaupré could not comply. So a few days after the establishment of the Beaupré Province, the temporary English minor seminary in St. Ann, Montreal, under John McPhail, with students going to Loyola College, became the first official English-Canadian Redemptorist minor seminary. The first step in an institutional division between the French- and English-speaking Canadian Redemptorists had been taken.

There remained the problems of the novitiate and the major seminary. In 1912 the Baltimore Province had sixteen Canadian priests, five brothers and, together with novices and students, thirty-seven Canadians ready to form a Canadian vice-province. Beaupré had ten English-speaking priests, four brothers and, with students and novices, a total of thirty-one. Baltimore had newly built, large educational institutions, enough to share with several vice-provinces. Their foundations in Quebec City, Toronto, and Saint John were strategically placed to form the backbone of a new vice-province. Furthermore, the Americans were able to offer Redemptorist education in English on the same continent, in the nearby states of Pennsylvania, Maryland, and New York. This important fact tipped the balance towards the Americans taking over the English-Canadian field.[14]

Father Provincial Lemieux of Beaupré quietly went to New York City to meet the American consultor general and the Baltimore provincial. Lemieux asked that the Americans accept the burden of English education for all English-Canadian Redemptorists. If the American provincial wished to form an English-Canadian vice-province, Beaupré was willing to cede St. Ann's in Montreal to Baltimore. If the Baltimore Province or the English Canadians wished to expand into western Canada, Beaupré would hand over the houses of Brandon and Yorkton in exchange for permission to found a French mission house in the eastern United States. The French Canadians could give French missions and staff French houses, while the Americans and the English Canadians could give English missions and staff the English houses. The Americans refused to give up their Franco-American territory, but accepted the rest of the proposal. Lemieux gave up any claim to a French mission house in the United States and prepared the way for an English-Canadian vice-province. In the early summer of 1912, the agreement was made public:

> An English-speaking Canadian Vice-Province
> depending from [sic] the Baltimore Province is rec-
> ommended for the reason that such a Vice-Province
> would be of the greatest advantage not only for the

greater spreading of our Congregation in Canada, but also for the extension of the Catholic Faith amongst the English-speaking Canadians and for the good of souls, especially in the great North West of Canada.[15]

The new vice-province contained the houses of St. Peter's in Saint John, St. Patrick's in Quebec City, St. Ann's in Montreal, and St. Patrick's in Toronto. Toronto, as the future centre of a Canada-wide English province, became the vice-provincial residence and headquarters. All Canadians in either the Baltimore or the Beaupré provinces who wanted to join the new vice-province had to signal their intention in writing. Negotiations between Beaupré and Baltimore over western Canada were left to the future. The bilingual Beaupré Province had come to an end after only one year of existence. Henceforth, it would restrict itself to the French language.

William Brick (1855–1935)
The first vice-provincial of the Toronto Vice-province.

William Brick, the former rector of St. Patrick's, Toronto, became the first vice-provincial. Born in 1855 in St. Louis, Missouri, he had been ordained in 1881 and was known by the large number of Canadians – John Kane, Peter Costello, George Mylett, and James McCandlish, for example – who passed through his hands when he had been novice master, prefect of students, and rector in Annapolis and Ilchester, Baltimore's houses of formation. He then became rector in Toronto and showed financial sense in paring the large debt on the new church left by the former rector. As former provincial Elias Schauer stated to the father general: "He is a worthy son of St. Alphonsus in every respect. He is unassuming, thoroughly humble, blindly obedient, loving towards all and strictly conscientious. Praying, studying and commitment to duty are constantly stirred up within him. He is punctual in the observance of all the rules and cannot stand to see them abused by anyone."[16]

George Daly was sent to replace McPhail as rector of St. Ann's, Montreal, and John McPhail went to Toronto to take up his new position as consultor and the unofficial representative of the former Beaupré English Canadians. Stephen Connolly became rector of St. Patrick's, Toronto, and Brick's second consultor, the unofficial representative of the Baltimore Canadians. Connolly and McPhail quickly agreed together on how the vice-province should develop – rapidly. Their goal was the creation of an independent Toronto province.

George Daly was ecstatic. "This separation of our Order in Canada on language lines blazed a new trail which in the course of years other orders were to follow." Religious and secular newspapers picked up the story and trumpeted that it was "A Move in the Right Direction."[17] It seemed as if a new era had begun for the English-Canadian Redemptorists and that this vice-province would endure. In the Toronto house of St. Patrick's, the first large book of chronicles begun in 1881 was closed and a new one opened, to begin with the new vice-province, on 4 August 1912.

London, Ontario (1912)

McPhail turned to the bishop of London, Michael Fallon, then the leader of the English party within the Canadian Catholic Church, and solicited the offer of a foundation in Windsor. A house in Windsor, just opposite the American house in Detroit, would protect the important southwest Ontario missions for Canadian Redemptorists and keep the Americans out of Canada. McPhail also agreed with Fallon about the English future of the Catholic Church in the London diocese and in Canada, and Fallon promised to back the English-language Redemptorists as much as possible. The bishop sent a formal invitation to the Redemptorist superiors to establish themselves in London itself. Although London was rather close to Toronto, McPhail and Connolly agreed that London was an excellent missionary centre strategically placed to serve all of southwestern Ontario.[18]

Their superiors, Brick and the American provincial, Joseph Schneider, were convinced by McPhail and Connolly that London, in the more pleasant southern Ontario climate, would be an excellent place to establish a house of studies, a minor seminary or, later, a major seminary. The Baltimore Province immediately loaned Toronto $30,000 to buy thirty acres of land for a minor seminary and to begin building a house and church.[19] McPhail bought land, hastily built a temporary house and a small church, and dedicated them both to St. Patrick. Connolly exclaimed in the Toronto Annals, "Thus was the dream entertained [by] Redemptorist Missioners, fulfilled, their fervent prayers answered." Of the four altar boys at the first mass, three went to the minor seminary, and one of them, Joseph O'Donnell, became a Redemptorist priest.[20]

Brick soon discovered that McPhail was a poor builder and a worse administrator. Although Connolly proudly wrote in the Annals that McPhail was appointed the first superior of the new house in London, this never came to pass. During the opening ceremonies Brick named Peter Doyle, an American, to be the first superior. Among the Toronto Redemptorists, rumours circulated that McPhail was passed over because the house and the church were too ramshackle, or McPhail too inflexible as a superior – both of which would have been true. McPhail's superiors recognized that he was an excellent missionary and that it would be a waste of talent to tie him to administration.[21] London became an important missionary house, and Brick brought McPhail along to the Newfoundland missions. But the precedent of naming American superiors to the Canadian foundations worried Connolly.

St. Patrick's Community, London, Ontario, 1924
Redemptorists sent to London spent most of their time giving missions and
retreats.

The English Canadians who left the Beaupré and Baltimore
provinces for the Toronto Vice-province were eager to go on the
English-language missions, which were multiplying across eastern
Canada. The Newfoundland missions were one example. Led by
William Brick, the Redemptorists sailed in small boats from outport
to outport. Heralded by bagpipes, horns, and conches, Daniel
Holland, John McPhail, and James McCandlish braved the winds, fell
into the waves, were thrown out of their beds when their railcar
jumped the tracks, slept on pine boughs or rough boards, and ate
quickly, sparingly, or badly in order to get through the work. When
travel seemed impossible, local men took the place of horses and
brought the missionaries in buggies, sleds, or catamaran rafts from
church to church. The priests were welcomed as saviours by
Catholics desperately in need of confession; penitents walked over fifteen miles twice a day to attend a mission; women kissed the missionaries' feet, and Bonne Bay asked the government to change its name
to Holland, in honour of the visiting Newfoundland Redemptorist.

The real work, the real cost, and the real triumphs were not in the sermons, which were successful in attracting both Catholic and Protestant, but in the confessional where the missionaries listened and tried to reintroduce God into the Newfoundland towns and outports wracked by alcoholism, theft, murder, incest, rape, and other soul-destroying problems. In nine months and nine days, the four Redemptorists held thirty-five missions, four retreats, with over thirty thousand confessions, administered the temperance pledge to over three thousand, and erected twenty-five wooden crosses to remind the people of their promises to reform and of God's promise to forgive.[22]

The Americans and Our Lady of Mount Carmel, Toronto (1913)

St. Patrick's parish, placed in downtown Toronto close to the railways where immigrants ended their travels, often cared for several language groups. The original American Redemptorists cared for the Germans, since they were often themselves German or Americans of German descent. Less well-known is their involvement with Italian Canadians. The Redemptorist Bishop John Neumann had established the first Italian parish in North America in his diocese of Philadelphia in 1852. The Redemptorists in Toronto, fully conscious of their origins in Naples, welcomed the Italian immigrants. Italians may also have been attracted to the Redemptorists for their popular Italian devotions to St. Gerard and to Our Lady of Perpetual Help. Moreover, individual Redemptorists, such as Cyril Dodsworth at St. Patrick's, were fluent in Italian.

Cyril Dodsworth was the son of an Anglican minister who had become a Roman Catholic during the Oxford movement when Cyril was a young boy. The Dodsworth family, like many Anglo-Catholic families, fled British prejudice, and lived on the continent. Educated in Italy, Dodsworth joined the Redemptorists, and was sent to the United States. Eventually transferred to St. Patrick's, Toronto, he cared for the Italians in the city. The Italian Society of the Immaculate Conception patronized the church; Italians were hired as workers in the parish; and the Italian community began to consider St. Patrick's their own parish by 1900.[23]

When Dodsworth died in 1907 and the new St. Patrick's church was ready, Archbishop Patrick McEvay asked that the old St. Patrick's church be leased to the Italians who were moving into the parish in massive numbers. The Redemptorists sent Lawrence Jung in 1908 to organize the first Italian parish, but before he arrived the archbishop had already named a diocesan priest. Within five years, the number of Toronto Italians grew to such an extent that one parish could not handle them all. The diocesan priest was sent to establish a second parish, and the care of Mount Carmel was given back to the Redemptorists. In 1913 Arthur Coughlan from New York, Domenico Viglianti from Rome, and in 1914 Umberto Bonomo also from Rome arrived to care for the parish of Our Lady of Mount Carmel, which soon outstripped St. Patrick's in numbers and activities.[24] The American Redemptorist combination of North American parish organization, a melting-pot approach to the many Italian regional groups, and a gradual integration of immigrants into Catholic urban life worked well for Our Lady of Mount Carmel.

Americans in the Canadian West

Father General Murray fully intended to establish a Redemptorist vice-province in western Canada after establishing the Toronto Vice-province. He planned, as did McPhail and the Beaupré provincial, Alphonse Lemieux, to take the Belgian houses of Brandon in Manitoba and Yorkton in Saskatchewan and join them to houses to be founded rapidly by Baltimore in western Canada for a new western vice-province. However, when Lemieux formally offered Brandon and Yorkton to the Americans as the nucleus for an English-language western province in exchange for the coveted Franco-American mission field, not only did the Americans refuse to give up their mission field, but the Belgians also protested vigorously: "To give the North West to the Americans means the death of the work and the ruin of a great number of souls," Achille Delaere declared, "for the Americans have only one goal and that is to anglicize every race that comes to America."[25] They begged their superiors to save the Ukrainian work already begun. While their superiors searched for a compromise, the Belgians remained under the

French-Canadian Beaupré Province. Yet, with the prairies growing and changing so rapidly, this arrangement could not last long.

The Canadian hierarchy had received an Eastern-rite Ukrainian bishop, Nicetas Budka, who toured the Redemptorist foundations in western Canada in late 1912 and energetically attracted Ukrainians away from Protestant proselytizers. Unfortunately, Budka proclaimed that Eastern-rite Catholics wanting ordination should in future be educated in Ukrainian, preferably in the Austro-Hungarian province of Galicia where most Eastern-rite Ukrainian Catholic Canadians originated, so that the Ukrainians would not feel that the Latins were trying to assimilate them. Besides alienating Ukrainian Catholics from other parts of the Ukraine, Budka made it clear that he barely tolerated the Belgians or their Ukrainian students. After much anguish, the Belgian Redemptorists wrote to their superiors for help.[26] Father General Murray called a conference in Rome in May 1913 to thrash out the problems of the Canadian west.

The French Canadians and the Belgians called on the eager Americans to take over the responsibility for Latin-rite Catholics in western Canada, while the Belgians would dedicate themselves solely to the Ukrainians. Lemieux again gave up his request for a French mission house in the United States and merely sold St. Gerard in Yorkton and St. Augustine in Brandon to the Americans. Canada's linguistic divisions did not expand beyond the Canadian border. In recognition that French-Canadian pastors in the United States would not call on the Americans if they could not get French-Canadian Redemptorists, Baltimore allowed Beaupré's missionaries to work occasionally in the United States.[27] Since the western houses were meant to help the Toronto Vice-province become a Canada-wide English-speaking province, the Baltimore Province charged the $90,000 purchase of Yorkton and Brandon to the Toronto Vice-province.

The Belgians closed their mixed English, French, and Ukrainian minor seminary in Brandon. In the hope that a house in the Ukraine would supply Eastern-rite missionaries to Canada, the Belgians established their first house in the Ukraine in August of 1913. Delaere moved to a new mission house in Yorkton, Our Lady of Perpetual Help, dedicated solely to the Ukrainians. The Belgians withdrew from all further work among English Canadians.[28]

Under the Americans, Brandon and Yorkton went into an immediate decline. Many Belgians and French Canadians had worked there for thirteen years, spent huge amounts of money, built imposing buildings, and had buried some of their confreres there, but the Americans complained they arrived to find nothing but empty mission churches. They credited Lemieux for being shrewd enough to know when to leave; they never thought that their own reluctance to provide services in any language other than English would not attract many of the immigrants. The French Canadians and the Belgians did leave flourishing French, Polish, German, and Ukrainian parishes and mission churches. The English parishes and missions, however, were not well attended, since there were still too few English-speaking Canadians, and that is what the American superiors found.[29] While they eventually learned English, Canadian immigrants often succeeded in maintaining and handing on their languages, traditions, and cultures to their children. The American Redemptorist as well as the American church's pastoral strategy of English Catholic assimilation and homogeneity did not work immediately in the western Canadian parishes.

Americans and Canadian Redemptorist Education

After the London difficulties and now with the problems of Canada's west, the Americans believed that English Canada was far from attaining its own provincial independence. Father Provincial Joseph Schneider of Baltimore wrote to Father Patrick Murray asking to be released from the obligation to build and staff a novitiate, a minor, and a major seminary for the Toronto Vice-province. He rightly claimed that the expense and personnel required would use up all available resources. Schneider proposed to expand Baltimore's minor seminary and the major seminary at a much lower cost and with hardly any increase in teaching personnel. He also proposed closing the minor seminary established at St. Ann's, Montreal, to avoid duplication of effort and to avoid "bringing in customs and traditions not in accordance with the customs and traditions of the Congregation." He rejected McPhail's idea that Jesuits could educate Redemptorists. Murray and his consultors agreed that it would be best to keep all training in the hands of Baltimore, mainly because the Baltimore Province needed the Canadian students to help fill and pay for its own recently built educational institutions. A common education would help to create strong friendships and unity between Americans and Canadians, especially if, as the Americans assumed, the vice-province seemed likely to remain part of the Baltimore Province for many years to come. "As to a Juvenate [minor seminary or high school], Novitiate and Studentate [major seminary] of the Vice-Prov[ince] no one expected that the erection of these institutions could be made at once," Fidelis Speidel, the consultor general from North America, declared, "Besides (inter nos) that phrase was put in the circular rather to please the Canadians and pacify them."[30]

The English Canadians protested against the decision to educate the Canadians with the Americans. A common political culture and loyalty to the British crown brought English-Canadian Catholics to see themselves as different from the Americans and having a greater right to work in Canada. Canadians in the Baltimore Province, especially Stephen Connolly, had spoken to Father General Murray about moving Canadians to Canada to participate in the heady goal of shaping Canada's future. "Canada for the Canadians!" was their rallying cry. McPhail wrote more soberly: "It is impossible to plant the same spirit here as in the United States. The Belgians tried to make French Canadians Belgians and failed. The spirit of religious will always reflect something of the country."[31] With American education and American superiors, Daly asked whether Canadians needed to become Americans in order to become Redemptorists? Baltimore had already closed Montreal's minor seminary and absorbed the Canadian students; did this mean that the Toronto Vice-province itself might eventually be closed? Daly insisted that social life and government were different in British Canada; education of Canadian Redemptorists had to take place in Canada under knowledgeable Canadians. Connolly calculated that sending boys to the United States would cost the Toronto Vice-province even more than keeping them in Canada. Although Baltimore would save money, Toronto would suffer.[32] McPhail predicted that "the Americans are going to be for the English Vice-Province just what the Belgians were for [the] old [Canadian] Vice Province": a brake on Toronto's growth.

Nonetheless, the English Canadians were short of men and money to educate their own people. The American superiors ordered the Canadian students to go to North East, near Erie, Pennsylvania, for their minor seminary studies, to Ilchester, Maryland, for the novitiate, and to Mount St. Alphonsus Seminary in Esopus, New York, for the major seminary. Until English Canada had the men, the money, and the buildings, education would be in the United States.

In Canada itself, relations between the Americans and the Canadians deteriorated. One of the reasons why a Toronto vice-province had been rejected back in 1911 in favour of the bilingual province was the belief that joining American and Belgian-trained English-Canadian Redemptorists would cause problems. This was all too true. After his London problems, McPhail quarrelled constantly with Vice-provincial William Brick, especially during the difficult Newfoundland missions which exhausted both of them. Connolly began to ignore Brick, who really had no power, and sent his advice directly to the provincial of the Baltimore Province. When the Americans transferred all of their American missionaries back to the United States in August of 1912 to help raise monies for the Baltimore Province's building projects, the Canadian protests increased. Speidel dismissed the complaints and took aim at Connolly who, it was rumoured, might become Toronto's first Canadian vice-provincial, and at McPhail, who was said to be smarting from his public disgrace in London: "First they cry Canada for Can[a]dians and then they complain that the American Missionaries were recalled. It seems to me it is only a few of the older men that cause the disturbance and that not for their love for Canada, but because they were disappointed in their ambition to be Rector or Superior somewhere."[33]

After Baltimore named American superiors not only in London, Ontario, but in Brandon and in Yorkton, while continuing to charge these houses' debts to the Toronto Vice-province, the Canadians asked to be consulted about the superiors being named within the vice-province. Not only were there doubts about the financial ability of those sent to care for the Canadian houses, there had been a delicate balance between Baltimore men and former Beaupré men which was rapidly tipping in Baltimore's favour after 1912, especially in Canada's west. The grumbling disgusted the American provincial even more, since to criticize a superior's decisions was democracy, not obedience to authority.[34] Brick, however, could not stop the complaints. Although he was the vice-provincial, his own provincial consciously or unconsciously undermined his authority by rarely consulting him, and by making all of the decisions for Canada.

The fact that Canadian students were costing the Canadians more to educate in the United States meant nothing to the Americans, since they were saving money by charging the Toronto Vice-province the high fees. Besides, they argued, the education was better in the United States. In all, the Americans continued to treat the Toronto Vice-province exactly as if it were part and parcel of the Baltimore Province and Vice-provincial Brick merely a figurehead. Canadians were paying for everything: students, London, and western debts, and had no say in how or where the students were educated. Since the London incident, Canadians no longer had any say in how or where houses were accepted, built, or managed. The Canadian solution was to have American money pay for the Canadian institutions but allow the Canadians to run their own affairs independently of the Baltimore Province, on the grounds that Canadian Redemptorists knew what was right for Canada.

The Vice-province of St. Boniface that Never Was

The disputes over education, personnel, and money escalated from 1913 to 1914 when the Baltimore provincial decided that Americans should establish a western vice-province separate from the Vice-province of Toronto, taking all of western Canada permanently out of eastern Canada's control. The American authorities had staffed the western houses mainly with Americans and believed that Canada's west would develop very much as did the American west. Looking closely at Canada's immigration, almost everyone could see that many who went to western Canada did so only because the United States no longer had free land and an open frontier. Western

Canada was just like the western United States, the Americans argued, but only a generation behind. In fact, many new Canadians were merely Americans who had moved across the border into the open lands of Canada. Baltimore's Redemptorists felt themselves at home in western Canada. Furthermore, all of the American rectors appointed to Brandon and Yorkton rarely consulted Toronto and sought decisions directly from New York. Decisions were faster this way, since mail going immediately across the border would then travel more rapidly to the Baltimore provincial in New York than if it were sent over the Great Lakes to Toronto's vice-provincial. Return mail also jumped right over the Canadian consultors who could delay decisions by being at odds with American decisions.

At the same time, Connolly sent McPhail west to look for possible sites for Redemptorist foundations. McPhail used his immense missionary experience and knowledge of Canada to open negotiations for places in Saskatoon and Edmonton, stating that the Redemptorists had to get into those dioceses immediately, as land values were rising. Negotiations for Calgary, Vancouver, and Victoria could wait until later when the Redemptorists had more men. When the provincial of Baltimore opened negotiations with the archbishop of St. Boniface for a house in Elmwood, East Kildonan, near Winnipeg, McPhail and Connolly voted against accepting it. First, Brandon already guaranteed a presence in Manitoba. Second, both Yorkton and Brandon were in the St. Boniface archdiocese, saturating the English mission field, and Yorkton should probably be closed, now that the Ukrainian-rite Redemptorists were established in another Yorkton house. Finally, the archbishop was making difficulties about the Redemptorists' traditional request to own and operate the parish without trustees.

Anxious to gain Elmwood so as to have a third house and thus enough for a separate western vice-province, the Baltimore provincial became furious at the delays the Toronto Vice-province put in his way.[35] In spite of Toronto's reasoned opposition, and in spite of the fact that a trustee system would be in place and the Redemptorists would not own the church, Father Provincial Schneider appointed a superior, Augustine Duke, to establish the parish of St. Alphonsus, Elmwood, and gave him permission to buy land and begin building, the expenses to be charged to Toronto. Duke arrived without a single penny and was greeted in a novel way. He "came upon a group of young children, who seemed astonished at his appearance. Father Duke said to them: 'My dear children, I suppose you never saw the like of me before.' They all answered in chorus: 'No, Mam'."[36]

Since Toronto's finances and personnel could not handle Elmwood, Baltimore boldly proposed that a western vice-province be established immediately with the St. Alphonsus foundation in Winnipeg as the third house. The Toronto Vice-province would be restricted to eastern Canada. The Americans proposed taking over the debts on Brandon and Yorkton, staffing the west entirely with Americans, and relieving the eastern Canadians from any responsibility in western Canada. Schneider and his consultors named the proposed western Canadian vice-province after Saint Boniface, the patron saint of Germans and of the archdiocese which had invited the Redemptorists into all three foundations – Brandon, Yorkton, and Winnipeg.

The Roman authorities were willing to endorse the proposal, since a western Canadian vice-province had long been planned. Loud Canadian complaints did not stop Rome from giving permission for Elmwood, but it did delay the western vice-province. Questions, however, were raised not only in Redemptorist circles in Rome, but in the Roman curia's Sacred Congregation for Religious over the speed and the procedure being used to establish new Redemptorist houses in western Canada. A vice-province with three heavily indebted houses, one not even canonically founded or built, seemed hasty. Besides, Father General Murray wrote Schneider, having only one vice-province in English Canada was not as bad as having two.[37]

Frustrated in their plans for a vice-province in western Canada, the Americans then refused to accept any of McPhail's proposed foundations in Edmonton or Saskatoon on behalf of the Toronto Vice-province, for fear of "seriously jeopardizing the common observance and seriously crippling the work of the missions in the United States and Canada."[38] Strained to find money for their other projects, the Americans also refused permissions for all projects in eastern Canada. Stephen Connolly, the rector in Toronto, was denied permission to finish decorating the interior of St. Patrick's church. Daly, the rector in Montreal, was refused permission to renovate St. Ann's church. Charles McCormick, rector in Saint John, New Brunswick, could not build a new school. James Woods, rector in Quebec City, was not allowed to complete the superstructure of the new church – English Quebeckers would have to make do with a basement church. The American superiors stopped all building, all spending, and all activities in the vice-province unless explicit written permission was obtained from the provincial and from Rome.[39] Significantly, all of these eastern foundations were under Canadian superiors.

Reports that the Canadians, even American-trained ones, were circulating a petition to bring the Canadian students back to Canada in order to force the building of an English-Canadian minor seminary astonished and angered the American provincial even more. As the irascible provincial, Joseph Schneider, wrote to Father Murray: "to find such disloyalty to the Province is more than I can bear ... to think that these same men received their education and all that they have from the Province and then stoop to such despicable measures."[40]

When the offer of Elmwood seemed about to be withdrawn by the diocese, the Americans hastily accepted the temporary care of the pro-Cathedral, Our Lady of the Rosary, in Regina in the hopes of a permanent foundation there. The Canadians again angrily petitioned Rome to stop the Americans from accepting any houses in western Canada unless the Canadians were consulted.[41] This way, the vice-province at least had a say in the burdens jeopardizing the future of the Toronto Vice-province.

After only two years of existence, the vice-province had acquired over $120,000 in debt, land in London for a minor seminary which was never begun, two declining parishes in the archdiocese of St. Boniface, and debts in Winnipeg. Yet the Baltimore Province had already sent a superior to take over the pro-Cathedral of Regina, in spite of the fact that no contract had been signed. The more they relied on American Redemptorists to staff western parishes, the less likely would Toronto ever become a province.

The English Canadians believed that Redemptorists should be educated in Canada, adapt to Canadian conditions, and become or be Canadian. The Americans, however, believed that Canadians were just like Americans. They were all driven by the haunting thought that, if they did not act as their view of Canada demanded, vast numbers of new Canadians living outside traditional parish and diocesan structures would lose their immortal souls unless the Redemptorist missionary was there to offer them salvation in their own culture and in their own language. These differing visions caused misunderstanding and mistrust. Some of the Canadians, notably McPhail, Connolly, and Daly began to label all of the American Redemptorists "Germans" and proudly called themselves British. By the summer of 1914 these competing visions in western Canada created a deadlock among the Canadian and American Redemptorists that could be ended only by one of two solutions: dissolution of the Toronto Vice-province or formation of an independent English-Canadian province.

On 4 August 1914, Britain declared war on Germany.

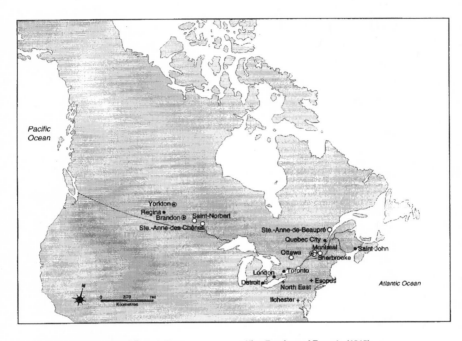

Pacific
Ocean

Yorkton ◉
Regina ●
Brandon ◉   Saint-Norbert
Ste.-Anne-des-Chênes

Ste.-Anne-de-Beaupré ○
Quebec City ●
Montreal   ● Saint John
Ottawa   Sherbrooke
London
Detroit   ● Toronto   + Esopus
        North East   Atlantic Ocean
Ilchester +

N
0   370   740
Kilometres

○ **Province of Canada (1911) Foundations**
St. Anne-de-Beaupré (1878)
St. Ann's, Montreal (1884)
Sacred Heart, Hochelaga, Montreal (1895)
St. Augustine's, Brandon, Manitoba (1898)
St. Gerard's, Yorkton, Saskatchewan (1904)
Bayswater, Ottawa (1905)
St. Alphonse d'Youville, Montreal (1910)
Notre-Dame du Perpétuel-Secours, Sherbrooke, Quebec (1913)
Saint-Vital, Saint-Norbert, Manitoba (1913-1916)
Saint-Anne-des-Chênes, Manitoba (1916)

● **Vice-Province of Toronto (1912)**
St. Patrick's, Quebec City (1874)
St. Patrick's, Toronto (1881)
St. Ann's, Montreal (1884)
St. Peter's, Saint John, N.B. (1884)
St Augustine's, Brandon, Manitoba (1898, transferred 1913)
(1913-1924)
St Gerard's, Yorkton, Saskatchewan (1904, transferred 1913)
(1913-1991)
St. Patrick's, London, Ontario (1912-1975)
St. Alphonsus, East Kildonan, Manitoba (1914-1993)
Holy Rosary, Regina (1915-1927)

+ **Baltimore Province educational institutions**
North East, Pennsylvania: minor seminary
Ilchester, Maryland: noviitate seminary
Esopus, New York: major seminary

The Second Vice-Province of Toronto, 1912–18

5

The Formation of the Toronto Province, 1914–27

Between 1914 and 1927 a new generation of Redemptorists came forward to fill the houses, doubling the number of those working in English Canada. The price for growth was education in the United States and a close imitation of the successful American Baltimore Province model of Redemptorist life and mission in North America. Yet English-Canadian wartime nationalism allowed English-Canadian Redemptorists to strike a balance between North American uniformity and Canadian needs in order to build their own identity. In spite of its financial problems, the Toronto Vice-province attained provincial autonomy and its own educational institutions, and began to expand rapidly into western Canada. By 1927 it seemed time even to have a Canadian direct the fortunes of the Redemptorists in English Canada.

The Great War

As part of the British Empire, Canada was automatically at war in 1914. While the Baltimore Province marched ahead with building projects in the United States as well as in Puerto Rico, all work in Canada was postponed. Wartime construction and enlistment took up all available workers and drove prices beyond the Redemptorists' reach. The war also interrupted communications between Toronto and

New York. Letters to people with German names, such as to Father Provincial Joseph Schneider, were opened, delayed, or destroyed at the border by Canadian government officials. Canadian Redemptorists born in Germany fled to the United States to avoid Canadian internment camps. Young men travelling to the Redemptorist schools in the United States were stopped at the border by officials eager to keep eligible military recruits from leaving Canada. To avoid any breaches of confidentiality, the Canadians no longer sent important matters to New York, but directly to Rome, through the diplomatic immunity afforded the mail of Rome's apostolic delegate to Canada.[1]

Since many American Redemptorists were of German descent, American Redemptorist sympathies were with the German-speaking countries. Moreover, as long as the United States remained neutral, the American Redemptorists in Canada were suspect foreigners, reporting regularly to the Royal Canadian Mounted Police and kept under close watch by zealous Canadian patriots. When many Austrians, Germans, Bohemians, Romanians, Russians, and Ukrainians were interned in Canada, the Redemptorists withdrew their German-American members from the public eye and promoted English-speaking Canadians. George Daly, for example, kept his rectorship at St. Ann's, Montreal, in spite of Charles Kelz's cutting criticisms of his spendthrift habits. Baltimore dared not replace Daly with Kelz; anti-German sentiment in Montreal might object to the Toronto-born Kelz's German name. So, for the first few months of the First World War, the Toronto Vice-province was forced to live, work, and develop separately from the Baltimore Province.

By the summer of 1915, all these difficulties forced the Baltimore authorities to consider breaking up the Toronto Vice-province and withdrawing from some of the Canadian foundations. Roman authorities, however, had long considered that the only solution to Canada's particular geographic, political, and linguistic problems was the establishment of an English-Canadian province independent of American control.[2] As a compromise, Toronto's entire vice-provincial council was replaced: the ineffectual vice-provincial, William Brick, was transferred back to the United States, and both of his Canadian consultors, Stephen Connolly and John McPhail, were removed from any position of authority.

A former Baltimore provincial consultor, Arthur Coughlan, was pastor of the Italian parish of Our Lady of Mount Carmel in Toronto. Although the war harmed the Italian parish when some of the men went back to Italy to serve in the army, and created incredible stresses within the Italian community over questions of Canadian citizenship and loyalty, the families and activities in the parish of Mount Carmel still outstripped St. Patrick's, Toronto. Coughlan's success in integrating Italians into the North American parish and having Italian, American, and Canadian Redemptorists work together harmoniously marked him out for greater responsibilities. He became rector of St. Patrick's parish, which controlled the land and buildings of Our Lady of Mount Carmel, and replaced Stephen Connolly as vice-provincial consultor.

The second consultor was Sinon Grogan. Born in Sillery, Quebec, in 1857, Grogan had attended St. Patrick's church in Quebec City before entering the minor seminary in the Baltimore Province. One of the first Canadians to join the Redemptorists, he was ordained in 1888 and had been part of the short-lived first Vice-province of Toronto. Stationed almost constantly in Toronto, he had devoted himself to the care of the parishioners and to the sick in nearby St. Michael's Hospital. His piety was remarkable. Slowly, after unusual or unexplained cures occurred among the patients he visited, he developed a reputation as a miracle-worker. Growing deafness put a stop to his confessional work and to his hospital visits, but he turned to preaching and promoted weekly devotions to Our Lady of Perpetual Help at St. Patrick's church. His preaching and his reputation drew crowds, which revived the declining parish of St. Patrick's. While Our Lady of Mount Carmel had surpassed St. Patrick's in parishioners, attendance at St. Patrick's devotional services outstripped any of the other parishes in the Redemptorist vice-province.[3]

The new vice-provincial was a relative newcomer to Canada. Patrick Mulhall, born in New York in 1861, had studied at the minor seminary in North East, Pennsylvania. Despite his own great piety and faithful devotion to the Rule, he became fearful of the burden of ordination and left the Redemptorists. Six years later his vocation to the priesthood and to religious life proved so strong that he rejoined

Patrick Mulhall (1861–1922)
The second vice-provincial and the first provincial of Toronto was responsible for building St. Mary's College, Brockville.

the Congregation. Although recurring illnesses slowed him down,
his maturity, organization, deep piety, self-discipline, and work
experiences marked him out to become rector of Saratoga, a mission
centre and retirement house for the sick. He was then transferred to
Toronto to help pare the continuing debt on St. Patrick's church,
direct its mission band, and transfer the old church to the Toronto
Italian parish of Our Lady of Mount Carmel. He succeeded in reducing the debts and created an environment where both St. Patrick's
and Mount Carmel's parishes could flourish while sharing land,
buildings, and personnel.[4]
    The only two Canadians who had been prominent in the first
years of the vice-province, George Daly and James Woods,
remained superiors. Woods had dedicated himself entirely to Quebec
City and had not actively participated in the grumbling and the politics of the previous three years; he was reappointed as rector of

Quebec City. Daly's lack of financial caution, however, earned him a demotion to the smaller foundation in Regina, notwithstanding protests from the archbishop of Montreal, Paul Bruchési. Mulhall's firmness in handling Bruchési, prominent Montreal lay people, and Daly, while installing Charles Kelz as Montreal's rector during the war in spite of his German name, gained Mulhall the respect and trust of his American superiors. English Canada was in strong hands.

Mulhall also quickly gained the confidence of most of his Canadian confreres. He reassured them time and again that Redemptorists were missionaries first and parish clergy second. To James Woods, who thought that Mulhall neglected the parishes that were the building stones of the Baltimore Province, Mulhall wrote: "We are bound by contract to take care of the souls in our parishes – but we are bound by *Vow* to labor for the most abandoned souls – especially by giving *missions*." Missions in the vice-province rose from fifty in 1915 to over a hundred in 1916.[5]

Mulhall also displayed his strong talents in financial matters, battling the Baltimore provincial over Toronto's debts. On the one hand, Mulhall threatened to declare bankruptcy and let Baltimore seize the western houses, which, he declared "were not taken ... with zeal for the glory of God, but through spite against the Belgium Province – to keep them out of the field."[6] On the other hand, he reassured the Redemptorists working in western Canada that the future of the Congregation and of the English Catholic Church in Canada depended on them, not on the French-Canadian Redemptorists. Under such leadership, the vice-province grew steadily, with an average of four novices each year. Roman authorities were happy to see that the complaints and problems of the preceding years were at an end as most English-Canadian Redemptorists united behind Mulhall.

A few English-Canadian Redemptorists, however, believed Mulhall was doing too little for Canada during the Great War. The bishops were pressuring the Redemptorists to provide chaplains for the front line. Many English Catholics and some English-Canadian Redemptorists were glad of the chance to show that Catholics were loyal to Britain and were as good citizens of Canada and of the Empire as any Orangeman. Canadian Redemptorists such as George

Mylett volunteered to be wartime chaplains. George Daly travelled the prairies speaking on behalf of enlistment.[7] Unknown to Mylett and to Daly, Mulhall privately begged the Baltimore Province to allow a Canadian to serve as a military chaplain, or the future of the Redemptorists in Canada would be jeopardized. The bishop of London had cancelled all missions until the end of the war and the other archbishops and bishops resolved not to allow anyone to give missions in Canada, unless they furnished war chaplains. But Schneider refused. When the United States joined the war in April 1917, Schneider then provided chaplains to the American army and commanded every community, including the Canadian houses, to add three Hail Marys to its night prayers for the chaplains. The Toronto Vice-province was still not allowed to provide even one chaplain to the Canadian government.[8]

While Mylett quietly conformed to Mulhall's instructions to work for souls and not for recruits, Daly continued his public work on the prairies. He incorporated the Redemptorists in each of the prairie provinces, became the go-between for the delicate transfer of the Brandon and Yorkton properties from the French-Canadian Redemptorists to the English Canadians after the sale in 1913, and maintained good relations between the French-speaking bishops and their increasingly English-speaking parishioners. He began a series of popular Sunday-night sermons in Regina for non-Catholics, who formed the vast majority of Canadians in the west. He even appeared on a public platform with Prime Minister Robert Borden in support of Canada's war effort. His vision of how Roman Catholics should adapt to western Canadian conditions in order to be accepted as full citizens in a predominantly English and Protestant country drove him to push Catholics to take a prominent place in the emerging Canadian nation.

Although all were convinced that Daly was doing good work in calming Protestant bigotry and in establishing the Redemptorists in western Canada, some of Daly's activities upset his eastern superiors. When Daly received the gift of a car to travel around Regina, his scandalized superiors investigated this supposed breach of his vow of poverty, found that the streetcars could travel from one end of Regina to the other in ten minutes, and ordered Daly to give up the car. Daly complied very slowly and reluctantly. Daly's carefully cultivated friendships with politicians, Catholic and non-Catholic, which proved so useful for incorporating the Redemptorists, embarrassed his superiors when Daly appeared in the newspapers and on war recruitment platforms.

Mulhall cautioned Daly that Redemptorists were supposed to be more interested in souls than in recruits, but Daly's travels and lectures continued and the vice-provincial became convinced that Daly had "no idea of religious life. He wants to be in the public eye all the time. He cannot content himself at home with his community."[9] Mulhall and the Roman consultors decided that Daly, with his mania for cars, telephones, and politics, could not be trusted to embrace poverty, self-sacrifice, and obedience. In spite of repeated warnings, Daly's continual adaptation of religious life to Canadian wartime conditions on the prairies forced Mulhall to transfer him in 1917 to the Maritimes to work as a missionary out of the Saint John house. When Daly complained that Maritime mission work affected his health, he was reassigned to quieter, less strenuous and even less public retreat work, but still in the Maritimes.

Brockville, Ontario

There were more serious problems than Daly's wartime activities. During the war the number of young men asking to join grew, but the American minor seminaries were full. The Toronto Vice-province had a quota of 25 per cent of the Baltimore Province student body, although more Canadians were applying to enter. The candidates being sent for education in the United States cost the Toronto Vice-province fully 50 per cent of its total budget, yet the Baltimore Province raised fees and ended all subsidies for Canadian students, charging Canadians the same as Americans. The students and their families rarely paid anything, so the Toronto Vice-province found itself with an even greater financial burden. As a stopgap measure to save money the large buildings in Brandon were again pressed into service as a preparatory school, this time to educate westerners for the St. Louis Province minor seminary in Kirkwood, Missouri.

Unfortunately, some Canadians who graduated from the minor seminaries were refused entrance into or were dismissed from the novitiate. Since the novitiate was the place where individual candidates began their Redemptorist life, the quota in the Baltimore novitiate cut off the supply of men to the Vice-province of Toronto. The American consultor general, Fidelis Speidel, vetoed Toronto's decision to send its novices to St. Louis and ordered the novices back to Baltimore. Rome and Baltimore were sure that only unworthy candidates were being rejected; Toronto was not so sure.[10]

Obviously English Canada needed its own institutions. There was land in London and in Sillery large enough for a minor seminary, but it was decided that neither place would do; the London property was too small, while Quebec was too cold. Mulhall and his consultors petitioned to sell the Sillery property and have the money go to buying a more suitable site. Unfortunately, Rector James Woods of Quebec also petitioned that the money be used to build a new monastery for the community in Quebec City. So much money had been taken out of Quebec City for the needs of the western houses, Woods argued powerfully, that Quebec City was entitled to some compensation. The authorities in New York decided that the Toronto Vice-province could certainly use a new house in Quebec City that would serve both as a residence and as a novitiate.[11] The Roman compromise, however, was to allow Quebec City to build a new house – but one that would be too small to be used as a novitiate.

Encouraged by the Baltimore provincial, Woods nevertheless embarked on a grandiose building scheme that would make the house almost as imposing as the church he had begun. Unfortunately, only the basement of the church was dedicated in 1915 and it had cost so much during wartime inflation that a new residence had to wait for another rector to raise more money. The community in Saint John, however, sent all of its money to Mulhall for the new minor seminary. As a result, Mulhall removed Woods as rector in Quebec. This meant that if Stephen Connolly had not taken Daly's place as rector in Regina, not a single Canadian from the previous years would have been in a position of authority in the entire Toronto Vice-province.

All of the Redemptorists became involved in a lengthy search throughout Ontario for the best possible site for a minor seminary. On 10 October 1917 Mulhall signed the purchase papers for a plot of slightly more than 180 acres fronting the St. Lawrence River, just four miles east of the city of Brockville, which boasted a Catholic hospital, a railway, and a ferry to Ogdensburg, New York. The land cost over $25,000, some of the money coming from the sale of the Sillery property. On 16 May 1918 four Redemptorists – Mulhall, Coughlan, Grogan, and Brother Mark (Francis Daly) – visited the land, said mass in the farm house, and hung crucifixes and pictures of Our Lady of Perpetual Help "so that under the protection of Our Blessed Redeemer and His Blessed Mother of Perpetual Help success may crown our efforts for the future welfare of the CSsR in Canada."[12]

The Province of Toronto (1918)

The Roman authorities had informed Mulhall that an English-Canadian province would only be formed if he and his consultors unanimously requested it and if the educational institutions were ready. With the divisions brought about by the First World War, with Baltimore no longer sending men or money into Canada, and no longer subsidizing or even accepting some of the Canadian students, there were no reasons for a formal connection with the Baltimore Province. In late 1916, one year after assuming office, Mulhall and his consultors petitioned Rome to establish the Toronto Province. The Baltimore provincial also agreed. The Baltimore Province had obviously become too big for one man to govern and the houses of the Toronto Vice-province formed over 25 per cent of the province. Geographically, English Canada formed over 70 per cent of the Baltimore Province and the American provincial could not hope to visit the distant Canadian houses on any regular basis. While Rome deliberated, Mulhall asked the vice-province to add three Hail Marys to the night prayers in honour of Our Mother of Perpetual Help and of her mother, St. Ann, for a special intention – the creation of a province. But the answer to Toronto's prayer was no. Rome informed Mulhall that no decision about Toronto would be taken until the end of the war. Novices and students were to continue going to the Baltimore Province.[13]

Exactly one year later, at the beginning of 1918, the Toronto vice-provincial council repeated its request for provincial status. Mulhall formally announced the purchase of the land in Brockville for the foundation of a minor seminary and that a novitiate would be held in the large house in Saint John, New Brunswick. Should the Baltimore Province remit some of the interest and debt on the western houses – already totalling over $150,000 – and allow some of the American fathers to remain in Canada for a time, then a Toronto province could be established. This time Toronto's prayers were heard. On Pentecost, 19 May 1918, Mulhall was named Toronto's first provincial with Coughlan and Grogan as his consultors.

Mulhall's first act as provincial was to appoint Peter O'Hare as an army chaplain to serve in Regina, Saskatchewan. The second order of business was to set up a fundraising campaign to raise $750,000 to build the minor seminary, a novitiate, and a seminary "for the formation of Redemptorist missionaries for the Dominion of Canada." Families, friends, and Redemptorist parishioners in eastern Canada formed a Liguorian Society to help. Even Toronto's Massey Hall was rented for a benefit concert by the Knights of Columbus. Unfortunately, the campaign brought in a grand total of only $35,000.[14] Even though the contractors' tenders to build the Brockville minor seminary were all over $400,000, the Toronto Province nevertheless went ahead with the building.

On 2 August 1918, the feast of St. Alphonsus, Mulhall turned the first sod for the new minor seminary. Officially named for Our Lady of Perpetual Help, among the Redemptorists it would be called St. Mary's College, in memory of St. Mary's minor seminary in the Baltimore Province. The sod-turning came mere days after the Baltimore Province had refused to accept any new Toronto students into their minor seminary, ostensibly for lack of space, but really "on account of their spirit of independence." It seems that with their own authorities far away in Canada, the Canadian students sometimes felt a little freer to flout the rules. The Baltimore authorities claimed that the Canadians were into almost every "racket," whether pranks, practical jokes, smoking, late-night discussions, or reading prohibited magazines. With the Russian Revolution fresh in everyone's minds, the Canadians were labelled the "Bolsheviki." In November three unrepentant Canadian students were ignominiously expelled from the Baltimore minor seminary.[15]

Although the postwar period brought autonomy to the English-Canadian Redemptorists, it also brought setbacks. Five Redemptorist priests returned to the Baltimore Province and one to the Belgian Province. Within days of each other, three Toronto Redemptorists died. Thomas Scollon, a student, caught typhoid fever, was professed on his deathbed, and died in October 1918. A week later, Father Francis Corrigan, only three years ordained, died in the influenza epidemic sweeping the continent. The epidemic also claimed Patrick Brennan while he was studying in Oconomowoc, Wisconsin. With six departures and these three deaths, the personnel of the Toronto Province was reduced by more than 10 per cent in its first year.

One other death a year later had an even greater effect on the Toronto Province. Baltimore's father provincial, Joseph Schneider, died suddenly in early February 1920. Mulhall seized the opportunity to travel to the funeral in New York and ask for a loan. Unlike Schneider, who had turned down Mulhall's every request to reduce Toronto's debts, the interim provincial, Edward Weigel, a former rector of St. Peter's in Saint John, New Brunswick, generously forgave the interest due on the western houses, promised space in the educational institutions of his province, and loaned more money.[16] The Toronto Province breathed easier.

The general labour unrest of the immediate postwar period meant that Brockville was not ready for 1919. The Toronto Province therefore spent more money and rented a house in nearby Prescott to house most of the minor seminarians.

> Unannounced half a hundred young men and half a dozen priests suddenly enter[ed] the town and conceal[ed] themselves in an old dilapidated building by the water-front. Strange noises emerged from the building. Bells were heard ringing at various times of the day and night. There was much loud talking and

laughter, then much singing and again a great deal of prayer services … So the talk went the rounds and the conclusion reached was, that [the Redemptorists] were the "Holy Rollers." This belief was evidently founded on the coincidence of our arrival with that of R.C. Horner, the Holy Roller organizer, who held his meetings … not far west of the Mansion House.[17]

Brockville's community and students, c. 1923
Many of the young men pictured entered the Congregation. Fr. Charles Kelz, the director, is on the bottom left.

The students were split between two lower classes at St. Ann's rectory, Montreal, and four upper classes at Prescott in the "Mansion House" on the waterfront. The Mansion House held fifty-three students and a staff of seven Redemptorists, while the Montreal house held five Redemptorists caring for thirty-five boys. In May 1920 the Prescott house was abandoned. The older students were sent to clean out the debris in the partly finished minor seminary, which still had no electricity or running water. A week later the younger Montreal students arrived in Brockville and Brockville's first class graduated. Meanwhile, the debts grew.

St. Mary's College was finally dedicated and declared finished in September. Weigel came from New York to celebrate the mass and Stephen Connolly gave the sermon. Six hundred visitors, almost eighty students, parishioners, and choirs from Redemptorist parishes, and Canadian Redemptorists from across North America attended. Unfortunately, weakened partly by the stress that went into building Brockville, Mulhall was too ill to attend.

Brockville became the cradle of the Toronto Province. Meetings and province-wide consultations were held at St. Mary's College, the province's largest institution. By 1922 eight fathers and four brothers were stationed at Brockville and, although "one or two of them ... are not thoroughly fitted for teaching," and senior students sometimes taught the juniors, the province was too young and the average age of the fathers too low to expect more. In 1924 twelve clerical candidates entered the novitiate, all but one graduates of St. Mary's College.[18]

In January 1918 there were fifteen brothers and fifty-one priests in the Toronto Vice-province. The vast majority was under the age of fifty. In fact, eight of the brothers had entered during the war, and twelve priests had been ordained during the war, while twenty-three out of the fifty-one priests had been ordained since the creation of the Vice-province of Toronto in 1912. Mulhall opened the first novitiate in 1919 for four brothers under Father Joseph Jacqmin for one year in Montreal. Father Anthony McBriarty replaced him the following year and held the brothers' novitiate at Brockville. From 1920 to 1927 twenty-two brothers were professed and by 1927 there were twenty-six brothers working in the province. In 1919 Saint John was filled with the second novitiate under William Hogan. The veteran missionary drilled the seven young fathers in the traditions of Redemptorist mission work, but the parishes used up all of the graduates and Mulhall suspended the second novitiate. When there were enough fathers to form a second novitiate in 1922, they went to the Baltimore Province. In 1924

Hogan led another Canadian second novitiate class, at the large new house in Quebec City where the second novitiate stayed for the rest of this period. Creating its own institutions helped the Province of Toronto grow.

Arthur Coughlan (1920-27)

Shortly after the opening of Brockville, Mulhall sent in his resignation and returned to the Baltimore Province, where he died in 1922. Father General Murray appointed Mulhall's consultor, Arthur Coughlan, as provincial to serve out Mulhall's three-year term.[19] Coughlan patterned everything on the Baltimore Province. The Baltimore Statutes were adopted almost in their entirety and republished as the Toronto Statutes in 1926. Coughlan merely appended useful form letters, mission prayers, circular letters, and advertising all produced by the Baltimore Province. The small house in London, Ontario, founded as a mission house, was gradually brought up to

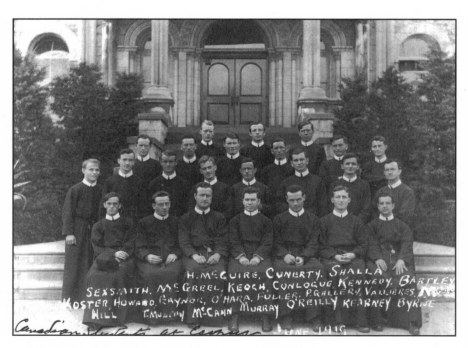

The Canadian students at Esopus

Baltimore's ideal of a parish centre, with extensions to the church and a new monastery, in the hopes that it would eventually become a resting place for aged or sick members of the Toronto Province.

Until 1921 clerical novices or candidates for the priesthood were sent to Baltimore. Then lack of space in Baltimore finally forced Toronto to bring the novices back to Canada. The young men went to Saint John, New Brunswick, under Peter Costello, but not before Coughlan carefully tailored the novitiate to follow the Baltimore Province traditions exactly. To give the Saint John foundation the atmosphere of a novitiate, the private chapel attached to St. Peter's rectory underwent major redecoration and renovations in 1922, while the church grounds, formerly cow pastures, were improved with gardens, walks, and a replica of the grotto at Lourdes. The playing field, begun in 1914, was improved, but baseball was banned by Roman visitors who worried that the noise and distraction would upset the novices and the religious exercises. There is no evidence that the novices or even the Redemptorists at St. Peter's had complained; the ball-playing started again and even attained semi-professional status.

Description of a daily prayer schedule kept by Brother Raymond (John Gomes) who participated in the first brothers' novitiate in the Toronto Province.

Students on St. Patrick's Day at St. Mary's, Brockville
Along with languages, literature, public speaking, group sports, history, and geography, learning how to organize impromptu processions and parades was part of the training necessary to any young man in public life. It also helped to lighten the strict regimen in the minor seminary.

Local Catholics encouraged Redemptorist high spirits. The young men of Saint John enthusiastically welcomed the novices in the early 1920s with a "ghost raid" by sheet-covered young men trying to frighten the novices with firecrackers and gunfire. Arthur Coughlan led the defence with pitchers of cold water poured from the upper stairs. The annual raids, led by Edward Hansen, ended when one of the ghosts was badly injured by a falling pitcher still filled with water. Some of the ghosts later entered Brockville and, eventually, the novitiate.[20]

Baltimore's decision in 1927 to dismiss some Canadian students from the seminary in Esopus for high jinks relating to a secret smoking ring, reading unauthorized magazines, and going around in automobiles without permission led Arthur Coughlan and his consultors to decide that Toronto should have its own seminary. Only in that way could Toronto have any control over its theology students. It was time to bring the Canadians home.

The Toronto Province's First Seminary: St. Ann's, Montreal

St. Ann's in the Montreal of the 1920s was still very much an Irish working-class parish. The Irish Self-Determination League even made an appearance with the Sinn Fein flag in 1920. When changes in municipal and railway lands threatened to wipe out the residential areas of St. Ann's, there was an attempt in 1922 to replace the declining Montreal parish with one in the new town of Mount Royal, but the archbishop of Montreal's reluctance caused Coughlan to keep St. Ann's rather than risk not having a place in Montreal at all. The "attendance at the services is quite large [over 4,000], so that it seems to me it will take many years for the parish to be practically wiped out, as some predict will happen. The parishioners are mostly of the poorer classes," Coughlan argued, and the Redemptorists should work with them, as St. Alphonsus would want.[21] St. Ann's did not seem an ideal place for a seminary, but it had extra rooms as fewer Redemptorists were needed to care for the smaller parish. St. Ann's monastery in Montreal became a temporary seminary, from 1925 to 1930, with Francis Hill, James Fuller, and Leonard McGuire as the lecturers.

The many outings, the poetry, the oratory, the meetings with parishioners, the escapades from the upper windows of St. Ann's, the clandestine smoking, and the punishments and expulsions of the unruly ringleaders all became part of the oral history of the Toronto Province. To some extent, these experiences helped to lighten the intensive spiritual training and bind the Redemptorist students closer together. Young men who had met and played and studied in Brockville fought off ghost raids together in the novitiate and then studied at St. Ann's. The stories, reputations, and nicknames were fixed for ever. Of the nineteen students in the first seminary class at St. Ann's, twelve were still in the Congregation twenty years later, two having died as Redemptorists. These were, as Francis Hill later wrote, the "Nazareth days" of the Toronto Province.[22]

Young and adventurous, Hill embarked on a doctorate in theology at the same time as he worked as student prefect (monitor). Leonard McGuire, socius (assistant monitor) to the students and teacher in ethics, spent his spare time writing the brisk-selling little

book *Oatcakes and Sulphur*, which set out to prove the existence of
God and justify the nature of the Church, with examples taken from
Canada. Fuller taught the natural sciences while trying to overcome
the chronic insomnia that crippled him with fatigue and depression,
but which also allowed him to see and worry about the nightly comings and goings of his colleagues and charges. Other young teachers
– two from the Baltimore Province – added to the generally high
spirits of the teaching staff, not to mention the students themselves.

The search for a more suitable Canadian seminary site had
been going on for some years, and the possibility of sending students
to England, Ireland, or even Vienna had been explored. A former
Baptist College in Woodstock was for sale and although it was in
rather poor condition, Father Provincial Coughlan opened negotiations to purchase the property.[23] In the meantime, Coughlan, over the
protests of his consultors that such work was unseemly, gave Father
Ken Kennedy at Brockville permission and encouragement to found
the *Saint Mary's College Review*, an annual magazine started in 1926,
to occupy the time, energy, and talents of the many young men, both
Redemptorists and students, who had a taste for light literature.[24]

The West

Distance has always isolated the west. In the postwar period western
Canadian conditions continued to demand special attention and a different missionary strategy on the part of the Redemptorists. Primitive
conditions in the west also forced the Toronto Province to keep older
fathers in the more settled foundations of eastern Canada. Although
worried about the lack of training younger Redemptorists had, superiors regularly sent newly ordained Redemptorists west, which gave
a different complexion to Redemptorist life in western Canada. The
saying in eastern Canada was that the young Redemptorists leaned
out of their railway car windows and tossed the Rule and their canon
law books onto a growing heap somewhere in Lake Superior before
reaching the house in East Kildonan, Winnipeg.[25]

With settlers moving farther westward into Alberta and
British Columbia, the Redemptorist houses in East Kildonan and
Brandon in Manitoba and in Yorkton and Regina in Saskatchewan

were too far away from the new population centres rising farther west along the railway lines. The Redemptorists wanted to move to Edmonton as soon as possible, but the question was where to find the men and the money to establish a new house.

Coughlan turned first to American examples. The western American St. Louis Province had instituted a railway chapel car ministry, which travelled throughout the western United States. Coughlan and his consultors believed that such a roving ministry would suit the Redemptorists in Canada. He also attempted to imitate the Baltimore Province by establishing a Polish mission band for western Canada. While there is no evidence that much came of these efforts, his attempt to establish a North American Italian mission band at Toronto's Our Lady of Mount Carmel parish might illustrate what happened.

Roman and Baltimore authorities decided that the United States, with its larger Italian population, would be a better base for the missionaries. So eventually the Italian Redemptorists at Our Lady of Mount Carmel were transferred to the Baltimore Province, leaving at most one Italian-born Redemptorist and one Roman-trained and Italian-speaking English-Canadian Redemptorist in Toronto to care for the parish.[26] These disappointments brought Coughlan to search for other ways to work in western Canada.

The attitude of eastern Canada's English Redemptorists and of the English-Canadian Catholic Church in general to Catholicism in the west could perhaps best be seen in the early history of the Sisters of Service. A Catholic school teacher, Catherine Donnelly, came to Arthur Coughlan for advice on how she, along with a few others, "might devote her services to the religious welfare of neglected Catholics in Western Canada." In his many conversations and prayers with her and with Archbishop Neil McNeil of Toronto, the idea grew of a distinctly Canadian religious institute adapted for Canada's needs. The Sisters of Service, acting as nurses, teachers, and social workers, were to help immigrants in isolated areas adapt to Canada while remaining Catholic. The new congregation was placed under the patronage of Our Lady of Perpetual Help and formally began on the feast of the Assumption, 15 August 1922, with four novices including Catherine Donnelly, and a novice mistress loaned from the Sisters of St. Joseph.[27]

Coughlan was too busy to direct the foundation of a religious congregation. He turned to the one man experienced in leadership, education, missions, spiritual retreats, immigration, and the west – George Daly. Coughlan knew that Daly could never become provincial – he conceded as much to Rome – when he suggested that Stephen Connolly might become Toronto's first Canadian provincial. Nevertheless, Coughlan felt that Daly was the finest Redemptorist produced by Canada.[28]

Coughlan showed his admiration for Daly's ideas by subsidizing half the publication costs of a book of essays and speeches Daly had given while in western Canada. Then Coughlan recommended the 1921 book, *Catholic Problems in Western Canada*, to the entire Toronto Province and asked that it be read, promoted, and sold. Challenged in part by the Protestant vision of a Christian Canada, Daly wove together plans for Church expansion, organization, the assimilation of immigrants, the need for separate schools, a Catholic university, and a Catholic press. Such plans mirrored the thinking of the Catholic hierarchy in Toronto and the Toronto-based Catholic Church Extension Society. These were the Catholics most threatened and influenced by the surrounding English Protestant culture. The book won Daly, the Redemptorists, and Roman Catholics a measure of respect from prominent Canadians, both Catholic and Protestant, because Daly borrowed so many ideas from Protestant missionaries and applied them to Catholic missions. He wrote in several of his works, "Fas est ab hoste doceri!" (it is good to learn from the enemy).

Coughlan invited Daly to Toronto in 1922 to preach at the opening services to celebrate the newly redecorated interior of St. Patrick's church. Afterwards he kept him in Toronto as an informal consultor. When American solutions did not work out, Coughlan turned to Daly for advice on how to deal with Canadian problems.

Although Coughlan originally believed that the Sisters of Service would only need help from the Redemptorists for one or two years, he remained the Sisters' spiritual director until 1927. Daly enthusiastically and successfully guided them in temporal matters, allowing them to establish a new novitiate in the wealthy area of Rosedale, Toronto, in 1927. Daly also succeeded in gaining the

Sisters canonical status, with their own province, consultors, and novice mistress in 1928. Once Coughlan retired from his position as spiritual guide to the Sisters, Daly continued as both their temporal and spiritual guide after 1927.

The Sisters of Service became a providential outlet for Daly's many talents, wide-ranging vision, and his desire to blend religious with Canadian life. Writing, travelling, and consulting people across Canada on behalf of the Sisters, he would also gather information and negotiate new foundations on Toronto's and on occasion Beaupré's behalf. With the Sisters of Service, Daly put his writings into action and worked tirelessly to integrate new Canadians into the English-speaking Catholic community.[29] To continue his work, he begged his superiors to fight the rumours and possible moves to have him made a bishop in western Canada. He remained based in Toronto, close to the Sisters of Service, to the Catholic Truth Society, to the Catholic Church Extension Society, and to Toronto's Archbishop Neil McNeil.

Toronto's Community in 1923

Daly's influence in Toronto and the Toronto Province's continual work in the archdiocese, as confessors to many of the other religious congregations and as chaplains to the hospitals, tied the Toronto Province Redemptorists more firmly to the archdiocese and its plans for English-Canadian Catholicism, making Toronto more than just the administrative centre of the far-flung Toronto Province, but the ideological centre as well.

Eventually, the Sisters of Service found themselves in the same Canadian mission fields as the Redemptorists, running schools, student residences, catechetical and religious correspondence programs, small hospitals, and visiting new immigrants in port or in their homes. Women relatives of men who had joined the Redemptorists could sometimes be found among the Sisters of Service, practising similar devotions and creating a stronger "family" resemblance between the Toronto Redemptorists and the Sisters of Service. The membership continued to grow and, in 1981, there were over one hundred and twenty Sisters, most of whom worked in eastern Canada.[30]

Redemptorists had been giving missions on the west coast since 1887. As recently as 1916 three missionaries left Toronto to visit Vancouver, and they had been favourably impressed by the growth in population and by the mild climate, suitable for older Redemptorists or those unable to stand the cold. Coughlan sent George Daly to Vancouver in 1922 to open negotiations for a Redemptorist foundation. Daly's work bore fruit in 1923. When the Benedictines prepared to leave the Vancouver area, Archbishop Timothy Casey asked the Redemptorists for replacements. The Redemptorists sent John Frederick Coghlan, who had family in Vancouver, to establish a house in the Benedictines' old area of Kerrisdale near the Fraser River. Coghlan instead urged that the Redemptorists take the Point Grey area, but without the care of the students who would attend the university planned for West Point Grey. While Redemptorists were heavily involved in teaching in their own institutions preparing young men for ordination, they did not feel themselves called to care for other students. The need for training missionary priests at times justified – barely – their own educational institutions; it did not justify taking over the chaplaincy of students on the campus of a secular university.

A temporary chapel was set up in an abandoned Protestant church being used as a shoe repair shop. The nature of the west in those days can be seen in the comment in the Redemptorist chronicles that "The proprietor of the premises was an active Free-Mason and the key of the place was kept by a Baptist next door."

Out in the Point Grey forest, Father Harry McGuire boosted Father Coghlan up onto the highest stump so that he could look around at the land for the parish. The two young men prayed and planted medals of St. Alphonsus, St. Clement, St. Gerard, and Our Lady of Perpetual Help in the ground to obtain their blessings on the site. Our Lady of Perpetual Help, Vancouver, was canonically established on 18 October 1923. Father General Patrick Murray had enthusiastically approved of the Vancouver foundation so that the Toronto Province would stretch from the Atlantic to the Pacific and proposed to visit it at the first opportunity. A house in town was rented mere days before he arrived and the beds were brought in during his evening meal, causing him to proclaim that a miracle had taken place. A new church opened in November 1925, a new hall followed

Our Lady of Perpetual Help, Vancouver.

in February 1926, a new monastery began in June 1926, and a new school completed the parish plant in 1927. Such rapid expansion, typical of western Canada in the 1920s, was financed with staggering debts charged to the eastern houses.[31]

The far-western missions and personnel shortages brought the Redemptorists to give St. Augustine's in Brandon back to the diocese. The parishioners had begun to complain of the Redemptorists' overly cautious financial management. The complaints led to the election of lay trustees in 1919 who then pushed for an enlarged parish hall in 1920, a new school in 1921, and a new addition to the school in 1923. The Redemptorists opposed these additions, because it seemed to them that the parish had never and probably would never pay the school sisters' salaries nor the costs of the buildings. They had long subsidized the entire parish plant and salaries. While Brandon had been used as a minor seminary for western vocations, and as a centre for Polish missions, the Redemptorists had been willing to remain and subsidize the parish. With the Baltimore Province unable to send any Polish missionaries and with Brockville in place, Brandon was no longer needed. The Redemptorists took the parishioners' criticisms as an invitation to leave.[32]

St. Alphonsus, Edmonton
Edmonton's strategic location on several transportation routes made it a natural foundation for a missionary congregation.

Leaving Brandon gave the Redemptorists the necessary men, furniture, and books to establish St. Alphonsus Liguori parish in Edmonton on 29 February 1924. Edmonton quickly became a mission centre for Alberta and a pastoral centre for mission chapels stretching north of Edmonton to the Vilna, Smoky Lake, and Radway districts.

Although Regina was much more central for the prairie missions, the Redemptorists were unhappy with the obviously diocesan and temporary nature of their work in the cathedral. Although it had begun as a short-term assignment in 1915 to help with a temporary shortage, the archbishop gave no sign of replacing the Redemptorists or of giving them another place in his archdiocese. These parish years at Regina, with George Daly and then Stephen Connolly, were nonetheless most successful in attracting western candidates, and the Redemptorists were reluctant to force the issue.[33] Finally, when it became obvious that Regina would not have another English Catholic parish soon, or ever, the Redemptorists returned the cathedral parish to the diocese and accepted a parish farther west, in Moose Jaw in 1927.

By 1927 the Toronto Province had seventy-six priests in eleven houses, fifty-six professed students and seven priests in studies. This was almost double the number of priests and triple the number of professed students the Toronto Province had in 1918. The province had also more than doubled its missionary work: in 1927 it had given one hundred and twenty-eight missions, twenty-seven renewals, ten novenas, ninety tridua and quaridua (three and four day devotions), and sixty-three retreats to priests, religious, nuns, and students. Observance of the Rule was generally excellent in the eastern houses and always so in the houses of formation at Brockville and Saint John. Observance declined gradually going west, until the Vancouver house was reached and the third and lowest rating of "mediocre" was earned. The smaller houses in western Canada found it difficult to bring enough men together to perform their religious exercises, while Fred Coghlan in Vancouver rarely wrote any financial accounts. But in fervour and in apostolic ministry, every house in the Toronto Province always gained the grades of good or excellent.

When the province began, its debts totalled over $250,000. With the advent of Edward Weigel as provincial, the Baltimore Province forgave most of its interests and loans to the Toronto Province. Even so, Brockville's total cost was just over $330,000, not including maintenance of the property and the care of the students. Toronto borrowed more money from the Baltimore Province to pay for Brockville and the new western houses of Vancouver and Edmonton. After ten years, the financial books showed that little had changed, despite Baltimore forgiving yet another $100,000 in loans and interest. The Toronto Province during the boom times of the 1920s had not reduced its debt load and still groaned under a mountain of debt.[34]

In spite of debts, the Redemptorist vocation appeared marvellous and attractive: "to become living images of our Most Holy Redeemer, in order to continue the great work of redemption begun by Him during His mortal life ... to do for the people of our time and country what Jesus Christ Himself did for the people of the Holy Land during His mortal life."[35] The number of students continued to increase beyond the levels reached during the war.

The only fault anyone could find with the Toronto Province was that it was young and suffered from a general lack of formation in Redemptorist traditions. Mulhall and Coughlan were forced to push young men into positions of authority and into the western mission fields years before they believed them seasoned enough. In reaction to their lack of confidence in their own Redemptorist identity, English Canadians modelled themselves closely on the Baltimore Province and its interpretation of the Rule. Both Mulhall and Coughlan insisted on strictness in following the Rule and the traditions of the Baltimore Province. Older members of the Toronto Province who had come from the Belgian and Beaupré provinces were increasingly kept from positions of authority, causing some discontent. Daly, however, continued to argue that his former students in the Beaupré Province, after they were educated further in Baltimore's institutions, were the hope of future unity. Redemptorist ideals, Belgium's missionary spirit, Baltimore's educational and parish structures, and English-Canadian nationalism combined into a powerful and well-organized religious movement in Catholic Canada. Lack of money meant nothing to those with faith.

In the private memorandum that Father General Murray wrote on his canonical visit of 1923, he noted that the two elements of the province, the Baltimore and the Beaupré graduates, were being welded into one; he could see hardly any differences between the two, if, indeed, they ever existed. Although everyone in 1923 asked for a Canadian provincial, he decided that Father Coughlan was the best man for the position in 1924, but a Canadian, Stephen Connolly, could replace him if needed. The province had elected Connolly as their representative to the 1921 Roman General Chapter. His creditable performance in Rome, his Canadian nationalism tempered by his Baltimore education, his experience as rector of St. Patrick's in Toronto and as a vice-provincial consultor, his continued work for students, and above all, his ability to follow the Rule made him acceptable to everyone.

Daly had alienated many with his independent ways. However, he continued to write, to speak, and to influence people. He wrote to Rome insisting that Canadians from the Belgian Province be represented in the provincial council. Coughlan, on Daly's recommendation, promoted other Beaupré alumni, such as Edward Walsh and Donald MacDougal, although not Daly himself. Daly did not become provincial, but he directly influenced the attitudes of the Toronto Province. Coughlan wrote to Rome that "Father Daly is a man of unbounded influence in the entire Dominion ... There is no priest in Canada, secular or religious, who is so influential and so much in demand."[36]

To keep Daly in Toronto and please the archbishop who wanted his services, Coughlan annulled Daly's promotion to the rectorship of Edmonton and retained him in Toronto without any duties. This gave Daly even more time for his travels, writings, and meetings. In the province and in Rome, there was no doubt as to who was the "power behind the throne."[37] It was sometimes hard to tell which tradition, Baltimore's or Belgium's, dominated in the Toronto Province.

It still came as a surprise to learn how influential George Daly had become. He had correctly gauged the needs of the Toronto Province and urged a young candidate to start a new regime that would take the Toronto Province beyond American or Belgian labels. The Baltimore-trained Stephen Connolly, long considered Baltimore's candidate to become the first Canadian-born provincial, did not get the promotion. In 1927 he was already over sixty years old. In May 1927 the news was received that Daly's brilliant former student, a Canadian, the forty-one year-old Gerald Murray was to be the new provincial, with two equally young Canadians, John Barry and John Kane, as his consultors.[38] Arthur Coughlan was transferred to Quebec City, protesting feebly at the inexperienced nature of the new council. The "American invasion" was a thing of the past.[39] A new and younger generation of Redemptorists had arrived in Canada and they were all Canadians.

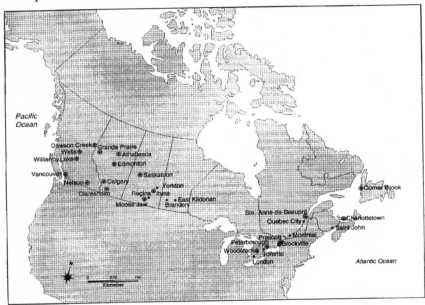

• Foundations Prior to 1918

Western Canada

St. Augustine's, Brandon, Manitoba (1898-1924)
St. Gerard, Yorkton, Saskatchewan (1904-1991)
East Kildonan, Manitoba (1914-1993)
Holy Rosary, Regina, Saskatchewan (1915-1927)

Eastern Canada

St. Patrick's, Quebec City (1874)
St. Patrick's, Toronto (1881)
St. Peter's, Saint John, N.B. (1884)
St. Ann's, Montreal (1884-1970)
St. Patrick's, London (1912-1975)

⊛ Foundations Between 1918 and 1945

Our Lady of Perpetual Help, Vancouver, B.C. (1923)
St. Alphonsus, Edmonton, Alberta (1924)
St. Joseph's, Moose Jaw, Saskatchewan (1927)
St. Mary's, Yorkton, Saskatchewan (1928-1931)
Sacred Heart, Ituna, Saskatchewan (1928-1931)
Our Lady of Perpetual Help, Calgary, Alberta (1929)
St. Joseph's, Grande Prairie, Alberta (1932)
St. Mary's, Saskatoon, Saskatchewan (1935)
Our Lady of Perpetual Help, Dawson Creek, B.C. (1936-1960)
Sacred Heart, William's Lake, B.C. (1938)
Blessed Sacrament, Nelson, B.C. (1939-87)
St. Gabriel's, Athabaska, Alberta (1940-1966)
Holy Rosary, Wells, B.C. (1941-1948)
St. George's, Claresholm, Alberta (1941-1947)

Juvenate, Prescott, Ontario (1919-1920)
St. Mary's College, Brockville, Ontario (1920-1969)
Holy Redeemer, Charlottetown, P.E.I. (1929-1975)
St. Alphonsus Seminary, Woodstock, Ontario (1930-1957)
Holy Redeemer, Corner Brook, Newfoundland (1931-1947)
St. Clement's Juvenate, Toronto (1942-1947)
St. Alphonsus, Peterborough, Ontario (1944-1984)

The Toronto Province, 1918–45

6

Moving from East to West, 1927–45

Once established in the east, the missionary energies of the English-Canadian Redemptorists turned west. From 1927 to 1945 only three foundations were established in eastern Canada. In the same period twelve foundations were accepted in the west: four in Saskatchewan, four in Alberta, and four in British Columbia. Western Canada became the scene of several struggles to adapt eastern Canadian Redemptorist life and ideals.

Gerald Murray (1927–30)

Gerald Murray was born into an Irish Catholic home in Montreal in 1885. He had attended Beaupré's English minor seminary in St. Ann's in 1896, but was unsure of his vocation. He then entered Loyola College in Montreal to see something of the Jesuits. After graduation in 1905, however, he returned to Beaupré to teach for a year before entering the Redemptorist novitiate held in Hochelaga, Montreal. He attended the Redemptorist major seminary in Ottawa, was ordained in 1910, and joined the Toronto Vice-province in 1912. Having completed his second novitiate in Annapolis, Maryland, he was sent to Rome in 1913 for further education. The outbreak of the First World War cut short his studies, but he was granted a doctorate in philosophy in his one year at Rome instead of the usual two. Sent to Baltimore's major seminary in Esopus, New York, in 1914, he taught philosophy and moral theology, as well as French and elocution, for ten years.

Baltimore at first turned down Canadian requests to have him transferred back to Canada, since his knowledge and skills were greatly appreciated. Murray successfully negotiated the solution to the Beaupré and Baltimore rivalry over the Franco-American mission field by tactfully remarking that Baltimore did not have the qualified manpower to keep all of the Franco-American missions for itself. He was finally transferred from Esopus to the key position of Brockville rector in 1924. There were rumours that he had difficulties keeping the unruly boys in line, but after Charles Kelz's reputation as a man who thought all boys were "canoes needing to be paddled," Murray's slow, easy-going ways were a welcome change. His obvious ability to represent both the American and the Beaupré traditions was such that George Daly and Rome judged him able to become the first Canadian to unite and head the Toronto Province in April 1927.[1]

Although he was inexperienced and Father General Murray advised him to start nothing new, Murray had little inclination and less choice to do otherwise. Only the richest parish, St. Patrick's in Quebec City, could afford a building program, and a new hall and renovations to St. Brigid's Home emptied even those parish funds. As the Great Depression closed in, Gerald Murray contemplated the province's vast debt and gladly took Father General Patrick Murray's advice. He and his consultors started nothing new but merely built on Arthur Coughlan's initiatives.

Woodstock (1930)

First, Murray and his consultors consummated the previous administration's negotiations for Woodstock Baptist College in the London diocese. It took two years, but the Redemptorists finally acquired the property, buildings, and fixtures in 1929 for just over $60,000. The need was great, because the overcrowding and disciplinary problems in St. Ann's temporary seminary had continued. With relief, the first community – Leo Sexsmith, Ladislaus Wojciechowski, Arthur

Woodstock Baptist College
All that remains today are the trees. (Courtesy of the Canadian Baptist Archives, McMaster Divinity College, Hamilton, Ontario)

Conlogue, George Michel, and Arthur Ryan – moved from Montreal to the quiet of spacious Woodstock and began teaching classes in September 1930. With thirty-six acres of rolling pasture and woods on the Woodstock property, there was enough room to contain the energies of a hundred students, should that happy day ever arrive. In recognition of Arthur Coughlan's influence and standing in the province, he became the first rector of St. Alphonsus' Seminary, named after the Redemptorist major seminary in Esopus, New York.

Lack of money forced the Redemptorists to turn much of the seminary into a farm. Students and novices helped the brothers with the farm work. Perhaps it was a useful education; several of the students appreciated the peaceful atmosphere which allowed them time and space to grow into their lives as Redemptorists.

Apostolate of the Pen

Murray also followed Coughlan's lead in the apostolate of the pen. The Annals of Ste-Anne-de-Beaupré in the 1930s published over eighty thousand copies monthly in French, and over twenty thousand in English, half going to the United States, Ireland, Scotland, and England. Members of the Toronto Province had a standing invitation to send material to the Annals and some accepted. Clayton Kramer, for example, later wrote short pieces of moral theology in the "Answer of the Month" section for almost twenty years under the pen name of Father Robert Mark.[2]

Leonard McGuire's successful *Oatcakes and Sulphur* encouraged his brother Henry in Quebec City to launch the publication of an erudite, expensive, and therefore short-lived monthly, *The Patrician*.[3] The experiment raised such enthusiasm that James McCandlish asked Gerald Murray for permission to start a more popular magazine in Toronto to spread devotion to Our Lady of Perpetual Help beyond the weekly devotions at the Redemptorist parishes. A twenty-four-page magazine designed for a wide Catholic family readership, named *The Eikon*, was first published in October 1928 under the editorship of Patrick Gallery. Gerald Murray wrote the first article while the other well-known Toronto speakers and writers, George Daly, John Keogh, and Bernard Coffey, contributed the remaining articles to the successful first issue.

The Eikon gave space to aspiring English-language Redemptorist poets and writers from around the world. Naturally, Toronto Province authors were most often in prominence. Brother Reginald, the religious name for the Oxford-educated Charles Greenall and the assistant editor for many years at *The Eikon*, published several devotional poems. Father Augustine Bennett, who wrote under several pen names, published his poetry in local and international religious newspapers and magazines after they first appeared in *The Eikon*.[4] The magazine's goal was reached: if the membership lists of the Archconfraternity of Our Lady of Perpetual Help are any evidence, devotion increased.

Within two years *The Eikon* had reached a paid circulation of six thousand. The subscriptions allowed the Redemptorists to finance the printing of almost sixty thousand further free copies every month in 1932, but in the following year and for the rest of its existence, Depression realities forced the Toronto Province to print no more than twenty-five thousand free copies. Although the higher-brow *Patrician* was cancelled, several members of the Toronto Province felt the need for such a publication. Woodstock professor Arthur Ryan suggested that the Toronto Province publish a digest of significant articles and books especially for Redemptorists. *Homo Apostolicus*, with articles, summaries, digests, and reviews by the Woodstock faculty began in 1936 in stapled, mimeographed form. These publications, *The Eikon* for the laity, the Brockville *Review* for students, and *Homo Apostolicus* for seminarians and priests, encouraged a generation of young Redemptorists to publish and be read by as many people as possible.

Other Foundations

Despite financial constraints, the Toronto Province under Gerald Murray established two new foundations. The bishop of Prince Edward Island, Louis O'Leary, brother to the Edmonton archbishop, offered land and money for a new parish in Charlottetown. Murray saw Prince Edward Island as "a nursery of priests" and that many candidates would come to the only religious congregation for men on the Island. George Daly negotiated the agreement, but Toronto's money problems dictated the terms: the diocese would own the church, while the Redemptorists owned only their own monastery. The parish of the Most Holy Redeemer, Charlottetown, began 6 May 1929, under Father Joseph McGreel. By 1938 not only had the Redemptorists helped the parish build and decorate a church, they also offered lay-retreats with the Sisters of St. Martha.[5]

At the same time, Murray urged the acceptance of a parish in Calgary. He argued that Calgary, as the only major western city without a Redemptorist presence and without any religious clergy, would also attract students and allow for more missions in the area. Calgary's house began in April 1929 under Isidore Shalla, and the parish was renamed Our Lady of Perpetual Help. A basement church, a mission, a census, and the devotions all began within days. In 1931 the Redemptorists also took on the care of Holy Trinity parish, Forest Lawn, Calgary as an outmission of Our Lady of Perpetual Help.[6]

Rome reluctantly accepted both Charlottetown and Calgary since they had been initiated by Murray's predecessor, but begged Murray not to think of any more foundations until the Toronto Province had fewer debts.[7] The Roman officials had good reason to urge restraint, for Gerald Murray faced a more pressing challenge. Not surprisingly, it was one put together by George Daly.

The Ukrainian Vice-province of Yorkton, 1928–31

In 1922 Daly met the apostolic delegate to Canada and, in the course
of the conversation, was invited to report on the Ukrainian question
in western Canada. The "Private and Confidential Report Presented
on Demand to His Excellency the Apostolic Delegate, on the
Ruthenian [Ukrainian] Problem in Canada" was, true to Daly's form,
neither private nor confidential, since Daly wrote, copied, and
showed it to Provincial Coughlan, to the Belgian provincial, to the
superior general, and to several Canadian bishops before sending the
final draft to the apostolic delegate. It summarized English-Canadian
Catholic thinking.

Daly called for the removal of the Ukrainian-Catholic bish-
op, Nicetas Budka. At the outbreak of the First World War, Bishop
Budka had urged Ukrainians to support Austria. When the British
Empire declared war on Austria, Budka was forced to retract. Many
English Canadians could not forget or forgive Budka's first loyalty.
Daly declared Budka's appointment a mistake and a failure, since
public opinion had turned against him and by association against the
Catholic Church. The younger generation of Ukrainian Canadians
were conscious of Canada's low opinion of them and their clergy
and succumbed to the temptation to change their names, speak only
English, and join Protestant churches.

Daly's solution was the gradual assimilation of Ukrainian
Catholics into the English-language Latin-rite Church. To do this, he
suggested that each Latin-rite bishop be in charge of the Ukrainians
in his own diocese. All obstacles to the transfer of Eastern-rite
Catholics to the Latin-rite were to be removed. Daly also argued that
the Toronto Province could help in this assimilation by taking over
the Ukrainian-Catholic missions of western Canada.[8]

This was not an outlandish request, because the Belgian
Redemptorists, along with the Eastern-rite Order of Saint Basil,
were intimately bound up with the Ukrainian work in the minds of
the Canadian bishops. Since their incorporation into the Ukrainian
Vice-province of Lviv in 1913, the Belgians had established a novitiate, a minor seminary, and a religious monthly newspaper, as well
as dozens of churches, schools, and an orphanage. By 1919 there

Poster announcing lecture and slide show: "Ten Years in the Ice" by Fr. Van den Bossche, CSsR, (Father Bosky). Money raised in Belgium went to support the work in Canada. (Courtesy of the Archives of the North Belgium Province) were substantial Redemptorist foundations in Yorkton and Ituna, both in Saskatchewan, and in Komarno, Manitoba, with mission fields and churches covering the prairies, enough for a separate Canadian vice-province.

In the chaos of the First World War, communication with the European houses of the Vice-province of Lviv had been cut off, and in 1919 Achille Delaere was named vice-provincial with residence in Canada.[9] In 1921 the Lviv Vice-province was canonically divided into two vice-provinces, one in Europe named Lviv, and the other in Canada, named Yorkton with Delaere as Yorkton's first vice-provincial. A dozen men had done an incredible amount of work in Canada, but the need for help was growing as individuals grew older and the Belgian Province was again busier elsewhere in the world and could not promise men or money to Canada.[10]

The war years and the postwar period had created a heightened Ukrainian nationalism, jeopardizing the Belgian work. Germans, Poles, and Russians had fought over, in, and through the Ukraine. The Soviet Union's 1928 collectivization policies created

Sacred Heart, Ituna, Saskatchewan

famine and further chaos across the area. Ukrainian nationalism and isolationism increased. Even in Canada, Ukrainians rejected the Belgians as strangers and outsiders. Bishop Budka excommunicated some of the ultra-nationalists, but it did not help the situation.

In 1926 Daly had written to Father General Patrick Murray to promote the idea of assimilating the Canadian Ukrainian missions as the only solution to the loss of souls to the Protestant churches. He asked that the Yorkton Vice-province be given to Toronto with himself as Toronto's delegated visitor to oversee the integration of the Belgian and Ukrainian Redemptorists as well as the Ukrainian Catholics into the English-Canadian Catholic Church.[11] At first Daly received no support for his ideas. As the situation on the prairies worsened, however, he won over the American consultor general, Fidelis Speidel, and the Belgian consultor general, Franciscus Ter Haar. Speidel proposed Daly's solution to Gerald Murray and Ter Haar wrote to the Belgian provincial that it was a possible solution to his manpower shortage in western Canada.

In 1927 there were only eleven Redemptorist priests, four of them Ukrainian, and six brothers, working with the Ukrainians. With few missions, few recruits, and exhausted men, the Yorkton Vice-province had already closed its Komarno foundation, its minor seminary in 1926, and the newspaper in early 1928. No longer welcome among the Ukrainian Canadians, the Belgian Redemptorists turned their thoughts to Poland, where their knowledge of Ukrainian, so similar to Polish, would be useful. The Belgian provincial came to believe that the Yorkton Vice-province could simply be dissolved and the two houses of Yorkton and Ituna merely transferred to Toronto. Putting the best face on the deal, the Yorkton Redemptorists thought Toronto could provide men, education for their students, and English priests for the Ukrainian children who were assimilating into the English culture. Toronto's own manpower was growing rapidly with Brockville graduates. Although only Daly was arguing for it, the plan had merit. Father General Patrick Murray approved the transfer on 18 December 1927.

Negotiations between Belgium and Toronto now began in earnest. Toronto wanted the Belgians to be replaced by Redemptorists from the Ukraine in order to establish better relations with the Ukrainian Canadians and to teach the Toronto Redemptorists the language and the rite. The Ukrainian Redemptorists did not want to go over to Toronto, because they were aware, through Daly's writings and talks, of Toronto's intention to anglicize and latinize the Canadian Ukrainians, something they feared would alienate every Ukrainian from the Catholic Church. Consequently, Toronto and Belgium agreed that the Belgians would be gradually replaced by English-Canadian Redemptorists and Ukrainian-Canadian Redemptorists educated in Toronto's institutions. Yorkton's considerable assets in land and buildings would not be sold to offset Toronto's own large debts, but would be kept whole as a vice-province under Toronto. The Yorkton Vice-province was formally attached to the Toronto Province on 25 January 1929.

When Gerald Murray sent George Daly to negotiate the property transfers, Daly finally learned about the Ukrainian Redemptorist fears for their people's loyalty to Catholicism if there were any attempts to assimilate them; Daly hastily wrote to Murray to ask that no English be used in the houses and no attempt made to anglicize or latinize the students or the parishioners. Everything, as he had often said, had to be slow and natural.[12] Unfortunately, Daly's letter came too late.

The man chosen to head up the Yorkton house of St. Mary's was Edward Walsh. Born in 1880, one of the last St. Ann Montrealers trained in Belgium, Walsh had been a pioneer English-speaking Redemptorist in western Canada. Walsh was superior of Brandon between 1915 and 1921, rector of Toronto between 1921 and 1924, and minister in Brockville until 1927. At almost fifty years of age, Walsh felt himself unable and unwilling to learn Ukrainian. He also firmly believed in a vigorous policy of anglicizing the Ukrainian people and bringing them into the Latin-rite. Walsh immediately began preaching missions in English in the villages and towns around Yorkton. Daly and Murray were aghast, but Walsh found a powerful protector in the Baltimore provincial, James Barron, named the official visitor on behalf of the Roman authorities. Barron recommended Walsh's views in an official report to Rome on the Toronto Province and the Ukrainian question.[13]

Walsh had been chosen for Yorkton in part for his knowledge of Belgian ways, but he and the Belgian, Achille Delaere, clashed immediately. Delaere insisted that Redemptorists become Ukrainians while Walsh wanted the Ukrainians to become English Canadians. Although the Ukrainians were indeed learning English and their children would eventually become English-speaking Canadians, Walsh and the English-Canadian Redemptorists over-looked the fact that it was easier for a few Redemptorists to become Ukrainian than for the students and their parents to become English. Young and old still needed religious services in their own language and in their own rite. As Delaere and other Belgian and Ukrainian Redemptorists knew, Redemptorists had to deal with Ukrainians speaking Ukrainian then and there, and not Ukrainians speaking English and attending the Latin mass in a generation's time.

The tension and squabbles could not help but affect the young men Toronto sent to Yorkton. James Grannan arrived in Yorkton in February 1929, and Michael MacIsaac and Lucian Howard were sent in the fall of 1929 to learn the language and the rite. All three recent-ly ordained Maritimers found the experience demanding and frustrat-ing. Their instructions from Gerald Murray and Daly said one thing while Walsh did another and sent them to preach missions in English. Compounding the difficulties was the fact that there were no English-Ukrainian grammar books or dictionaries in the Yorkton house. The house library had several Latin-Ukrainian, German-Ukrainian, even French-Ukrainian books, but none in English. Grannan said his first mass in the Eastern rite in September, but all three men had so many difficulties in adapting their lives to a new language and a new rite that they naturally fell in with their superior Edward Walsh's views that the language and even the rite were hardly necessary. The English Canadians requested permission for bi-ritualism – that is, to perform the Eastern liturgy in public and the Latin rite in private or when among Latin-rite Catholics. Rome refused the permission on the grounds that it showed that none of the Toronto Redemptorists was willing or ready to give up the Latin rite to dedicate himself entirely to the Ukrainians. The Ukrainians themselves, Delaere insisted, would doubt the good faith of the Toronto Redemptorists and suspect that they had come to anglicize and latinize them, which would have been the truth.[14] So the three young men were again left to study in Yorkton, although they had already decided to attend no more classes.

Gerald Murray tried to break the deadlock by sending the young men to Galicia for more intensive training. He called for volunteers. Not one of the three men stepped forward. All declared their willingness to go if ordered to do so, but none believed himself able to learn much of the difficult language. When Murray called for volunteers from the rest of the students in the Toronto Province, only Regina-born Daniel Ehman, of Russian-German parents, came forward. Some months later, after an enormous personal struggle, Grannan also volunteered. None was sent. It was already clear that the Toronto Province had failed in its work with the Ukrainians.

By 1930 Delaere and the Ukrainian Redemptorists agreed that the Ukrainian Canadians needed Ukrainian priests or they would leave the Catholic Church. With only Grannan celebrating in the Eastern rite, and poorly at that, all of the English-Canadian Redemptorists made a bad impression on the Ukrainians around Yorkton. Walsh and Howard were pulled off the work and the most advanced students, Grannan and MacIsaac, soon to be joined by Dan Ehman, were sent to the foundation in Ituna, Saskatchewan, for further study. Grannan and MacIsaac preached more missions in English while Ehman, at the request of the Latin-rite bishop, began to work among the Polish Catholics. Delaere left for Europe stating he would return once the English Canadians had left the Ukrainian field.[15] The Ukrainian Redemptorists asked for the Yorkton Vice-province to be rejoined to the Vice-province of Lviv so that it could recruit and educate their members in Europe until such time as they received candidates from the Ukrainian-Canadian people.

The Toronto Province could not help western Canadians in the Eastern rite. The solution to this problem, however, would become clear only under Gerald Murray's successor.

Peter Costello (1930–36)

The number of priests in the province had increased from seventy-six to one hundred and fourteen in just three years, the debt had stopped rising, two new houses and a major seminary were founded, *The Eikon* was a success, and the two Ukrainian houses in the west had been taken over. In February 1930, after preparing the slates for the next three years, Murray was called to Ottawa to meet with the apostolic delegate. On arrival in Ottawa he was informed that he was named bishop of Victoria, British Columbia, and commanded to accept. Murray's name was out of the running for provincial superior.

What lay behind this appointment? Murray's time in Rome, his knowledge of Italian, English, and French, his experience as rector of Brockville, and even the few years as provincial of a religious congregation with important foundations in western Canada, would all have recommended him. Daly probably brought Murray's name to the attention of those consulted for the names of possible bishops. One story states that Murray met and impressed the Canadian apostolic delegate on the train one day. Finally, it was time for a Redemptorist bishop in Canada. Their importance to Canada was growing steadily as English, French, and Belgian Redemptorists fanned out across the country, in an increasing number of parishes, missions, and retreats.

It was a gain for the Canadian church and a loss for the Toronto Province. After the large and extensive responsibilities Murray held for the Toronto Province's many priests, parishes, and missions, he moved to a narrow strip of land and a poor diocese with only thirteen secular and nine religious priests to care for twelve thousand Catholics. St. Patrick's parish in Toronto alone had a larger staff for as many Catholics. Undoubtedly what Roman pundits had hoped and predicted came to pass. Redemptorists promised Murray money, men, and advice should he need any. The little diocese of Victoria had gained not only a bishop, but a religious congregation. Murray immediately asked for the loan of one Redemptorist, George Coffin, to establish a census of the diocese.[16]

As his replacement in the Toronto Province, Murray and his consultors recommended either Charles Kelz or John Kane. Charles Kelz, with his reputation as an intellectual and a good administrator, was known to be a Daly opponent. John Kane, a Daly man and Murray's consultor, was more loved. But neither Kelz nor Kane was chosen. The former provincial, Arthur Coughlan, suggested the novice master, Peter Costello, as the one man not part of any clique who would insist on regular observance while setting an excellent example himself. Official visitors from the Baltimore Province agreed. Costello took the oath of office on 12 May 1930. He was to preside over the English-Canadian Redemptorists during the worst of the Depression, the glorious celebrations surrounding the Redemptorists' fiftieth anniversary in Toronto in 1931, and the Redemptorists' own two hundredth anniversary in 1932.

Although born in St. Patrick's parish, Toronto in 1876, Peter Costello had spent most of his youth in the Baltimore Province studying in the minor and major seminaries and working in New York City. Later rector of Saint John, New Brunswick, and then of Quebec City, he became the first novice master of the clerical candidates in Saint John because of his insistence on the Rule as lived in the Baltimore Province. After becoming provincial, Costello continued to promote American uniformity.[17]

Murray had been constrained by lack of time and money: Costello was faced with worse problems. Murray's cautious financial administration combined with year-round work on the part of

Peter Costello (1876–1940)
A son of St. Patrick's parish, Toronto, and the first choir novice-master of the Toronto Province

an increasing number of Redemptorist missionaries and parish priests had reduced the debts of the individual foundations by over $100,000. Unfortunately, with donations to the Redemptorists having dried up with the summer crops, Costello could not help defaulting on loans the Toronto Province owed to the Baltimore Province.[18]

In 1934 officials in the Sacred Congregation for Religious rebuked the Redemptorist father general for bad financial administration in not paying down the principal or even the interest on loans contracted by the Redemptorists in English Canada. The scolding was duly passed down to Costello. In an attempt to raise money, Costello tried to establish an annuity plan for the lay friends of the Toronto Redemptorists. Rome turned him down coldly, pointing out that Toronto and other provinces usually squandered the principal as well as the interest. Foundations such as the Purgatorian Society instituted years before as a combination mass foundation, prayer society, and fundraising organization, were bankrupt, and left later generations of Redemptorists with nothing but obligations and no income. Costello instituted a cent-a-meal program in early 1936, asking friends of the Redemptorists to drop a penny in a box placed on the dinner table at each meal. The money went for the education of Redemptorist missionaries and to poor relief in Redemptorist parishes.

More importantly, he and his treasurer, Father John Muldoon, centralized all of the extra income from individual foundations into the provincial treasury. This had been the solution to the Baltimore Province's financial problems of the 1880s and now became the solution to Toronto's problems. It also helped when the Baltimore provincial, Andrew Kuhn, who had once been stationed in Toronto, dismissed most of the defaulted debt and reduced the interest payments.

The Loss of the Ukrainian Missions

Costello inherited a Ukrainian Redemptorist mission wracked by internal squabbles. Until native Ukrainian-Canadian priests came forward to take over from the Belgians and the English Canadians, nothing could be done. James Grannan, Michael MacIsaac, and Daniel Ehman had not yet learned enough Ukrainian to take over any duties except the catechism of the English-speaking Ukrainian children in Ituna. Costello began sending the Ukrainian-Canadian minor seminarians to Brockville, the novices to Saint John, and the theology students to Woodstock in order to Canadianize them. The remaining Belgian Redemptorists, however, threatened to go back to Europe immediately if Toronto planned to ruin the mission by actively anglicizing the Ukrainians, encouraging them to join the Latin rite, and alienating those too old to learn English.

Both MacIsaac and Ehman were still unable to speak the language well enough to be accepted by the Ukrainians. Archbishop of Regina James McGuigan pressured them to turn their attention to the Polish and German Catholics in the region. To see English Redemptorists sent for the Ukrainians working for the Latin-rite Poles instead of learning more of the Ukrainian language and the rite infuriated the Belgian and Ukrainian Redemptorists. Costello in turn hardened his attitude toward the Ukrainian Redemptorists and declared himself more than willing to let every Eastern-rite Redemptorist go back to Europe. He expected a small schism among the Ukrainian people, "But that will be nothing new. Schism is in their blood!"[19] Costello encouraged his seminarians to learn some Ukrainian, but he decided not to ask Rome to allow more of his men to go over to the Eastern rite. The Toronto Province would remain completely Latin.

The Roman authorities in the Sacred Congregation for Oriental Churches faced a similar problem in Poland between Latin and Eastern-rite Christians and feared the schism more than Costello. They decided on 19 October 1931 to transfer the Canadian Ukrainian houses back to the Belgium Province prior to dissolving the Yorkton Vice-province and uniting the two Canadian houses to the Vice-province of Lviv in Ukraine. The Ukrainian mission in western Canada kept its own language, its own rite, and stayed far from the charge of Latin-rite assimilation. Yorkton and Ituna received Ukrainian missionaries from Europe and began to recover.[20]

Giving up the Ukrainian vice-province freed the English-Canadian Redemptorists from a huge burden they had been unable and in some ways unwilling to handle. One question remained: where to send the many enthusiastic priests coming out of Woodstock that had been promised to the Ukrainian mission and had been studying the languages necessary for the work?

In 1931, only a decade after the Great War had driven many German Canadians to hide their origin and claim another country or language as their own, there were still almost half a million people in Canada who claimed German descent. Although the Redemptorists had been formally charged with the care of Germans in Toronto since 1881, the second generation had adopted English, just as the German-American Redemptorists had been replaced by English-speaking and Canadian-born Redemptorists. There is no record that a Toronto Redemptorist had given a sermon in German in over a generation. St. Patrick's parish was in the heart of the immigrant district, however, and German Catholic immigrants continued to show up at the church. The now elderly Father John Kane, who had learned German in the Baltimore Province, heard the occasional confession in German and realized that the number of people requiring the sacraments in German was on the increase.

In 1927 Toronto asked the Baltimore Province for the loan of a German-speaking father. Paul Stroh arrived in 1929 as pastor of the Germans in the archdiocese, formally organized the first German congregation in Toronto, and established the first parish council in the Toronto Province. The work grew so rapidly that a second Baltimore man, George Foerst, was needed to help the exhausted Stroh. In 1930 six hundred people regularly attended mass in St. Patrick's church basement and were soon moved into the church itself. The Redemptorists with the help of the Sisters of Service then established the Catholic Settlement House at 131 McCaul Street to provide the immigrants with medical, educational, social, and recreational services. By 1933 the number of baptisms among the young immigrant Germans of Toronto stood at more than 10 per cent of the total from all of the parishes of the Toronto Province. The Germans formed St. Patrick's largest group, surpassing the English congregation by two to one, and formed 50 per cent of the administration of St. Patrick's People's Cooperative Store. Shortly after coming off the Ukrainian work, Dan Ehman was assigned to help Paul Stroh.

Our Lady of Mount Carmel, the Italian parish that had taken vigorous root under diocesan care in old St. Patrick's church, continued to grow. The Redemptorists hoped that the Italian parish would eventually move out of Our Lady of Mount Carmel to make way for the growing German congregation. When the Italian Franciscans at nearby St. Agnes church lobbied to take over Our Lady of Mount Carmel, the Redemptorists did not care to have two religious communities using the same land and buildings. With the thought that the Italian Canadians would assimilate into English Catholic society and revitalize the English congregation at St. Patrick's, the Redemptorists took over Our Lady of Mount Carmel in 1937. James Grannan was put in charge as it was thought that Italian Redemptorists, missionaries all, had no experience in parish administration.

Although some assimilation took place, neither the German nor the Italian congregations were declining; they were growing every year. By 1935 even Provincial Costello realized that the Canadian Catholic Church would be composed of a multitude of languages and began to recommend the study of Polish and Hungarian as well as French, Italian, and German among the students. Father John Naphin was sent to study Cree with the Oblates of Mary Immaculate, two English-Canadian Redemptorists were sent to Europe to study Polish, and one was sent for Italian.

Young Redemptorist students and priests also began to realize that languages had a usefulness in western Canada far beyond the classroom. For example, in Calgary the parish held twice as many Italian families as English-speaking ones. Ukrainian, German, Hungarian, Polish, French, and Dutch families together outnumbered the English two to one. At the very least, language training would help Redemptorists to hear confessions. An earlier generation of English-Canadian Redemptorists had polished their English to preach among the Irish immigrants of eastern Canada; now the study of other modern languages became part of Redemptorist training. While it remained firmly committed to the Latin rite and used English, the Toronto Province slowly changed from one dedicated only to English-speaking Catholics in Canada to one open to other immigrant groups. The Ukrainians first and then the number and variety of immigrants pouring into Canada and overwhelming the structures of the Church in Canada convinced the Redemptorists that there were other neglected members of the Church needing the Redemptorists.

Corner Brook, Newfoundland (1931)

For generations of Redemptorists, Newfoundland had been a mission territory. Foundations had been regularly offered in the St. George's diocese, but lack of men, Newfoundland's isolation, and lack of transportation essential to any missionary work had prevented the Redemptorists from doing more than send occasional mission bands. Gerald Murray declared to Rome that the Toronto Province's "hearts go out to the truly abandoned souls there" but it could not help just yet. When Bishop Thomas Renouf of St. George's placed his request for Redemptorists directly to Pope Pius XI, the Redemptorists were instructed to establish a foundation in Newfoundland. Warned by Peter O'Hare and William Hogan, who were experienced missionaries in Newfoundland, the English-Canadian Redemptorists went to Newfoundland fully aware of the difficulties they would face.[21]

Rectory, Corner Brook, Newfoundland

Corner Brook had been considered as the possible episcopal seat ever since 1925 when British investment in a sawmill caused a population boom in the area. Over $40,000 in debt, the parish was nonetheless near a railway and had a recently built church, school, convent, and parish hall. Advised by Father General Murray to send four men – two for the parish and two for the missions – Peter Costello appointed Father Bernard Coffey to begin the pioneer work. He became so popular that the western section of Corner Brook was eventually named Mount Bernard. The Redemptorists were the only religious priests on the island and soon staffed a house with six to eight men to care for the parish of Corner Brook, outlying mission parishes in the area from Bonne Bay in the north, Kitty's Brook on the east, Crow Gulch in the west, and missions throughout the island. When Father James Fuller visited Coffey's successor, James Dwyer, in 1936, he described a typical trip to Bonne Bay.

> About 5 P.M. we set sail on a schooner from Curling [now part of Corner Brook] for Bonne Bay. Of course the boat was an hour late in leaving and they had to blow the fog horn to call the crew from a nearby tavern where they were having their last drink. With a mixed cargo of gas and groceries we at length pulled away from the wharf [at] five miles an hour. When about an mile or two down the Bay we had to stop for oil. The worthy crew had forgotten it. At the mouth of the Bay the engine broke down and we were stalled for three hours. It was ten P.M. when they got going again. They also hoisted the sail to increase speed. We lay down on the bare deck. At least I thought it was bare till I found I was sleeping on the anchor chain which had made sundry impressions on my ribs. The night was not cold though a brisk wind was blowing. We had our overcoats on. I don't think I slept more than a few minutes at a time but Father [James] Dwyer's snores kept time with the engines.[22]

That eight to twelve hour sea trip now takes less than an hour by car.

Grande Prairie, Alberta (1932)

Shortly after the Yorkton Vice-province was given back to Belgium in December of 1931, Bishop Joseph Guy, OMI, of the Apostolic Vicariate of Grouard in the Peace River District northwest of Edmonton called on Provincial Costello to take over part of the district. The bishop's own Congregation of Oblates of Mary Immaculate were unable to send any more men into the area. The growing English, French, German, and Polish immigration had made the Peace River area significantly different from the native missions in which the Oblates traditionally worked. It had become more suited to a centralized religious community such as the Redemptorists. White settlers now outnumbered the native and Métis in the area by two to one, yet there were over thirty Oblates caring for the natives and no diocesan priests.

Father Daly undertook the negotiations and Father Provincial Costello sent John Cunningham to establish the Redemptorists in the new parish of St. Joseph's at Grande Prairie, Alberta, in March of 1932. A parish of roughly fourteen hundred kilometres with sixty Catholic families and seventeen hundred inhabitants called for more Redemptorists; Cunningham was joined in the summer of 1932 by Isidore Shalla to work for the Polish and German immigrants and Austin McGuire to work with the English settlers.

McGuire began a series of radio broadcasts to reach the distant settlers and organized annual plays dealing with Irish themes. Some years there was not a single person with any connection to Ireland in the play; but that was the nature of the English-Catholic Church in Canada and the kind of church promoted by the Redemptorists of the Toronto Province in the first half of the 1930s. For many Redemptorists and their parishioners, Irish Catholicism was the only model of English-language Catholicism in Canada.

Saskatoon, Saskatchewan (1935)

Like other parishes on the prairies, Our Lady of Victory, also called St. Mary's, in Saskatoon had been established by the Oblates and transferred to the diocesan clergy in 1931. When Gerald Murray was transferred to Saskatoon to become its first bishop in 1933, he immediately saw the need for more clergy and invited his Redemptorists. St. Mary's parish, Murray declared, was the largest and the poorest. Officially English, it also contained many families that spoke French or German. The church had a debt of $74,000. It seemed tailor-made for the Redemptorists. Nine men had just finished their second novitiate, and there was an immediate need for more work. Father Fred Coghlan became the first superior of St. Mary's, which was canonically established on 9 May, 1936.

Gerald Murray also quickly gave his approval for a federated college proposal long promoted by George Daly and the English Catholics of the city and long opposed by the French-Canadian Catholics. St. Thomas More College, in the care of the Basilian Fathers from Toronto, affiliated with the secular University of Saskatchewan and was formally established in 1936. Daly shuttled between Saskatchewan's bishops to assure them that this affiliated college was in all Catholics' best interest. English-speaking Catholic students of Saskatchewan now had an alternative to the separate, French-Canadian Catholic system and a Protestant-controlled secular education. Daly's earlier predictions that the west would form

St. Mary's, Saskatoon

part of the English-speaking world was coming to pass and the French bishops now listened to his arguments. Although English-speaking Catholics sometimes sat uneasily between French-speaking Catholics and English-speaking Protestants, they now had a way of gaining higher education and influencing Saskatchewan's history.[23]

James Fuller (1936–47)

In 1936 Rome named yet another novice master to succeed Costello as provincial. James Fuller was born in Quebec City in 1893 and ordained in 1918 just days before the Toronto Province was created. He attended the 1918 second novitiate class in Saint John but was not sent on missions because manpower was so scarce. He was sent to Prescott and then Brockville. In 1924 he became part of the teaching staff of the temporary major seminary at St. Ann's, Montreal. He returned to Brockville, this time as rector in 1927. His reputation as a close follower of the Rule and his general success in the education of young men earned him the position of novice master under Murray in 1930.

His success in shepherding young men through the Redemptorist educational institutions was no mean thing. In 1936 he had had over forty-five brother novices, twenty-five of whom were professed. Among the priest candidates, he had prepared seventy-three novices, seeing sixty-three professed and forty-seven of them going on to ordination. In a province made up of more than two hundred professed members, Fuller had given religious training to over a third of the members. American and Roman observers chose him in 1929 and in 1934 to accompany official visitors sent to examine the province. His job was to examine the financial books, introduce the visitor to different people, and answer the visitor's questions about Canada. The 1934 visitor, the American consultor general Christopher McEnniry, was so impressed with Fuller that he regularly wrote to him after the visitation for more information about the Redemptorists in English Canada and occasionally entrusted him with confidential tasks. By the time Fuller succeeded Murray at the young age of forty-three, over half of the province had received some education from Fuller.

Yet, in keeping with the ascetic tradition of humility and self-effacement among the Redemptorists, Fuller himself believed that in all those years he had been a failure. He had been unable to stop the shenanigans in St. Ann's, Montreal; over 50 per cent of the boys he knew in Brockville never went to the novitiate; many of the brother novices did not persevere in the Congregation; and he worried constantly that the many men he had recommended for profession were really not the stuff of which good Redemptorists were made.[24] He had never been on missions; he was young, and he suffered from depression and insomnia.

Rome, however, knew from the last official visit that Toronto did not need a missionary as provincial. Missions were booming as Redemptorists overcame cold, heat, hunger, thirst, and exhaustion to give missions in the most remote areas of Canada. Through the report of the 1934 official visitor, Rome knew that the discontent with Costello's years of emphasis on external rules and observance was spreading and Toronto above all needed a spiritual man who could teach the province the values of religious life and the reasons behind the rules. Prudently, Rome also gave the young provincial two experienced advisors.

The first was the well-liked and well-travelled George Mylett, who traced his vocation to Sinon Grogan, had served at Grogan's first mass, and preached at his funeral in 1934. Born in Quebec City in 1877 and ordained in 1902, Mylett served as a missionary in Puerto Rico, and was best known for promoting baseball. He had formed the first Puerto Rican ball club, the nursery of later great professional American ball players. In Canada as a missionary in London and as rector in several of the houses, most notably Montreal during the years boys were educated there, he also promoted sports in Canada as an excellent way of building character in young men. Now close to sixty, overweight, diabetic and jovial, he held the affection of the men educated in the Baltimore Province who had known him as a missionary, sports fan, and as a kind superior.

George Daly became the second consultor. Now sixty-three years old, he was still, as Costello reported to Rome, "energetic, progressive, and well known in ecclesiastical circles," although Costello added that "as a Redemptorist, he rates rather low. He does not work for our Province, comes and goes pretty much as he likes and has a rather free hand in anything he wants to do." Still, he had negotiated almost every foundation in western Canada, and he had a following in the province, "men he had as juvenists [students] in Beaupré." To bring this Beaupré group closer to the province, Costello had very reluctantly proposed Daly as consultor.[25]

Rome was much more impressed with the fact that Daly had been elected by the Toronto Province to be its representative to the Redemptorist General Assembly in Rome. In Rome he had been an active, alert, and eloquent participant, in English, French, and Latin, unlike Costello. Daly's many qualities must have impressed his Roman hosts. His popularity, his knowledge, his experience, his reputation as a founder of a women's religious congregation, and his contacts brought them to look a little more critically at the many negative reports that had been sent to Rome by Daly's American superiors, and to remember the many positive reports by his former Beaupré superiors. The call for Daly as a provincial who could inspire the men was getting louder. If not provincial, an older, wiser, more religious Daly could become provincial consultor.[26]

Fuller inherited a strong province. Despite Brockville's capacity to absorb any amount of money without showing much physical improvement, it did produce educated young men eager to test a Redemptorist vocation. In 1937 Brockville sent eighteen of its graduates to the novitiate, the largest since the college was founded. Eight candidates also entered to become brothers. Missions were all on the rise as the increasing number of priests were able to accept more invitations. In one year, missions went over the two hundred mark.

Fuller also inherited a good financial balance sheet. Costello's desperate attempts to raise money through the cent-a-meal campaign, the Purgatorian Society, *The Eikon* and a volunteer women's "Chain-Bridge" for the benefit of Redemptorist educational institutions, had almost halved the debt load. Fuller then built on these initiatives by founding the St. Alphonsus' Associates open to all. As more young boys were sent to Brockville or to Woodstock, there were more families and alumni willing to support the private educational institutions of the Redemptorists. Fuller rarely had to worry about raising money; he let the provincial treasurer, John Muldoon, do that for him. He and his consultors spent it in a good cause: the west. Muldoon had not been consulted about Fuller. He might have stated that Fuller's administrative experience was confined to Brockville, and Brockville always cost money. He might also have said that Daly's recommendation of Fuller as provincial meant that money would always take second place to other considerations.

British Columbia

Costello had already accepted Grande Prairie in the Peace River district. By 1935, however, Anglican competition brought Bishop Guy of Grouard to urge the Redemptorists to take Dawson Creek in British Columbia as well. In 1936 Fuller gave permission for the Grande Prairie Redemptorists to take over Our Lady of Perpetual Help, Dawson Creek, from an overworked Oblate missionary. With only thirteen families, most of them speaking English, it became one of Grande Prairie's outmissions. Brother Thomas Labelle arrived in 1937 and, as he had done in other foundations, used his carpentry and other building skills to rebuild and decorate the church and rectory. In 1945, when Dawson Creek was separated from the Vicariate of Grouard and joined the Vicariate of Prince Rupert, Fuller petitioned Rome to have the Redemptorist community canonically established.[27]

The Toronto Province also expanded into the Cariboo Country of British Columbia, first by missions out of the Vancouver house and then by taking over Sacred Heart parish on the request of the archbishop of Vancouver. As the Vancouver Annals stated on 21 April 1938: "Off to Cariboo; Fr. Cunningham shouldered his rifle and with fountain pen in pocket headed for William's Lake to establish a Redemptorist House. The Cariboo is open." The first superior, Russell Conway, became a tough-talking pioneer priest who attended People's Forums to denounce communism in Spain and the Soviet Union, and was known to knock a man down for immoral behaviour.[28]

When the Nelson district in southeast British Columbia was made a separate diocese from the Vancouver archdiocese, the new bishop, Martin Johnson, uncle to three Redemptorist seminarians, met with George Daly to ask for help from the Sisters of Service and from the Redemptorists. Fuller first sent Frank Sullivan and then Gerald Murphy to help in the Sacred Heart missions. After several discussions about Revelstoke, Slocan, Nelson, East Trail, and Fairview, an agreement to make a foundation in Fairview, a suburb of Nelson, was signed when Bishop Johnson went to ordain one of his nephews at Woodstock. The building of the Church of the Blessed Sacrament and the residence proceeded at a furious pace and between 1937 and 1942 seven churches were built in the area. Nelson was canonically established as a Redemptorist house in 1939.[29]

By 1938 Fuller's expansion created a debt of almost $500,000. John Muldoon was furious at such a lack of financial caution, but as the Roman authorities explained to Muldoon, the financial problems in Toronto were the same as others world-wide. "Your Province is going through the difficult stage just now on account of the necessity of making foundations in the strategical parts of the country while the Bishops were willing to give them. By hard luck the crisis came just at the same time. If you can pass through this safely, the future will be splendid."[30]

This did not calm Muldoon's astonishment at the many strictly parish foundations being accepted in western Canada, "multiplying small, weak communities unnecessarily."[31] He fingered Moose Jaw especially as a financial disaster. The archbishop of Regina, James McGuigan, had discovered some minor debt on the parish that had compounded interest over the years; McGuigan promptly shifted the debt from the diocese onto the Redemptorists.[32] Every western house, however, came in for some of Muldoon's criticisms. The Depression on the prairies affected every Redemptorist house, but unlike in the east where financial constraints kept construction to a minimum, the buildings kept going up.

Obviously Fuller and the Toronto Province Redemptorists had developed a love for western Canada, thinking it a place for real missionary work. As Fuller said, the difficult work united the Redemptorists and fostered true charity among them. The foundation of Dawson Creek, so near to Grande Prairie, brought Provincial Fuller's name to the fore as a possible bishop for the Peace River area.[33]

Brothers' retreat, Montreal 1941
Left to Right: sitting: Nicholas, Raymond, Gerard, Victor, Fr. C. McCormick, David, Michael, Joseph, Allan. *Second row:* Vincent, Reginald, Paul, Robert, Lawrence, Wilfred, Daniel, Cornelius, Matthew. *Third row:* Augustine, Edward, Anthony, Oswald, Leo.

By the end of 1940 there were over ninety fathers working in nine eastern houses and thirteen mission stations. Forty fathers worked in twelve western houses and eighty-nine mission stations. Most of the forty brothers worked mainly in the educational institutions of the east. Parish missions climbed to over two hundred weeks, seven thousand sermons were delivered, half a million communions were distributed, and three quarters of a million confessions were heard. Ordinations were topping ten a year. Although Fuller sometimes feared that the active missionary life was overwhelming the contemplative religious life, he continued to promote more activities. He appointed John Keogh to organize the lay retreat movement throughout the Toronto Province. Starting first in Charlottetown, where the movement had already begun with the Sisters of St. Martha, Keogh spread the retreat movement to the poor of Montreal, Quebec, and Toronto houses. The Circolo Columbo hall, the popular social centre for the Italian parish of Our Lady of Mount Carmel, became the site for closed retreats for unemployed men in the summer of 1939. Keogh established a Toronto Retreat League, and finally a national Retreat League of Our Lady of Perpetual Help that lasted a few years.

MISSIONARY
VADE MECUM

CONGREGATION OF THE
MOST HOLY REDEEMER

TORONTO PROVINCE
1940

The Redemptorist missionaries' manual
The Latin inscription on the coat of arms is the motto of the Congregation: "With Him Is Plentiful Redemption."

The Second World War

In 1935 the Nazi authorities in Germany had put members of religious orders on trial. When the Canadian government had put an embargo on all trade, letters, and packages between Italy and Canada after Italy's conquest of Ethiopia, the Redemptorists were forced to send and receive their mail from Rome through neutral countries. Redemptorists along with other religious men and women were murdered in Spain during its Civil War. By 1938 Fuller was anxiously asking different provincial superiors whether a war was coming and whether it was wise to send his men to study in Europe. German Sudeten refugees, all of them Social Democrats and nominal Catholics from Czechoslovakia, were accepted into Canada and were sent on to the Peace River district. Redemptorists who knew German – Raymond Horn, Stan Goetz, and Joseph Owens – were sent to catechize the children and to convert the adults from their mild form of socialism to a deeper appreciation of Catholicism.

When war did break out in September of 1939, there were five English-Canadian Redemptorists studying in Europe. Victor Crean and Neil Corbett were in Poland and Matthew Meehan, John Harrington, and Francis Dales were in Italy. Each had been carefully instructed to make his way to England or Ireland to sail for Canada when war broke out. The Canadians in Poland braved several dangers in escaping to Ireland, but many of the Polish Redemptorists they left behind did not survive the war. Fuller wired the nervous Redemptorist students who had fled Italy for Ireland to return to Italy and finish their studies. Italy did not declare war on Canada until June 1940.[34]

The Canadian government was persuaded by the apostolic delegate that the larger monasteries were austere enough and isolated enough to house German and Polish religious priests as enemy

Joseph Owens teaching catechism to Sudeten children
The Social Democratic emphasis on education made the parents grateful for the Redemptorists' work with their children, although the parents resisted abandoning their own socialist beliefs.

prisoners. In this way, several Pallottine Fathers spent the war at Woodstock instead of in a Canadian concentration camp. The Toronto Province enjoyed the teaching and cosmopolitan influence they gave to the seminary and the Pallottines avoided the unpleasant conditions of a prison camp. An Italian Franciscan sent to Woodstock, however, decided that the Redemptorist regime was too austere and he made his escape to the still-neutral United States.[35]

At home, the war's immediate impact was on the Redemptorist government. Father General Murray reappointed Fuller and delegated all of his authority save the right to appoint Fuller's successor for the duration of the war: "So you can take whatever action ... you think best ... May God and our Lady strengthen and guide you." Fuller was reappointed again in 1942 and for an unusual fourth term in 1945. He was fully responsible for the appointments for all of Canada from 1939 to 1945 and was also asked to draw up the slates for the Baltimore Province and the Vice-province of Puerto Rico in 1945.[36]

The war affected every house in the province. The Redemptorists at Saint John offered Our Lady's Camp at Chapel Grove as a temporary home for refugees. At the other end of the country, in 1942, Dawson Creek became mile zero for the Alaska Highway built by American Army engineers. The population of the town tripled and the traffic and the money transformed the region. Redemptorists in Peace River were never again as isolated as they were before the war. When Italy entered the war, parishioners from the Italian parish of Our Lady of Mount Carmel were interned and the parish itself went into decline. As military casualties mounted, attendance at the devotions to Our Lady of Perpetual Help shot up. It reached ten thousand at the Wednesday devotions in St. Patrick's church, Toronto, although there were fewer than seventy-five families in the parish.

Several dioceses sent men as military chaplains. To fill the gaps, Fuller and his consultors took over St. Gabriel's parish in Athabaska, Alberta on 14 July, 1941, and two other parishes for at least the duration of the war: Holy Rosary in Wells, British Columbia, on 29 June, 1941, and the parish of St. George's in Claresholm, Alberta, on 6 July, 1941. The Redemptorists worked in small chapels scattered through the hills of British Columbia and were inspired, as one Redemptorist chronicler wrote, by the thought that among "those towering mountains are souls to be enlightened, souls to be freed from sin, souls hungering for the bread of life, souls to be consoled and strengthened, children to be baptized, catechized and reared up in the faith."[37]

The Closing of Brockville

Between 1920 and 1941 five hundred and twenty-six young men attended St. Mary's College in Brockville and just over 40 per cent of them went on to novitiate. One hundred and thirty-seven, or 26 per cent, were eventually ordained as Redemptorist priests.[38] These impressive figures do not reveal that, since the depth of the Depression, enrolment at Brockville had declined. There may have been a combination of reasons for the crisis at Brockville. More and more, excellent public and Catholic schools offered education nearer home. Also, although the Redemptorists offered bursaries to any who could not pay, perhaps the theoretical cost was enough to keep some boys away.

Undeniably, the Second World War attracted some English-speaking young men to postpone a religious commitment or to sublimate it to join the war effort, as the propagandists presented it, to save Christian civilization. Certainly, while fifteen men presented themselves at the brothers' novitiate between 1939 and 1945, one or other to escape the war overseas, fifteen brothers also left the Congregation between 1939 and 1945, one of them explicitly stating he was joining the troops. Almost no students or priests left, but the number of newly professed students from 1939 to 1941 declined significantly from the large classes of the Depression years.

Fuller decided that the staff of seven professors, four brothers, and three missionaries could be better employed elsewhere. He closed St. Mary's College, sent the remaining students to Loyola College in Montreal, and rented the building to the government. The following year, when student numbers began to rise again, they were sent to study at St. Michael's High School and at St. Michael's

College run by the Basilians in Toronto. A few Redemptorists stayed on at a rented house in Prescott waiting for the day when Brockville would reopen.

The Vice-province of Edmonton (1945)

From 1927 to 1941, George Daly had seen the Toronto Province grow from a small group of English-language Canadians heavily influenced by the United States to a Canada-wide religious congregation with members working in a dozen languages. From ten monasteries it had grown to twenty-five. In under fourteen years, the Toronto Province had gained almost a hundred members and its first bishop. In the First World War the Toronto Province could send barely a single chaplain to the government; now thirty-one were on their way. Daly believed that the English-Canadian Redemptorists of the Toronto Province had a glorious future in Canada and were well positioned to influence Canada after the war. He also believed it was time for a separate English-Canadian Redemptorist province in western Canada.

In 1938 at the provincial consultation held in Montreal Daly had presented a paper advocating a vice-province for the west. The recommendation was soundly defeated, twelve votes against five, with four abstentions. In 1944, the same proposal was again defeated, twenty-one votes to eleven. The western superiors and their communities in domestic meetings declared that there were insufficient men and money for too large a field; they needed the east and its educational institutions. Yet, despite the near unanimous opposition of everyone in the west, Daly's arguments finally won out. Fuller and his two consultors, Patrick Gallery and Fred Coghlan, proposed a vice-province in 1944. So many foundations and the distances between them brought Toronto to beg Rome to take some of the load off the administration and name a major superior for western Canada. The official visitor, Edward Molloy from the St. Louis Province, agreed. The triennial appointments of 20 August, 1945 announced the creation of the Edmonton Vice-province. One of George Daly's recruits from Regina, Gabriel Ehman, became the first vice-provincial.

Silver Jubilee of the Toronto Province,
Listed vertically: seated (left to right): A. Hochard, D. Miller, F. Fagen, J. Fuller, G. Murray, M. Gearin, L. Laplante, A. Ferland, G. Daly. *Standing below steps:* Goetz, Madigan, Licking, Dietz, McKenna, Huber, Hayes, Mann, Routhier, Dwyer, T. Murphy, W. Murphy, Coghlan, O'Donnell, Vallieres, D. Ehman, Kane, G. Ehman, Brocklehurst, Molloy, Boulet, Cunningham, C. Johnson, Rolls, Gallery, Feehan, W. James, Harper, Fisher, Powers, Egan. *On steps, beginning on lowest step:* Kroetsch, Jos. Murphy, Bourbeau, McCullough, Coholan, Barry, J. Murphy, Kenny, Doucet - Mallett, Lussier, Cain, Redmond, Fleming, Sexsmith, Coffey, Washington

Woodstock, Ontario, January 1944
- Gallagher, Koster, DeVine, McCann, Coll, Collison, C. Killingsworth, Blackmore - G. Murphy, R. McKenna, Bro. Dominic, Spicer, Muldoon, Lambert - J. Byrne, Meehan, Hill, Bro. John - B. Johnson, McElligott, Harrington, McDonald, Arsenault, Conway, O'Deady, Bedard. *On top platform:* Monaghan, Glavine, Bro. Clement, Phelan, Bro. Allan, Bro. George, Delaney, Thomas, Stephens, Chidlow, Cunerty, G. Owens, O'Connor, Bro. Augustine, Campbell, Coyne, L. Murphy, Bro. Paul, Connaughton, Boyle, Tobin, Rekowski, MacGillivray, Langi, Scullion, Moreau, Griffin, J. James, Hennessey, Huard, Beland, Quinn, Skaluba, McCandlish, Bro. Liguori,

7

"This Spirit of the World," 1945–57

T hirty-one English-Canadian Redemptorists eventually participated in Canada's military effort during the Second World War.
A few were civilian chaplains; twenty spent their time as chaplains on training or repatriation bases in Canada or Newfoundland;
eleven went overseas. Many of these spent time in Iceland, Ireland,
Scotland, and England, and a few served in the shifting fronts of
Belgium, Holland, France, Italy, North Africa, and Germany. They
shared the same battle conditions as the troops and the medals and
promotions testify to the work of these men. Three, Arthur Ryan,
William Enright, and Daniel O'Sullivan, were promoted to the rank
of major in the army. The air force had two wing commanders,
Edward Howard and Edward Gillen, one squadron leader, Thomas
Coyne, and the bulk of the part-time Redemptorist chaplains. In the
navy, one Redemptorist, Michael MacIsaac, became chaplain of the
fleet, while a second, Cecil Moreau, was awarded the Order of the
British Empire for bravery under fire.[1]

All were strongly marked by the experience. Most kept their
humour, as seen in their letters to the *Yank Club* newsletter published
by the St. Louis Province. Some became more committed to their
religious vocation, as the insanity and carnage everywhere rein-
forced their disgust with the secular world; one left the
Redemptorists to marry in England; a few became alcoholics. Others

Mass at sea by Father Cecil Moreau

became convinced that the war "is doing God's work in its own way" by encouraging men to prepare for death, think of God, and go to confession. Some tried to forget the war; others could not and the experiences continued to haunt some of them in nightmares and in hallucinations later in life.[2]

Redemptorists were asked to stay on in the military after the war ended. The apostolic delegate offered the Redemptorists the apostolate of the sea with the merchant marine since the Redemptorists were the only religious community with foundations in almost every important naval centre. The air force wondered if the Redemptorists, with so many men in the air force, did not look on that service as an "adopted child." The Roman Catholic military bishop, C.L. Nelligan of Pembroke, used the Redemptorists as an example to other religious communities to promote chaplaincy recruiting; at one point there were more Redemptorists than any other religious priests in the armed forces.[3]

The chaplains' return from the military had an impact on the Redemptorists. During the war, students, young priests, novices, and even many of the older men were relatively insulated from the day-to-day events. The cloister, few newspapers, even the absence of a radio in most of the houses kept much of the war from reaching the Redemptorists. But personal letters, death among family members fighting in the war, and the sight of some students, novices, brothers, and priests leaving for the war profoundly impressed those left behind. When the chaplains returned, their new experiences, attitudes, and opinions helped to transform the Redemptorists of English Canada.

While in the army Father Arthur Ryan had correctly predicted to James Fuller that "There are so many of us in the armed forces now that the province will be taking on a military atmosphere after the war, with military terminology, discipline, etc. substituted for the Alphonsian." He and several other Redemptorists did not find that a bad idea since, inspired by the Jesuits, St. Alphonsus had also adopted "a rather military set-up from the beginning."[4]

A camaraderie sprang up among the ex-chaplains who supported each others' efforts to implement their views on how the Church and the Congregation should deal with a postwar world that was so different from the smaller, parish-based world of the past.[5] Other Redemptorists, however, became fearful of this self-assured, aggressive, almost arrogant attitude. Fuller, aware of the toll military work had taken on his men, began to withdraw the Redemptorists from chaplaincy work as soon as the war ended. He then sent the returning chaplains on retreat to relearn the routines of religious life. There was a concerted effort throughout the Congregation to stamp out "this spirit of the world" brought back to the monasteries by the chaplains.

The wartime experiences were so valuable and so overwhelming that the Redemptorists had to take them into account as they dealt with the new moral problems created by the war. While a scheduled moral theology debate in the thirties might discuss theft, in 1946 the Redemptorists debated the legitimacy of the atomic bomb. During such debates, the returning chaplains naturally had an advantage and overcame some of the uneasiness their return had caused among their confreres. For example, Ryan's outstanding war record as an army major and his organizational abilities brought some to complain that he was being wasted in out-of-the-way Grande Prairie.[6]

The missionary-minded element in the province, led by George Daly, promoted the military chaplains. Daly's followers and students had already embraced the "spirit of the world"; they readily accepted technology, travel, and the adaptation of Redemptorist life to the good the world had to offer. Now joined by some of the ex-chaplains, this newly strengthened group pressed for a reduction in the many parishes Fuller had accepted and an expansion of Toronto's missionary effort.[7] As a consequence, some of the military chaplains were given positions of authority and Ryan was sent to reopen Brockville. To care for those military chaplains, such as Mike MacIsaac, who stayed on in the forces and were often in Ottawa, Fuller immediately opened discussions with Archbishop Vachon of Ottawa for a mission house, a parish, or a retreat house. In March 1947 Henry Bartley became superior of the province's first mission house, St. Clement's, in Ottawa.

The Redemptoristines

The military chaplains helped to introduce a women's order to English Canada. The cloistered Redemptoristine nuns, the Order of the Most Holy Redeemer, were founded in Italy in 1731 by Sister Maria Celeste Crostarosa. While more contemplative and ascetic, Redemptoristine spirituality is similar to that of the Redemptorists. Both Maria Celeste and Alphonsus had the same spiritual director; Maria Celeste greatly influenced Alphonsus Liguori to found a missionary congregation for men and the earliest Redemptorists adopted much of the Redemptoristine Rule, the twelve monthly virtues, for example. The Redemptoristines themselves later developed a special devotion to Our Lady of Perpetual Help. The ties between the two religious families are so close that, to this day, Redemptorist historians debate whether Crostarosa inspired Alphonsus or vice versa. There is no doubt that the Redemptoristines, relying mainly on dowries in the beginning and then on the work of sewing, religious painting, and the baking of altar bread, slowly spread their apostolate of prayer in the wake of the Redemptorist expansion.

The French-Canadian Redemptorist Province of Ste-Anne-de-Beaupré was the first to invite the Redemptoristines to North America, and a convent had been established in Beaupré by three nuns from Marienthal, Dutch Limburg, in 1905. In 1947 the Redemptoristines in Beaupré had thirty-six members. No convent in

English Canada or in the United States had yet been established, and English-speaking women drawn to contemplative seclusion were still directed to join other orders.[8]

As the Redemptorists participated increasingly in the active missionary life, Fuller longed for the more contemplative dimension of Redemptorist life. He agreed enthusiastically with the military chaplains' suggestion to establish the Redemptoristines in English Canada so that their prayers would help the work of the Redemptorists. He sent Father Basil Wallace Malone, then a chaplain in England, to speak to the Redemptoristines in Chudleigh, Devon.

After failing to interest Bishop Bray of Saint John and Archbishop Murray of Winnipeg, both of whom thought that the nuns would not find enough work in their dioceses, Fuller then turned to one of his penitents, the archbishop of Toronto, James McGuigan. He proposed loaning the Redemptoristines a house on St. George Street once the resident students returned to Brockville and promised any financial help the Redemptoristines would need so that they would not be a burden on the archdiocese. Four nuns left

The Redemptoristines at Barrie

Chudleigh in July 1947 with the understanding that in Canada they were to become self-supporting as soon as possible. After a stream of Redemptorists and Sisters of Service helped to put the house in order for the nuns, the Redemptoristines established the monastic enclosure on 21 October 1947.[9]

Vocations grew at a tremendous rate, requests for vestments and artwork grew equally quickly, and the foundation flourished. From their arrival in 1947 to their move to a larger house in Barrie, Ontario, in May of 1951, twenty-six women were received, all but five remaining until vows. Twenty-four women made the move to a more spacious house in Barrie. Fuller declared "that bringing the Redemptoristines to Canada was the most popular thing that he ever did."[10] By such steps the influence of the ex-chaplains continued to grow.

The English-Canadian delegates to the 1947 General Chapter in Rome
Left to right: James Fuller, Gabriel Ehman, and John Keogh.

Daniel Ehman (1947–52)

Having brought the Redemptorists through two major wars, Father General Patrick Murray called a General Chapter to submit his resignation on 26 April 1947. In office since 1909, he was eighty-one years old and although he would live until 1959, he believed it was time to pass the burden of government to younger men. With Gabriel Ehman and John Keogh, respectively Edmonton's vice-provincial and Toronto's elected representative, Provincial Fuller left for the General Chapter. Rumours whirled that he would remain in Rome as the consultor general for North America while Keogh would return to Canada to become provincial. No Canadian had ever been consultor, and Fuller was North America's most experienced provincial, enjoying Father Patrick Murray's confidence.

On Fuller's recent official visit in the United States, he had insisted on strict observance of the Rule, something which many Americans thought was impossible in North American parishes. The American Redemptorists reacted against Fuller by voting for John Keogh as consultor; so Keogh stayed in Rome and Fuller returned to Canada. A new problem now faced the Redemptorists. With Keogh gone, who could Fuller recommend as his own successor? He and Keogh decided on Daniel Ehman, Gabriel Ehman's older brother. Foreseeing the criticisms that could be made at having brothers holding both the provincial and the vice-provincial positions, Gabriel tried to block the move and offered his own resignation. In the end, Daniel took office as provincial in August of 1947 and Gabriel remained in Edmonton as vice-provincial.[11]

Born in 1903, Dan's life was in many respects similar to his brother's. Son of a prosperous German-Russian immigrant family settled near Regina, Saskatchewan, he graduated from St. Mary's Separate School, Regina, in 1915. He was influenced by George Daly and Stephen Connolly, and went to St. Joseph's College in Kirkwood, Missouri, and later to St. Mary's College, Brockville. An avid musician and sports fan, he early demonstrated uncommon energy and stamina and participated actively in all plays, concerts, and games. Judged "most worthy" by his novice master, Peter Costello, Ehman was ordained in 1928. Volunteering for the

Ukrainian-Canadian missions, he was sent after his second novitiate to learn Ukrainian in the Yorkton Vice-province, where he impressed many by his ability. He also managed to alienate some by dividing his attention between the Ukrainians and the Polish Catholics in Ituna on the insistence of Archbishop McGuigan of Regina. When the Ukrainian Vice-province of Canada was transferred from Toronto to Belgium, Ehman was sent on the missions out of St. Peter's parish in Saint John. In 1932 the Catholic Women's League of St. Peter's asked for a Redemptorist to help organize a Catholic Action group. In response, Dan Ehman founded the Christian Family Spokes' Club, an integrated discussion and social group which expanded rapidly to over two hundred members. In June of 1934 his superiors took him off the missions at which he had been so successful and named him pastor of the German Catholics of Toronto. Even as pastor he nevertheless continued to give popular missions in English and in German.[12]

Daniel Ehman (1903–75)

Dan Ehman's energy allowed him to replace both Paul Stroh and George Foerst, both of whom returned to the Baltimore Province. To reinforce the Germans' Catholic identity and to resist the twin appeals of communism and nazism, he organized the first Katholikentag (Catholic Day) ever held in North America and annual pilgrimages to the Martyrs' Shrine in Midland. He helped to establish a German Hall, directed the Catholic Settlement House for immigrants, and successfully collected money during the Depression – no mean feat – to pay for a janitor, social worker, and secretary at the Catholic Settlement House.

The Settlement House illustrated the Redemptorists' concern for family life and the practical application of their missionary sermons. Beyond helping German and other immigrants, it soon housed a day care centre, a pre-natal maternity clinic, a baby clinic, a tonsil clinic, a kindergarten, and a credit union. The Felician Sisters had recently arrived from Buffalo for Toronto's Polish parish of St. Stanislaus Kostka. Ehman invited them to take charge of the Settlement House work. Ehman also established a cooperative funeral society and had land rented as a playground for children near the Settlement House. Lastly, he founded the League of St. Gerard, which spread around the world, gaining hundreds of thousands of members, to promote devotion to the "Mothers' saint" and to combat birth control and abortion.[13]

During the war Ehman adroitly handled the hostilities facing German Canadians and German-speaking Redemptorists and took on the pastoral care of the German internment camp in Mimico. With money from both the German congregation and the Redemptorists, he also bought farm property in Richmond Hill north of Toronto. Named Perpetual Help Farm, the land became a popular parish picnic area and campground. Since the Redemptorists would care for the property and handle all of the legal niceties, especially during the war when the German congregation had no hope of incorporating itself to take possession, Dan Ehman had ownership and control vested in the Redemptorists.[14]

After the war and even as provincial, he continued to participate in the German congregation, and requested Redemptorists from Europe to care for the Italian and German communities. This was not merely a labour of love; the German congregation, with almost seven thousand parishioners, had become by far the largest congregation in the Redemptorists' Toronto Province.

The Sisters of Service regularly sent the Redemptorists lists of Italian and German immigrants landing in Halifax or Quebec City who were heading for Toronto, and a Redemptorist often met the immigrants at Toronto's train station. The Italian parish of Our Lady of Mount Carmel had long suffered from a constant turnover in staff and from previous attempts to assimilate the Italians into English-Canadian life as quickly as possible so that the parishioners could attend St. Patrick's. Under Dan Ehman, with his larger views of Canadian citizenship, peace descended on both the German and the Italian parishes. Father George McKenna, Italian pastor from 1945 to 1947, was renamed to the parish and founded the Italian Immigrant Aid Society in 1951. As a long-serving pastor, Father William Kroetsch continued Ehman's work in the German congregation.

Ehman himself promoted devotion to Our Lady of Perpetual Help by writing whenever he had time. Before becoming provincial, he published over fifty articles and stories in the Redemptorist's magazine, *The Eikon*, and its successor *Mother of Perpetual Help Magazine*. As well, he wrote poems, songs, and edited popular works. Ehman's pamphlet, *I Pray to Mary*, had a print run of thirty thousand copies in 1950 alone, the year when the dogma of Mary's Assumption was defined. Long before the end of his life, he had become the Toronto Province's most published author.

The *Mother of Perpetual Help Magazine* had almost four thousand paid subscriptions when Fuller left the provincial's job. Ehman had begun the *League of St. Gerard Semi Annual Bulletin* in 1937 and its successor the *St. Gerard News*. As provincial, he combined both magazines and united the devotions to Our Lady of Perpetual Help with the Archconfraternity of the Blessed Virgin and St. Alphonsus into a new *Madonna Magazine*. Circulation doubled. Half a million copies of the picture of Our Lady of Perpetual Help were sent out to interested people. Ehman then concentrated on establishing parish shrines to Our Lady. He appointed special preachers, and by 1950 one hundred and fifty-two Perpetual Help shrines had been established in Canada. Since the devotions were short (between twenty to thirty minutes in length), in English, and encouraged participation and singing, they were a simple and practical way to promote the popular piety preached on the missions. Devotions to Our Lady of Perpetual Help continued to multiply in parishes across the country and the icon hung on many more walls in Canadian Catholic homes.[15]

The Redemptorist apostolate expanded into other forms of communications. While radio had been an experimental medium in the 1930s on the prairies, by the 1940s its usefulness had been proven. Arthur Ryan gained experience as a radio announcer and preacher over the British Broadcasting Corporation in 1943 while a military chaplain in England. When he was in Grande Prairie he organized the popular weekly program, "The Faith of Millions," as well as the Catholic Radio League. "The Faith of Millions" ran for more than a decade with an audience of twenty thousand. After Ryan left for Brockville, the radio network catapulted Father Martin

Canada's media priest, Matthew Meehan, working at the CBC

Foley to popularity in western Canada with "The Catholic Hour." Ehman then appointed Father Matthew Meehan to work with the CBC to produce radio programs on family life. In 1950 Bishop Francis Ryan of Hamilton invited Father Meehan to do weekly radio programs for his diocese. In 1957 Father Meehan made the jump into television and international fame on Hamilton's CHCH-TV, participating in thousands of radio and television shows, as host, commentator, or interviewer, covering events from the Second Vatican Council to Pope John Paul II's travels.[16]

Dan Ehman was an enthusiast who sometimes did not follow the Rule or think things out before throwing himself into parish projects. Indeed, the news of his elevation to the provincial's chair dumbfounded many of his colleagues. For years he had regularly gone missing from the community's spiritual exercises as he rushed from one project to another. When his appointment was announced at table in St. Patrick's, Toronto, he was not even in attendance. One of the Redemptorists at table joked that he was up in his room, reading the Rule for the first time. Most Redemptorists, however, recognized that he authentically embodied both the zealous missionary and parish aspects of Redemptorist life in English Canada.

Ehman inherited twenty-four houses, eleven in the east and thirteen in the west. There were two hundred ordained Redemptorist priests, twenty-three professed students and thirty-nine brothers. The sixty-five fathers in the west cared for a further one hundred and fourteen outmissions and said mass in thirty private homes. The east had one hundred and thirty-five priests and few outmissions, but the numbers included priests who were sick, studying, teaching, and/or in administration, caring for a further thirty major seminarians and sixty minor seminarians. In 1946 there had been over two hundred weeks of missions, reaching almost one hundred thousand people. Financially, the province was in great shape. Since the Depression there had been over $100,000 in donations and the military chaplains had brought an equal amount in salaries. Most of the old debts had been paid off. Fuller knew that the Toronto Province needed new mission fields, a new novitiate and, eventually, a new seminary. What was needed to put Fuller's plans into action was Ehman's energy.

Ehman's first challenge was to choose a new mission field. The Beaupré Province had taken on the French Indochina mission in 1925 and began what became the Vietnam Province. The Toronto Province was too small to think of sending missionaries anywhere then, but longed to do so. Fuller and his consultors instead lobbied Rome to gain the right to work for groups handicapped by racism in Canada. In 1940 Fuller enthusiastically passed on the Edmonton archbishop's request for a foundation among the "coloreds" in northern Alberta. In 1941 he followed this up with a request to take up the work for the poor and abandoned coloured people of Montreal who had formerly been under Redemptorist care in the British West Indies. Both proposals died when other work intervened.[17]

The 1947 General Chapter declared that foreign missions "be recognized as a genuine ministry of our Congregation." The new superior general, Leonard Buijs, called on the entire Congregation to embrace the foreign missions. Then the vice-provincial of Roseau, Joseph Hermans, an old classmate of Daly's, wrote Fuller for help in the West Indies. Fuller sent Fathers James Dwyer, Joseph Dever, and John Lambert to preach missions on the islands of St. Kitts, Antigua, Monserrat, Dominica, and Nevis and for parish work in Basseterre on St. Kitts, and Tyrells on Antigua. In his report, James Dwyer recommended that the Toronto Province take over the entire work from the Belgians. While there were already twenty-five Belgians, including two bishops, working in the West Indies, the islands were part of the British Commonwealth and English was commonly spoken. English-Canadian Redemptorists would be better prepared for the work in the West Indies than Belgians who had little or no parish experience.[18]

Before these plans for the West Indies could be implemented, another urgent request intervened.

Maizuru, Japan (1948)

Ildebrando Antoniutti, the apostolic delegate to Canada, had passed on Pope Pius XII's "keen desire" to see missionaries go to Japan "where, at the present time, circumstances seem favourable to the

Catholic Apostolate." Prostrate after the atomic bombs, administered by the American Army of Occupation headed by General Douglas MacArthur, Japan had revoked Shintoism as the official religion and proclaimed religious freedom. Fuller volunteered the Toronto Province.[19] When three men in the Toronto Province were asked to begin the study of Japanese, word of the impending mission got out and volunteers came forward, many of them former military chaplains such as Arthur Ryan. Missions to non-Catholics and to Japan had been present in St. Alphonsus's writings but, of course, could not find expression in the Naples of his day. A mission to Japan offered new possibilities for heroism when western Canada seemed to be saturated as a mission territory. Toronto jumped at the chance to go to Japan.[20]

The American Redemptorist military chaplain in Japan, Milton Girse, passed on information about a possible mission field in the diocese of Osaka, then under Bishop Paul Taguchi. Fuller wrote Taguchi that the Toronto Redemptorists knew nothing of the work, the language, or the conditions, but "We are prepared to do almost any kind of work offered us as long as we could preserve community life. We will accept parishes or try to open mission stations among the pagans. We are prepared to send five or six almost at once."[21] Taguchi offered the Redemptorists a choice between specialized work in the cities of Osaka and Kobe or parish and quasi-parish work in the Tango and Tamba districts in the Kyoto Prefecture. These two districts included the cities of Maizuru, Miyazu, Ayabe, and Fukuchiyama, and the villages of Kuchiono and Mineyama. Although the population ran into the hundreds of thousands, the Catholics numbered only in the hundreds. A former naval base and shipyard facing the Sea of Japan, Maizuru was the largest Catholic centre with a parish of about two hundred and fifty Catholics and a Catholic school for girls run by the Japanese Sisters of the Visitation. Many of the Catholics were women who had graduated from the Catholic girls' high school and the recruitment of Japanese into the active congregations of sisters was a growing success. Before the war, the districts had been under the care of the Paris Foreign Missionary Society but now only three Japanese priests were taking care of the whole district.[22]

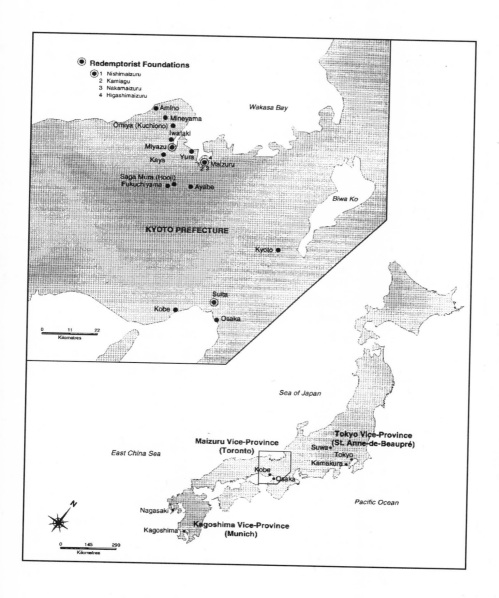

The Maizuru Mission, Japan, 1948–82

When Fuller heard that the French-Canadian Redemptorists were to go to Japan too, he hesitated and thought again of the mission in the British West Indies. Toronto's new provincial, Dan Ehman, was informed that the conditions would be hard and that Bishop Taguchi had an unflattering reputation as having been one of the most outspoken supporters of the former Japanese imperial government. The American Redemptorist military chaplain, Henry Sutton, assured Ehman, however, that there was great work to be done and that there was room for both English and French Canadians.

In December 1947 Ehman decided that the Toronto Redemptorists would go to Japan and chose James Fuller to be the mission superior. Fuller had practically no family left, enjoyed everyone's full confidence, and could decide whether the Redemptorists would take over specialized work in the cities or parish work in the countryside of the Osaka diocese. The Japanese departure ceremony, a high-spirited event carefully preserved on tape and film, illustrated the missionary hopes of a generation of English-Canadian Catholics. Cardinal James McGuigan of Toronto presided while six bishops, ten monsignors, and over one hundred priests were in attendance. Many spoke at the occasion, among them Archbishop Gerald Murray of Winnipeg and Father George Daly. Fuller declared that it was time for Canada's Redemptorists to reach beyond the Pacific Ocean much as Europe's Redemptorists had crossed the Atlantic to Canada.

Fathers William James and Raymond Horn accompanied Fuller. William James, from Saint John, New Brunswick, just turned thirty and recently ordained, was considered brilliant and zealous. Thirty-seven years old, Raymond Horn, born in Yorkton, Saskatchewan, had been teaching in Woodstock and was known to have a gift for languages and to be indifferent to any kind of poverty or hardship. These three Redemptorists – a former provincial, a man from western Canada, and one from eastern Canada – were carefully chosen to represent the entire province. Both Fuller and James left in June 1948 while Father Horn followed after he finished teaching at St. Alphonsus Seminary in Woodstock. Charles Brocklehurst and Thomas Carr in 1949, Titus Campbell and Brother George Pope in 1950, and then Patrick Hennessey and David Weir in 1951 were sent to join the original three. In all, sixteen English-Canadian Redemptorists, fifteen priests and one brother, would be sent.[23]

Fuller and James soon learned that they were only two of two hundred and forty-eight priests and brothers who had arrived in Japan since the end of the war. Redemptorists from the Beaupré Province had been in the country since May 1948 and met Fuller and James at Yokohama port, to Fuller's keen disappointment at not being the first Canadian Redemptorist in Japan. Even the Beaupré Redemptorists had been beaten by the American Redemptorist military chaplains who had already preached the country's first Redemptorist missions and retreats.

Fuller found some evidence to support the rumours about Bishop Taguchi. He was not popular with either the foreign or the Japanese priests, or with the American or Japanese authorities. There were even rumours that he dealt in the black market. On the other hand, Fuller was strongly impressed with Taguchi's ability, his progressive ideas and building plans for the future, at a time when many of the other Japanese bishops were at a loss to know what to do in the postwar situation. Taguchi walked a fine line between the many factions present in Japanese society; he also successfully ran an entire diocese with no money. Fuller recommended that the Redemptorists ask for a forty-year contract so that the money that the Toronto Province put into the diocese would not be immediately appropriated by the bishop for other uses.

Unknown to the Redemptorists, Bishop Taguchi had a special fondness for them. He had been taught in Rome by the famous Redemptorist canon lawyer and moralist, Cornelius Damen; he had another well-known Redemptorist, the scripture scholar, moralist, and general consultor, Franciscus Ter Haar as confessor; a third Redemptorist, Cardinal Willem Van Rossum, had been prefect of the Sacred College of Propaganda when Taguchi studied there. He wanted the Redemptorists not merely for the financial help they could bring to his diocese but for what they could bring in the field of moral theology in the delicate days of postwar reconstruction where morals were changing rapidly.[24] The Maizuru mission officially began on 14 July 1948. Fuller had made an excellent choice; Taguchi was eventually named a cardinal.

The many small churches in the rural Tango and Tamba regions would mean splitting the mission band into small groups or even into individuals working alone. The urban areas, however, were devastated by the war and Fuller could not see how any work could be done there by the English-Canadian Redemptorists for years to come, even with massive amounts of money to build churches and residences. After he accompanied the bishop on a confirmation tour, Fuller opted for the countryside. In June 1949 the Toronto Province signed an agreement with Taguchi in which they named a Maizuru regional superior whom the bishop then appointed as his vicar. The Redemptorists were still free to give missions, retreats, or spiritual exercises.[25]

Fuller then embarked on an ambitious building program, hiring an interpreter and clerk to carry through negotiations with the Japanese government. The Visitation Sisters of Nissei High School in Kamiagu, Maizuru, loaned him two buildings behind their school, and these became the first St. Clement's Monastery. Within a year Fuller had bought the property in Kamiagu and more land in Kaya, Fukuchiyama, Naka Maizuru, San no Maru, and a tuberculosis hospital run by the Visitation Sisters. From 1950 to 1953, chapels, churches, and combination church-halls, called dendobas, went up in Amino, Fukuchiyama, Iwataki, Kaya, Kuchiono, Saga Mura (Hooji), and Yura. A new monastery went up at San no Maru and became the mother house and novitiate for the Maizuru mission. The total amount of money sent by the Redemptorists to Japan up to 1952 was just over $20,000. In comparison, the subsidy sent to Brockville in 1951 alone was also slightly more than $20,000. Fuller, however, had received grants from the Propagation of the Faith and spent almost $50,000; he believed he had no choice but to buy and build while land was cheap.

For the first year, naturally, the labours were almost entirely in English among the other religious communities and the American soldiers. The missionaries also taught English and western culture in the local schools, in order to present the Bible and Catholicism. Almost from the beginning, prayers, benedictions, and the rosary were said in Japanese. The Japanese Buddhist tradition of reading sermons from prepared texts greatly helped the Redemptorists overcome language difficulties during their first years. They gave lectures on the dignity of human life, the marriage law of the Church, and the evils of communism and birth control.

The members of the Toronto Province only vaguely suspected the difficulties of working in Japan. In one outstanding example, Fathers Fuller, Horn, and Carr participated in a mass baptism of about two hundred people gathered in Saga Mura by one of the Japanese secular priests. It became an international media event. Unfortunately, many of the people thought that baptism was a way of showing their anti-communism or a means of getting the priests to build a Christian university or a church in their town. When these rewards did not immediately appear, the Catholic "betrayal" of Saga Mura was published in *Asahi*, the largest Japanese newspaper.[26]

Some of the missionaries also found it hard to adjust to a totally non-Christian and non-English environment. Fuller thought it easier to deal with non-Japanese priests and bishops and bemoaned what he perceived to be the incompetence of the indigenous clergy and hierarchy. In fact, in September of 1940 the foreign-born bish-

Saga Mura mass baptism, with Raymond Horn (1911–85)

ops working in Japan had tendered their resignations to the Holy See and were replaced by inexperienced Japanese-born bishops. Furthermore, because of language difficulties, the Redemptorists sometimes found their contacts with the Japanese restricted. While Fuller had learned Japanese for day-to-day conversation, he had turned sixty years old in 1953 and still needed an interpreter for writing and dealing with the government.

Fuller also brought English-Canadian models of Redemptorist life and church architecture to Japan. The Maizuru mission rules were identical to Toronto's in every way except for the fact that the Maizuru men were allowed to wear a white habit in the summer. For example, the church in Higashi Maizuru was modelled after the church of Our Lady of Perpetual Help in Vancouver. Outmission stations, well known in western Canada and in Newfoundland, became the solution to the many parishes of the Maizuru area. In contrast, French-Canadian Redemptorists adopted the European-style central Redemptorist mission foundation in Tokyo to preserve community life, but built in an entirely Japanese fashion, spoke only in Japanese, and integrated into Japan as fully and as quickly as possible.

The younger English-Canadian Redemptorists were more successful in integrating into Japanese society. These went to professional language schools, unlike the first missionaries who had to pick up the language through use, private study, and more or less competent tutors. All of these efforts seemed to be rewarded in March 1953 when three Japanese were professed as brothers at Kamiagu after a novitiate directed by Father Fuller. The progress of the work in Japan nevertheless seemed painfully slow.

New Foundations

Associated with the military chaplains' postwar promotion of the Redemptoristines and of the Japanese mission was the establishment of the parish of Our Lady of the Assumption, Toronto. As Toronto's downtown core became more heavily industrialized and less residential, St. Patrick's parish had already lost most of its English population. It catered increasingly to office workers who attended services on their lunch hour and new immigrants who lived in the crowded tenements. Veterans were buying homes in the suburbs. So Cardinal McGuigan invited the Redemptorists to accept the new parish of Our Lady of the Assumption in Forest Hill Village, now a part of Toronto. In 1947 four hundred families needed to be organized and a church and school built.

Ehman wrote to Superior General Buijs that the foundation would gain Cardinal McGuigan's goodwill, give an outlet for work to the many semi-retired priests crowding St. Patrick's, provide an insurance against the possibility that St. Patrick's might close down because of the demographic changes in the city core, and be an excellent source of students and of income since the area had a high number of middle-class families. Ehman's consultors were enthusiastic, and one explicitly stated that the Redemptorists needed a wealthy urban parish to finance the foreign missions. Buijs conceded, but only on the condition that the Redemptorists never treat Assumption as if it were only a parish. The parish was to be staffed with seven or eight fathers in order to make it into a missionary centre. Above all, it was never to have any debts that would affect any other project. In 1950 Francis Cunerty was named the first superior and called the parishioners to meet in a nearby theatre. Cardinal McGuigan laid the church's cornerstone in November of 1951 and the church opened on 20 July 1952.[27]

Few of the hopes for the parish ever materialized. Although a few young men went to Brockville and the Redemptorists subsidized their education, they never went on to profession. Although the area had a small, wealthy class of Catholics, the parish itself amassed debts; the church alone cost over $300,000 while the temporary rectory, a former private home, cost over $15,000 and was too small for the Redemptorists. One of the brothers even had to sleep on the living-room sofa. Because of cost overruns, a new rectory planned in 1952 was never completed, even though two of three floors were finished in 1955 at a cost of over $70,000. Demographically, the area continued to be heavily Jewish. Catholics at Our Lady of the Assumption certainly could not help to pay for the Redemptorist missionaries in Japan when they had to pay for their own church. The semi-retired Redemptorists stayed at St. Patrick's, because the dynamic new parish with young families needed younger Redemptorists. A strong parish community had nonetheless been created in an area of Toronto where a single diocesan priest might have met failure.

In a search for a more contemplative and rural environment, the Redemptorists decided in 1944 to move the novitiate from Saint John, New Brunswick. When the military moved out of Brockville, the novices moved in for lack of a better place and waited while one place after another was rejected as too small, too urban, or too expensive.

Fuller finally settled on Peterborough, but postwar costs drove building prices sky-high, so he postponed the novitiate idea. He nonetheless continued negotiations for a parish because of Peterborough's great demand for missions and clergy and his belief that the Toronto Province needed space for the returning military chaplains. In the meantime, he bought "Ennismore," a farm on Harrington Island in Buckhorn Lake as a vacation spot for professed students. Under Daniel Ehman, in 1947 the parish of St. Alphonsus Liguori was established in Peterborough, a church was built in 1949, a school in 1950, and the cloistered monastery of the Precious Blood Sisters began a foundation in 1952. Although the provincial council discussed building a monastery large enough for a community and a novitiate in Peterborough, it never materialized.

The northern Ontario mining region around Kirkland Lake and Timmins had been, in the eyes of the Redemptorists, in dreadful need of missions. Fuller had considered a mission house in northern Ontario that might double as a quiet novitiate site, but the war intervened. After the war, lumber companies employed displaced persons, many of them Polish Catholics, but also Lithuanians, Ukrainians, Latvians, Estonians, and Russians. Ehman proposed to build a novitiate in Sudbury. Bishop Ralph Dignan countered with the offer of a parish. Ehman enthusiastically asked for Roman permission to establish the foundation, arguing in his usually emphatic way that "THE MOST ABANDONED SOULS IN CANADA ARE IN THE LUMBER CAMPS OF NORTHERN ONTARIO." They were prey to communists so that even the Protestant owners of the lumber companies offered to help the Redemptorists.[28] When the Redemptorists learned that

Bishop Dignan wanted the English-speaking Redemptorists to help crowd out the French priests, both John Keogh in Rome and Dan Ehman in Toronto hesitated at first to become "pieces in a chess game of clerical politics between the French and the English."[29] But when Bishop Dignan promised to create a territorial English parish and allow the Redemptorists full authority to promote their devotions, they hesitated no longer. They arrived in July 1949, bought land, and started building a church. The novitiate did not move to Sudbury.

With houses in London and in Woodstock, the Redemptorists were fully part of the English-Canadian Catholic Church's growth in the London diocese. Under Ehman, the Redemptorists founded yet another house in the same diocese. The driving force behind an English-Canadian Redemptorist foundation in Windsor was Father John Lambert, who lobbied constantly with Ehman and the bishop of London, John Cody, to get the Redemptorists into his home town. When the bishop offered the large and well-established Holy Rosary parish in 1951, Ehman and his consultors were unanimous in recommending the place. The Redemptorists were already well known in Windsor and the devotions to Our Lady of Perpetual Help were popular. Windsor itself was a good centre for missions in southwestern Ontario. Since Windsor has a significant number of French Canadians, the Beaupré Redemptorists were also interested in a Windsor foundation, which spurred the Toronto Redemptorists to lobby Rome to get into Windsor first and safeguard the mission territory. Father General Buijs, however, turned down all of Ehman's requests for further parish foundations that year, whether in Windsor, Ottawa, or Hamilton. He believed the Toronto Province was already over-extended with parishes far from the missionary nature of the Redemptorists. Nor could he accept the implicit rivalry with the French-Canadian Redemptorists.[30]

The following year Father Lambert again urged Bishop Cody of London to offer another parish, this time Lambert's home parish of St. Alphonsus, Windsor. Founded in 1865, the parish was now in the business section of the city with its own hall, an eighty-five-year-old church, a large rectory, and a parish school staffed by Ursulines.

Reluctantly, Rome gave permission when it realized that the French-Canadian Redemptorists would not be invited into Windsor, the scene of continued English- and French-Catholic clergy rivalry.

As St. Ann's parish in Montreal continued to decline, the Redemptorists feared they would find themselves without a foundation in Montreal, still the largest city in Canada and with an important number of English-speaking Catholics. Fuller and then Ehman therefore explored the possibility of moving the novitiate to one of the suburban areas of Montreal. In the spring of 1950 the L'Abord-à-Plouffe estate property became available. The land, about one hundred and sixty acres along Rivière-des-Prairies, had a three-storey stone house. Within a month, with the help of an adroit realty agent, Ehman abandoned all plans for a novitiate in either Peterborough or Sudbury. He argued that the Redemptorists should buy the property in the hopes of selling sections of it to pay for the purchase. On Father Mike MacIsaac's suggestion, the house was renamed Marianella in honour of St. Alphonsus Liguori's birthplace and also in honour of the dogma of Mary's Assumption. It was solemnly opened on 15 August 1950.[31]

L'Abord-à-Plouffe novitiate

Ehman found himself asking for further permission to build a separate chapel because the thick stone building could not be enlarged or renovated. While waiting for permission, Ehman tried desperately to sell off land; he succeeded in selling only one of the houses. In Rome, the costs horrified the consultors and no further permissions were granted. Without permission for a new building, Ehman found himself forced to buy back the recently sold house at a higher price so as to have enough room for the many novices. Twelve had been professed in 1950 and fifteen candidates arrived at L'Abord-à-Plouffe for 1951. When Ehman then requested permission to renovate the repurchased house, bringing the proposed total cost of the L'Abord-à-Plouffe novitiate into the range of $250,000, Father General Buijs rebuked him and vetoed any further novitiate plans.[32]

Ehman realized he had earned the reputation of a reckless enthusiast and a poor administrator, both in Canada and in Rome. Yet he had followed Fuller's plans: the withdrawal of the military chaplains, the introduction of the Redemptoristines, the creation of the Japanese mission, and the Montreal novitiate. He had spent lavishly in London, Sudbury, and L'Abord-à-Plouffe. He had placed Redemptorist communities in some of the few English-Canadian mission fields remaining to the Redemptorists in Canada, even battling for the bilingual fields of Windsor and Sudbury. Rome saw little but the competition and the costs.

After six years of criticism from his confreres and now from Father General Buijs, Dan Ehman begged to be taken off the provincial's job and sent on the missions where he felt he belonged. There were many candidates to replace him: Frederick DeVine, rector in Woodstock, received the highest marks but had little experience outside of education. George O'Reilly in London seemed too young at thirty-seven. Gabriel Ehman in Edmonton was seriously considered until someone said there had been "enough Ehman" already. The Redemptorists needed a leader and an administrator. Arthur Ryan was named the new provincial in December of 1952. Dan Ehman went to Windsor and then to Saskatoon to work as a missionary, as he had asked.

Arthur Ryan (1952–61)

Over the years Ryan had developed a formidable reputation. Long known to be a man of superior intellect, his novice master wrote in 1924 that he had a fervent interior and a cold exterior. He had changed little in a quarter-century. Born in 1904 in Saint John, New Brunswick, professed in 1924, and ordained in 1929, he had a thoroughly Redemptorist background. Educated for a year in St. Mary's minor seminary in the Baltimore Province before attending the juvenates in Montreal, Prescott, and Brockville, he then returned to the United States for major seminary studies in Esopus. He became one of the first Canadian Redemptorists to study in Rome and received a Ph.D. in philosophy from the Angelicum. He also spent a summer at Fordham University studying economics.

The Baltimore Province's John Hosey, the official visitor to Toronto in 1950, cautioned that Ryan was still somewhat unmindful of others' feelings and opinions. He was regularly in the forefront of the unrest that had demanded changes in Redemptorist life before the war. He was a proud, critical, even cynical man who demanded much from himself and from those around him. His cutting way of speaking had earned him the reputation of "a stinker" and "very unpopular." He once wrote proudly that some thought of him as "a nasty old bugger, which of course I am." Students and lecturers who had known him in Woodstock before the war remembered his swift and ruthless logic.[33]

The war had transformed Ryan from a disgruntled, critical thinker into a believer in the philosophy of organizational management which permeated the armed forces. After the war he applied modern theories of sociology, psychology, and administration and became known as a progressive rector of Brockville. Father General Buijs appointed him to chair the 1951 joint North American meeting on Redemptorist formation. He adopted a military vocabulary, and words such as plan, operation, blitz, rank and file, personnel, and manpower were often on his lips and in his letters. Following in Daly's footsteps and encouraged by what he learned in the army, he favoured new technology, allowing radios, televisions, and film projectors as a means of continual education. His own leanings to the

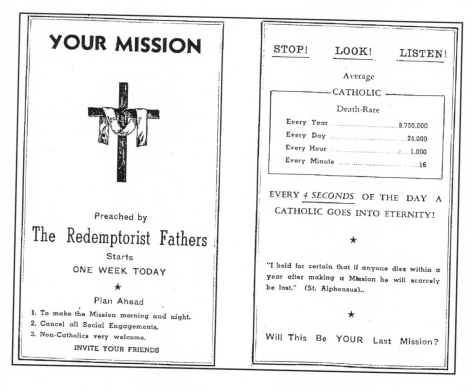

YOUR MISSION

Preached by

The Redemptorist Fathers

Starts
ONE WEEK TODAY

★

Plan Ahead

1. To make the Mission morning and night.
2. Cancel all Social Engagements.
3. Non-Catholics very welcome.

INVITE YOUR FRIENDS

STOP!   LOOK!   LISTEN!

Average
— CATHOLIC —
Death-Rate

Every Year	8.750.000
Every Day	24.000
Every Hour	1.000
Every Minute	16

EVERY *4 SECONDS* OF THE DAY A
CATHOLIC GOES INTO ETERNITY!

★

"I hold for certain that if anyone dies within a
year after making a Mission he will scarcely
be lost." (St. Alphonsus)..

★

Will This Be YOUR Last Mission?

Mission leaflet, *c.* 1950s

military did not go so far as to blind him to Redemptorist needs. While the whole world might accept everything the cold war military demanded, Ryan was still a critical thinker. He refused all requests by the military for chaplains. The Toronto Province itself needed every man.

As provincial, he created staff positions. He had learned in the military that a complex organization should have specialized staff workers, as well as the front-line missionaries and parish priests. He set up permanent committees on apostolic work, building, finance, regular observance, personnel, education, and Japan. He named himself and his two consultors, Norman Killingsworth and George O'Reilly, as heads of individual committees. Ryan established the vocation director's office as a key staff position and made sure that qualified people filled it. By 1955 over a hundred young boys applied to go to Brockville. He founded Madonna House in 1956, at 426 St. Germain Avenue in North York, Toronto, originally to house the provincial staff which had grown too large for St. Patrick's rectory. The administrative staff included those working for the *Madonna Magazine*, the missions, the League of St. Gerard, devotions to Our Lady of Perpetual Help, the Japanese missionaries, the financial offices, and the confreres living or studying in other countries. In 1957 his staff succeeded in revising the statutes of the province, untouched since 1926. By the time Ryan left the provincial's job, another building next door to the Madonna House was ready to become the provincial residence.

Staff positions and a staff headquarters meant nothing without Redemptorists. Ryan's thinking about reorganization centred on increasing the personnel. By 1953 two hundred and eighty-four English-Canadian Redemptorists worked in Canada, the British West Indies, and Japan, of whom forty-six were brothers and two hundred and four were ordained priests. Students made up the remainder. Although the average age was still only forty-three, it was a full ten years higher than at the foundation of the province. Although student numbers were higher than ten years previously, the fact remained that the number of priests themselves had not increased. But Ehman had accepted the Japanese missions and seven new foundations between 1947 and 1952, giving back to a diocese only one small foundation (Wells, British Columbia). Ryan therefore inherited a growing personnel problem.

At first, relying on statistics that a significant number of students would persevere in the Congregation and eventually help with the personnel crunch, he tried to recruit temporary help from other provinces. He jokingly bribed the English provincial with a case of Canadian rye whisky on top of the cost of a man's education in England in order to have the English provincial transfer one of his men to Canada.[34] He failed.

Ryan did succeed in obtaining two men from the Naples Province, Francesco Di Chio and Antonio Montecalvo, to work in Our Lady of Mount Carmel. He also began negotiating with the German provinces for men to care for the German parish. In the meantime, German-speaking priests from other congregations, such as the Jesuit Peter Mueller, and the Pallottine Nicholas Haering (who began his connection with the Redemptorists as a prisoner of war) helped out in the parish. By 1955 Fathers Karl Schindler and Emil Urban arrived from the Sudetenland Vice-province of Karlsbad, Czechoslovakia, which had been scattered by the communist takeover of 1946.

Ehman also left Ryan a difficult situation in Newfoundland. During Fuller's time, the bishop of St. George's had demanded that the Redemptorists vacate Corner Brook so that he could make it his episcopal see. The bishop, Michael O'Reilly, traded the parish of St. Joseph in St. George's for Corner Brook in 1947. In spite of the severe jostling they had received in the bishop's unilateral decision, the Redemptorists decided to stay in Newfoundland. They were the only religious priests there, and there was much work to be done in helping the diocesan priests on the island.

To anchor their position, the Redemptorists in April 1950 accepted the parish of St. Alphonsus, Whitbourne, offered by Bishop O'Neill of the Harbour Grace diocese to his Redemptorist cousin, Father Gerald Murphy. As in Ehman's other projects, the costs in Whitbourne began to mount. When Brother Anthony Pittman warned Father Ehman that Gerald Murphy had some wrong ideas about architecture, Ehman demanded that the brother learn obedience; and, unfortunately, mistakes were incorporated into the building.[35] Whitbourne became an important mission centre for the east coast, but Ryan was faced with two houses in Newfoundland when one was enough for the missions. Ryan had the Redemptorists leave Corner Brook and began negotiating for the parish of St. Teresa's in St. John's to replace the small and badly built mission house in Whitbourne.

Another difficult decision focused on the novitiate. Ryan looked at the L'Abord-à-Plouffe novitiate and at St. Ann's parish, both in the Montreal archdiocese, and decided that St. Ann's was much the better foundation since six to seven thousand people attended the Tuesday Perpetual Help devotions. The house was again becoming an active mission centre for the English-speaking Catholics of Quebec and of eastern Ontario. John Bennett broadcast

Family rosary broadcast from St. Ann's
These weekly broadcasts gathered personalities from around the world to lead English Montrealers in prayer. This 1954 picture shows the members of the Detroit Red Wings hockey team praying the rosary behind William Power, later the Bishop of Antigonish. (David Bier Studios)

the family rosary daily over a local radio station. Since L'Abord-à-Plouffe was finally becoming a popular suburb, its sale in 1956 recouped the money spent by Ehman on the site. The novitiate moved west to Senneville, still in the Montreal suburban district, near Ste-Anne-de-Bellevue.

Although Ryan preferred Quebec's Catholic atmosphere, Senneville proved a temporary novitiate site. The Senneville municipality restricted the number of people living on any piece of land, and then the land itself was threatened with expropriation for a major gas pipeline. Dr. and Mrs. Heffering, friends of the Redemptorists, offered to donate their Black Angus beef farm in Keswick, near Lake Simcoe, Ontario. The total cost of a new building to house thirty novices came to over $500,000 and another $250,000 went for the agricultural equipment to run the attached farm. St. Gerard's novitiate in Keswick opened on 10 October 1958.

Chapels, churches, schools, and halls also needed to be built in western Canada. The Edmonton Vice-province needed to borrow $100,000 for a school extension in the Vancouver parish. East Kildonan needed a hall and church sacristy. Calgary needed a new church. Yorkton needed a parish hall and a new school. Edmonton needed a new school. Before leaving the provincial's chair, Dan Ehman allowed the Edmonton Vice-province to spend $500,000 on a new church in Edmonton. With the help of Father John D. Lockwood as the provincial treasurer, Ryan found the money and paid the debts.

In contrast to Fuller and Ehman who had previously promised any financial help necessary to make the Redemptoristines and the Japanese missions a success, Ryan put them both on a budget. He suggested to the Redemptoristines ways of making money in the creation and sale of devotional items such as the Little Infant Jesus of Prague statues, popularized in western Canada by Father Joseph Celustka. Ryan also restricted the supply of missionaries to Japan, insisted that the mission had to recruit from the Japanese people, and discouraged any further foundations until the number of personnel warranted them. He instructed Fuller to stop expanding, to sell the monastery in Kamiagu, to give the tuberculosis hospital to Our Lady's Missionaries or whatever congregation of sisters would take it, to hand over the two kindergartens to the Redemptoristines and to concentrate on missions in the Japanese language.

Ryan had a point. With ten priests in 1956, the mission had three canonical foundations, several parishes, chapels, halls, schools, and a hospital, all in one diocese. There was still not one Redemptorist comfortable enough to preach missions in Japanese and not one ordained native Japanese priest. He and Fuller then recommended that the available Munich Province Redemptorists move into the south of Japan around Nagasaki since the Toronto Province did not have the men to go there.

The Major Seminary

Ryan's decisions were leading to one main goal: a major seminary. There had to be enough money to build one, enough qualified people to staff it, and enough students to make it worthwhile. The 1944 consultation of the province's rectors had discussed the creation of the western vice-province, the reopening of the Brockville minor seminary, a new novitiate, and the establishment of a mission house, all of which were now realities. There remained one item on the 1944 agenda which neither Fuller nor Ehman had been able to address: the major seminary.

Ryan detested Woodstock. While his criticisms about the ramshackle place had been aired as early as 1934, his experiences in 1936 turned his distaste into fixed hostility. The town tried to impose a poll tax, which hit the seminary hardest of all since the tax was based on live bodies, not income. It then proceeded to arrest each member of the seminary staff and prosecute them one by one for non-payment. Fathers Bernard Coffey, Arthur Ryan, and Edward Walsh all were taken to court. The town succeeded in convicting and fining Father Edward Walsh. When he refused to pay on the grounds he had no money, some of the town officials and citizens argued that he should be jailed. Father Fuller and the entire seminary were convinced that "bigotry was at the back of it." The magistrates could not understand the vow of poverty and had to be convinced that no money would be forthcoming. Further, the town would spend more on feeding and housing the whole seminary in the town jail than it could raise in an already unpopular poll tax. This incident and others brought several Redemptorists to label Woodstock a "black, Protestant" town and to call for a new seminary elsewhere.[36]

Since then, Fuller and Ehman had postponed building a new seminary in Woodstock for lack of money. When Ryan returned from military service, although he was the most qualified man available, he refused to be considered as the next rector of a Woodstock seminary he detested. He argued that Redemptorists had to break free of their traditional seminary training and gain academic degrees, to be better prepared for teaching, graduate work, or the missions in the modern world. Ryan's superiors, however, saw that the quiet atmospheres of Brockville and Woodstock allowed some individuals to mature and test their vocation further. Ryan's attempt to move Brockville's final year, one unnecessary for a high school diploma, to the seminary would mean allowing graduating high school men into the novitiate a year earlier. Gaining academic degrees would mean tacking on yet another year to the major seminary, delaying the entry of the Redemptorist into the active ministry. In all, Ryan's plans would mean bringing younger men into the Congregation and keeping them at their studies longer.

There the debate stood until Superior General Buijs visited Toronto in 1951 and insisted on a good library, affiliation with a Catholic university, and more theoretical rather than practical training.[37] Woodstock began to purchase audio-visual equipment, biblical maps, and new books. By the mid-1950s forty-three Redemptorists had university degrees, nine of them had completed doctorates, and one, Joseph Owens, had an international reputation in neo-Thomistic philosophy. More were sent for higher studies. Ehman then named a building committee to plan for a new seminary in Woodstock, but ran out of money and time to do anything.

Shortly after Ryan's appointment as provincial, the Basilian-run Assumption College of Windsor became a university. Ryan approached the Basilian Fathers, who were perhaps Canada's best English-speaking teaching congregation, to explore affiliating St. Alphonsus Seminary in Woodstock with the new university. Affiliation would gain the bachelor of arts degree and a level of education demanded by many diocesan seminaries, teachers' colleges, and graduate schools. Redemptorists with a B.A. could attend any of these institutions after seminary without further undergraduate studies. Removing that last year of Brockville studies also created more space in the minor seminary for the new students recruited by the vocation director.

To institute these changes, Ryan contemplated a radical departure. He argued that since the province had planned to rebuild the ramshackle Woodstock college, long condemned as a fire hazard, it could just as easily build the college in Windsor, in the same London diocese as Woodstock. Buijs cautioned Ryan that keeping all of the students together, from first-year undergraduate to final-

At the end of second novitiate class and pastoral year, St. Ann's, Montreal, the young priests are given their mission crosses and a blessing before being assigned to their mission fields or parishes.

year theology, might create more stresses than a single institution could handle. The Redemptorists also planned to have an extra pastoral year to coincide with the second novitiate, which meant that the Redemptorists would undergo yet another year of education before entering the ministry. Adding a full undergraduate program would strain the resources of the seminary to the breaking point.

In negotiations with Assumption University, it was agreed that the two institutions would have common examinations, although the Redemptorist theology students would be taught mainly by Redemptorist lecturers while undergraduates would take most of their courses at the university. It was assumed that if student numbers increased, the proposed Redemptorist house of studies in Windsor would eventually become an entirely undergraduate institution. Toronto's Redemptorists assured Father General Buijs that they intended to build another house for theological studies.[38] In August 1953 Rome granted Ryan, as John Keogh said, his "big chance ... to make or break yourself as a Provincial" in the building of the Windsor seminary.

After Ehman's financial extravagances, the Toronto Province was not able to finance the seminary. As well as closing houses, Ryan called in 75 per cent of the liquid assets of each foundation and asked every member to practise further poverty. He then undertook a fundraising campaign. The first such campaign since the building of Brockville, Ryan entrusted it to a professional organization, the Community Counselling Service, and recruited prominent lay people to head it. The Liberal party politician, Senator Charles Power of St. Patrick's, Quebec City, became general chairman for eastern Canada and Walter Thom of Moose Jaw chaired the campaign in western Canada. Prime Minister Louis St. Laurent, a long-time patron of St. Patrick's church in Quebec City, kicked off the campaign. The total campaign raised over $1 million, a third of which came from the Redemptorist parishes in Toronto, half coming from the other eastern foundations, and the remaining sixth from western Canada. Within the province, all other fundraising, renovation, or building projects ground to a halt as everyone concentrated

Gerald Grant in his cell in crumbling Woodstock

on the final stage of the seminary campaign: Operation Blitzkrieg. In contrast to the amateurish Brockville campaign of 1919 which fizzled out in a matter of weeks, Ryan's use of professional fundraisers made the Windsor campaign a resounding financial success.

Some Redemptorists continued to question Ryan's single-minded drive to leave Woodstock, a place that had been successful in training a generation of priests. They wondered about the impact the new emphasis on money and administration would have on Redemptorist life. In the provincial consultation of 1944 the province's representatives had voted against a new place of studies and a new novitiate site. But by 1954 the novitiate had been moved four times and Woodstock was destined to close. Opposition was useless; when logic did not sway anyone, Ryan required obedience.

The Redemptorists tried mightily to obtain land near Assumption University, but failed. Reluctantly, the province purchased land along Cousineau Road nine kilometres from Assumption University for $47,000. Construction began in 1956,

Arthur Ryan breaking the ground for Holy Redeemer College
Windsor's Eastern Construction Company won the contract for Windsor and for its smaller twin, Keswick.

Holy Redeemer College, Windsor, aerial view

and costs soon rose to $1,680,000. Holy Redeemer College opened officially in October 1957 with eleven lecturers, six professed brothers, and three candidate brothers as maintenance and support staff, seven priests in their final year of theology, nineteen other students in theology, and twenty-one students in philosophy, for a total of sixty-seven people. Ryan rejoiced: "At last we shall be able to vacate this tumbling-down former Baptist college which we have dignified for the past twenty-seven years with the name of 'St. Alphonsus Seminary'." Ryan had the Woodstock buildings demolished, and the land sold. When a local history society had a plaque installed on the spot with not a word written about the Redemptorist stay there, he again felt himself vindicated in leaving Protestant Woodstock.[39] The ceremonies in Windsor were grandiose.

By the end of the 1950s the entire provincial structure had reached full maturity. There were over three hundred and thirty men, including novices and professed students, a provincial staff, statutes, minor seminary, novitiate, major seminary, parishes, publishing house, parish and foreign missions stretching across Canada and into Japan, all of it debt-free. With the Sisters of Service to help in the parishes and the Redemptoristines praying for success, the Toronto Province appeared to be a magnificent structure marching toward the conquest of all English Catholic Canada and beyond.

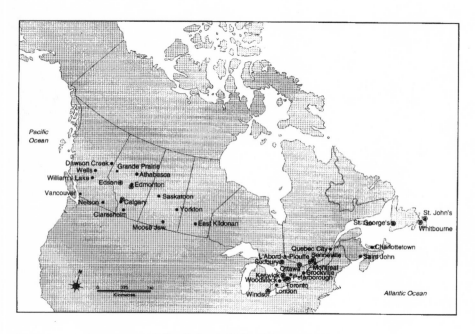

⊛ **New Redemptorist Foundations (1945-1961)**

Western Canada
Edson, Alberta (1949-1985)
Holy Redeemer College, Edmonton, Alberta (1960-1970)
Holy Trinity, Forest Lawn, Calgary, Alberta (1961)

Eastern Canada
St. Joseph's, St. George's, Newfoundland (1947-1953)
St. Clement's, Ottawa, Ontario (1947-1954)
Marianella, L'Abord-a-Plouffe, Quebec (1950-1956)
St. Gerard's, Senneville, Quebec (1956-1957)
Holy Redeemer, Minnow Lake, Sudbury, Ontario (1949)
Our Lady of the Assumption, Toronto (1950-1995)
St. Alphonsus, Whitbourne, Newfoundland (1950-1971)
St. Alphonsus, Windsor, Ontario (1952-1984)
St. Theresa's, Mundy Pond, St. John's, Newfoundland (1956)
Our Lady of Perpetual Help (Madonna House), North York, Toronto (1956)
Holy Redeemer College, Windsor (1957-1995)
St. Gerard's Novitiate, Keswick, Ontario (1957-1966)

The Toronto Province, 1945-61

8

The Years of the Second Vatican Council, 1958–65

J ohn XXIII was elected pope on 28 October 1958. Almost immediately, he began thinking about a council to bring the Church
up to date. The almost revolutionary changes among the
Redemptorist and all religious institutes in the Catholic Church
brought about by the Second Vatican Council were in no way sudden, except to individuals who had closed their eyes to the coming
changes. The Church had long been moving towards a restructuring
of religious life in the modern world. In the First International
Congress of Religious at Rome in 1950, Pope Pius XII had called for
them to adapt themselves "to the style and needs of the time and the
people."[1] The Redemptorists under Father General Buijs had already
enthusiastically begun to modernize their religious life.

Unfortunately, Father Buijs died suddenly in June of 1953. A
General Chapter met in Rome to elect a new superior general. It was
felt that it was time for an American, because the missionary, finan-
cial, and numerical vitality of the Congregation had shifted to North
America. Toronto Provincial Arthur Ryan's reputation gained him
several votes as a serious candidate for superior general. Instead,
however, the Chapter elected William Gaudreau of the Baltimore
Province, who had spent the years 1939 to 1950 as superior of the
Vice-province of Campo Grande, Brazil. Born in the archdiocese of
Boston, he was of French-Canadian descent, spoke French as well as

English as a youth, and had spent some years on the bilingual English-French missions of New England. He was thought acceptable to French Canada's Beaupré Province and to other French-language provinces. In Brazil he had shown himself an able administrator and a capable linguist. It could be argued that Gaudreau represented both the American parish traditions of the Congregation and the new foreign missions promoted by Father Buijs around the world. There were those, however, like Ryan who knew Gaudreau personally, having studied with him in Esopus, who suspected that his many years in Brazil had isolated him from the new movements in the Church and in religious life.[2]

In contrast to Buijs's openness to change in the early 1950s, Gaudreau set a more conservative tone for the remainder of the decade, consolidating much that was old and instituting little that was new. The same could be said of the Catholic Church as a whole, as Pius XII and many of his cardinals became increasingly conservative with age. This perception made an old and essentially conservative John XXIII appear liberal when he called the council. Ryan himself had also become less collegial and more authoritarian, forgetting to delegate, bypassing his consultors, and ignoring his standing committees. He immersed himself in the details of every project, and so completely dominated everything that he violated a basic management principle: he did not allow his own men to develop themselves as leaders. If anything needed to be done right, he felt that he had to do it himself and let others know about their failings, too. His criticisms spared no one, not Dan Ehman, not James Fuller, not any of the rectors, missionaries, or students. He demoralized some of his men. They saw their lives reduced to statistics, fundraising, and constant pressure. Some began to wonder whether they would not be happier in diocesan ranks, or even in leaving the priesthood to get married. By 1958 Ryan himself realized his shortcomings and strongly suggested that a new provincial be named. He had accomplished what he had set out to do: build a new seminary. Now there was a need for new leadership.[3]

By the end of 1958 there were one hundred and seventy-six men in sixteen foundations in eastern Canada, seventy-five men in thirteen foundations in western Canada, eighteen men in three foundations in Maizuru, and sixty-two professed students in various stages of studies.[4] The parishes across Canada were booming as young families crowded the churches. In Newfoundland a new church was rising in St. Teresa's parish and its slum area was gradually being transformed into a good place to live. The Whitbourne outmissions were being rebuilt and strengthened. A new church was planned in Charlottetown. St. Patrick's in London held four masses back-to-back on a Sunday morning, creating a traffic jam in the parking lots. Holy Redeemer in Sudbury added a new section to the rectory. The devotions to Our Lady of Perpetual Help brought in thousands across the country. Father Matthew Meehan became rector of St. Patrick's, Toronto, in 1959 at the height of his radio and television work. The *Madonna Magazine* flourished with a dozen sidelines in religious goods. The Co-Redemptorist Association was reaching its zenith with six thousand members. Brockville entered into the mainstream of high school life with public plays, athletic events, and oratorical competitions. With the new winds of change brought into the Church by the new pope, there was excitement and energy throughout the province. Gaudreau, impressed with Ryan's accomplishments, reappointed him for a third three-year term. Ryan and the Redemptorists of the Toronto Province then faced a much greater, more exciting challenge than building a seminary. They were called to live through the Second Vatican Council.

The Council

The ecumenical council was announced in 1959 by John XXIII and finally began on 11 October 1962. Many Redemptorists assumed that it would follow the later trends of Pius XII's pontificate and be a doctrinal council enhancing Mary. Following the Redemptorists' example in the United States, Ryan appointed Tim O'Sullivan to canvass Canada with a petition to make Our Lady of Perpetual Help patroness of the Second Vatican Council. When O'Sullivan died in 1960, Ryan then appointed Father Edward Kennedy as the province's first public relations officer and Father Fred Coghlan to work on the Perpetual Help movement. When the council moved from the scholastic tradition towards biblical and socio-ethical con-

cerns, it became clear that a dogmatic definition of Mary as media-
trix of all graces would not be made. The Redemptorist campaign
faded away.

One of the activities which Redemptorists could claim to
have given continuously to the Church since their founding was the
study and practice of moral theology. This now came into its own.
Since the mid-nineteenth century, most manuals of moral theology
had become more or less technical discussions of sin.[5] In Canada
this development was compounded by the fact that few priests had
actually read Alphonsus's moral theology but contented themselves
with summaries, manuals, and glosses. There had been only one
incomplete translation of his works into English. Most clerical students found his writings on asceticism and devotion, especially to
Mary, much easier to read than the moral theology that had brought
Alphonsus the title of Doctor of the Church. The spirit of his moral
theology lived on less in the Church as a whole than in individual
Redemptorist confessors who continued to offer compassionate
moral guidance and who continued to attract penitents to the confes-
sionals of Redemptorist churches.

The council encouraged moral theology students to revive
the moral theology's pastoral element which had always been present in St. Alphonsus's work but had been overshadowed by the
canon law elements that form part of the study of moral theology.
Moral theology took note of new developments in biblical studies,
the humanities, and the social sciences, especially psychology and
sociology. There also grew a renewed appreciation of the "supernat-
ural foundation of Christian morality on the ethos of love and its
being made concrete in the Sermon on the Mount."[6]

The best-known proponent of these renewed trends was the
German Redemptorist, Bernhard Haering. After the Second World
War Haering received his doctorate in sacred theology not from a
Roman university but from the University of Tuebingen, Germany,
and became professor of moral theology and pastoral sociology in
the Redemptorist institutions of Gars am Inn and in the Alphonsian
Academy affiliated with the Lateran University. His dissertation, *The
Law of Christ*, united the new scholarly trends into a single work
and emphasized love rather than law as a determining principle in

theology. Haering's reputation grew throughout John XXIII's pontificate and he was named an expert or "peritus" to the council.

English Canada's Redemptorists invited Haering to speak to them in 1963 as he toured North America, and they briefly considered introducing Haering's *The Law of Christ* as the textbook for Windsor's moral theology course. It became a popular supplementary text. The Redemptorists heard Haering insist on "the gentle heart" that must run through all rules and authority. "The law of Christ is infinitely more than a mere written code: it is primarily the law of the loving God written in our deepest being and existence, 'in our understanding and on our heart.'" There was to be no legalism, conformity, regimentation, or terrorism.[7] Coming from his experience in a medical corps in the Second World War, Haering had long pondered the relationship of authority to obedience and how Germany's obedience had led to mass murder. Haering taught that the authority of God's love required mutual responsibility, not blind obedience. From this renewed knowledge of the different kinds of obedience possible in religious life, dialogue, reasonable acts, and personal responsibility began to influence the understanding of obedience and the exercise of authority. Father General Gaudreau disagreed. In several circular letters, he re-emphasized a traditional view of obedience, denouncing the trend for individuals to determine the reasonableness of orders given by superiors. Obedience, Gaudreau wrote to the Toronto Province, is required even when unreasonable. The Rule stated that a subject could inform a superior of matters of which the superior was perhaps unaware before giving his order. No dialogue was necessary.[8]

When the Redemptorist students returned in September 1963 to Holy Redeemer College in Windsor from their summer holiday, they enthusiastically began their academic year with a five-day retreat preached by Haering. Within the highly structured and traditional format, Haering introduced his ideas and the new liturgical practices that incarnated his ideas: a dialogue mass, a Bible vigil, mass with communion in both kinds, and a solemn high mass, vespers, and compline all in English. These now common practices were revolutionary in 1963. Vernacular in the liturgy was approved only in principle at the council and the practice came only two years later. In Windsor, Haering's *Law of Christ* was read during meals and the vernacular was used in the liturgy for the next month.[9]

Haering returned to Rome, where his reputation as a modern prophet continued to grow. In North America his writings on sexual ethics, especially on responsible parenthood and birth control, were widely read by bishops, priests, and laity. Nonetheless, rumours of moral relativism dogged Haering and other teaching members of the Congregation in Rome. In Windsor some of the Redemptorist lecturers began to complain that Haering's ideas and anticipations of liturgical innovations undermined authority and that the students were confused and unbalanced from too much "undigested Haering."[10] The students read, debated, anticipated liturgical changes, and demanded further experiments.

Missions

The council accelerated a re-evaluation of missions in the province. The standard mission still lasted eight or ten days to overlap two Sundays, and always discussed salvation, mortal sin, general judgment, and hell. Renewals, which stressed the love of God, were infrequent. From 1939 to 1949, only 20 per cent of all missions were followed with a renewal. After the Second World War, Father General Buijs urged Toronto to adopt the model of the longer European missions which lasted a minimum of fourteen days, and to experiment with different sermon topics, perhaps patterned after the Jesuits' Ignatian exercises, so as to reach non-Catholics. These suggestions were enthusiastically accepted. Radio missions, Cana conferences, inquiry classes, and Catholic information centres increased, especially in western Canada. The basic traditional mission system did not change, however, because the new superior general, Gaudreau, forbade any changes in the mission sermon topics.

Ryan nevertheless saw a need to rework parish missions to new sociological conditions. The fact was that the Redemptorist "blood and thunder" parish mission was no longer as popular as it once was. So Ryan conscientiously followed Gaudreau's strictures and changed only the externals of the mission, not the contents, but he also trusted the seminary to produce intellectually capable people who could adapt to Canada's future needs. The younger men were given more room in their work and lifestyles. The seminarians in 1957 held their own mission day. To the question whether the Canadian parish mission was alphonsian, they answered that it was not. They urged a shift in the missions, from fear to love. Some of the younger lecturers gave a more detailed critique in 1960 which stated much the same thing. In western Canada, Father Bernard Johnson, observing that few people were asking for the traditional mission and fewer people were being reached by it, also argued that the Redemptorists should abandon the small parish missions based on fear and move towards the model promoted by Archbishop Montini, later Pope Paul vi. In Montini's 1957 monster mission in Milan, almost a thousand voices, clerical and lay, preached the good news of salvation.[11]

In opposition to Ryan and Johnson, some of Toronto's missionaries pointed out that the new missions and retreats, as impressive and exciting as they were to priests who read deeply in council documents, did not move people to repentance. Nevertheless, the new liturgical changes proposed by the council had to be introduced to the parishes. By 1961 some of the Toronto Province was ready to try something new, and even older-style missionaries such as Dan Ehman argued that Redemptorists had to move with the Second Vatican Council beyond Joseph Wissel's use of fear and towards Bernhard Haering's use of hope. The missionaries divided into two groups: those who favoured new methods and sermon topics, and those who preached the old.[12]

Edmonton

Father Johnson's enthusiastic endorsement of new mission methods, as opposed to Ryan's more cautious implementation of Gaudreau's strictures, was part of a larger struggle between western and eastern Canadian Redemptorist superiors. Although 1958 saw Ryan reappointed for a third term, Johnson replaced Gabriel Ehman as vice-provincial of Edmonton.

Ryan's relations with Gabriel Ehman had never been good. On first being named provincial, Ryan had immediately vetoed

Ehman's suggested appointment list for western Canada and personally rearranged the postings – something that had never been done by previous provincials. In theory, western Canadian Redemptorists, two-thirds of whom were easterners anyway, could not be distinguished from their eastern counterparts. Except for the west's many outmissions, the Edmonton Vice-province was fully part of the Toronto Province. In practice, Edmonton had become functionally autonomous. The working principle had been that the provincial assigned men to the west and the vice-provincial assigned them to a particular foundation.

Ryan's appointments caused confusion and Gabriel Ehman reminded him that western communities were so small that even minor changes upset delicate balances among the rectors, consultors, and subjects. Ehman was more explicit to Rome, demanding that Ryan's rulings about western Canada be ignored on the grounds that the Edmonton vice-provincial had been granted the rights of a major superior by former provincial Fuller with the permission of the former father general, Patrick Murray. He labelled Ryan's appointments disastrous.[13]

Another point of friction was the western minor seminary. Ryan had imposed a quota on westerners going to Brockville. So in 1956 the Redemptorists purchased over a hundred and fifty acres overlooking the North Saskatchewan River near Edmonton as the first step toward a western Canadian minor seminary. In the meantime, in 1957 Gabriel Ehman sent twelve western boys due to enter grade nine to St. Louis College, Moose Jaw, and the following year twenty-seven westerners in grades nine and ten went there. On 3 September 1960, Edmonton's Holy Redeemer College opened its doors to sixty-five young men, eleven Redemptorist priests, and eight brothers. The college was dedicated in an impressive ceremony on 9 October 1960, with Gabriel Ehman as its first rector.

Naturally, Edmonton had been annoyed at Toronto's quota. The quota made it difficult to generate any fundraising enthusiasm in the west for eastern building projects while the western minor seminary was also being built. Gabriel Ehman claimed that money and men from the west should stay there, on the grounds that western Canada was poorer and more Protestant than eastern Canada.[14] Ryan countered, as did previous provincials, that the west often got younger, healthy men, because travel to the outmissions was very hard and the small western houses did not have the space and could not afford anyone who was ill. Furthermore, the east paid for all medical, educational, and travel bills which the taxes on the western houses hardly reimbursed, even if they were paid, and often they were not. As for the major seminary and the new novitiate being built in the east, it was meant to serve the entire province, east, west, and Japan.

Faced with Gabriel Ehman's reluctance to do anything for the Toronto Province as a whole, Ryan decided that Edmonton should become a separate province. Ehman protested vigorously that Edmonton had too few men and too large a debt at $350,000 to support all of the foundations and educational institutions needed for a province.[15]

**Superiors' Meeting at Holy Redeemer College, Edmonton, 1960
with the statue of Christ the Teacher behind.**
Standing left to right: F. Lawless, D. Langi, E. Quinn, G. Campbell, G. McKenna, J. MacGillivray, J. Naphin, L. Murphy. Seated: D. Pankhurst. J. Spicer, G. Gunnip, G. Ehman, N. Corbett, B. Johnson, G. Feehan, P. Scullion, F. Lane.

Ryan pushed for Bernard Johnson to replace Ehman as vice-provincial in order to have a younger, more flexible man in place. Johnson had been born in Toronto and grew up in Paris, Ontario. He had a thoroughly eastern training in Brockville and Woodstock, having had Ryan as a teacher in Woodstock. Johnson was Ryan's kind of Redemptorist: intelligent, versatile, and competent. He had proved himself as an editor of *The Eikon* magazine and as a rector in William's Lake and in Edmonton. Ryan trusted him to do what needed to be done. Ehman privately wrote to Rome that while he would like to see a province in western Canada to solve the problems arising from the past nine to ten years (without mentioning that these were Ryan's years), he could predict success only if Toronto granted $100,000 and left in the west all of the men born in the east. No easterner should be allowed to return east for ten years unless a westerner could replace him.[16]

Ryan became angry at Ehman's demands, pointing out that the west did not really appreciate the number of men and dollars that went into the novitiate and the seminary. Moreover, western Canada had not paid for anything since 1953, while all monies raised in the west went back west. Nonetheless, he promised the necessary men and money "out of charity." Caught between Ehman and Ryan, doubting the wisdom of separating western Canada from Toronto, Johnson hesitated and delayed. Ryan grew more furious and requested Rome to ignore Johnson and raise the Edmonton Vice-province to provincial status immediately. Edmonton had named its price; Toronto had met it. Now Rome should in justice meet Toronto's demand. As the mother province, Ryan relentlessly argued, Toronto knew what was best for Edmonton.[17]

The Edmonton Province was created on 16 July 1961, with Bernard Johnson as provincial and Neil Corbett and Grattan Feehan as consultors. Sixty-six priests and sixteen brothers entered the Edmonton Province, over half of them easterners. It was Ryan's last act. He volunteered for Japan but was sent to St. Ann's, Montreal, to study the parish and the Redemptorists' future in Montreal.

George O'Reilly (1961–64)

In July 1961 George O'Reilly was named provincial. As a young man, he had been judged one of the best missionaries the province had and became Ryan's first mission coordinator. Considered an intelligent man of excellent judgment, he had just missed being provincial on account of his youth when Ryan was named, but he was later made a provincial consultor. He became rector in Peterborough and then in London, and had demonstrated administrative skill in building a new church even while negotiating with a bishop who wanted to split the parish into two. As provincial consultor, he had been in charge of building the Windsor seminary. He went on to become the prefect of students in Windsor. Many people thought that he succeeded in bringing the students to a better appreciation of Redemptorist community life during the rapid changes of the ecumenical council and the transition from a rural, cloistered Woodstock seminary experience to the urban, public university system in Windsor.

George O'Reilly (1915–92)

O'Reilly and his consultors immediately set a new tone. The fact that Ryan was gone meant that some of the tension with Edmonton disappeared. O'Reilly revived the staff committees Ryan had allowed to lapse and generally moved the province away from a centralized and authoritarian leadership model to a more consultative and participative model of religious government. He cancelled the centralized and unwieldy mission coordination system and placed the missions back into the hands of the house rectors and senior missionaries who were closer to the missionaries and to the people who asked for them.

The province began to send men to Japan again. Because the Japanese missionaries were spread so thinly, understaffing and overwork had led to health problems and heart attacks. Charles Brocklehurst's sudden death in early 1961 came as a terrible blow. By early 1962 both James Glavine and Thomas Carr had suffered heart attacks from overwork. While the German Redemptorists' Kagoshima mission in the south and the French-Canadians' Tokyo mission in the north had been given vice-provincial status, Maizuru could not think of it even as late as 1962 for lack of men. Ryan had too long refused to send men to Japan. Under O'Reilly, young men fresh from seminary were sent to revitalize the Japanese mission. In contrast to the former competition with the French-Canadian Redemptorists, Toronto's missionaries entrusted their seminary formation to the French Canadians in Tokyo and began to plan for a united Japanese province with a united seminary and a united novitiate.[18]

With Gaudreau from Brazil in the superior general's chair, and with Canadian bishops sending missionaries to South America, the Redemptorist Congregation and the students in the Toronto Province turned their attention south. O'Reilly helped to establish a national Portuguese parish in Our Lady of Mount Carmel church in Toronto. Two men from the Toronto Province joined men from the Edmonton Province in the district of Bahia, Brazil, in 1968.

In his last report, Ryan had thrashed around for new ideas and mentioned the possibility of phasing out the brothers, *Madonna Magazine*, the Purgatorian Society, and St. Mary's, Brockville, all tagged as expensive and unsuccessful. He also proposed a Toronto

Province retirement home in the Bahamas. O'Reilly vetoed these suggestions. While the magazine, the Purgatorian Society, and the minor seminary were indeed expensive and could be considered peripheral to Redemptorist life and mission, Ryan's suggestion of refusing vocations to the brotherhood was shocking. Brothers had been part of the Congregation since its founding.

Still, the brothers had sometimes been treated as servants rather than brothers in the same family of God. Over the years, continuous formation of the brothers, obligatory spiritual conferences, readings, and translations of circular letters into the vernacular for the brothers who could not handle Latin had all but disappeared, so that the educational differences between the priests and the brothers had increased. Buijs complained about this two-tiered social hierarchy in the Congregation; William Gaudreau encouraged it. In Toronto, as elsewhere, different work schedules had brought separation to its logical conclusion in separate novitiates, recreation periods, and common rooms. Ryan tried to upgrade the education, status, and apostolate of the brothers, but Gaudreau and the prevailing attitudes in the Church, in society, and among the priests in the Congregation kept the brothers in their traditional positions. Ryan came to believe that the brotherhood could not coexist with the fathers in the modern world.[19] O'Reilly, however, encouraged the brothers to form panel discussions as a means of eventually breaking down the segregation. In 1964 the brothers began a short-lived newspaper, *The Redemptorist Brothers' News*, to promote their vocation.

The future suggested that the brother could become a missionary in his own right, as a catechist or a liturgical leader. Between 1961 and 1965, seventeen brothers were professed. The end of segregation, however, also meant that the brothers were exposed to new developments in the modern world, causing great unrest. In the same years, seventeen brothers left the Toronto Province, two died, and sixteen joined the Edmonton Province, from which many requested their dispensation. O'Reilly was held partly responsible for the one-third decline.

As provincial, O'Reilly made other decisions that were equally divisive. He approved the invitation by the new prefect of students, Victor Crean, to the controversial Bernhard Haering to

**Brother Ambrose (Cecil Chisholm) coaching altar boys
at St. Patrick's, Toronto**

speak in Windsor. Concerning missions, O'Reilly boldly wrote to the superior general that the old type of Redemptorist mission "confined to one particular parish, especially in the city, is no longer the effective agent of salvation that it was in the past."[20] He asked Edward Boyce then in Lyons, France, to study the general mission held there so that he could introduce its sociological components to Canada. He also instructed the editor of the *Madonna Magazine*, James Bennett, to update the magazine with biblical, liturgical, lay, and ecumenical aspects so that it would be in "harmony with the whole Church which is undergoing a profound renewal." To pay for the new articles, new format, and photographs as well as the hiring of lay writers, the subscription price doubled to two dollars. He encouraged the entire province in biblical studies, spiritual reading, study of the Second Vatican Council, personal responsibility and dialogue. O'Reilly seemed just the man to update and lead the Toronto Province into the post-conciliar period.

London's General Mission

When the parish of St. Teresa of the Child Jesus in Mundy Pond in the archdiocese of St. John's was offered by the archbishop, Ryan recognized it as a desirable foundation for a religious congregation and as a centre for missionaries and retreats, so the Redemptorists accepted this foundation in October 1956. St. Teresa's became the centre for a massive diocesan-wide mission, with over twelve missionaries who heard forty-nine thousand confessions in a Catholic population of fifty-seven thousand people. Under the title of "The Making of a New Creature in Christ," it incorporated new technologies, television, radio, and newspaper advertising and articles, on a regional basis. It had mixed success, because the missionaries were so overworked they could not reach everyone. Father Martin Foley

Book launching of *A Demographic Survey of Essex County and Metropolitan Windsor* by Rudolph Helling and Edward Boyce
Left to right: Rt. Rev. P.A. Mugan, pastor of Christ the King parish, Windsor, Dr. Rudolph Helling of the University of Windsor, Bishop G. Emmett Carter of London, Hon. Mayor John Wheelton of Windsor, and Father Edward Boyce, CSsR, March 1965

suggested that London or Windsor would be a more appropriate centre for a regional mission so that more Redemptorists and other missionaries, such as the Passionists or the Vincentians, could reach more people on an individual basis.[21]

Following Foley's recommendation, in the spring of 1964 O'Reilly wrote to Bishop Emmett Carter of London about holding a general mission in London or Windsor. Carter, well known for his work in religious education in Quebec, wanted a catechetical centre in the diocese. In exchange for the loan of Father Emmanuel Demerah to establish the centre, Carter enthusiastically accepted Edward Boyce to direct a general mission to help update the Church in his diocese according to the Second Vatican Council.[22] It was decided to hold the general mission in Essex County, including the city of Windsor. The province sent twelve men to a course taught by Bernhard Haering at the Missionary Institute in Detroit, Michigan, to study modern approaches to parish missions, moral theology, and the impact of Vatican II on the missions. Redemptorists from neighbouring provinces were invited to participate in the mission, to take place once the sociological studies and preparations were completed in 1967.

John D. Lockwood (1964–68)

In spite of these signs of renewal, George O'Reilly was not renamed provincial in 1964. He had been suffering from health problems throughout 1963 and had participated little in drawing up the slate mailed to Rome by acting provincial William Murphy. Although O'Reilly fully expected to stay on for another three years, and many people in the province hoped he would stay, his health, the puzzling departures of brothers and students from the seminary, and continuing problems with western Canada brought Father General Gaudreau to set aside O'Reilly's proposed appointments and raise John D. Lockwood from the treasurer's to the provincial's chair.[23]

Born in 1906 in Vancouver, John Lockwood had been educated there before going to Brockville. His family could not pay for his education and he counted on an unreliable benefactor; the worries made for a tense period. His own doubts about his vocation sur-

John Lockwood (1906–91)

faced during his novitiate and in the year before his ordination. In both cases he trusted in obedience to his superiors who had assured him that his doubts were unfounded. Shortly after ordination and second novitiate, he was sent to study the Antigonish cooperative movement. From 1935 to 1941 he helped establish Toronto's St. Patrick's study clubs and the Central Toronto People's Cooperative store. During the Second World War he enlisted as a navy chaplain and served in Halifax, Esquimalt, and Prince Rupert. After the war he spent time in Edmonton, and from 1947 to 1953 was rector of St. Mary's, Saskatoon, where a large, successful credit union was established.

Although Ryan was chosen provincial in 1952, Lockwood's solid administrative skills, his experience as a military chaplain, his western popularity, and his reputation for fair-mindedness brought his name also into consideration for provincial, western vice-provincial, or even the first provincial of western Canada. Ryan brought Lockwood east to Toronto as the provincial treasurer where he was responsible for much of the financial work leading to the Windsor

seminary, the new novitiate in Keswick, and Edmonton's minor seminary. Lockwood developed a tough, autocratic image, but in reality,
he was much less self-confident than O'Reilly in the new world of
Vatican II.

Rome reappointed two experienced eastern consultors,
William Murphy and John Harrington, to be Lockwood's consultors.
Murphy, a short, fiery preacher, had completed a course of studies in
Montreal-area Sulpician institutions before going to the
Redemptorist novitiate. He eventually became one of the Toronto
Province's top missionary preachers and master of the second novi-
tiate, training the younger generation of missionaries. Later he was
named bursar at Holy Redeemer College, Windsor, where he came
to know something of the students and of the seminary.

Born and raised in Saint John, New Brunswick, John
Harrington's keen mind was known to many, as were his pastoral
experiences as a military chaplain and in the Italian parish of Our
Lady of Mount Carmel. As rector of Our Lady of the Assumption
parish in Toronto, he had demonstrated excellent financial acumen in
wiping out the debt. At fifty-four, Harrington was the youngest of
the three men.

Looking over the past five years, Lockwood reported that all
was well and that O'Reilly had left a strong province. Together,
Lockwood and the consultors sat down to consider their first order
of business, one given them by Father Gaudreau: the "problems
relating to the personnel of the staff and the community of the
Seminary."[24]

The Seminary

The first class graduated from Holy Redeemer College with B.A.
degrees from Assumption University in 1959. The move from
Woodstock to Windsor was apparently successful. Still, the higher
academic standards required of every candidate for the priesthood
created tensions. The young men juggled studies on a university
campus, studies at Holy Redeemer College, the requirements of
Redemptorist community life, and an extensive prayer life.
Religious life was disrupted whenever university classes conflicted

with Redemptorist holidays. Furthermore, on 21 January 1960 Ryan affiliated the theology lecturers with Assumption University, soon to become part of the University of Windsor, so that the theology students would receive the degree of Bachelor of Theology after their B.A. The daily schedule changed constantly in response to university class times and Redemptorist regular order disintegrated.

Urged by Ryan, all of the lecturers gradually raised their own teaching standards. He continually examined the seminary teaching and caustically remarked on "out-moded and sterile" methods. Both students and lecturers were sent to Europe and the United States for higher studies. He made it clear that the seminary was not a vocational school for training priests but a centre for ideas to educate the whole province.[25] The standards went up again, as did the tension.

Teaching staff of Holy Redeemer College, *c.* 1957
While the students saw the Redemptorist lecturers as old, the average age of these men in 1958 was under forty. *Left to right: sitting:* Alphonsus Thomas, Raymond Powers, Gerard Owens, Kleinnert Johnson. *Standing:* Edward Crowley, Arthur Alexander, Clark McAulay, Thomas Traynor, D'Arcy Egan.

Many of the ideas in the seminary naturally came from the United States. Windsor was so close to the United States, and Canada was so much influenced by events there, that the students were constantly exposed to American developments. The noon meal was postponed so that the community could see John F. Kennedy, the first Catholic president of the United States, take the oath of office. At one point in 1961, the television was on most of the day so that people could watch the first American astronaut; in 1962, the same thing repeated itself for John Glenn's triple orbit of the earth. The undergraduate students launched a short-lived creative writing magazine in January of 1963 in which American political events dominated the longer articles. Kennedy's assassination disrupted the seminary as everyone watched the televised event. Significantly, many of the students were in Detroit at the time, listening to lectures at Wayne State University. The American civil rights and race riots of 1964 and 1965 had a profound impact on people in Windsor and the Redemptorist students followed the events closely.

Above all, important ideas were coming from the Vatican Council. Students themselves were starting to demand that their lecturers update their teaching to take these new developments into account. The lecturers were well aware of the council's developments, but could not institute them until authorized to do so. Even the introduction of the vernacular into the liturgy was only a council proposal, while the 1962 Apostolic Constitution, *Veterum Sapientia*, re-emphasized that seminary education was to be conducted in Latin.

With John XXIII's death in June of 1963 and the election of Paul VI, a period of greater instability seemed to take over the Catholic world. The new pope gave few clues as to which direction he wanted the council to go, further confusing Catholics. The students avidly read the commentaries by outstanding writers, such as Karl Rahner, Yves Congar, and Bernhard Haering. The *New Yorker* writer "Xavier Rynne" broke the secrecy around the debates in Vatican II and chronicled the struggles between the conservative and the liberal forces, the author obviously favouring the liberals. Rynne was a pen name to protect the author, but rumours – accurate for once – circulated that he was none other than the Redemptorist

Baltimore Province Father Francis-Xavier Murphy, then in Rome.[26] The students also followed the creation and activities of the Secretariat for Christian Unity, "always the engine of progress in the Council," to which the Canadian Ukrainian Redemptorist Archbishop Maxim Hermaniuk had been named. While the lecturers gave papers on various aspects of the council, the students and young fathers at the seminary published their own *Council Notes*, favouring liberal views. It was an exciting time for everyone.

The tension over the changes in the seminary might have become a source of creativity in the right people, but Ryan, as Gabriel Ehman had already warned the Roman authorities, sometimes made disastrous mistakes in his appointments. In 1956 he replaced William Wyllie as prefect of students, the man responsible for discipline, with the genial and well-liked missionary John S. MacDonald. MacDonald had developed a heart condition and needed a rest from the missions. Ryan also believed that the students needed a true Redemptorist missionary as a role model.[27]

Unfortunately, the new prefect and the lecturers did not work well together. John S. MacDonald favoured a liberalization of the rules in the seminary and granted privileges, such as wine and beer at a Christmas party, that the lecturers opposed. Over the next few years, to rebuild harmony within the seminary, the offices of prefect and assistant to the prefect changed hands several times. The highly qualified lecturers could not be so easily replaced. There were continual battles over student discipline between a usually temporary student prefect, who had legitimate authority but little experience, and the usually permanent lecturers who had no authority but a great deal of power from their entrenched positions in the seminary. Ironically, the many changes and the different approaches to discipline and to the religious life confused the students even further. The students interpreted the rules as laxly as possibly as they searched for a more mature and modern way of being Redemptorists. The lecturers saw these actions as a challenge to authority and leaned further towards the strictest interpretations.

The first warning sign to Father General Gaudreau that not all was not well in the new seminary came in the form of the "Truth and Love" movement during Ryan's time. A group of seven or eight

Redemptorists, mostly very young, loosely associated through correspondence, had been greatly taken by the writings of the English Dominican priest, Gerald Vann, on the subject of charity, chiefly in religious communities. Gerald Vann (1906–63), a moralist and spiritual writer, blended Thomistic philosophy and theology with the humanism current in the 1920s and 1930s. Vann himself was invited to lecture at the Catholic University of America from 1959 to 1962 and became a Catholic author in great demand. The younger Redemptorists applied Vann's ideas in analysing the zeal, community life, and spirit of charity in the Toronto Province and found them wanting. Two of the group were lecturers in the seminary, and they in turn influenced some of the older students to bring a more psychological and humanistic appreciation to religious life. The divisions between these two lecturers and the rest of the staff and between the students for and against the movement became acrimonious. Nine professed students left the Redemptorists from the seminary in 1959, the highest in the history of the Toronto Province. Ryan reported to Gaudreau that "Many of the Fathers in the upper age brackets have not helped … towards the best solution of this 'problem' because of the intolerance they have shown towards members of the group."[28] The whole incident would later contribute to more serious conflicts.

Since he could not remove the entire staff, Ryan removed the two lecturers from the seminary in 1959. They could not be replaced and the students were forced to take more courses at the University of Windsor. This caused a further breakdown in community life at Holy Redeemer College as the students found their work, identity, and responsibility less directed toward the Redemptorists and more to the University. Problems in religious life were discussed not with Redemptorists but with university professors, some of whom had little understanding or sympathy for the stresses the Redemptorist community was suffering in its integration into the University of Windsor.

Relations between the students and the remaining lecturers continued to deteriorate. Although the two lecturers were gone, the older students, often the intellectual leaders in the seminary, continued to influence the incoming younger students. Students fresh from the novitiate, having just taken vows of poverty, chastity, and obedience in the Congregation, found themselves confronted by a renewed, more refined evaluation of religious life, priesthood, and the Redemptorist Congregation. Father Cornelius McElligott, a popular and studious novice master, published his lengthy study of the vow of perseverance in 1963. The book, an uneven work, sold poorly and was quietly forgotten.[29] Some of the Windsor lecturers were dismissive of McElligott's academic work, distrusted the novices he and his successor, Martin Foley, had recommended, and worked to weed them out, causing greater stress and conflict in the seminary. New Redemptorists, surrounded by doubting students, taught by suspicious lecturers, in a Church that daily debated the nature and meaning of religious life and priesthood, began to question their own perseverance in a religious family that seemed less a family than an institution. After receiving their B.A., some took steps to leave the Congregation; others were asked to leave.

When George O'Reilly replaced MacDonald in 1959, he treated the students as adults and placed them on their honour in the observance of the rules. Naturally, some individuals ignored the rules, but on the whole the situation began to stabilize. When O'Reilly became provincial in 1961, Edmonton became a province, too. The same situation repeated itself, with western students calling on their provincial directly over the head of the prefect, and with eastern students occasionally calling on their former prefect, O'Reilly.

After problems with individual Ukrainian students, the Ukrainian Redemptorists had been informed in December of 1961 that the seminary was crowded and that there would be no room for them in the future. The Ukrainian students gradually withdrew from the life of the seminary. In June of 1964 the remaining ten Ukrainian students left for the Yorkton Province's new seminary. While the Windsor seminary had been crowded and plans had been discussed to add a new wing in the early 1960s, by 1964 it was far from full and the departure of the ten Ukrainian students left a gaping hole. With fewer students now in residence, every departure became much more visible and influential on the remaining students. The new prefect, Victor Crean, tried to reimpose some semblance of discipline on the students in simple things such as silence, lights out, and prayer periods, while his assistant, Gerald Grant, relied on the students' maturity. The students, still caught between university and religious life, asked for more free time, more time to study, more dialogue, fewer class hours, more visits to their families, and a greater family spirit instead of the institutional spirit that prevailed. The students had moved very far from St. Alphonsus's insistence on obedience above all. Although the authorities decided to allow the students to go home during the summers and gain experience in manual and social work to broaden their experience of the world, they also blamed Grant for counselling the students in lax views of obedience and removed the one man in the seminary the students had begun to trust.[30]

The 1964 appointments removed Victor Crean and made Gerard Owens prefect of students; fifty-three years old, he had already been rector of Holy Redeemer College from 1952 to 1961. Still, he had recently completed his doctorate in Rome, had attended speeches at the Second Vatican Council, and was prepared to work hard at bringing the young and the old together. Unfortunately, he found that the chasm between the Redemptorist authorities and the students was too deep; to the students he seemed too old and too much part of the old crowd.

More serious was a new obstacle in the way of trust. Previous generations of Redemptorists had accepted that superiors could read their mail and monitor their conversations in the interests of childlike transparency and submission to authority. Letters, except those dealing with matters of conscience, were traditionally handed between superiors and individuals in unsealed envelopes, but few superiors bothered to read the many letters that came and went. With new technology, nineteenth-century fatherly supervision in the seminary had become administrative oppression, with students' telephone conversations tapped, as well as letters opened and read, and people watched and followed. The immorality of such secretive actions was not yet clear, but the lecturers in part justified their actions and based their recommendations to dismiss students on their findings.[31] Once the students suspected that private conversations were being overheard and perhaps used to decide their fitness and their future,

Owens could do nothing to overcome the unhealthy atmosphere of mistrust and silence. Owens had once received the nickname "Nails" for his athletic ability, but the students believed him hard as nails in his inflexibility in interpreting the Rule.

Relations between the students and the lecturers deteriorated so much that all communication ceased. Both conservative-minded and liberal-minded students left, some with the thought that the Church had changed and others complaining that it was not changing quickly enough. The Congregation itself seemed to be moving backwards into an increasingly oppressive dark age while the university students were moving forward into the Vatican Council's promised updating of religious life.

To inculcate the correct view of obedience as submission, the authorities sent Robert Macdonald to preach a retreat. Macdonald, one of the province's well-known missionaries, believed that a sermon was "an instrument for combatting firmly and decisively certain specific sins."[32] He was asked to deal with the specific sin of religious disobedience. Afterwards, he reported that only a small group of five or six students had peculiar ideas about obedience. This group had walked out of his conferences until ordered to return. Macdonald recommended that these students, "the focus of the infection," be dismissed.

The retreat itself, however, was traumatic for all of the students. The heavy-handed treatment of modern theories of obedience as sinful and the appeal to return to the traditional view and practice of obedience, as well as Macdonald's calls for the students to choose one side or the other and to follow their choice either in leaving the seminary or in going on to ordination, brought several to consider leaving immediately. The contrast with what was being taught by Bernhard Haering and by the Vatican Council could not have been greater. Overlooking the fact that religious life is an ascetic vocation, some of the students began to think that a true priestly or even a Christian vocation could not be found within the Congregation of the Most Holy Redeemer. Eighteen students left the seminary shortly after Macdonald's retreat. Even the Windsor newspapers picked up the fact that the Redemptorists were suffering a steadily increasing haemorrhage.[33] Although George O'Reilly's three-year tenure as provincial had been troubled by seminary problems, those years seemed a golden age in comparison with Lockwood's first term of office.

The Brief

Flailing about for communication and reassurance, the students took to visiting and consulting the members of the Essex County Renewal mission team at St. Alphonsus, Windsor. After listening to several of the students, Edward Boyce requested permission from Lockwood to report his findings to the superior general in Rome. But when Boyce arrived in Rome, Gaudreau had left for Mexico, despite his scheduled appointment with Boyce. Some of the other officials with whom Boyce met were surprised at Gaudreau's inaction, and sympathetic to Boyce's concerns. Indeed, the European provinces were undergoing similar upheavals. They encouraged Boyce to gather signatures for a brief outlining the problems in the province. As one European stated, the father general would be forced to react, because "Americans understand numbers."[34]

On his return to Canada, Boyce and other interested people drafted a brief. It went through several versions and the least accusatory one was accepted as the final draft by the London mission team. The brief was eventually signed by forty-three fathers, including the London mission team, by four other fathers in separate letters, and by three brothers. Senior members of the Toronto Province, such as Bernard Coffey, James Grannan, Gregory Murphy, Arthur Ryan, William Wyllie, rectors such as Frank Maloney, some of the younger missionaries, such as Boyce himself and Ervin Williams, those who had studied in Rome, such as Raymond Corriveau, and the former provincial, George O'Reilly, all supported it. It requested that the superior general himself visit the province to solve the seminary's problems.[35]

The provincial consultors, Bill Murphy and John Harrington, wrote scathing analyses of the brief as an attack on legitimate authority, based on misinformed hearsay and leading to further division and disquiet.[36] True, the brief did help to identify and divide the two groups in the province, but when it also stated there was a lack of communication, no one could deny that charge. Over half of the fathers who had signed the brief eventually left the Congregation. Toronto's mass exodus would later be duplicated to a lesser extent throughout the Redemptorist Congregation and among religious institutes throughout the world.

Edmonton's provincial, Bernard Johnson, watched the students' flight from Windsor with growing panic as he realized that almost every student from the west was leaving the Congregation. It seemed as if Toronto was chasing the western students out of the Congregation. In a lengthy meeting and then in a long letter, Johnson questioned the competence of the staff and demanded a say in how the seminary was run, but Toronto's administration rebuffed the requests and tended to ignore his calls and letters. Communication broke down between the two provinces.[37]

The truth was that Toronto's administration was unhappy that Johnson was still making impromptu visits to Windsor, further undermining its own authority over the students. Johnson then unilaterally appointed a westerner, Mansell Blair, to accompany the western seminarians and novices. He also wrote a letter in support of the brief, placing the blame for Toronto's problems more squarely on individual lecturers, Ryan's bad judgment in the past, as well as on the general situation in North America among Roman Catholics during the Vatican Council. Privately, he suggested an official visit from Rome to the Toronto Province to correct the problems, since Toronto seemed unable or unwilling to do so on its own. He nonetheless feared that things had gotten so bad in Toronto that renewal along the lines of the Second Vatican Council would only come through "an inevitable and scarred revolution."[38] The staff denied his allegations, blamed much of the lack of communication and discipline on the student unrest throughout the world, and suggested that Johnson stop panicking, stop interfering, stop undermining their efforts, talk to the lecturers as well as the students to get both sides of the story, and perhaps transfer his students elsewhere if he could not trust the seminary. Johnson began to make arrangements for the western students to study at the French-Canadian Redemptorist seminary in Aylmer and suggested that all of the students be pulled out of Windsor and sent elsewhere to get away from the unhealthy situation.[39]

Diaspora

By the spring of 1965 the unrest in the province was so great that it finally became clear to both Lockwood and to his consultor, Harrington, that student disobedience was a symptom, not the disease. Insisting on obedience to club people into submission to older ways of thinking was not working. On one day alone, Lockwood received requests for laicization from three young priests, none of them in studies. After speaking with the authorities in Edmonton and with the lecturers in Windsor, Harrington came to a new understanding of the difficulty. He traced the breakdown between the students and the lecturers to the growth of the new empirical sciences of sociology and psychology that were transforming theology, religious life, and the Redemptorist students, while the lecturers were defending the "monastic, scholastic, deductive clerical education of the past." To help welcome the new breed of Redemptorist into the Toronto Province, Harrington called for new leadership that would accept and use these trends. While Lockwood recognized some of the truth in Harrington's analysis, Murphy did not. But they all could agree on one thing to satisfy the students, the lecturers, western Canada, and their own consciences: ask Gaudreau himself to come to make a formal visitation.[40] Lockwood felt out of his depth with the student situation and found it hard to make a decision. He had always relied on unanimity from his consultors and relied on Gaudreau when there were differences of opinion. The search for unanimity, of course, meant delay or, worse, immobility.

Gaudreau sent Raymond Schmitt, the provincial of the St. Louis Province, to conduct an extraordinary visitation. On 17 October the dispersal of the students was proposed to the seminary staff. William Murphy argued that transferring all of the students would kill the seminary. Others argued that getting rid of a few students would not work any better than in the past and would probably provoke further departures. Lockwood again asked Gaudreau to visit the seminary, but Gaudreau absolutely refused to meet with the students or the lecturers; he tried to appear impartial, although he risked being arbitrary.

May I ask you then always to place the right emphasis on this specialized work of ours which is to reach out and seek neglected souls principally by means of missions. Otherwise I fear that if we put exaggerated stress on other means, however good in themselves and even though duly approved by our Constitutions and Traditions, our missions will cease to be the principal and first means which St. Alphonsus had in mind when founding the Congregation. Essentially and primarily we are a missionary Order and all of us wherever we may be should strive might and main to make and keep the missions our specialized work, our own particular Redemptoristic way of bringing to men the way of salvation.

William Gaudreau C.SS.R.
Superior General and Rector Major.

Statement by Father General Gaudreau on the missionary nature of the Congregation.

All Redemptorists agree on the missionary nature of the Congregation. The debates between the "new breed" of Redemptorists and the older generation, such as Gaudreau, were about method. Gaudreau's statement hung in several Redemptorist bedrooms around the world and might have been penned by any of the younger missionaries in the Toronto Province.

If the problem was not obedience, the students would obey this order and go to where they were sent. If the University of Windsor or the lecturers were part of the problem, sending the students elsewhere would save some of the vocations. In the long run, the returned students would bring back to the Toronto Province new experiences, languages, and a wider view of the Congregation. In an attempt to satisfy some of the student demands, Lockwood asked Gaudreau to remove Father Murphy, who had been adamant in his criticisms of the students, and name Gerry Grant in his stead as a provincial consultor. Gaudreau objected that it would undermine authority by acceding to the students' requests. To Boyce, Gaudreau wrote a reprimand for his action in dividing the province further with the brief.[41] All of these actions in the name of authority would drive more young Redemptorists out of the Toronto Province, but as Ray Schmitt said, "St. Alphonsus was so right 'rather a dozen good Redemptorists than a hundred poor ones.'"[42] This presupposed that those who left were poor Redemptorists.

On the morning of 18 November 1965 Lockwood met with the entire seminary body and announced the dispersal. There was no dialogue and no appeal. Three were sent to the Aylmer Seminary in the Ste-Anne-de-Beaupré Province; four went to Oconomowoc, Wisconsin, in the St. Louis Province; four went to Esopus, New York, in the Baltimore Province; three went to Echternach in Luxembourg; four went to Gars am Inn, in West Germany; two went to Shrewsbury, England; and two to Galway, Ireland. Of these twenty-two men, fourteen were ordained, but most eventually left the Congregation. The Redemptorists, however, could not see the future that morning. The lecturers were transferred one by one to other jobs, and the rector left the Congregation. Soon, nothing remained but the building, a few lecturers under contract to the University of Windsor, a few brothers to keep the building standing, and a few arts students who took all of their courses at the University. The Toronto Province had lost what it had taken a generation of Redemptorists to build. The seminary was gone.

Traditional obedience required every Redemptorist to be ready to leave at a moment's notice and the closing of the seminary was a successful example of traditional obedience. The news of the

Windsor closing spread throughout the Congregation, and student revolts against authority were repeated in some of the other seminaries, most notably in Oconomowoc, Wisconsin. The same tough attitude towards the students was immediately implemented in the St. Louis and Baltimore provinces.

Whether these dispersals were successful in better preparing the students for their future in the Congregation and the Church is another question, impossible to answer. Almost none of the students stayed in the Congregation. The reasons for leaving were as varied as the men who left. Overall, the one thing that can be said is that the unsettled state of the Church, of the Congregation, and even of the nature of religious life and of priesthood brought each member to reconsider his former commitments. There was a "confusion not only about the nature of religious life in general (as a social institution), but also about the charism, mission, membership, and structures of individual communities and the attempts of individual religious to live out their religious commitments," a confusion which continued for the rest of the twentieth century.[43]

9

"The New Breed," 1965-75

On the same morning as the dispersal of the Windsor students, John Lockwood began the updating of the Toronto Province. He announced to the rectors who had gathered for a provincial consultation that it was time to rebuild. Lockwood established three commissions: one on ministry, one on clerical formation, and one on the formation of the brothers. The province's rectors decided that renewal and dialogue would be improved with a certain amount of democracy and therefore voted further members to the commissions.[1] Together, the elected and the ex-officio members began an incredible amount of work in studying and redefining the Redemptorist identity and mission in English Canada. The history of the Redemptorists of English Canada for the decade after the end of the Second Vatican Council is a history of renewal in the face of declining numbers.

The decline continued rapidly after the close of the Vatican Council in December 1965. The *Toronto Star* of 23 April 1966, in an article appropriately titled "Exodus," wondered whether the Redemptorists may have been the hardest hit of all Canadian religious communities. The article might have been right. Between 1965 and 1970 forty-six priests and students formally left the Toronto Province and a dozen more left without even requesting their dispensation. Twenty-seven Redemptorists died in the same period, while only twenty joined. The brothers fell from fifty to thirty. In all, the Toronto Province suffered a net loss of almost seventy-five people, or almost 40 per cent, falling from over two hundred members in 1965 to just over one hundred and thirty at the end of 1970. The Edmonton Province suffered a similar decline. In summary, the Redemptorists of English Canada had lost over half of their members since the start of the Vatican Council.

The Commissions

As part of their re-examination, the Redemptorists of Toronto reopened the same debate that had consumed them ever since they had opened their first house in North America. The Commission on Ministry asked: what was a missionary congregation doing in parishes? It proposed that the English-Canadian Redemptorists move out of some of the parishes and found a new mission house "for the 'New Breed' of missionaries." Arthur Ryan complained,

This procession of the Sodality of the Blessed Virgin Mary, Toronto, in the early 1960s and other Redemptorist-sponsored devotions in parishes across Canada made the move away from parishes incomprehensible to many Redemptorists.

"How history does repeat itself!"[2] This so-called new breed looked very much like the old type of European Redemptorists who had trouble accepting the American parish. As for the Europeans themselves, they were finally accepting parishes, at the same time as the English Canadians were again questioning them. For older Canadian Redemptorists, to abandon the parishes automatically meant the end of any Redemptorist presence in Canada. For Boyce and the younger missionaries, this was a moot point, since there were dramatically fewer Redemptorists available to staff them. In the Edmonton Province, St. Gabriel's foundation in Athabaska closed in 1966.

The seven-member Commission on Ministry, headed by Edward Boyce, and the Commission on Clerical Formation, headed by Arthur Ryan, finally agreed on one crucial point: some parishes should be given back to their dioceses in order to free Redemptorists for missions. Where and when would be decided later.

Although the Brothers' Commission recommended greater efforts in recruiting new candidates, the Clerical Commission recommended closing all of the formation institutions: St. Mary's minor seminary in Brockville, St. Gerard's novitiate in Keswick, and Holy Redeemer College in Windsor. These recommendations, following the recommendation to close some parishes, further alarmed and polarized many members of the Toronto Province, some seeing in it another step toward suicide or, worse, a plot to hasten the death of the Toronto Province.[3] If the formation system closed down, how could the province recruit and renew itself?

The Redemptorists again reached a middle ground and decided to accept new applicants only if they had completed college degrees. The experience of the previous ten years showed that novices accepted immediately after high school had a poor record of persevering in the Congregation. In effect, the Redemptorists in both eastern and western Canada deferred their novitiates from 1966 to 1969 in order to give applicants from the minor seminaries time to get a degree before entering the novitiate. The novitiate at Keswick closed in 1966.

On his return from Rome, Lockwood met with the Provincial Assembly of March 1967, often labelled the Easter Meeting, and made a momentous announcement. Father General William

Gaudreau had granted permission to experiment in the apostolate and in community life. These changes would help the Redemptorists revise the constitutions and rules of the Congregation in line with the decrees of the Second Vatican Council. The Easter Meeting became the Toronto Province's first parliament. Since dialogue, democracy, and collegiality were still new to almost everyone, and hardly acceptable to some, chaos descended as many people tried to voice their opinions or refused to speak. Almost all community prayers and activities ended as individuals went their own ways, and most of the annals and chronicles of the daily activities of the foundations and their parishes, kept faithfully since 1874, stopped. There is almost nothing recorded of the many short-lived individual and community experiments with prayer, religious exercises, or other adaptations of the Rule. Events, experiments, and the many comings and goings were happening too quickly for any chronicler.

The Redemptorists were encouraged in their many experiments by the Second Vatican Council and by Pope Paul VI himself. The council had previously declared that all religious communities, in their "pursuit of perfect charity" through the evangelical counsels of poverty, chastity, and obedience, had to adapt and renew themselves "to the modern physical and psychic conditions of the members and, as required by the nature of each institute, to the needs of the apostolate, to the requirements of culture, and to social and economic conditions."[4] After the council, the pope continually challenged the religious communities of the world to adapt to the world while remaining faithful to their founders. It was an immense although beneficial challenge. For example, the Vatican Council's decree on liturgy allowed the adoption of the vernacular. Accordingly the Redemptorists adopted English in community prayers. While it stripped away some of the beauty of the Latin language, the use of English revitalized the prayer life of the brothers, many of whom had sometimes misunderstood or had never known what was being said before.

The Redemptorists had already held a 1963 General Chapter to revise their constitutions and rules, but that chapter had done little except to patch up the constitutions by abandoning some out-of-date rules. Pope Paul VI issued norms for the implementation of the renewal of religious life in August 1966, emphasizing fidelity to the gospel, the charism or special grace and spirit of the founder, and the needs of the modern world. The Redemptorists had to face another General Chapter, called for 1967. Redemptorists around the world began to study the essential charism and works of the Congregation. Toronto's Commissions on Ministry and Formation prepared for the perennial challenge of applying the spirit of the Congregation to the contemporary situation in Canada.

The Redemptorists of North America asked the Toronto Province to study and discuss the first and perhaps the most important section of the constitutions: "The End of the Congregation." As just one example of the work that went into the revisions of the constitutions, at the 1967 Easter Meeting Lockwood immediately recommended that such an unhappy title be changed to: "The Purpose of the Congregation." The "End" of the Congregation briefly became "The Vocation of the Congregation" and, finally, the 1982 Constitutions settled on "The Mission of the Congregation of the Most Holy Redeemer in the Church." Every word, every sentence, and every section underwent the same scrutiny and change after 1967. Every change had a far-reaching theological, spiritual, and day-to-day impact on the way the Redemptorists would henceforth see themselves.[5]

The Toronto Easter Meeting of 1967 also reaffirmed the traditional unity of apostolic ministry and of personal sanctification: the salvation of one's own soul went hand-in-hand with the salvation of others. While certainly not an original idea in North America, where parishes often interfered with a close observance of the Rule, Toronto further declared that religious life should be structured according to the needs of the ministry, not according to Redemptorist traditions or personal desires for sanctification. Traditions could not take precedence over the calls of the ministry, such as parish work, or Redemptorists would become increasingly divorced from the actual challenges and needs of the Church. While the works would change, the Redemptorists were confident that their spirit of alphonsian zeal in imitation of Christ would remain to distinguish them from other congregations. Closer attention to ministry would also lead to holiness. In response to these suggestions by

Toronto and other provinces, the Congregation as a whole decided that the constitutions would henceforth restrict themselves to general norms, while each province would draft new provincial statutes in accordance with local conditions.

In May 1967 Gaudreau announced the triennial appointments. It created a sensation. While Lockwood, now sixty-one, was renamed provincial, both of his consultors were changed for younger men. Underscoring the importance of the younger element in the province, the popular former Windsor student adviser, Gerald Grant, became the first consultor. At forty-five, with his doctorate in psychology now completed, he represented a bridge between the older and the younger generations and their different approaches to religious life.

Edward Boyce (1968–70)

The choice of a second consultor was a greater surprise. Edward Boyce, the director of the London General Mission, the author of the Windsor brief, had been born in Saint John, New Brunswick, in 1932. He had attended St. Peter's School in Saint John and then left for St. Mary's, Brockville. He was professed in Montreal in 1952 and ordained in 1957. His theology studies in Windsor were followed by his second novitiate at the pastoral institute in Montreal. After preaching missions from 1959 to 1961 out of Montreal, he pursued further studies in sociology and general mission techniques in Lyons, France, and then worked as a parish priest in Prince Edward Island from 1962 to 1964. Since 1964 he had been working in Windsor. He had presided over the Ministry Commission since 1965. Considered as a possible consultor as early as 1965 when William Murphy tried to resign in protest at the commissions' recommendations, in 1967 Boyce became the leader of renewal in the administration of the Toronto Province. He and John Madigan began a "Redemptorist Survey for Renewal" that interviewed Redemptorists and bishops about needs and priorities in the province.[6]

The general mission in Windsor came to an end in 1967. As Boyce reported to the newspapers, unlike the general area mission of

Newfoundland of the late fifties where there were insufficient numbers of missionaries, "There were too many missionaries [each spending too little time on the mission] and they didn't know the people enough."[7] Boyce proposed that future missions would have Redemptorists training local diocesan priests, establishing ecumenical efforts to reach every denomination in a geographic area, holding fewer and shorter parish surveys, and investing in more advertising. The diocese successfully adapted the sociological studies, grouping parishes into pastoral zones with different pastoral approaches, which in turn led to more effective diocesan planning and better informed leadership. The bishop of London, Emmett Carter, asked that a general area mission be given to Middlesex County, which included the city of London.

In December 1967 Gaudreau, now aged seventy, announced his resignation. Lockwood had often offered Gaudreau his own resignation, partly because he felt that he could do nothing to help the province, but also out of fear that the province, perhaps even the Congregation, was dying. There was desperate need for new, more confident leadership to carve out a place for a reformed Redemptorist mission in the renewed Catholic world. With Gaudreau gone, Lockwood now presented his resignation to the new father general, Tarcisio Amaral of Brazil. Lockwood stressed the need for a provincial from the new breed of Redemptorists, capable of leading the Toronto Province into the future. In view of his own age and his inability to unite the different generations in the province, Lockwood boldly proposed that the Toronto Province experiment further with democracy by actually electing his successor.[8]

Amaral agreed. A chapter of forty-eight members, half of them elected and the other half ex-officio, met in January 1968 to elect a new provincial and a new administration. Lockwood first referred to the recent Roman General Chapter that had elected the chapter secretary, Tarcisio Amaral, to replace Gaudreau. He spoke on the need for new leadership, and then pointedly named Edward Boyce as the provincial chapter's secretary. Boyce immediately received twenty-two out of forty-eight votes. The balloting became tense as the chapter added two more members, one to represent

Japan and another to represent the brothers. The second ballot did not give Boyce the necessary two-thirds majority. Matthew Meehan, formerly rector of St. Patrick's, Toronto, and to some extent a conservative candidate, gained some votes. On the third ballot, Meehan's candidacy peaked and declined enough on the fourth and deciding ballot to give Boyce his two-thirds majority. At thirty-five, the youngest provincial in the Congregation, Boyce also became the first elected provincial in the history of the Congregation. When confirmed by Rome, Boyce composed an oath of office that pointed the way to renewal.

> I, Edward Boyce, duly elected and approved Provincial of the Toronto Province, of the Congregation of the Most Holy Redeemer, do hereby swear, with the help of God and my confreres, to uphold the spirit of the Congregation according to the mind of the Church and our Holy Founder Alphonsus. So help me God.[9]

In the future, the Redemptorists would be asked to think more about the spirit of the Congregation than its laws and its traditions; more about the mind of the Church and St. Alphonsus than what the Church and St. Alphonsus had actually done in the past.

As provincial, Edward Boyce delivered several papers and talks describing what he saw as the "signs of the times." He explored ways religious communities could respond to the signs and become relevant. In June 1968 Boyce issued a policy paper which stated the need for change and adaptation in several elements of Redemptorist life. Two memorable statements summarize his key thoughts. First, "Modern man has been dramatically described as a surfer. His world is waves of change. He rides the waves." Second, "Those who hope and pray that things 'will settle down' are doomed to unhappiness." Both statements argued for a positive approach to change. The rest of the statement promoted Redemptorists as missionaries, formed according to the spirit of St. Alphonsus, rather than modelled on his works. Alphonsus, Boyce reminded his readers, was above all dedicated to the most abandoned of souls, not to their institutions. The contemporary world demanded different work but always the same spirit: a missionary vocation.

Such reasoning emphasized deinstitutionalization so that Redemptorists could gain more mobility and flexibility for the missions. Although buildings and parishes were important and Redemptorists would continue to maintain them, the spirit was to be at all times a missionary one. Authority and responsibility, even in the matter of personal expenses and budgeting, were delegated so that individuals could grow in personal responsibility for their practice of poverty. Community was necessary for individual growth and the province's common goals.[10]

In an oft-repeated and sometimes misunderstood statement, Boyce proposed that the Redemptorists "separate to unite." Deep differences of opinion about the kind of missions, the kind of life, and the kind of future the Redemptorists should have divided them everywhere. Boyce proposed that these groups should, in theory, separate from each other and form new, united communities to work toward the common goal of mission to the English-Canadian Catholic Church. In general practice, it meant that younger Redemptorists would live with like-minded younger Redemptorists and older Redemptorists would live with like-minded older confreres. Parish-minded Redemptorists would live together in parishes while missionaries would live in mission houses. While the statement was well received as a working document, some saw it as a complete revision if not a destruction of their lives as a religious community. Separation created further divisions and mutual incomprehension.[11]

The year 1968 was the fiftieth anniversary of the foundation of the Toronto Province. The celebrations fostered the feeling that the Toronto Province, in spite of problems, led the way into the future of religious life. Redemptorists around the world were closely watching Toronto's first elected provincial and were prepared to elect their own. Bernard Johnson of Edmonton teamed with Boyce to present a common Canadian approach at the North American regional meetings discussing changes in the Redemptorist Rule. Johnson borrowed Boyce's modern language for his Christmas message of 1968 and prepared Edmonton for a province-wide election.

Father Grattan Feehan became Edmonton's first elected provincial. Boyce's flair for striking phrases and his thoughts on the future of Redemptorist and religious life made an impact far beyond the Congregation. Both the Sisters of Service and the Sisters of Charity of St. Vincent de Paul invited Boyce to analyse their congregations and make recommendations for their own renewal. His statements about the new sociological trends in religious life were published and repeatedly cited.[12]

In faithfully copying the restructuring of the Roman General Chapter, the Toronto chapter tried to move away from the hierarchical models of the past. The province tried to institute co-responsibility by adding four councillors to an expanded provincial council. The new council thus had a Consulta proper, comprising the provincial and his two consultors (also called the ordinary provincial council) for routine and confidential matters. Four councillors joined the three Consulta members in a seven-man extraordinary provincial council to discuss major matters such as implementing chapter decisions, drawing up major appointments, negotiating property transactions, establishing or suppressing foundations, and formulating general policy for formation, vocations, apostolates, and experimentation.[13] To offset any arbitrary decision, the four council members could theoretically outvote the Consulta. Within the Consulta itself, the two consultors could outvote the provincial. The new council immediately acted as the administrative body for the province.

As one of its first acts, the council closed down the *Madonna Magazine*. In 1960 there had been seventeen thousand paid subscriptions.[14] In the turmoil of the Vatican Council, a devotional magazine became less popular, and by 1967 subscriptions had fallen to ten thousand. This was still a respectable number, but production costs had risen dramatically, because the magazine now maintained a separate building, lay employees, and expensive colour printing. The year 1967 saw a net loss in the operation of the magazine. After forty years of almost continuous monthly publication promoting devotion to Mary as Our Lady of Perpetual Help, the *Madonna Magazine* came to an end in April 1968.

The Toronto Province council also closed the Italian parish at Our Lady of Mount Carmel, which then had fewer than thirty families. Other Italian parishes flourished in the Toronto suburbs, so the need for Our Lady of Mount Carmel had vanished. The church became a Chinese Catholic centre in 1970 under diocesan care.

When the Redemptorists finished consolidating their work, they began to experiment with new forms of Redemptorist religious life.

Experiments

The Commission on Clerical Formation had recommended that the missionaries be formed in a new kind of second novitiate at the Divine Word Institute in London, Ontario, where Bishop Emmett Carter and Bernhard Haering were guest lecturers. The Commission on Ministry, for its part, recommended that the new missionaries be grouped into bands of four men, the first such band to be stationed at Holy Redeemer College. It would serve as a model mission house and as a help to the general mission of the City of London. Each mission house would be renamed a pastoral renewal centre, and every member stationed in such a centre had to be prepared to work as a missionary.

The Windsor team of missionaries unfortunately found it difficult to integrate into the life of Holy Redeemer College. The college also found it hard to adapt to the new missionaries since it already suffered from the tensions between lay arts students and professed theology students. The mission team transferred to St. Alphonsus, Windsor. New conflicts between missionary and parish lifestyles and schedules then brought the team to move to a house in the city. The mission team travelled in eastern Canada wearing secular clothes, encouraging school children to call the priests by their first names, and introducing audio-visual materials and a lighter atmosphere to the mission. Some controversies erupted among more conservative-minded parents and clergy who objected to late-night meetings, group confessions, communion in the hand, a more casual approach to church authority, an increased emphasis on personal conscience, and the lesser emphasis on heaven, hell, and original sin. Father Charles Coughlin of American radio fame and now in Detroit where the missionaries often visited, reportedly called the

Canadian mission team, "the satanic sons of St. Alphonsus." The team felt it was merely preaching according to the spirit of the Vatican Council. The controversies and complaints involved several dioceses questioning the team's orthodoxy. Bishop Carter of London at first parried the complaints from the other dioceses by stating that the Redemptorists often overemphasized the value of shock treatment. Privately, he informed Provincial Boyce that he did not care to spend his time protecting the Redemptorist mission band stationed in the London diocese.[15]

Unfortunately, these criticisms were echoed by fellow Redemptorists. Many opposed the team's methods and their outspoken attacks on the traditional Redemptorist mission, education, and government in the province. The team consciously invited debate by advocating greater flexibility and representation in government, greater shared responsibility, and an immediate withdrawal from both Brockville and Holy Redeemer College. By March 1969 the mounting criticisms forced Boyce to suspend the renewal team's missions, to the great bitterness of its members. By 1972 all four young men had left the Congregation. This experiment became a warning to later teams of the difficulties in creating a radically new form of mission and in winning a place for it within both the Redemptorist Congregation and the English-Canadian Catholic Church.

A similar experiment involved the brothers. In their earlier attempts to be accepted and integrated into the Redemptorist mission, the brothers at first restricted themselves to protesting their second-class status in such small things as the signs and stationery describing the Congregation as the "Redemptorist Fathers." Under Lockwood, the brothers gained the right to keep their baptismal name in religion instead of being given a new name. Individual brothers followed courses and obtained certificates in a variety of disciplines, such as hospital care. In 1967 the idea that the brothers could actually participate in the Redemptorist mission in more than an auxiliary role took hold and individual brothers began to explore special apostolates. They all approved a 1968 worker experiment in downtown Toronto which created a separate brothers' community inspired by the priest-worker experiment of the 1940s and 1950s.

Three brothers and a priest lived together, but they did not work in a church or parish. They took jobs in factories and hospitals so that they could share their lives with others. One priest, Father Ralph McQuaid, was the diocesan chaplain to the Young Christian Workers. One of the brothers helped McQuaid in the Y.C.W. and worked with alcoholics. Another brother cooked in a senior citizens' residence. Their salaries went to support the house and the community needed very few subsidies from the Toronto Province. Their influence in opening up the active apostolate to the brothers was immense. Unfortunately, it did not last. The young brothers who volunteered for this new apostolate felt that their thinking and their lives had cut them off from the Congregation. They left the Congregation and the experiment ended after a year.[16]

That is not to say that the experiment had no consequences. Father McQuaid found that many of the poorer workers in Toronto were recently arrived European immigrants and Maritime Canadians looking for better jobs. He went on to found the Apostolate of the Maritimers. This personal apostolate concentrated on helping those who were uprooted from their Maritime homes and had not yet found a place in Toronto. McQuaid established a store-front drop-in "Atlantic Centre," and worked with a social worker to help fix broken lives, broken homes, and the alcoholism that often accompanied both.

At the same time that the Apostolate of the Maritimers began, the Redemptorists founded an experimental team ministry in Nova Scotia, the one province where the Redemptorists had not yet established themselves, but which had had a growing percentage of Roman Catholics and a number of Redemptorist candidates over the years. Halifax, the seat of the archdiocese, and home to a third of the 286,000 Catholics in the province, was the logical place to begin. A house was established in Springhill in August 1968 to care for the parish of St. John the Baptist and two nearby prison farms for a three-year period. The Redemptorists withdrew three years later; there was not enough work in Springhill to keep more than two men busy, hardly enough for a community. Furthermore, the Redemptorists could not guarantee a long-term commitment on the part of any one man for the difficult chaplaincy work which the archbishop had requested.[17] The prison apostolate, however, did become a long-term commitment on the part of individual Redemptorists. For the rest of the twentieth century, one or more Redemptorists could be found in prison chaplaincy.

Another well-publicized experiment, begun in Montreal in 1968, soon took precedence over the traditional parish approach. Some of the younger priests wishing "to work in an urban apostolate with the special purpose of attaining those people who are indifferent to the Church and are not reached through present structures ('secular man')" proposed a house in Montreal. The Lakeshore Experimental Project with three priests was established in Pointe Claire in the west end of the island of Montreal. This team began to establish parish councils, conduct parish opinion surveys, create ecumenical chaplaincies in local apartment buildings, lead parish adult education programs, provide individual counselling, and introduce marriage encounter weekends to the Montreal archdiocese. The men threw themselves into community activities such as the West Island Social Action Committee, the YMCA, the Federation of Catholic Charities, and juvenile court. In 1970 one of the priests, Clarence Kenney, was hired by Northern Electric as a counsellor but tragically died soon afterwards in a car accident. In his memory, the foundation was renamed Kenney House. When the province of Quebec restructured its educational system to encourage post-secondary technical and professional education (the CEGEP system), the non-denominational John Abbott College was founded for English-language post-secondary education. Paul Curtin became one of the pastoral animators and participated in the design of the college.[18]

Montreal's St. Ann's foundation continued to decline, mainly because demographics and urban highway planning squeezed the area dry of any residential housing. The Redemptorist foundation closed in September of 1969, the parish was broken up the following year, and any land not expropriated by the City of Montreal over the years was returned to its original owners, the Sulpicians. To maintain a parish presence in Montreal, Father Raymond Fitzgerald went to St. Richard's parish in Côte-St-Luc to help with the delicate change from a French to an English parish, and Martin Foley replaced him in a temporary assignment that lasted twenty years.

The problem of staffing foundations and experimental apostolates with a declining Redemptorist membership was temporarily allayed by closing St. Ann's. The Lakeshore Experimental Project, with its mission to "disillusioned" urban humanity, became the English-language Redemptorists' Montreal presence and one of the most exciting events in the lives of those who participated in it.[19]

In June of 1969, Boyce was re-elected provincial by vote of the whole province. Ninety-five per cent of those eligible to vote did so and Boyce obtained 81 per cent of the vote. It was a high measure of approval for the expanded, more collegial council, for the experiments in Nova Scotia and Montreal, and for Boyce's overall missionary emphasis. These elections brought few changes in leadership: Richard Bedard was again elected first consultor and Frank Maloney second consultor. In the turmoil of the years after the Second Vatican Council, it seemed as if the Toronto Province had successfully redefined itself as a missionary presence in Canada.

The Church, however, never stood still. The Sacred Council for Religious and Secular Institutes in early 1969 totally reordered the entire section of the 1917 Code of Canon Law concerning novitiate and formation. In November the Sacred Council declared that lay brothers could not hold governance positions in clerical institutes comprising both priests and brothers. The Toronto provincial chapter thereupon recommended a temporary suspension of the recruiting of brother of candidates and declared a moratorium on building projects. By April of the following year no clerical or brother novices remained, and the novitiate was suspended.

Closing St. Mary's College, Brockville

The decision to close St. Mary's College originated in Ryan's provincial visitation of 1961 and it had been revived in the 1966 Commission on Ministry chaired by Boyce. In 1966 the province was split: half of the men wanted to keep the minor seminary, and half wanted to sell it. Against Brockville were the facts that it was expensive, that it used up valuable men, and that other congregations had a vocation for teaching, while the Redemptorists did not. In Brockville's favour was the fact that the vast majority of priests in

St. Mary's Choir, Brockville, directed by Mageste Santopinto

the entire history of the Toronto Province had come out of Brockville. After 1920 only thirteen or fourteen young men out of over five hundred and sixty joined the Redemptorists without ever having attended Brockville. In recognition of these figures, the Redemptorists built a new combination gym and auditorium, Macdonnell Hall, for over $200,000 and dedicated it in 1962. A new faculty building was built in 1963 for over $300,000, while renovations of the older buildings in 1964 cost another $60,000. Brockville nevertheless produced fewer young men for the novitiate, and there were fewer Redemptorists available to teach there.

The number of Brockville students dropped because young men and their families continued to favour local high schools over residential private schools. Few families now sent a boy away from home for education unless he needed special education. Fewer young men therefore learned much about the Congregation and did not have the chance to consider a Redemptorist vocation. To fill the fast-emptying building the Redemptorists opened Brockville to young men who were considering a vocation, although not specifically to the Redemptorists, but the numbers did not increase. The college stood practically empty, and it seemed with every new departure from the Congregation that the Redemptorists would need to spend more money in hiring lay teachers.

The chapter of January 1968 which elected Boyce as the new provincial voted to close Brockville by a vote of forty-four to two. The provincial administration tried to sell the property for what it had cost over the years: $2 million. This was unrealistic, especially since the evaluation was considerably less. Boyce and his consultors learned that no educational group could even afford such a price and finally agreed to sell the property for $650,000. The only interested buyers at the time, the Texas-based Bereans, a Congregationalist movement originating in Presbyterianism, signed a lease-to-own agreement in 1969. Incorporated as Grenville Christian College, the Bereans developed close ties with the Anglican Church of Canada, excellent relations with the Redemptorists, and provided a private Christian secondary-school education that was the envy of many. The Redemptorists at the time, however, received some sharp criti- cism from a less than ecumenically-minded columnist in the *Catholic Register* for letting the college go to Protestants.[20]

Every minor seminary in every Redemptorist province and in almost every religious community faced the same situation. Residential private schools had fallen out of favour with the Catholic public. Enrolment declined even at Holy Redeemer College, the ultra-modern Edmonton minor seminary. In 1969 not one of the mere thirty-seven students had the intention of joining the Redemptorists. When enrollments declined further and the costs of keeping the building rose, the Edmonton Province followed Toronto's lead and closed its college in the summer of 1970. The college then became a retreat and adult education centre.

The Redemptorists of the Toronto Province tried to remain active in the Kingston archdiocese of which St. Mary's College had been so long a part. They had recently established a parish using the college chapel in 1965 for the Catholics of Maitland near the col- lege. After the Brockville College was sold and the parish closed, the Redemptorists took over the newly created Blessed Sacrament parish in Amherstview with the mission of St. Linus in Bath and a chaplaincy in Collins Bay Penitentiary. Russell Conway cared for the parish of the Annunciation in Enterprise, Ontario, also in the archdiocese. True to their definition of the Redemptorist missionary vocation as one demanding a temporary or short-term mission-like presence, the parishes were returned to archdiocesan care in 1972. Since then the Redemptorists have maintained a presence in the Kingston archdiocese by prison chaplaincy work.

A Year Out

When novice master George Glover requested his dispensation from the priesthood, the last and most important aspect of the entire Redemptorist formation program fell apart. Of the seven novices who had begun in August of 1969, five had already left and another was preparing to leave. There were only two novices left at 422 St. Germain Avenue, the provincial residence in Toronto, and some students attending St. Michael's College at the Toronto School of Theology while living at 70 Edith Drive. For lack of anyone else available, and in the belief that young people should be with young people – perhaps as a last-ditch effort in coping with the younger generation – twenty-seven-year-old Paul Curtin from the Lakeshore Experimental Project was named novice master in January 1970. He continued to work in Montreal and commuted to meet with the students.

Curtin found the remaining students casual, almost indifferent towards community, authority, eucharist, and ordination. They had had only two common liturgies in the previous month and had made no effort to meet for common prayer or recreation. Perhaps the students unthinkingly reflected the attitudes of the novice master who had just left the Congregation and the priesthood. Quite definitely, the seminarians were living their lives as individual university students without any reference to Redemptorist life or community. Whatever the students' motivation, Curtin's first report suggested closing down the novitiate. There were serious doubts in his mind about the validity of the novitiate year already half completed. Closing the novitiate would give the Redemptorists some time to reshape their own lives and educational program before inviting people to join them.

The provincial council was dismayed at the preliminary report but immediately accepted it. Four members on the council proposed to close not only the novitiate program but the entire formation program for a year and send the students home to think about their commitment to the Congregation. The three other councillors recommended transferring the students to another province. Boyce himself argued for the more radical proposal because "it was one thing for students to be challenged 'verbally' on a university campus and something else when all supports are removed and students have to maintain themselves over an extended period of time in face of the world at large." Boyce swayed the council. The final decision declared that:

> In view of the many tensions and misunderstandings generated by:
> 1. a breakdown in effective dialogue and communication
> 2. difficulties indigenous to small group living for students
> 3. problems experienced in relating studies at the Toronto School of Theology with an effective program of Redemptorist formation, and
> 4. the fact that no acceptable program of Redemptorist formation has yet been devised to answer present needs,
> the Council has unanimously decided to suspend the formation program for students in theology from May 1, 1970 to September 1, 1971.[21]

The outraged students wrote to the council that stopping Redemptorist formation did not necessarily have to mean stopping studies in theology. For those students who had finished their novitiates in previous years, becoming Redemptorists had already delayed studies towards ordination and ministry by at least the novitiate year. To delay studies for ordination even further was incomprehensible. In fact, the problems in the formation program lay more with the Toronto Province not providing competent people and not knowing where it was going than with the students, all of whom had already demonstrated their commitment through years at Brockville, a year in novitiate, or the past year at the Toronto School of Theology. It was illogical to stop Redemptorist formation when one of the problems identified was the lack of Redemptorist formation on the university campus. Why could not Toronto send its students to another Redemptorist province? All in all, it seemed to the students and to many of the priests that the Toronto Province was intent on repeating the Windsor dispersal of 1965, by having the students assume responsibility for its own personnel problems.[22]

The councillors, for their part, were being battered by the loss and departure of many of their former school friends, co-workers, and confreres, all brothers in religion. They doubted the spirit of the Redemptorist formation the young men had received from those who had recently left. The councillors reasoned that the students needed to be tested and decided that only those prepared to make sacrifices for their commitment, such as another year of novitiate after spending a year away from the Congregation, would be accepted. The council refused to renew the temporary vows of the students or to recommend them to permanent vows. None of the temporarily-professed students returned. Not surprisingly, removing all supports for religious life and ordering people to leave failed to create any commitment on the part of the abandoned students. After the students left, the Redemptorists, especially Raymond Corriveau, began the slow work on a new formation program.

In spite of these problems, Boyce reported on 21 June 1970 that the Redemptorists were now ready to face the future. The English-Canadian Redemptorist involvement in the religious life of Canada continued to grow. One Redemptorist, Gerald Grant, worked as director of research for the Canadian Religious Conference, which united every religious community in Canada; another, Emmanuel Demerah, was director of English publications for Novalis, a Catholic press. Boyce identified disunity as a continuing problem, but in a telling phrase, he described the division as one between those who were mission-minded and those who were maintenance-minded. To promote the missions, Boyce argued that the province needed to get out of maintaining parishes in the same way it had withdrawn from its educational institutions. Toronto needed a list of priorities that would determine which parishes the Redemptorists could give back to their dioceses, in order to free men for missionary work.

The day after making this report, Boyce announced his resignation and left the Congregation. The morale in the province could hardly sink lower. The major seminary had closed, the minor seminary had been sold, the students had been dispersed or expelled, dozens of priests had left, including the vocation director, the novice master, and now the provincial himself. The value of Boyce's year-long sociological study and final report on closing parishes in the Toronto Province was overlooked, even rejected, in the reaction to his departure.

Boyce's resignation was not unexpected in Rome. Roman authorities had recently informed him that the Canadian bishops took exception to his many public statements. The Redemptorist authorities had also been surprised at his stance on several issues contradicting St. Alphonsus's own views. Boyce had strongly supported lifting the requirement of celibacy for diocesan priests, with the idea that a married diocesan clergy would be sufficiently different from the celibate religious orders to give candidates for ordination a clear choice. But on 24 June 1967 the pope had issued *Sacerdotalis Coelibatus*, which dashed hopes that the Catholic Church would soon have married priests. Boyce had also argued for the restructuring of the Ontario Catholic separate school system on the New Brunswick model, which had a single provincial administration for all school boards. Such a system, Boyce argued, would promote ecumenism and save separate school money for other purposes. The bishops, school trustees, and school boards of Ontario immediately denounced Boyce for promoting the "abolition" of their schools. Articles calling him a crackpot and a renegade appeared in the press. Boyce's immediate response to the opposition was to harden his position. "To give in to such pressures," he wrote, "would be to countenance the end of renewal in the Church."[23]

Boyce thought of issuing a public rebuttal to the criticisms but eventually decided to resign and leave religious life. He had come to realize that he could do nothing more within the

Congregation's structures. He himself had become an obstacle to change for some of the older members in the Toronto Province. As the author of the Windsor brief of 1965, then as a consultor, and even as provincial, he had never been trusted or accepted by a significant number of Redemptorists. They saw in him the author of the collapse of the entire formation system, and even the instigator of a larger plot to destroy the Redemptorists. His departure would add to the difficulties the Redemptorists and the Church were facing in maintaining their present structures, but in some small way, through God's providence, Boyce hoped it could bring the province, the Congregation, and the Church to accept further change for the better. In fact, Boyce's election to the provincial chair and his subsequent departure forced his opponents to turn their attention and their individual commitments away from any fallible authority figure, even a provincial, to the spirit of St. Alphonsus embodied in the Redemptorist Congregation as a whole and to the Church embodied in the people of God. His departure furthered a spiritual renewal in the province which his staying could not accomplish. In a way, this was exactly the goal Boyce and the new breed of Redemptorists hoped to achieve. A tentative unity began to grow among the remaining members.

Richard Bedard (1970–72)

Vicar-Provincial Richard Bedard automatically became acting provincial with Frank Maloney and Kleinnart Johnson as his acting consultors. Bedard had been the vocation director under Arthur Ryan in 1955 and had been part of the successful recruiting drive to fill Brockville with one hundred young men. In 1956 he had accepted the position of Japanese treasurer, by which he raised money for the Japanese missions. He had a heart condition which restricted his activity after 1959, but the Vatican Council and the incredible changes of the 1960s saw him supervising the experiments, especially as Boyce's vicar-provincial. Boyce had spent much time travelling to local communities or attending the General Chapter in Rome, and Bedard had frequently been the acting provincial. Therefore an element of continuity prevailed. Bedard, Maloney, and Johnson had

Richard Bedard (1916–86)

all participated in the previous decisions. The Provincial Chapter of September 1970 confirmed Bedard in office and elected Frank Maloney and Raymond Corriveau as consultors.

Bedard dedicated himself to rebuilding the province. He believed that decentralization had gone too far; too many people had gone off on solo apostolates and they were asked to rejoin the province in common projects. The province therefore became less fragmented, more cohesive, and developed better morale. Next, Bedard's administration ended the Redemptorist second novitiate program with the Divine Word Institute, since the institute had been subjected to criticisms, directed notably at Redemptorist lecturers such as Boyce.

Finally, Toronto settled its long-standing squabbles with Edmonton. Edmonton's students were yet again orphaned in 1970 by Toronto's decision to close down its formation system and the Edmonton Province was forced at great expense to establish a house of studies for the western students at 1303 King Street in Toronto so that its students could continue their courses at St. Michael's College.[24] These Toronto-caused expenses added to those Edmonton suffered from its minor seminary, Holy Redeemer College, which cost more as a retreat house than expected. Although Provincial Grattan Feehan searched for a buyer, interest charges on loans climbed, and the college could not be sold, especially in Alberta in the early 1970s before world oil prices made Alberta wealthy. Bedard explicitly set aside the argument that Toronto did not owe anything to Edmonton and stated that charity and mutual help were always necessary amongst Redemptorists. Because of several years of excellent fiscal prudence, Toronto's finances were in great shape. Grattan Feehan, in negotiations with Bedard and treasurer Frank Maloney, cleared up the final questions about Edmonton's stake in Windsor with Toronto buying out Edmonton's claim. This settlement and the sale of the Edmonton college in 1974 eased Edmonton's financial problems and improved relations between the east and the west.

While Bedard tried to apply the brakes to experimentation in order to rebuild a fragmented province, his consultors favoured even more experimentation. Dedicated advocates of the missionary vocation of the Congregation, both Frank Maloney and Raymond Corriveau demanded that the Redemptorists withdraw from some of the parishes in favour of experimental communities.[25] Boyce had already begun the withdrawal from Whitbourne in Newfoundland. There were only forty families in the parish, and the diocese had enough priests to staff it properly. The Redemptorists already had St. Teresa's parish in St. John's, which was large enough to support a full community and missionaries for the rest of Newfoundland. The Redemptorists agreed to sell their Whitbourne property at a loss to the diocese of Grand Falls and the bishop gave permission to withdraw. The last Redemptorist, Father Paul Doucet, left on 15 August 1971.

After prolonged balloting and painful discussions, the chapter of 1971 voted to follow through on Boyce's parting recommendations and withdraw from two more foundations by the following year, not only as a response to personnel shortages but to free men for the missions. The chapter asked the council to look at each foundation and judge the local church's need, the local Redemptorist community's opinion of their work there, the parishioners' evaluation of their work, the mission field attached to the foundation, and the ability of the Redemptorists to staff the foundation. In effect, the Redemptorists voted to return their wealthiest parishes to the dioceses that were best able to care for them. The Redemptorists looked at closing Charlottetown, Sudbury, Assumption in Toronto, Holy Redeemer College in Windsor, Peterborough, Saint John, and London, in that order. Holy Redeemer College could not be sold for anything approaching what it cost to build, because no one could afford it. The building took on a new role as the province's retreat house in 1972. In 1981 the novitiate also moved to the college to make use of its excellent facilities and library.

Redemptorists committed to individual parishes scrambled to create new, experimental ministries tied to their favourite parishes. At first, the Peterborough parish of St. Alphonsus under James Farrell succeeded. Farrell requested a team apostolate, because the diocese had asked the parish for a number of missions and retreats, a retreat centre, school or prison chaplaincy, or an adult spiritual education centre. The Edmonton Province loaned Gabriel Ehman for the retreat centre so that he could establish a similar house in western Canada. With Edwin McSherry and Emmanuel Demerah, Ehman planned the renewal centre in the former Peterborough rectory. Now renamed Emmaus House, it was to be a centre for preaching, devotions, medical-moral ethics consultations, missions, retreats, marriage encounter sessions, counselling, and prayer.[26]

Although the chapter voted to close two foundations, Bedard could not bring himself to comply. After withdrawing from every educational institution they had ever built, withdrawal from parishes seemed like suicide to too many Redemptorists. Against Corriveau and Maloney's insistence on the need to withdraw, Bedard joined the rest of the province in opposing the move as "a regressive step." He argued that parishes had become a tradition of the Congregation in North America and a move to disengage from them would lessen the credibility of Redemptorists with bishops "especially at a time when most dioceses are equally hard pressed for parish personnel." Bedard saw that even the idea of closing a parish foundation, no matter how logical from a missionary angle, upset the province's morale and would cause further dissent. Since more than half the men were strongly in favour of working in the exciting parish environment created by the Second Vatican Council, Bedard swayed his council to set aside the chapter's decision.[27]

Unfortunately, these years of controversy were very stressful for Bedard. He suffered another severe heart attack, and on doctors' orders, withdrew from administration.

Alphonsus Thomas (1972–75)

On the day he was born in 1920 Alphonsus Thomas was baptized by a Redemptorist at St. Patrick's parish, Quebec City, and as a young boy he attended the parish schools there. Since the Redemptorists were the only English-speaking priests he knew, he could not conceive of the priesthood apart from the Redemptorist Congregation. His novice master marked him out as sincere and earnest, with sane and practical judgment. His superiors agreed and sent him to study canon law at Laval University where he earned his doctorate in 1950. He taught in Woodstock from 1948 to 1951 before going to Rome for two years to study moral theology. He again taught in Woodstock and then in Windsor when the seminary was moved. When Windsor's theology program closed in 1965, Thomas became a hospital chaplain in Brockville, then a lecturer and chaplain at Marygrove College in Detroit across the river from Windsor. During all the years of turmoil, he had preserved a reputation of being objective, impartial, conservative, yet open-minded. He was elected provincial on the fourth ballot. Frank Maloney received the next highest number of votes and became the vicar-provincial.

Alphonsus Thomas was a compromise candidate, and it would be difficult for him to take any decisive action. Thomas knew it and said:

> To accomplish what may be expected of me, ... I would need to combine the zeal and prudence of St. Alphonsus with the practical dynamism of St. Clement and the miracle-working power of St.

Gerard, to say nothing of their outstanding holiness. To please all the confreres by agreeing with their divergent opinions concerning the priorities of our Redemptorist life and work, I would be involved in such contradictions that I would be in danger of becoming entirely confused. All I can promise is put whatever qualifications I have at the service of the Congregation to the best of my ability, and to trust in God to supply for my deficiencies.

I am fully aware that my election was by no means unanimous.[28]

Thomas never repudiated Boyce's statement that the various sections of the province had to separate in order to unite, but his style encouraged people first to unite. With this in mind, Thomas launched a discussion of the need for more prayer in the modern Canadian Redemptorist life. Prayer, he knew, was the foundation of Redemptorist life.

The chapter, which met after Thomas's election, accepted the decision to delay withdrawal from parishes, but it also urged the consideration of personnel shortages and of the province's desire to combine the parish apostolate with renewal preaching. It could not come to any conclusion and postponed the decision until April 1974. By this time the number of priests had dropped to ninety, and leaving a parish was more than a choice – it had become a necessity. Thomas, however, argued that the parish was the cell of the Church and should be the centre of Redemptorist energies and missions.[29] Before he would consent to close a parish foundation, he felt there were other things to accomplish.

He encouraged all of the missionaries, old and young, to meet and compare notes, mission outlines, and sermons. He argued that there was still a place for the traditional mission system and the traditional sermons about the basic truths of the faith, along with newer forms of preaching. The province's missionaries supported this stand. They soon reached agreement that the eternal truths were always valid, but that they needed to be applied in a contemporary manner and adapted to the locality.[30] A community-living workshop

"NO! You can't keep the water bed!
Christ walked on water. He never slept on it!"

The imitation of Christ takes many forms.
A Redemptorist Priest is one.

The Redemptorist Priests
Rev. Eugene O'Reilly, C.S.S.R.   721 Coxwell Avenue   Telephone (416) 466-9265   Toronto M4C 3C3

Redemptorist Promotional material, c.1970s,
by cartoonist Fr. Toby McGivern

in 1973, directed by the Passionist Father Conleth Overman, helped bring the members of the province closer together. Retreats in common for the brothers in October of 1974, and for the priests immediately afterwards, were preached by the Redemptorist Kevin Donlan of the Dublin Province.

Donlan's presence in the province illustrated another theme in Thomas's leadership: inter-provincial cooperation, almost unheard of in previous years. In 1973, the Toronto Province invited the Irish Redemptorists to take over a foundation or even all of Newfoundland. When the Dublin Province declined, Toronto turned to other provinces for inter-provincial loans of personnel and cooperation. Some of Toronto's men studied at the University of

Montreal while living in a house of studies established by the Beaupré Province. In the renewed formation program designed by Raymond Corriveau, the Redemptorists rented a house at 721 Coxwell Avenue in Toronto and established Gerard House for its novices and students. In 1972–73, Toronto, Edmonton, and Yorkton held a joint novitiate and in 1973–74, a joint house of studies. These efforts led to one man being ordained in 1972 and two men being professed in 1973. The Edmonton Province opened Casa Kairos in Toronto at 582 Huron Street from 1974 to 1977 for its own students attending the Toronto School of Theology.

The years 1972–75 also helped to resolve a problem that the Redemptorists had to some extent caused among the Redemptoristines.

The Redemptoristines

Not bound by the demands of the priesthood like many of the men's congregations, modernization began sooner amongst women's orders. Around the world, and beginning in the 1950s in the Barrie community, the Redemptoristines abolished the differences between lay and choir sisters and explored active ministries, similar to the Sisters of Service, to balance the contemplative life. Younger Redemptoristines began to participate more visibly in the active life of the Church through writings and publications.

At the same time, the Redemptoristines at Barrie created daughter houses. These required experienced yet energetic nuns, thereby depriving the Barrie mother house of valuable skills, experiences, and of some of its youth and energy. The English-Canadian Redemptoristines in 1957 founded a house near the Baltimore Province's seminary in Esopus, New York. This was swiftly followed by a house in Liguori, Missouri, in 1960 for the St. Louis Province, and a house in Australia in 1965. Two others were loaned to Japan for a year and a third was loaned to a monastery in Vienna and did not return for twenty years. All told, eighteen young women were sent, leaving twenty-five women at Barrie.[31]

The community had always relied on the Redemptorists for financial and spiritual help. But now the Redemptorists could not send a priest from Toronto to Barrie. They suggested selling the Barrie monastery to raise money and offered free land for a new convent in Brockville. Since St. Gerard's novitiate in Keswick was empty, the Redemptorists offered Keswick to the Redemptoristines during the construction of a new Brockville convent. Unfortunately, the Redemptorists then decided to sell Brockville. Such uncertainty, added to the tensions brought on by the changes in religious life, created many frustrated, "bitter and confused" nuns.[32] By 1970 there were fourteen in residence and an average of ten living outside the Keswick monastery, four in a Toronto satellite community, studying, working, and trying to live a contemplative life while in the world. One former prioress had joined the charismatic movement and worked with Brockville's Bereans.

To stabilize the situation, Rome asked the Redemptoristines living outside the monastery to make a choice: live a contemplative life at Keswick, leave the Redemptoristines, or join "an active Congregation or Institute suited to their aspirations; for example the Sisters of Service." If the situation did not stabilize by 1972, the Keswick monastery would be suppressed and all of the Redemptoristines would be forced to seek other homes. The women living outside of the Keswick community pointed out that Keswick was not a Redemptoristine monastery but a Redemptorist novitiate in which they were only guests.[33]

Thomas argued successfully that more time be given to the Redemptoristines to find a new home and that the stressful threat of dissolution be removed.[34] The Redemptorists had already voted to sell Keswick in 1971, and had offered it to the Redemptoristines, but the nuns decided it was too large for them to handle. Twelve Redemptoristines left Keswick in December 1973 for the Morrow Park Toronto house of the Congregation of St. Joseph Sisters. The Keswick novitiate building was then sold in January of 1975. Although the Sisters of St. Joseph thought the Redemptoristines were "the greatest"[35] and hoped they would stay, after examining over fifty places, the Redemptoristines found a site in Fort Erie, in the St. Catharines diocese. Seven Redemptoristines moved there in 1976, ten years almost to the day since they left Barrie, determined to rebuild their community and to live the interim Rules formulated according to the Second Vatican Council.

The Redemptoristines, on a smaller scale, had experienced the same fate as the Redemptorists; in the aftermath of the changes introduced into religious life by the Second Vatican Council, they lost 50 per cent of their sisters, all of them younger, and were reduced "to their more elderly members." Of course, elderly is a relative term: in the 1960s and 1970s it meant anyone over forty. By 1976 the Redemptoristines were established in their new home, and some of those living outside community rejoined the order one by one. Other interested women began to explore a contemplative vocation. For the rest of the twentieth century, the Monastery of the Most Holy Redeemer in Fort Erie stabilized with an average of eleven members.

Closing Foundations

At the General Chapter of 1973, the Toronto Province reported that the worst fears of the post-council years had been laid to rest and confidence in the Congregation's survival, if not in Toronto's survival, had begun to return. Better communication, community prayer, higher educational and age requirements for entrance into the novitiate, and the new emphasis on missions had all given the province greater unity and purpose. The centenary celebration in October 1974 of the Redemptorists' first foundation in Canada, held in Quebec City, was a joyful occasion and was followed by a special mass of thanksgiving in St. Patrick's, Toronto, on 17 November.

In previous years Toronto had led the Congregation in introducing democracy, experimenting with new forms of ministry, and had first felt the consequences of the Second Vatican Council. Thomas's administration in Toronto effectively ended further experimentation. The pendulum swung back to parish missions. The chapter of April 1974 resolved to withdraw from two parish foundations and one experimental project by 30 June 1975. While letters and protests flowed to Rome from the parishioners and some of the Redemptorists, both the Holy Redeemer foundation in Charlottetown and St. Patrick's foundation in London were suppressed on 21 January 1975. The Lakeshore Experimental Community also closed in July 1974, partly to offset the criticism that the experiments used up men and money that could go to the parishes, and partly because no team could be assembled to live there.

When Alphonsus Thomas received less than 50 per cent of the votes on the first ballot for a second term of office to begin in 1975, he withdrew from the balloting, as did several other council members, leaving Frank Maloney on the second ballot as the only clear choice. Maloney was confirmed in office by Rome on 15 April 1975. During the chapter in June that elected Maloney's council and consultors, the possibility of the Toronto Province's demise was raised and vigorously rejected. The Redemptorists would remain in English Canada. Closing a few parish foundations did not mean the end of the Toronto Province.

The democratic process and the introduction of politics into Redemptorist life created unhappiness. Some Redemptorists saw little of the will of God and more of the will of men who seemed scarcely obedient to the Rule. The Rule itself changed from year to year and was even ignored in favour of experiments. The more traditional followers became confused in seeing their superior dismantling the traditional structures of Redemptorist life in English Canada. The proposals of the Redemptorist new breed, embodied in Edward Boyce's position papers from 1968 to 1970, were far-reaching and radical for their time. For a few years, disunity and polarization hindered any common missionary goal. But with time the Redemptorists developed a stronger commitment to the spirit of St. Alphonsus and to the purpose of the Congregation in promoting personal spiritual discipline while ministering to the Canadian Church.

By 1975 the world, the Congregation, and the Redemptorists of English Canada had changed. Gradually the radical ideas of the 1960s were judiciously postponed, modified, and adapted by Richard Bedard and Alphonsus Thomas in eastern Canada and by Grattan Feehan in western Canada. The majority of Redemptorists accepted democracy because it fostered collegiality and co-responsibility more concretely than any Roman directive could have done. Although numbers continued to fall, they fell through the many deaths of the older remaining Redemptorists, not through departures.

The Toronto Redemptorists of 1975 also welcomed three novices and the ordination to the diaconate of two students, while Edmonton celebrated the ordination to the priesthood of two of their men. The newest generation of Redemptorists was now in a position to consolidate the arrival of the new kind of Redemptorist life and mission in English Canada. Some might say that little had changed. Although Redemptorist life and missions had changed in externals, to most people their purpose seemed very much the same: to be missionaries striving for continual conversion and perseverance in their own lives and in the lives of their fellow Christians. As always, parish missions and devotions, especially for the poor and abandoned of Canada, continued to distinguish the Redemptorist from other religious congregations.

10

"Emerging Stability," 1975–93

Redemptorist life had by now changed so much with the addition of committees and councils creating corporate leadership that some Redemptorists looked less at one person, the provincial, for leadership. Nonetheless, elections made provincials more firmly the representative and public expressions of the corporate Redemptorist and continued to be the focal point through which individuals expressed and used their talents.

Frank Maloney had joined the Redemptorists after his discharge from the army in 1946. Born in 1919, he was forty-six years old and rector of Holy Redeemer in Charlottetown during the 1965 dispersal of the Windsor students. He later served as a councillor, treasurer, and as a consultor, participating fully in the decisions and events from 1968 to 1975. Maloney's election as provincial meant that the Redemptorists had chosen someone who would continue the updating of the Toronto Province. Such continuity lasted through both the elections of 1978 and 1981 in which the province resoundingly re-elected Maloney on the first ballot. The more conservative element in the province greeted Maloney's arrival with some apprehension, since he openly supported the continuing revision of Redemptorist life.

Throughout these nine years, Desmond Scanlan was first consultor. Professed in 1953 and ordained in 1958, he had a master's degree in education and, at forty-three, had already proved his dedication to the educational institutions and traditions of the province, especially as student prefect in Brockville and as prefect and rector of Holy Redeemer College in Windsor after 1965. Desmond Scanlan's presence on the council reassured some of the more conservative members that their views would be heard. In 1984 Scanlan was elected on the second ballot when, for the first time, he allowed his name to stand for election as provincial. While he identified with the conservatives of the province, he had also been so much a part of the administration in the previous twenty years that Maloney wrote that there would be no break in the transition. Scanlan's own popularity was never in question; he was re-elected in 1987 and in 1990, serving until the elections of 1993 when he withdrew his name from the lists. Both Maloney and Scanlan had the confidence of most members of the Toronto Province, both those who wanted to adapt to modern conditions and those who wanted to preserve the older forms of religious life.

The careful balancing act between continuity and change could also be seen in the election of Edmonton's provincials. Grattan Feehan had become the first elected provincial in 1969, and made way for the forty-two-year-old Albert Sterzer nine years later in 1978. Born in 1936 and professed in 1956, Sterzer had been ordained in 1963, being educated almost entirely in the Toronto Province. After six years with Sterzer, Edward Kennedy was elected in 1984 to continue Sterzer's efforts to modernize the Edmonton Province according to the needs of the day. Born in The Pas, Manitoba, a nephew to Father Kenneth Kennedy of the Toronto Province, Ed Kennedy had been one of the most popular teachers and student prefects at Brockville in the 1950s and the early 1960s. The founder of *Communication* in 1962, a Redemptorist bulletin sharing news and views about the modernization of Redemptorist life and mission, he continued as editor of this short-lived effort even after he opted to join the Edmonton Province in 1963. He became involved in community affairs as the first director of the Edmonton Archdiocesan Catholic Information Centre in 1966 and then as an elected alderman in the City of Edmonton. As one of the younger priests interested in updating Redemptorist life in Canada, he corresponded with the authors of the brief which challenged authority and the traditional seminary formation in the Toronto Province during the mid-1960s. Kennedy served nine years as provincial until 1993. All of Edmonton's provincials served as provincial consultors before, and often served after, their terms as provincials. All of them had been formed in the Toronto Province.

In 1975 Frank Maloney inherited a province with ten foundations, ninety-eight priests, twenty-six brothers, and two students, as well as a Japanese mission with about twenty men. The average age was just over fifty-seven. About half the Toronto Province lived in Ontario, where almost half of all English-speaking Catholics also lived. In western Canada, Grattan Feehan cared for sixty-two priests, one deacon, two students, and ten brothers, with an average age of fifty-five. Edmonton's seventy-five members lived in thirteen foundations. In 1984, when Scanlan and Kennedy became provincials, total membership had fallen to one hundred and fifty-eight, and the

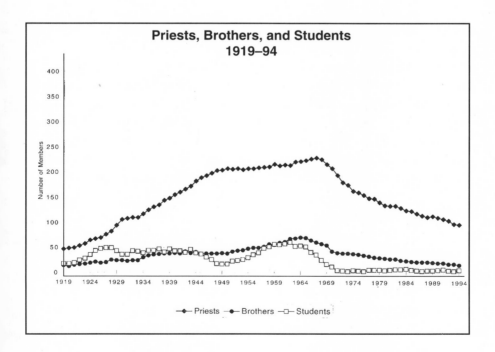

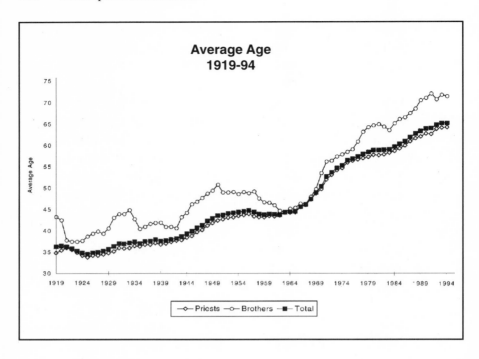

average age had crept up to sixty. At the beginning of 1993 the membership statistics were even more alarming. Just over one hundred and twenty members averaged sixty-five years of age. In the eighteen years between 1975 and 1993 the Redemptorists of English Canada declined by almost 40 per cent, while the average age increased by seven years. Clearly, in the minds of many Redemptorists, these years were years of decline and crisis.

Building Community

Maloney's efforts to strengthen the Toronto Province revolved around rebuilding community life. Redemptorists gathered the many chapter resolutions and provincial statutes written since 1968 into a single "Toronto Province C.Ss.R. Policy Handbook." Although some wished the traditional practices restored, Maloney announced the consensus of the province: there could be no going back to the old rules.[1] Although the Congregation's new Rule, the General Statutes, took effect on 1 January 1980 and were finally approved by the Holy See in 1982, the English translation arrived only in early 1983, just in time for further revisions in the light of the new Code of Canon Law promulgated by Pope John Paul II. Toronto and Edmonton then adapted their provincial statutes to the modern Church and Canadian conditions. Until then, the Redemptorists lived with some uncertainty as each community established its own particular rules. The Toronto Province set up a statutes commission which visited each community for discussion. The final text was approved by the General Curia in Rome in 1988. After years of solidifying community life, Maloney could take some satisfaction that the Redemptorists now had a renewed structure on both the general and the provincial levels to build their religious community.

Furthermore, although the Canadian Religious Conference had been in existence since 1958, Maloney brought the Redemptorists into a closer, active participation with the conference. This organization united the religious communities of Canada in studying common problems, such as education, departures, and aging. The hospitalization of elderly and disabled members had always been a major concern of the Redemptorists.[2] Increasing life expectancy and better medical attention made the need for chronic care facilities even more acute for everyone. St. Brigid's Home in Quebec City, Villa Maria Health Care Centre in Windsor, Providence Villa (now Providence Centre) and Lasalle Manor in Scarborough, Ontario and Rocmora Nursing Home in Saint John were all pressed into service for Redemptorists as were spare rooms in the nursing homes of other congregations. Maloney proposed as early as 1974 that Canada's religious communities pool their resources to provide long-term health and hospital care. The negotiations finally began to bear fruit in 1994 when over a dozen congregations, both men and women, and the archdiocese of Toronto agreed in principle to build a joint facility.

Maloney also scheduled workshops in 1976 led by Father Joseph Hurley of the Baltimore Province and Edwin Foley of the San Juan Vice-province. These workshops brought the members to explore Topics, Assumptions, Needs, Goals, Objectives, and Strategies (TANGOS). The workshops forced the Redemptorists to review their past. For many the 1976 sessions turned the page on the previous decade of acrimonious turmoil and brought them all to think about the future.

Finally, in 1978 the general assembly of the province asked the administration for help in establishing priorities for its future work. Maloney heard about a Goal Setting and Evaluation in Ministry (GEM) program used by the St. Louis Province. Father Bill Williams, who was in charge of the program, came in 1979 with a professional adviser, Charles Koop, to introduce new methods of planning for the future. Toronto's council composed a draft mission statement that described six goals: extraordinary preaching, realistic pastoral theology, community prayer, increased personnel, teamwork, and vocations to the brotherhood. By June 1980 a long-drawn out examination culminated in the province again defining itself in missionary terms. Maloney declared GEM helpful, but the Redemptorists could not agree on a uniform approach to preaching or on a uniform pastoral approach to alienated members of the Church.[3] In a word, the many workshops were good at confirming what Redemptorists thought about problems and goals, but were less helpful in finding solutions.

Nonetheless, the Toronto Province benefited from the workshop experiences, because the 1979 General Chapter in Rome directed all provinces to establish pastoral priorities by 1982. Toronto immediately set up a three-man committee in September 1980, moved to full study in May 1981 with a five-member committee, and by September 1981 prepared a document circulated to the entire province prior to the deadline. The provincial assembly ranked their pastoral priorities in the following order: formation, extraordinary preaching, and parish mission centres. In a fourth priority, the Redemptorists hoped that they could create a new, authentically Redemptorist outreach program. The rankings surprised no one; these had always been the priorities.

Formation

Formation and the promotion of vocations received first priority in the budgeting of both the Toronto and Edmonton provinces throughout the last quarter of the twentieth century. Besides subsidizing the students' tuition and their living expenses, in 1977 the Toronto

Province produced a thirty-minute film and five sets of film strips on Redemptorist life and work.

Maloney finished his first year as provincial in 1976 by accepting the final profession of the last two Brockville graduates to persevere in the Congregation, David Furlonger and Gerard Pettipas. A new era began that year with the acceptance of three novices who had never known the minor seminary at Brockville. Gerard House had become too small for all the novices and students, so the Redemptorists purchased 7 Howland Avenue in central Toronto in 1976. The students and novices moved into Howland Avenue's Gerard House in January 1977 and went for studies at nearby St. Michael's College and at the Toronto School of Theology. The move to what looked and felt like a private home and to a formation program geared to individuals and small groups attracted several young men in Toronto. When space at the new Gerard House became a problem, the Redemptorists took advantage of the situation to create a separate program for the novices, and the novitiate moved to Edmonton in 1979, to Ireland in 1980, and then to Holy Redeemer College in 1981. In 1986 one young man was sent to Beaupré for his novitiate year.

The 1974 sale of the minor seminary, Holy Redeemer College in Edmonton, allowed the western Redemptorists to purchase Scala House in Edmonton in 1975, replaced by Clement House in 1987. Similar to Toronto's Gerard House, it welcomed students and novices into a small group-setting while sending them for studies at the nearby University of Alberta.

The years from 1975 to 1984 were also years dedicated to the continuing formation of the professed members. Constantly having to deal with financial matters, Maloney often asked himself how a Redemptorist could live a vow of poverty in the materialistic culture of North America. With the sale of their minor seminaries and other properties, and with fewer students to support, the Redemptorists found themselves with available money for the first time in their history. After the Second Vatican Council, religious communities the world over had re-examined their lives and deepened their understanding of their vows. Toronto's Redemptorists began to re-examine the vow of poverty.

Addressing the January 1976 chapter, Maloney asked, "[H]ow do we, as Redemptorists of the Toronto Province in 1976 want to express the Vow of Poverty so that we can sincerely say to ourselves and to others that we are living the religious vow which we have professed?"[4] In February 1977 the chapter stated that the vow of poverty should be understood as "a radical attachment to the Lord expressed through the sign of simplicity and frugality of lifestyle minimizing ... needs for material goods." This goal was to be lived through periodic fasting and abstinence, constant generosity and hospitality, and moderation in food and drink.[5] Concepts of social justice also affected the Redemptorists' attitude towards the vow of poverty. As Canada moved into a recession in 1978, the Redemptorists urged each of their houses to exercise further financial restraint so that the money saved could be given to special projects of charity. The standard of living of Canada's lower middle class became a rough guide to living as a Redemptorist in modern Canada. More importantly, the Redemptorist view of poverty emphasized, as it had always done, a communal sharing of material goods, unlike the better-known Franciscan view of poverty as a lack of material goods.

The canonization of St. John Neumann in 1977 offered an occasion for the education of the public about the Redemptorists. Although born in Europe, John Neumann's entire priestly career had been spent in North America, most of it as a Redemptorist. The Redemptorist provinces of North America collaborated in promoting film strips, books, Catholic newspaper supplements, and memorabilia about St. John Neumann. While there is no evidence Neumann as a Redemptorist ever came to Canada, it is possible that he visited the German communities along the north shore of Lake Erie when he worked as a New York diocesan priest out of Buffalo. English Canada's Redemptorists enthusiastically entered into the celebrations culminating in a mass at St. Michael's Cathedral, Toronto, on 19 June 1977, with Archbishop Philip Pocock as celebrant and Father Matthew Meehan as homilist. Several Canadian Redemptorists went to Rome for the canonization ceremonies.

The rediscovery of the Congregation's roots continued. In 1979 a workshop on the history and the spirituality of the

Congregation by Baltimore's Father Joseph Oppitz and his book of assembled conferences sharpened Redemptorists' historical awareness.[6] The general government in Rome sponsored several workshops in history and spirituality throughout these years, leading up to the celebrations of 1982 marking the two hundred and fiftieth anniversary of the founding of the Congregation. The English-Canadian provinces began seriously to think of having their own histories written. In 1982 Redemptorists also celebrated the beatification of Father Peter Donders, a Dutch Redemptorist who spent many years among the lepers of Dutch Surinam until his death in 1887.

With Bernhard Haering as the leading moral theologian of the post-Vatican II Church, the Redemptorists and their graduate school in Rome, the Alphonsian Academy, had successfully reclaimed moral theology as a particularly Redemptorist work. They received an unexpected boost from Pope John Paul I. As Cardinal Luciani, Patriarch of Venice, the late pope had written a biographical, sometimes humorous recommendation of the study of Alphonsus's works on the hundredth anniversary of Alphonsus's elevation to the status of Doctor of the Church. In 1987, on the second centenary of the death of St. Alphonsus, Pope John Paul II wrote to recommend the saint's writings and the teaching of moral theology, as well as the missions to the poor that Alphonsus promoted. The Redemptorists in Canada held symposia, celebrations, and supported the writing of new biographies of their founder. The Edmonton Province assigned $50,000 a year for ten years to fund a lay moral theology chair at the Alfonsianum in Rome and established a $15,000 scholarship in Canada for moral theology doctoral studies by a lay person. All of these celebrations helped promote a sense of identity and allowed the Redemptorists to project this identity into the public arena.

The Japanese Missions

The main problem on the missions was as always lack of men. The Toronto Province turned down a Belgian request to take over their work in the Antilles in 1976 because of a lack of men. Edmonton's Casa Nova mission in Brazil formally closed down in 1985. Lack of men now forced Toronto to pull out of the Japanese mission.

The problems and the difficulties in directing Japanese affairs from Canada brought the Toronto council to raise the Maizuru mission with its three foundations and almost thirty professed members to a vice-province. On 4 January 1966, David Weir became the first Vice-provincial, with James Fuller and Robert Connaughton as consultors.

Unfortunately, the Japanese students began to leave, student reinforcements from Canada also left the Congregation, and Fuller himself was sent back to Canada because his health problems became a strain on the mission's resources. The three vice-provinces closed their own joint Tokyo minor seminary and student residence in 1970. This left ten older English-Canadian priests and one brother, together with a few Japanese brothers and fewer priests looking at the end of the Maizuru mission. The English-Canadian priests, most of them in their fifties, found it hard to share their authority with their three ordained but younger Japanese confreres. The fact that six out of nine Japanese Redemptorists were lay brothers created a triple barrier of age, nationality, and status between the English Canadians and the Japanese.

The Maizuru Mission, *c.* 1964
Standing left to right: Joseph (Hyozo Hamaguchi), Alphonsus (Shigeyoshi Yamaguchi), Dominic (Chikashi Makiyama), G. Pope, D. O'Rourke, B. Hutchison, F. Keogh, Michael (Shiro Yokota), Clement (Soichi Ura). *Sitting:* D. Weir, R. Connaughton, P. Hennessey, J. Fuller, W. James, R. Horn, J.

These problems were compounded by overwork and geographical fragmentation of the entire twenty-man Redemptorist mission in nine widely separate buildings. No community was possible, even if the Redemptorists wanted it. As many men lived in the single foundation of St. Patrick's, Toronto, as there were in the entire Maizuru mission. With the introduction of the vernacular, any new English-Canadian missionaries had further difficulty in adapting to the liturgy. With no community life to renew their spiritual lives, with no difference from diocesan priests to give them a separate identity, and with overwork, the Canadians lacked depth, focus, and energy.[7]

In November of 1978 the Maizuru chapter voted to return to become a mission region and Toronto voted to pull out of Japan entirely. Titus Campbell wrote to Bishop Tanaka of Kyoto that Toronto would withdraw from Miyazu as of January 1980. Some returned to Canada with relief, others in vigorous protest. A few English-Canadian Redemptorists stayed in Japan working either in the Tokyo or the Kagoshima vice-provinces.[8] Interestingly, some of those returning to Toronto and to Edmonton found it hard to adapt to Canadian Redemptorist community life and proceeded to find work in scattered parish settings not unlike the Maizuru mission itself. Each of Toronto's remaining Japanese brothers, priests, and students opted to join either Tokyo or Kagoshima. The lands purchased by James Fuller over the years were sold or given to the Tokyo Vice-province and the remaining money transferred to Canada. The vice-province was down-graded to a region on 15 December 1980 and suppressed 21 October 1981. On 13 April 1982 the Vice-province of Tokyo took over the Toronto Province buildings.

The last English-Canadian priest to leave Japan, Raymond Horn, wrote a letter that could serve as an epitaph for the Maizuru mission. English Canada's Redemptorists, he wrote, were unsuccessful in converting the Japanese and in preaching Redemptorist missions because of the language barrier, and simply drifted into diocesan work. Fuller had once stated that the Redemptorists were going to Japan to build the Church, not the Redemptorist Congregation. He was prepared to sacrifice everything, even their identity as Redemptorists, for the good of the Japanese church. Horn saw the sacrifice of the Redemptorist missionary identity at the very root of English Canada's failure.[9] In the 1980s and 1990s, however, several Japanese students in the Tokyo Vice-province came from the Maizuru region. Perhaps Toronto had been more successful than Horn had thought in creating a Japanese church strong enough to produce second-generation Redemptorists.

Parish Missions

The Redemptorists in Canada gave parish missions their second-highest priority. Edmonton's mission team was forced to find imaginative new ways to maintain and increase the Redemptorist presence in western Canada. With money saved from the sale of Holy Redeemer College, they were able to hire lay people, and Joan and Bob Williston became the first lay couple to serve on the Edmonton mission team. Redemptorists and lay people worked together to create a renewed mission combining Redemptorist traditions and Vatican II's theology of Church and evangelization.

In eastern Canada individual Redemptorists at first explored new missionary strategies. While the Toronto Province supported the marriage encounter movement as part of the Redemptorist preaching apostolate, individual Redemptorists explored the Movement for a Better World and the Charismatic Renewal Movement. Individuals occasionally came together to form mission groups, most notably a preaching group composed of Cecil Moreau, William Comerford, Paul Hansen, Donald MacLellan, and James Mason. These men believed that Redemptorists were called to be a form of "*Shock Therapy* within the church and within society" according to the spirit and intentions of St. Alphonsus.[10] The group could not rally much support, not because anyone disagreed with the approach, but because many of Toronto's Redemptorists looked for a united team of missionaries and a more uniform, identifiably Redemptorist mission. The dialogue between the members of the group and their critics became an important step in re-evaluating and creating a new, uniform Redemptorist mission.

The Toronto Province resolved to appoint "four men not presently engaged in preaching parish missions [to form a] mission community for at least 3 years."[11] Toronto's new team learned from the Edmonton and St. Louis provinces to update eastern Canada's mission system. The missions in both eastern and western Canada ran from Sunday to Thursday. At weekend masses prior to the mission the parishioners were invited to make the mission. On Sunday night the missionaries held a mission service without mass, preaching the good news of salvation and teaching the people about prayer. Monday morning saw a mission mass with the eucharist as the central theme. Jesus was forcefully presented on Monday night. A discussion about burning issues in family life, such as divorce and separation, followed the service. The Tuesday morning mass introduced Mary, while the evening service presented the kingdom of God. The people were then instructed on ways of forming one's conscience. Wednesday's mass held a healing service and the sacrament of anointing. The evening service discussed forgiveness and celebrated the sacrament of reconciliation (formerly called the sacrament of penance) followed by a social get-together. A closing mass was held on Thursday evening with the theme of discipleship, renewal of baptismal promises, and a mission blessing. Since Edmonton's missions had lay missionaries, more instructions were given about family life there. Toronto's missionaries handed out pamphlets on conscience, prayer, and annulments. Over the years, the sermon topics also included creation, justice, and peace.

Toronto's missionary report to the 1986 chapter was a significant comment on the changes that the Redemptorists had experienced since the Second Vatican Council. The mission had changed in one fundamental way: while its purpose was still to convert the people by "the experience of a good confession with a firm purpose of amendment," Canada's Redemptorists now combined the traditional mission with the traditional renewal to place new emphasis on Christ and the love of God. Preaching became much more biblically based and reminiscent of the renewal sermons preached before Vatican II. For example, missionaries still promoted devotions to Our Lady of Perpetual Help, but now spent more time on the biblical and Christological elements present in any healthy Marian devotion.

Damascus Road Singers
Left to right: Darryl McGinn, Eugene O'Reilly, Yaroslaw Dybka, and Paul

The externals of the mission, or the presentation of the instructions, the sermons, and the music, changed dramatically. Redemptorist students had always informally sung and had occasionally put on skits, plays, and operettas. Years of voice training together, through Brockville and then Windsor, led a group of Redemptorist Windsor students from the Toronto, Edmonton, and Yorkton provinces in March of 1964 to sing some folk songs for a public "hootenanny." The success led to a short tour around the London diocese.[12] By 1977 the collection of new songs and the increasing demand for Redemptorist music brought Eugene O'Reilly and Darrell McGinn, the authors of most of the music in the Toronto Province, to record the album "Damascus Road" in 1977. It was quickly followed by "All in My Hand" in 1978 and "Children of the Light" in 1985.

In western Canada the mission team began to write and produce music specifically for the missions. An English-Canadian Catholic Church hungry for an indigenous liturgical voice adopted some of Eugene O'Reilly's compositions for the *Catholic Book of Worship II* in 1980. The musicians were in constant demand and the music could be heard wherever a mission had been held. Eugene O'Reilly himself participated in over fifty of Toronto's missions and gave several hundred more on his own between 1984 and 1993. This alone brought many eastern Canadian Catholics to purchase records and tapes featuring O'Reilly's music. While the music in eastern Canada rarely raised enough money to support the missionaries, the sale of records and cassette tapes in western Canada did help to subsidize the missionaries there. Redemptorist music became an important part of the updating of the Church in Canada and part of the popular religion of Canada's English-speaking Catholics.

Beginning in 1975 in the west, and in 1983 in the east, the new mission teams spread out across Canada. Toronto's two-man teams averaged over twenty-five weeks of missions every year until 1993, while individuals continued to give their own missions, retreats, and renewals in schools and smaller parishes, sometimes creating a demand for a larger mission. Since Edmonton's teams averaged over sixty missions a year, hardly a parish in western Canada did not host one of the new missions. The Redemptorists again proved that a renewed Redemptorist mission after the Second Vatican Council had a welcome place in English Catholic Canada.

Parishes

Maloney often used simple memory tricks to remember his talks and get his points across. Once the four pastoral priorities were established in 1982, he warned that they would require greater commitment (C), self-sacrifice (Ss), and renewal (R) from every Toronto Province C.Ss.R.[13] With that warning, he deferred examination of the parishes and new projects to the provincial chapter of April 1983. With more men and money being dedicated to the first two priorities of formation and the missions, some painful sacrifices had to be made elsewhere. Every Redemptorist parish foundation came under intense scrutiny.

Nowhere was change more visible than in Quebec City. With the English Catholic population moving into the suburbs, the Redemptorists recognized that St. Patrick's in the heart of the city had little demographic future, but the sentimental attachment by many of Quebec's Irish Canadians, "even those who live too far ever to put foot into the church now or in the future" would likely "create a riot" if St. Patrick's itself were closed.[14] The election of a provincial separatist political party in 1976 stampeded some of the remaining unilingual English-speaking residents to leave the province. Young English-speaking adults found job opportunities more easily elsewhere in Canada or in the United States. Their parents followed on retirement.

In 1977 Father Clark McAulay pointed out to the parishioners that the parish had shrunk to three hundred members. Although volunteers came forward to help run the parish in a rejuvenated management committee, the Redemptorists felt unable to continue. The huge monastery building was at first offered to the Beaupré Province Redemptorists as a student house, but the discussions bogged down over whether the Beaupré Province could actually supply an English-speaking Redemptorist, much less take over the parish.[15] A significant number of English-Canadian Redemptorists believed that the English community of Quebec City still needed them; a 1980 chapter motion to pull out of Quebec City by 30 June 1981 received one vote less than the two-thirds necessary to pass. The next year, the chapter requested the Redemptorist administration to renegotiate the contract with the archdiocese of Quebec and place the Redemptorist presence in St. Patrick's parish on a short-term basis. The buildings and much of the land were sold, and the Redemptorists began to withdraw from the active management of the parish. Still, with 10 per cent of the Toronto Province in 1981 originally from Quebec, the English-speaking Redemptorists may not have felt ready to pull out from their first foundation in Canada and their only remaining one in Quebec.[16] When Father Martin Foley retired in 1993 from St. Richard's parish in Montreal, St. Patrick's in Quebec City became the Redemptorists' only English presence in Quebec.

After decades of delay, St. Patrick's in Quebec City finished the church's superstructure in time for St. Patrick's day, 1958. The architectural plans, drawn up before the First World War, were copied from those of the Redemptorist church of Our Lady of Perpetual Help, in Brooklyn, New York. Unfortunately the English-language population of Quebec City continued to move to the suburbs and used St. Patrick's church less and less. It was replaced by a smaller brick church in 1989.

Four foundations in Toronto held almost half of the Toronto Province's members, so the Toronto houses themselves came under intense examination. Gerard House, no matter how expensive, could not be touched, since it was one of the few hopes for the future. Madonna House with the administrative offices, and the attached Perpetual Help residence for retired, visiting, or missionary members, required relatively few people and served a useful role. Scanlan himself lived at Gerard House and worked as student prefect as well as provincial. Downtown, the German parishioners had long been the most important element in the parish of St. Patrick's run by William Kroetsch. Every time the question was raised whether it was time to close the German congregation, Kroetsch argued that the community was still alive, surprisingly, and that it would not disappear for another ten or more years. The German congregation demonstrated continued vigour in several ways; not least was its support of some of the Vietnamese refugees arriving in Canada in 1979.

When Ronald Delaney became rector of St. Patrick's in 1981, he at first accepted the common opinion that the German congregation was doomed and opposed it becoming a parish. The devotions to Our Lady of Perpetual Help drew in people from all over the city and especially from the downtown core, so that a German parish itself was unnecessary to the well-being of St. Patrick's. He changed his mind within three months and became the German congregation's firmest supporter, stating that "The German Congregation is of crucial value to the very existence of St. Patrick's itself." St. Patrick's in Toronto officially became home to two parishes, an English territorial parish and a German national parish as of 13 July 1982.

Nevertheless, some parish foundations had to close. Over the protests of many parishioners and of some of the Redemptorists themselves, both St. Alphonsus in Peterborough and St. Alphonsus in Windsor were chosen. In spite of thousand-signature petitions in protest, re-examinations convinced the Redemptorists that the parishes were financially healthy and the dioceses had the personnel to staff them. Toronto-based missionaries could easily reach Peterborough, while the entire London diocese could still be reached by the Redemptorists at Holy Redeemer College in Windsor. The Redemptorists took their personal belongings and books and left everything else behind. Both foundations were suppressed and the Redemptorist buildings and land were sold to the dioceses on 18 June 1984. As for the house attached to the parish of Our Lady of the Assumption, Toronto, the Redemptorists decided in 1983 that whenever they found it necessary to withdraw in view of the other commitments of the province, it would be the next to close. The parish was well-established, financially self-sufficient, and the archdiocese of Toronto had priests who could staff it. It was eventually announced that the Redemptorists would withdraw from Assumption in 1995.

Since Edmonton had more foundations, however, and only half the members enjoyed by the Toronto Province, no relief could be had by closing only one house. Edward Kennedy presided over the closing of the foundations in Edson in 1985, Blessed Sacrament in Nelson in 1987, and St. Gerard's in Yorkton in 1991. Even St. Alphonsus in East Kildonan closed in 1993, leaving not a single English-Canadian foundation in Manitoba, although both the French-Canadian and the Ukrainian Redemptorists had houses in that province, guaranteeing a Redemptorist parish presence in Manitoba. With twenty-three deaths among the priests and brothers from 1975 to 1993 and only four students who persevered to ordination to replace them all, the Edmonton Province had no choice.

New Projects

In its search for a new, authentically Redemptorist outreach program, the Toronto Province received a report from the Outreach Project Commission in November of 1982 which defined what such a program actually meant. The report declared that it had to be new either to the Redemptorists or to the local church, involve "explicit proclamation of the Word," especially in the form of preaching and ministering to the poor, meet the needs of the local church, be more stable than an experiment, and encompass some part of the Church not being reached by any other group, individual, or movement.[17]

　　The commission outlined several possible projects. First, the diocese of Thunder Bay requested a pastor, a mission director, and a priest for adult religious education. Second, the Redemptorists explored a media project whereby the Redemptorists would use Father Matthew Meehan's knowledge and contacts to enter the world of modern technological communications. Third, Father Provincial Maloney had strongly suggested that the Redemptorists replace their mission in Japan with Dominica in the West Indies. Each of these proposals was debated and dropped for lack of qualified men and money. Three other proposals, however, were eagerly adopted. The commission recommended creating another new community in Newfoundland, redeveloping Holy Redeemer College in Windsor as a full-time retreat centre, and entering the field of youth ministry.

The diocese of Grand Falls in Newfoundland had asked for help to relieve the pressure on the personnel-strapped diocese. Having left their parishes in Peterborough and in Windsor, as well as the Maizuru mission in Japan, some Redemptorists were available and excited by this request. Maloney committed the Redemptorists to supplying two priests and one brother to serve a number of parishes for three years or until the diocese could staff the parishes itself. On 19 August 1981 James Glavine, Paul Doucet, and Brother Albert Power took over the care of the parishes of Saints Peter and Paul in Harbour Main and St. Anne's in Conception Harbour. Father Titus Campbell took over the parish of Saints Peter and Paul in King's Cove. Newfoundland required no further special training or money, as did Japan or the field of electronic media communications. The men went to work in a traditional, parish apostolate familiar to every English-Canadian Redemptorist. The parishes were handed back to the diocese in August 1984.

Since its reason for existence as a student residence had disappeared, Holy Redeemer College in Windsor had been used for several things. By the 1980s individual Redemptorist brothers and priests began to see the college as a potentially "vibrant apostolic centre." There were still Redemptorists teaching at the University of Windsor, but now the college focus turned to retreat work. Marriage encounters, healing ministries, charismatic prayer groups, counselling, spiritual direction, and conferences all met there. How long the Redemptorists could afford to run the place with the brothers getting older every year was a constant worry. They began looking into the possibility of employing more lay people to maintain the buildings.

In western Canada, meanwhile, the Redemptorists established a Redemptorist Centre for Growth in 1985. Edward Kennedy had previously encouraged Raymond Douziech, who was completing his doctorate in psychology, to study the possibility of a counselling centre. Douziech was named the first director. Beginning originally in response to "the often expressed desire of the members of the Canadian Religious Conference, Western Region for therapeutic facilities in Western Canada for priests and religious needing help," Edmonton's Redemptorist Centre for Growth became a public counselling service, housing both highly trained Redemptorists and lay people in the areas of psychology, moral theology, and spiritual direction.[18]

Lay collaboration, formation, and a new Redemptorist outreach program came together in Edmonton's Redemptorist Moral Theology Bio-Ethics Consultancy under the directorship of Father Mark Miller. Graduates of the moral theology scholarship could be offered employment in an applied moral theology consultancy service specializing in bio-ethical situations faced by hospitals and other health-care institutions. Both the Centre for Growth and the Consultancy in Bio-Ethics had Redemptorist direction and financial sponsorship, but both also enlisted qualified lay psychologists and theologians.

In October of 1985 all of Canada's Redemptorist students met at Gerard House to plan their future, to discuss vocations, and to explore youth ministries. The following year Father David Furlonger and Brother Raymond Pierce proposed that the old ways of recruiting which concentrated on getting people "into the system" be replaced by a ministerial model which emphasized helping people "to make good decisions" about their lives.[19] Although such a change in recruitment strategy did not produce any more professed members, it led the Redemptorists to explore new ways of working with younger people. Toronto's Redemptorists later came across the Redemptorist Youth/Vocation Mission model proposed by South Africa's Redemptorist Father Kevin Dowling at the Justice and Peace Commission meeting in Oakland, California. When Father Douglas Stamp sold some of the Quebec City property, he suggested the possibility of using the money in a program with young lay people.

From these separate inspirations the vocation director, Gerry Pettipas, with Fathers Raymond Earle and Dermot FitzPatrick, launched a new form of lay ministry in 1988. "s.e.r.v.e." or a "Summer Endeavour in a Redemptorist Volunteer Experience" was a six-week summer program designed for young men and then extended to both men and women in 1991. Given room, board, and a small honorarium, the young men and women spent their days developing Christian community at Gerard House on Howland Avenue in

Toronto and providing services to volunteer agencies in the city. The program attracted a great number of volunteers who wanted meaningful service-oriented work, and perhaps a chance to explore a future in Church ministry. The numbers soon had to be limited to the funds and space available. Since 1988 twelve young adults annually have participated in Toronto's program, which became a model for the Edmonton and Yorkton provinces as well as for Redemptorists in Australia. The Edmonton Province began S.E.R.V.E. at Clement House in Edmonton in the summer of 1993 with Michael Xuerub, a graduate of Toronto's program, as one of the directors.

Father Michael Dodds was largely responsible for organizing S.E.R.V.E. from 1989 until he left to form a youth mission team with Pettipas in 1993. Pettipas and Dodds arrived in St. John's, Newfoundland, and established a team mission that visited five archdiocesan parishes and tried to foster youth organizations in them. In 1994, with three young adults recruited from the youth mission in St. John's, both Dodds and Pettipas moved to Saint John, New Brunswick. Bringing younger lay people on the missions or forming a youth mission team interested the Edmonton Province and both English-language provinces began discussions at collaboration.

While the youth missions were Toronto's first organized efforts at community with lay collaboration, the Redemptorists had previously worked with the laity mainly through a Co-Redemptorist Association as well as through the conferral of oblateships. The practice of admitting clergy and laity, especially the parents of Redemptorists, to a sharing in the prayers and good works of the Redemptorists had been in use from the time of St. Alphonsus. Besides sharing in the prayer life and the spiritual rewards due to Redemptorists, oblates also automatically enjoyed Redemptorist hospitality. Clement Hofbauer added the idea that the oblates were to collaborate actively in the Redemptorist apostolate.[20] Such an active confraternity never grew in English Canada, where it remained mainly an honorary position. Sometimes oblates were men who were too old to undergo a novitiate but lived in the community and did manual labour. In the 1920s Fred Reardon worked in St. Patrick's, Toronto, and when the London community was estab-

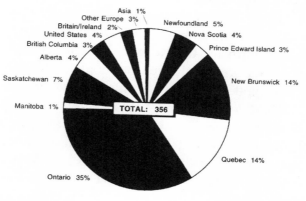

Priests by Place of Birth
1919 - 1994

Asia 1%
Other Europe 3%
Britain/Ireland 2%
United States 4%
British Columbia 3%
Alberta 4%
Saskatchewan 7%
Manitoba 1%
Newfoundland 5%
Nova Scotia 4%
Prince Edward Island 3%
New Brunswick 14%
TOTAL: 356
Quebec 14%
Ontario 35%

Born Outside Canada
9%

Born in Canada
91%

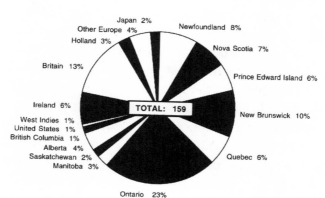

Brothers by Place of Birth
1919 - 1994

Japan 2%
Other Europe 4%
Holland 3%
Britain 13%
Ireland 6%
West Indies 1%
United States 1%
British Columbia 1%
Alberta 4%
Saskatchewan 2%
Manitoba 3%
Newfoundland 8%
Nova Scotia 7%
Prince Edward Island 6%
New Brunswick 10%
TOTAL: 159
Quebec 6%
Ontario 23%

Born Outside Canada
30%

Born in Canada
70%

lished, he went there as a cook. Yet the petition to have him made an oblate was made only in 1931, shortly before he died. By Arthur Ryan's time there had only been six other men and women named oblates, all after years of service with the Redemptorists.

After some initial hesitation, Ryan petitioned Rome to have nine of the most generous and constant supporters of the Redemptorists made oblates, including the Hefferings who had donated their farm for the Keswick novitiate.[21] After Ryan's time English Canada preferred to enrol people in the Co-Redemptorist Association, modelled after a similar association in the St. Louis Province. The Co-Redemptorist Association united the many bene-factors of the Redemptorists in 1961 shortly after the Windsor semi-nary was built and encouraged them to keep supporting Redemptorist vocations through donations and prayers. At its height in the 1960s the issue of turning the Co-Redemptorist Association into a third order was raised, but the question never went beyond the discussion stage. Since 1961 the Co-Redemptorists have donated over $1.5 million to the Redemptorists.[22]

Meanwhile, the number of oblates of the Most Holy Redeemer grew around the world, especially in mission lands. In these places, creating an oblate was more than a recognition for long years of service or of financial generosity. In some provinces it actu-ally became an unofficial third order for lay people at the beginning of their collaboration with the Redemptorists. Instead of a lifetime commitment, it has also sometimes become a recognition of a promise to collaborate for a period of time. In the twentieth century, when lay associations and secular institutes have grown in populari-ty, the oblates have become a flexible means for incorporating lay people into the Redemptorist apostolate. Toronto's Redemptorists hesitated to establish a third order, because lay people could support the Redemptorist mission as salaried employees, as volunteer Co-Redemptorists, and as honorary or as active oblates, without adding more categories of membership. The Edmonton Province, which had already instituted lay missionaries, however, established a chapter of lay associates in Saskatoon and hoped to expand the network throughout western Canada.

The Brothers

One group in the Redemptorist family continued to decline. Although there had been interested inquiries, Edmonton did not profess a single brother from 1975 to 1993. One joined Toronto in 1982. The notion of brothers as manual labourers no longer had the same appeal to young men in the late twentieth century. In past years, immigrants were attracted to the brotherhood, rather than to the priesthood, where their lack of formal education would prove to be a severe handicap. With immigration in decline and educational accomplishments rising, all young men in the 1975 to 1994 period were strongly encouraged to consider ordination in the Redemptorist Congregation, which overlooks the fact that ordination is not a necessary part of religious life. From their very beginning, however, the Redemptorists have been a clerical institute preferring to accept priests or candidates for ordination rather than those who have no intention of studying for the priesthood.

Since the brothers are the ones who have traditionally supported the missionary by maintaining Redemptorist institutions, the decline of the brotherhood in English Canada has gone hand-in-hand with the deinstitutionalization of the Redemptorists. As the brothers got older, it simply became too expensive to hire lay staff to replace them. Toronto's chapter of June 1991 realized that the special skills, dedication, and community provided by their brothers could not be replaced and decided to close Holy Redeemer College in Windsor. In 1994 the college was sold to a private school, to the sorrow of many Redemptorists in both east and west. The English-Canadian Redemptorists had divested themselves of every major educational institution they had ever had. They also no longer owned a single building in which they could all meet together.

Maloney summed up his years as provincial from 1975 to 1984 with the phrase "emerging stability."[23] He pointed to the positive signs and insisted that they outnumbered the negative ones. Indeed, the Redemptorists had moved beyond endless discussions about relevance, lifestyle, unity, and theological validity. From

1975 to the end of 1993, thirty-one people professed temporary vows in English Canada, and twelve men were ordained, but there was no hiding the fact that the Redemptorists in English Canada declined from two hundred members to one hundred and twenty. A quarter of everyone still with the Redemptorists were either too old and feeble or too sick to do much active work.[24] Still, as Maloney pointed out, proportionately fewer people actually left than in the previous decade; the decline in numbers was almost entirely due to mortality. While professions were low, they were increasing, as older men joined. Unlike in previous years where youths rapidly joined and just as rapidly left after a few years of subsidized education, older men, generally after university studies, now joined and most of them stayed. A dozen men were professed and six were ordained between 1984 and 1990, two in their thirties

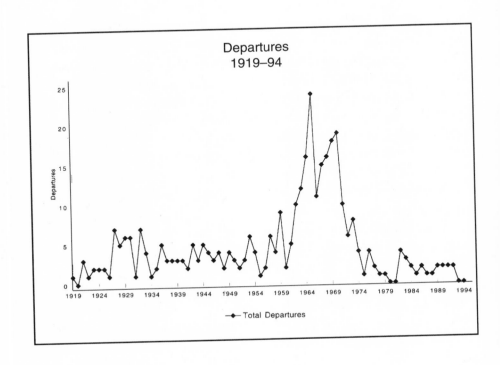

and one of fifty-seven. Not since their first years in Canada in the 1880s had the Redemptorists received or accepted applications from such diverse backgrounds: diocesan seminarians, priests, teachers, bricklayers, musicians, and grocery clerks. Such varied experiences gave the Redemptorists increased energy. By 1993 the average age had stabilized; it began to decline for the first time as these new members began to make their weight felt and younger men were attracted to these new examples of Redemptorist life.

Between 1975 and 1993 many religious congregations experienced chaos and crisis. Unsure about the meaning, contemporary relevance or mission of religious life, they found it difficult to cope with often rapidly declining numbers. The Redemptorists of English Canada, however, found renewed meaning, insisted on the relevance of faith and the eternal truths in a secular world, renewed their missions and their lives, and again began to attract men to the community.

In the summer of 1992 former Redemptorists were reunited in a weekend alumni gathering at Holy Redeemer College, Windsor. There were more former Redemptorists from all walks of life meeting at the college than there were Redemptorists working in English Canada. Former Redemptorists, the vast majority of them in service industries or educational institutions, spoke of their lives of service to their families and their communities, promoting Redemptorist prayers, devotions, or ideals. They were living proof of the influence the Redemptorists had beyond their own institutions. For some, the meeting healed old wounds; for others it was a celebration with old friends. It was an occasion to say goodbye to the old life symbolized by Holy Redeemer College and a time to meet the new generation of Redemptorists.

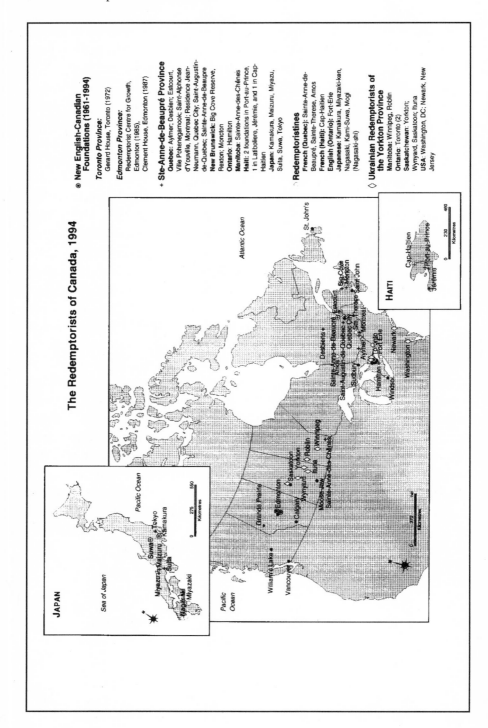

The Redemptorists of Canada, 1994

⊛ **New English-Canadian Foundations (1961-1994)**

Toronto Province:
Gerard House, Toronto (1972)

Edmonton Province:
Redemptorist Centre for Growth, Edmonton (1985),
Clement House, Edmonton (1987)

+ **Ste-Anne-de-Beaupré Province**
Quebec: Aylmer; Desbien; Estcourt, Ville Pohenegamook; Saint-Alphonse d'Youville, Montreal; Residence Jean-Neumann, Quebec City; Saint-Augustin-de-Quebec; Sainte-Anne-de-Beaupre
New Brunswick: Big Cove Reserve, Rexton; Moncton
Ontario: Hamilton
Manitoba: Sainte-Anne-des-Chênes
Haiti: 2 foundations in Port-au-Prince, 1 in Latiboliere, Jérémie, and 1 in Cap-Haitien
Japan: Kamakura, Maizuru, Miyazu, Suita, Suwa, Tokyo

◇ **Redemptoristines**
French (Quebec): Sainte-Anne-de-Beaupré, Sainte-Therese, Anos
French (Haiti): Cap-Haitien
English (Ontario): Fort-Erie
Japanese: Kamakura, Miyazaki-ken, Nagasaki, Kami-Suwa, Mogi (Nagasaki-shi)

◇ **Ukrainian Redemptorists of the Yorkton Province**
Manitoba: Winnipeg, Roblin
Ontario: Toronto (2)
Saskatchewan: Yorkton; Wynyard, Saskatoon; Ituna
USA: Washington, DC: Newark, New Jersey

Epilogue

Redemptorists are trained to preach. As missionaries, they are known through the spoken word. The old, warped phonograph records of the Japanese departure ceremony, a taped German sermon by Dan Ehman, a radio broadcast by Martin Foley in Saskatoon, or a television broadcast by Matthew Meehan in Hamilton can give some idea of who the Redemptorists were, but most of the voices are lost or, at most, preserved in point form in old sermon outlines. For a missionary congregation, every silenced voice means the passing of a small part of its being and its history.

Their constitutions, statutes, and discussions all describe what Redemptorists wanted to be and to some extent what they were. Desmond Scanlan cited the new constitutions and statutes to say that whatever particular work they would be doing, the English-Canadian Redemptorist missionary would "share in the mystery of Christ and proclaim it in Gospel simplicity of life and language, that they may bring to people plentiful Redemption."[1] Redemptorists zealously preach salvation to the poor and to the abandoned or they are not Redemptorists in Canada or elsewhere.

A history of the Redemptorists can have no conclusion, because their history is still being written in their lives. Furthermore, the history of a religious congregation is more than the spoken word or the sum of individual biographies, for there is that common spirit, and a common life, lived for common goals, only some of it preserved in countless buildings, churches, schools, books, tapes, photographs, and letters. Much of what Redemptorists are and were was also shared with the Church, particularly with their parishioners and with Catholic religious congregations and orders, such as the Sisters of Service and the Redemptoristines. Redemptorist devotions, to St.

Gerard and especially to Our Lady of Perpetual Help, are strong legacies evident from Newfoundland to British Columbia, from Windsor to the Peace River District. The numerous popular missions and the confessional work that went with them demonstrate how Redemptorist moral theology has affected English-Canadian Catholic daily lives from the 1830s to the present. These have been their contributions to English Canada.

As they enter the twenty-first century, the English-Canadian Redemptorists know they are a product of Canada's history as well as a contributor. The history of the Toronto Province is, to a great extent, the history of a generation in English-Canadian Catholic religious life. The First World War defined the English-Canadian identity of the Redemptorists, many of whom were of Irish backgrounds. These Redemptorists saw English-speaking Catholics as the most abandoned to whom they should offer God's redemption. After the First World War and during the Depression, English-Canadian Redemptorists adopted western Canada as the new mission field. The Second World War introduced the technology of the modern world to Redemptorist religious life and encouraged them to move beyond Canada to adopt Japan as the new mission field. The weight of immigration, new languages and cultures after the Second World War challenged English-Canadian Catholic certainties. Co-responsibility, democracy, even the laity, have entered the cloister since the Second Vatican Council. The decline in the numbers of Redemptorists since then has as much to do with the passing away of an entire generation of Irish-Canadians as with student dissatisfaction with older models of religious life in English Canada.

Canadian Redemptorist religious life has also shown that the English-Catholic Church is now centred in Ontario in general and the archdiocese of Toronto in particular. Demographically, the Maritimes, English Quebec, northern Ontario, and western Canada have become the periphery of central Canadian planning, since half of Canada's English-speaking Catholics live in Ontario and many of them live in Toronto. Western Redemptorists have sometimes rejected decisions made in Toronto, certain that western conditions demanded different decisions.

None of this is new to anyone familiar with Canada's political or economic realities. While they participated in the nationalism, regionalism, and linguistic divisions that have shaped Canadian life, the Redemptorists have been constantly moved by a sincere desire to evangelize and serve the most abandoned, wherever they could be found. Thus they formed the first linguistic division in their own Congregation, in order to serve the English-speaking Catholic missions of Canada better. Although they became an integral part of central Canada, Redemptorists continued to experiment, importing insights from other parts of Canada, notably the Antigonish cooperative movement, in order to overcome central Canada's limitations and to build new structures, new ways of life, and new apostolates to serve their people better.

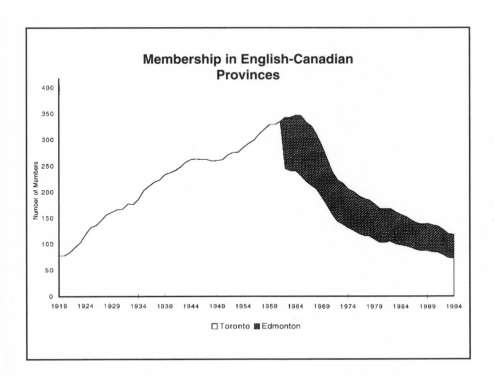

Raymond Hostie, in *The Life and Death of Religious Orders*, states unequivocally that if religious congregations do not renew themselves, they disappear as they become irrelevant to new situations. The Second Vatican Council unleashed a desire for renewal unprecedented in the history of the Roman Catholic Church since the Reformation. Renewal hit the Toronto Province more severely than any other province in the entire Congregation, not merely because of cultural and of regional stresses, but because its former parish-based missionary successes and phenomenal recruitment made its leadership resistant to change.

In part, the Redemptorist leadership, especially Father General William Gaudreau, had become prisoners of former missionary successes. When renewal came, the struggles between those who favoured modernization and deinstitutionalization and those who saw the continuing value of traditional institutions and forms of religious life and mission brought Toronto to suffer the largest decline of any Redemptorist province, vice-province, or region in the world.[2] Edmonton followed closely behind, since its formation program was so closely tied to Toronto's. The Vatican Council's renewal eventually challenged and permeated all of English-Canadian Redemptorist life so that Redemptorists abandoned their traditional educational institutions and many of their parishes to concentrate more on their missionary vocation.

In spite of cultural, regional, and administrative problems, Canada's Redemptorists have adapted the traditional forms of religious life and have found new ways to confront Canadian life in new outreach programs. Perhaps that is why their numbers and their average age in Canada have stabilized. They are preparing a new generation of missionaries for the future. The question whether the Redemptorists have something to offer English Canada in the twenty-first century other than a history of their efforts in the previous two centuries has often been raised and closely argued. The answer is in the attraction the Redemptorists have to men young and old, those who join and those who persevere.

After the Second Vatican Council, isolationist structures dividing the individual provinces into independent fiefdoms crumbled. Collaboration became the watchword of the 1990s as the four provinces in Canada sought to eliminate overlapping responsibilities, combine novitiates and educational institutions, give their students training in different cultures and regions, cooperate in mission activities, and integrate lay people with vowed religious. This trend encompassed not only English Canada's Redemptorists but every province in North America and the world. In Canada the needs of the large French and Ukrainian communities continue to keep the Beaupré and the Yorkton provinces administratively separate from the English provinces, but the Edmonton and Toronto provinces have fewer differences. Edmonton's provincial, Edward Kennedy, raised the question of reuniting the two English-Canadian provinces. Kennedy's and Scanlan's successors have taken up the challenge to reform English-Canadian Redemptorist life once again in the hope that the combined energies and different experiences of east and west will have a renewed impact on all of English Catholic Canada.

As the Redemptorists attract and adapt themselves to a Catholic world that knows little if anything of a Church before the Second Vatican Council, modern English-Canadian Catholics are calling forth another generation of Redemptorists to preach the eternal truths, teach moral living, build Christian community, and offer redemption and renewal to English Canada.

Appendix 1

List of members of the Toronto and Edmonton provinces (including the Maizuru and Yorkton vice-provinces), 1918–94

Abbott, Edward
Abbott, Robert Newman
Abrams, Charles
Adams, (John) Anthony
Alexander, Arthur Edward
Allan, William John
Allen, (Stanislaus) Ray
Andrews, John Geary
Archibald, Gerald Gregory
Arsenault, (Emile) Emile Joseph
Bachtalowky, Stephen
Bailey, Anthony
Baines, Richard
Bala, John
Bala, Joseph
Baldwin, Edward
Barbeito, Peter
Barnes, John Gerard
Barre, Wayne Ronald
Barry, John
Bartley, Henry
Beahen, Edmund
Beaubien, Arthur
Beckta, (Vincent) George

Beckta, Vincent James
Bedard, Richard
Benedet, Dino Nicholas
Beneteau, Kenneth Gordon Joseph
Bennett, Ambrose
Bennett, Augustine
Bennett, James
Bennett, John
Bernard, William Matthews
Berrigan, Michael Edward
Berti, (Louis) Oreste
Bielmeier, (George) Georg Franz
Bizon, Gerald Bronislaus
Blackmore, Matthew
Blair, Mansell John
Blanchard, Edward
Bogue, Daniel Bernard
Boland, Brendan
Bonokoski, Thomas Francis
Borsa, Francis
Boyce, Edward
Boyle, Edward
Boyle, Joseph Anthony
Boyne, Edward

Brady, Cecil A.
Brady, Patrick
Breen, (Frederick) John Thomas
Brehl, John Michael
Brennan, Patrick
Bresnahan, (Oswald) Michael
Briand, John Robert
Briand, Robert
Brinsek, (Cyril) Ivan
Brock, Charles
Brocklehurst, Charles
Brophy, (Jerome) Robert Timothy
Brost, Richard
Brouillard, Francis
Brown, Michael David
Brytan, (Reginald) William
Buckley, (Lawrence) Michael
Burke, (Benedict) John
Burke, John Francis
Burke, Kevin
Byrne, John K.
Cahill, (Stephen) Michael
Cain, Robert
Calarco, Paschal J.
Callaghan, Thomas Peter
Campbell, Gerard Hafey
Campbell, Titus
Cappellacci, Ross
Carr, Thomas
Casey, Francis Joseph
Casey, Thomas Andrew
Cassidy, (Jerome) Gerald Edmund
Cassidy, William
Celustka, Josef
Chanhao, James Term
Charlesworth, (Maurice) Charles
Chidlow, Thomas
Chisholm, (Ambrose) Cecil
Chisholm, (Gerard) Alexander
Clarke, Alfred
Clarke, Richard
Clarmont, Joseph Alexander
Cloran, James
Coady, Edward James
Coady, Michael Ross
Cochrane, (Denis)
Cochrane, (Dominic) Michael
Coffey, Francis Bernard
Coffin, George
Coghlan, John Frederick
Coholan, Edward
Coll, Denis
Collins, John Bernard
Collison, Paul Joseph
Comeau, (Linus) Leonard
Comerford, William
Conlogue, Arthur Edmund
Connaughton, Robert
Connell, Arthur
Connell, John Frederick
Connolly, Stephen L.
Connor, (James)
Conway, Russell John
Cookson, (Norbert) Charles
Corbett, Neil Adrian
Corcoran, James
Corkery, John
Corlett, Frederick J.
Corrigan, Francis
Corriveau, Raymond
Costello, Peter
Cottingham, David
Coulis, Christopher
Coyne, George
Coyne, Thomas Phineas
Coyne, (Thomas) Michael
Crawford, Joseph
Crean, Victor
Crowley, Edward J.
Crowley, Gerald

Cunerty, Francis Arthur
Cunerty, Francis Patrick
Cunnane (Keenan), (Henry)
Cunningham, John Joseph
Curtin, Paul
Cybulskie, Benedict
Dacey, (John)
Dale, (Arthur)
Dales, Francis Gerald
Dales, James John
Daley, Edmund
Daley, (Mark) Francis
Daley, Michael
Daley, William
Daly, George
Daly, (John) Richard
Darmawiez, (Vitus) Solomon
Davis, James
DeVine, Charles Frederick
Deane, (Thomas)
Delaere, Achille
Delaney, George Patrick Gerard
Delaney, John
Delaney, Ronald
Demerah, Emmanuel
Desilets, George Jules
Despres, Joseph French
Dever, Joseph
Dhaene, (Christopher) Peter
Diamond, (Malachy) John
Dieges, (Clement) John
Dietz, Oscar Julius
Dillon, Hugh Anthony
Dobbelsteyn, (Nicholas) Peter
Dodds, Michael
Doherty, Philip
Donato, Carman Peter
Donnelly, Ciaran
Donnelly, William
Donoghue, (Columban) John

Donovan, Merlin
Dore, John
Doucet, Marc Gerard
Doucet, Paul
Doucet, Ronald
Doucette, William
Douziech, Raymond
Dowling, (Xavier) John Douglas
Doyle, Edward
Doyle, Gilbert
Doyle, John William
Doyle, Thomas Edward
Drechsler, Gerald Patrick
Dubray, James Lawrence
Duffy, (Joseph) Vincent
Dunphy, (Francis) Joseph
Dust, Norman
Dwyer, James
Earle, Raymond
Edward, David Rundle Kenrick
Egan, Lawrence D'Arcy
Ehman, Daniel George
Ehman, Gabriel Joseph
Eldridge, Maynard Peter
English, Leo Gerard
Enright, Arthur Thomas
Enright, Joseph William
Evans, (Allan)
Farrell, James
Feddema, (Herman) Henry John
Fee, George
Feehan, Edward Grattan
Feehan, Leo Alphonsus
Field, Donald
Fisher, Paul
Fitzgerald, Joseph
Fitzgerald, Leonard
Fitzgerald, Raymond
Fitzgerald, (Vincent) Thomas M.
Fitzgerald, William

Fitzpatrick, Dermot
Fitzpatrick, Patrick James
Flaherty, (John)
Fleming, Gerald
Fleming, Henry
Fletcher, (Alphonsus) John
Foley, Martin
Forrestall, Michael
Fortier, Roch
Foster, (Bruce) Bruce Gregory
Fourchalk, Paul Lawrence
Fuller, James
Furlonger, David Paul
Galbraith, Frederick Dufferin
Gallagher, John
Gallagher, Joseph
Gallagher, Joseph Francis
Gallant, (Dominic) Dorice
Gallery, Francis
Gallery, Patrick
Gannon, (James)
Garcia, Ernest de Rama
Garvey, (Kevin) Matthew
Gaul, Francis T.
Gaynor, Wilfrid
Gilleece, Michael
Gillen, Edward
Gillis, (Philip) Francis
Glavin, Raphael
Glavine, James
Glover, George
Goakery, Charles
Godin, Clifford
Goetz, Stanley
Golden, John Gilbert
Goldrup, Joseph Keith
Gomes, (Raymond) John
Goodmurphy, Dennis Michael
Grannan, James Matthew
Grannan, James Thomas

Grannan, Richmond Louis
Grant, Gerald
Green, Francis
Greenall, (Reginald) Charles
Greene, Thomas John
Greenslade, John
Griffin, John Andrew
Grogan, Sinon John
Gross, Donald John
Gunnip, George Gerard
Hague, John
Hague, William J. Gerard
Haley, (Nicholas)
Hamaguchi, (Joseph) C. Hyozo
Hamasaki, Peter Katsuichi
Hamel, Edward Alfred
Hamel, Ernest
Haney, (Dominic) Harold
Hanlon, (William) James
Hansen, Paul Edward
Harding, (Joachim) John
Harmstone, (Bernard)
Harnett, (Lawrence) John Thomas
Harper, D. Gerald
Harrington, John Daniel
Harrington, (Victor) Daniel
Hartley, Thomas Joseph
Hayes, Jeremiah
Healey, Francis A.
Healey, (Sylvester) Gerard
Healy, James L.
Healy, Peter Joseph
Heaney, (Gabriel) William
Hebert, Remi Walter Joseph
Heffernan, Norman
Henchey, (Benedict) Hugh
Hennessey, Patrick
Hickey, (Paul) Vincent
Hicknell, Leo
Hicks, Arthur William

Hill, Francis
Hoeppe, Karl
Hoffman, (Simon) Edgar
Hogan, (Leo) Leo Michael
Hogan, William J.
Holland, (Alphonsus) William
Holland, Daniel
Horn, Raymond
Hovencamp, (Leon)
Howard, Edward
Howard, Lucian
Hrbolich, Francis Peter
Huber, Ronald Richard
Hughes, Walter
Hurtubise, (Andrew) Camille
Hutchison, Gerald
Hutchison, William Bruce
Insell, (Leo) John Bartley
Ivess, (Alban) Bernard Francis
Ivess, (Francis) Anthony
Jacqmin, Joseph
James, Joseph
James, William Patrick
Jimmo, Francis Kenneth
Johnson, Bernard Joseph
Johnson, Francis Claire
Johnson, Kleinnart
Josey, James
Josey, (John) Francis Alexander
Kane, John
Kassab, Jawad
Kathrein, (James) John Nicholas
Kathrein, (Luke) Carl George
Kathrein, (Mark) Daniel
Kearney, Francis
Keast, Richard Paul
Keindel, Gerald Edwin
Kelly, Arthur Jordan
Kelly, Charles E.
Kelly, (Edward) Leland

Kelly, John
Kelly, Thomas
Kelz, Charles
Kennedy, Edward Francis
Kennedy, Kenneth
Kennedy, Martin
Kennedy, Stephen John
Kenney, Clarence Glenwood
Kenny, John David
Keogh, Francis
Keogh, George
Keogh, John
Ketelaars, John
Kiely, J.
Kilbreath, Eric
Kiley, (John)
Killingsworth, Cecil
Killingsworth, Norman Joseph
Killoran, (Aloisius) Terrence Ch.
King, (Timothy) Peter Paul
King, (Robert) Kenneth R.
Kinsella, (Gerald)
Klein, (Ronald) Ronald John
Knapik, Joseph
Kondo, Clement Masahiro
Kopiakiwsky, Nicholas
Koster, Joseph Gerald
Kot, Joseph
Kramer, Clayton
Kroetsch, William
Kuc, Stanley
Labelle, (Thomas) Paul
Lambert, John Michael
Lane, Frederick Richard
Langi, Dominic
Lapierre, Paul Emile
Laton, (Alexander) William
Laver, Thomas
Lawless, Francis Daniel
Leacy, John

Leblanc, George
Leering, Albert
Leinweber, Douglas Arthur
Lelievre, (Liguori) Henri
Lemieux, Claude
Lenihan, (Francis) Thomas
Leonard, Arthur
Letang, (Brendan) John
Leusswik, (Paul) Bernard
Lewis, (Eugene) John David
Liska, Stanislaus
Lockwood, John David
Loftus, Albert
Logan, James Ronald
Lonergan, Thomas B.
Lopresti, (Lorenzo) Anthony
Loran, Hugo Gerard
Louch, David Richard
Luce, William
Luciani, Anthony J.
Lundrigan, (Raphael) Patrick
Lunney, Bernard Joseph Edward
MacDonald, (Allan)
MacDonald, Andrew Joseph
MacDonald, Archibald
MacDonald, Cameron
MacDonald, Donald C.
MacDonald, John Stewart
MacDonald, Robert
MacDonald, Wayne
MacDougald, Donald John
MacGillivray, Joseph Bernard
MacGregor, John Alan
MacIsaac, Charles Kenneth
MacIsaac, Michael Patrick
MacKay, Donald Charles
MacKerrow, Paul
MacKinnon, Angus
MacKinnon, John
MacKinnon, Neil Joseph

MacLellan, Alexander Archibald
MacLellan, Donald
MacLellan, Lewis
Madigan, John L.
Madigan, John J.
Mahoney, (Vincent) James
Makiyama, (Dominic) F. Chikashi
Mallett, Richard G.
Mallone, William
Malone, Basil Wallace
Malone, Francis Mathieu
Maloney, Francis
Maloney, Raymond
Mandrick, (Damien) Joseph
Mangan, Thomas Joseph
Mann, John Patrick
Mann, Roman
Mann, Walter Anthony
Marcina, Paul
Marino, Robert
Martin, John Patrick
Mason, James Bernard
Mates, Morton
Mayer, Stephen
McAulay, Clark
McAvoy, Reginald
McBriarty, Anthony
McCandlish, James
McCandlish, Leo
McCann, Andrew
McCarthy, (George) Francis
McCormick, Charles
McCormick, Gerard
McCormick, Joseph
McCullough, William Patrick
McDonald, (Alexis) Francis Gerard
McDonald, Archibald
McDonald, Charles Hickey
McDonald, Edward James
McDonald, Patrick James

McDonald, (Peter) Edw. Augustine
McDonald, Robert Bernard
McElhinney, Walter
McElligott, Cornelius John
McGee, Mark Darrell Stuart
McGillis, Neil John
McGinn, Darrell Francis
McGrath, Sinon Gerard
McGreel, Joseph Aloysius
McGuigan, William Joseph
McGuiness, Gordan Anthony P.
McGuire, Henry John
McGuire, Joseph Austin
McGuire, Leonard
McGurry, (Robert)
McHarg, (Peter) Donald
McIntyre, (Daniel) Joseph
McIntyre, (James) Frederick
McKenna, George Francis
McKenna, Robert
McKenna, Thomas
McLaughlin, Joseph
McLaughlin, William
McMahon, Howard Francis
McMullen, William
McNally, Raymond John
McNeil, Alexander
McNeill, Thomas Bernard
McNorgan, Gerald Anthony
McNulty, Douglas
McNulty, Gerald Edmund
McNulty, Thomas Michael
McPhail, John
McQuaid, Ralph
McSherry, Edwin Walton
Meehan, Edward
Meehan, Matthew
Melanson, (Rene) Francis
Mernagh, Michael Patrick
Mertz, David

Meyer, Edward
Michalski, Gary Warren
Miller, Mark Chester
Mitchell, (Benedict) Joseph
Mitchell, Joseph John
Moad, (William)
Mohan, Emmett J. Jos.
Molland, Robert Louis
Molnar, John Paul
Monaghan, John William
Mooney, James
Moore, (Cornelius) Thomas
Moore, Edward
Moran, Gerard
Moreau, Cecil
Morley, Thomas
Morrisey, Stephen Joseph
Morrison, (Paul) Norbert
Mountain, Francis
Moyes, (Leonard) George
Muldoon, John
Muldoon, Robert
Mullaly, Edward
Mullan, (Richard) James
Mullins, Francis
Mulroy, (Matthew)
Murphy, Aidan
Murphy, (Alphonsus) Robert
Murphy, Joseph John Leonard
Murphy, Gerald
Murphy, Gregory Joseph
Murphy, Michael Joseph Patrick
Murphy, (Patrick) Leo
Murphy, Paul
Murphy, Thomas Patrick
Murphy, Timothy
Murphy, William
Murray, Gerald
Murray, Michael Anthony
Murray, Terrence

Murray, Thomas
Mylett, George
Nadeau, Ronald
Naphin, John Cyril
Nash, (Andreas)
Nelder, Robert John
Nicol, Robert Joseph
Nishimoto, Albert Toru
Nishiuchi, Francis Kiyoshi
Nolan, James
Norman, Leonard
Nugent, (Eugene) William
Obertowich, Stephan
Osadec, Basil
Ouellette, (Dennis) Denis Edward
Owens, Gerard
Owens, Joseph
O'Brien, James
O'Brien, John David
O'Brien, (Peter)
O'Brien, Thomas
O'Connell, (Cornelius) John
O'Connell, (Paul) John
O'Connor, (Paul) William
O'Connor, Thomas Raymond
O'Deady, John
O'Donnell, David
O'Donnell, Joseph
O'Donnell, Robert
O'Flaherty, William
O'Hara, (Alphonsus) Gerard
O'Hara, Charles
O'Hara, Joseph
O'Hare, Peter
O'Hearn, (Eugene) Christian
O'Keefe, Barry Augustus
O'Reilly, Charles
O'Reilly, Donald Brian
O'Reilly, Eugene
O'Reilly, George Thomas

O'Reilly, John Michael
O'Rourke, (Bartholomew)
O'Rourke, Donald Martin
O'Rourke, Thomas Peter
O'Sullivan, Daniel
O'Sullivan, (Michael)
O'Sullivan, Timothy
Pankhurst, Douglas
Parks, (James)
Payer, Pierre
Peacock, (Dominic) Joseph Paul
Petryschen, Michael
Pettipas, Gerard
Phelan, James Michael
Pierce, (Gregory) Raymond
Pittman, (Anthony) Joseph
Plamondon, Robert
Plant, (Gerard) Garry
Poirier, Leger Joseph
Poliquin, Joseph Roger
Pope, (George)
Power, (Albert)
Power, (Augustine)
Power, (Dominic) Henry
Power, Donald
Power, Patrick Joseph
Power, William Patrick
Powers, Raymond
Primeau, Jean Claude Guy
Purcell, David Lawrence
Purschke, Douglas Joseph
Pyper, Terrance
Quinn, Edmund
Reardon, Joseph P.
Reddy, John Martin
Redman, Edward
Redmond, Joseph Gerard
Rekowski, Aloysius John
Reynolds, Cyril
Richards, (Francis) Thomas

Riopelle, (Martin) Denis
Riou, Robert Joseph
Roach, (Damian) Henry Francis
Rohatinsky, Stephen
Rolls, Leo Jeffrey
Rooney, James Patrick
Roth, Michael Dale
Roy, (Brendan) Louis
Ruta, Joseph Michael
Ryan, John Arthur
Ryan, (Stephen) Ronald
Salaga, Richard
Salmon, (Patrick)
Sandwell, (Bede) William
Santopinto, Mageste John
Savoia, Francis
Scanlan, Desmond
Schindler, Karl
Schmidt, Carl
Schofield, (Martin)
Scollard, James
Scollon, Michael Louis
Scollon, Thomas
Scullion, Paul Thomas
Scully, Edward A.
Sexsmith, Leo
Shalla, Isidore Ambrose
Sirianni, (Leonard) Francis
Skaluba, Francis
Sliva, Daniel John
Smets, (Modestus) Alphonse
Snoble, Russell Carl Joseph
Sozansky, (Onesime) Michael
Spicer, John Ewart
Stamp, Douglas Patrick John
Staniszewski, (Stephen) Szczepa
Starr, Paul Leo
Starr, (Vincent)
Steacy, William
Steele, (David) Angus

Steels, (Leonard) Charles
Stephens, Henry Kennedy
Sterzer, Albert Vincent
Stockton, Donald Alan
Stoeckel, Albert
Stoeckel, Rudolph
Stroebele, (Alfred) Albert
Stutskij, Joseph
St. John, Richard Harris
St. Pierre, Paul Joseph
St. Pierre, Philip John
Suckling, (Ernest)
Sullivan, Anthony
Sullivan, Arthur Joseph
Sullivan, Cornelius Francis
Sullivan, Gregory
Sutcliffe, (Leonard) Ivan
Swift, Herbert Thomas
Switalski, Bruno
Taggart, Bruce Joseph
Tanaka, Aloysius Kenji
Tedlock, F. Gerald Edwin Clifford
Thomas, Alphonsus
Timmony, (Patrick)
Tobin, Edward
Tobin, Roger J.
Toombs, (Philip) William Ernest
Tracey, Brian Peter
Travers, James
Traynor, Thomas William
Tugnett, Gordan
Uniac, (Gerald)
Ura, (Clement) Michael Soichi
Vale, Paul
Vallieres, Joseph
Vandersteen, Frank
Vandervoort, Peter Gerard
Vickers, (Gregory) Joseph Dennis
Voss, Reginald T.
Vozza, William Raymond

Wale Menard, Leonard
Wallace, (Wilfred)
Walsh, Dennis Joseph
Walsh, Edward
Weir, David Alexander
Welch, (Robert) Colin John R.
Welsh (Velycz), Gregory
Whalen, David Jerome
Whalen, Michael Carl
Whalley, William Lee
Wheeler, (Walter)
White, Patrick
Whitfield, (Francis) John

Wiley, Joseph
Williams, Frederick Ervin
Wingle, James Matthew
Wojciechowski, Ladislaus
Wolff, Ferdinand
Woods, James
Wright, Michael Paul
Wyllie, William Alfred
Yamaguchi, (Alphonsus) T.
   Shigeyoshi
Yamashita, (Gerard) Peter Tomiyuki
Yamashita, Paul Mineyuki
Yokota, (Michael) Joseph Shiro

Appendix 2

List of Redemptorists who were born or worked in English Canada but never joined an English-Canadian province, 1834–1994

Allard, Rene
Anderson, Archibald
Augenthaler, Charles
Banckaert, Henry
Barolet, Adelard
Barrett, Patrick H.
Bausch, Peter
Bayer, Benedict
Beaumont, (Patrick) Charles
Becker, (Maurice) Frank
Beil, John
Belanger, (Fidele) Emile
Bennett, John
Billiau, Alphonse
Boels, Henri
Bohn, Mathias
Boll, (Albert) Valentine
Bond, William
Bonia, Maurice
Bonomo, Umberto
Borgmann, Joseph
Borgonie, Florent
Bradley, James
Brandstaetter, Frederick

Breihof, Sebastian
Brick, William
Burke, Michael S.
Bye (Pye), (Gregory) James
Carbray, Paul-Felix
Caron, Arthur
Caron, Thomas
Catulle, Jan (Jean)
Cesare, Anthony
Chapoton, Joseph
Chin, Peter
Clauss, Joseph
Coen, (Hugh) Thomas
Condon, Michael
Conter, Antoine
Cook (Koch), Francis Joseph
Cooney, Thomas Lawrence
Cooper, Ernest
Corbett, John
Corduke, Michael
Corry, Fergus
Corsyn, (Eugene)
Coté, (Alfred)
Coté, Ovide

Coughlan, Arthur T.
Coulie, Joseph
Couvrette, Victor
Cronin, John
Crosby, William
Cuddihy, (Alban) James
Cullen, Bernard
Currier, Charles
Daels, (Sylvanus)
Daily, John
De Acetis, J.
De Ridder, Leopold
Debongnie, Charles
Decamps, Noel
Deckelmann, (Wolfgang)
Decoene, Joseph
Defains, Pierre
Delargy, Francis X.
Derenski, Julius
Derling, John
Devlin, (Majella) Francis
Di Chio, Francesco
Di Stasio, Giuseppe
Distler, Joseph
Dodsworth, Cyril
Dold, Louis
Donlan, (Patrick)
Donohue, Thomas A.
Dorawa, Raymond
Dougherty, (Terence) Joseph
Doyle, (Christopher) John
Doyle, Peter
Doyle, (Philip) Edward
Drouin, (Bernard) (Cyrille) Laur.
Dufresne, Eugene
Dugal, Paul
Duke, Augustine
Dumont, Eugene
Dwyer, Timothy
Englert, George

Fairbourne, (Arthur)
Feeney, James
Ference, Dennis
Fiset, Achille
Fitzgerald, John
Fitzsimon, Mark Bartholomew
Flynn, Edmund
Foerst, George
Fortier, Louis
Frings, (Richard) John
Fulford, John
Funk, Joseph
Gannon, Michael
Garant, Silfrid
Geiermann, Peter
Ghekiere, Joseph
Giesen, Henry
Girard, Pierre
Godts, Guillaume
Graham, (James)
Gregoire, Celestin
Gregoire, (Odilon) Joseph
Grimm, Eugene
Grix, (Florian) John Anthony
Groetsch, (Odilo) Andrew
Growchowski, Thomas
Guillo, John B.
Gunning, Andrew
Gutberlet, Francis
Haas, (Polycarp) Michael
Haetscher, Francis-Xavier
Haley, (Dominic) John
Halton, (Solanus) John
Hamelryckx, Joseph
Hanley, John
Hayden, John B.
Healey, Arthur
Heim, Henry
Heinemann, Charles
Helmpraecht, Joseph

Hendrickx, Alphonse
Hennes, Ferdinand
Henning, Joseph
Heslan (Hislin), (Xavier) Henry
Hespelein, John
Hickey, John
Hild, George
Hoelscher, Victor
Hofner, Lawrence
Holland, Edward
Holzer, Laurence
Hopkins, Bernard
Houle, (Gaetan) Guillaume
Hoyois, Jean-Baptiste
Hurley, (Edward) Thomas
Jaeckel, Nicholas
Jasinski, Francis
Jentsch, John
Jones, Alfred G.
Jones, Thomas A.
Jung, Lawrence
Kannamueller, Carl
Kauder, Christian
Kautz, Joseph
Kea, Henry
Kearns, (Linus) Mark
Kehoe, (Daniel) Daniel Clarence
Keitz, Joseph
Kenny, James
Kenny, Timothy Francis
Kern, Charles J.
Kinzinger, Hector
Kirchner, (Louis) Valentine
Klauder, Alexander Francis
Klennert, Frederick
Klingen, (Dominic) Francis-X.
Knecht, (Anselm) Adam
Koch, (Aloysius) Joseph
Kodisch, (Mathias) John
Kodisch, (Nicholas)

Kolb, Benedict
Konings, Anton
Krein, Stephen J.
Kreis, Adam
Krickser, Joseph
Krutil, Francis
Kuhn, Andrew
Kutter, (Joachim) Theodore
Laffineur, Camille
Lafrance, (Arthur) Eugene
Laliberte, (Romuald) Emile
Lamontagne, Edouard
Lamy, Theodore
Landherr (Justus) Joseph
Lava, Rene
Lawlor, John B.
Leclerc, Clement
Leclerc, (Pierre) Napoleon
Leibfritz, John
Leitheiser, Douglas
Lemieux, Alphonse
Lemieux, (Remi) Wilfrid
Lemire, Candide
Lentsch, Leonard
Leonard, Patrick
Lepas, (Ildephonse) Alphonse
Lietaert, Omer
Litzenburger, (Joseph) Henry
Loewekamp, William
Lortie, (Leon) Joseph
Loughnane, Thomas
Lover, James Francis
Maes, (Libert) Joseph
Maguire, John Edward
Mahoney, (Timothy) John
Mallengier, Adolph
Maloney, Martin J.
Martin, (Vitus) Hugh
Mayer (Meyer), (George)
McCabe, Hilton H. (Herb)

McCarthy, (Edward) Nicholas
McCarthy, Jeremiah
McClary, Frederick
McCormack, Thomas Joseph
McDonald, Dougal
McGinn, John Joseph
McGivern, Patrick
McGuire, Patrick
McInerney, Augustine J.
McLeod, Charles
McLaughlin, James
McMahon, Patrick Joseph
McMahon, (Patrick) Joseph
McManus, Bernard J.
McNamara, John
McPhee, John
Menard, Rodrigue
Mercier, J. Alfred
Merkle, (Cajetan) Joseph
Meunier, Joseph Paul Yvon
Meurer, Henry
Michel, George
Miller (Mueller), Francis X.
Miller (Mueller), Louis
Mohan, Henry
Molloy, Edward
Monstrey, (Idesbald) Louis
Montecalvo, Antonio
Moore, (Patrick)
Moran, (Ambrose) William
Muldoon, (Thomas)
Mulhall, Patrick
Mulheran, Eugene
Mulligan, Bernard
Munn, (Albert)
Murphy, James
Murphy, (Stanislaus) James
Mussely, Henry (Hendrik)
Nelligan, (Ambrose) Thomas
Neithart, Benedict

Niemann, Clement
Oates, Michael
Oberle, Francis
Ott, Charles
O'Callaghan, (Thomas)
O'Connor, Edward
O'Connor, William
O'Hagan, Alphonse
O'Keefe (Keefe), (Jeremiah)
O'Keefe, (Oscar) John
O'Neill, (Alexander) William
O'Neill, Francis
O'Regan, John Baptist
O'Reilly, Joseph P.
Paar, (Adam)
Pampalon, Pierre
Paquay, Servais
Paradis, (Eusebius) Edmond
Pazdziorko, Jozef
Pelletier, (Samuel) Achille
Perusse, (Achille) Eugene
Phelan, (Edmund) Edward
Philippe, (Désiré)
Pietsch, (Ubald) Aug.
Power, Edward
Power, John
Power, Nicholas
Quenneville, Alfred
Rathke, Charles
Reagan, Benedict
Reaume, (Hugh)
Rebhan, Conrad
Rein, James
Reisach, (Joseph)
Reiter, (Felix)
Renaud, (David) David Gerard
Reynolds, Thomas
Rheaume, Alfred
Rietvelt, Benedict
Rioux, Paul

Robinson, (Beatus) Joseph
Robinson, George
Rogers, (Daniel) Patrick
Rosenbauer, Michael
Rossbach, Philip
Saenderl, Simon
Samson, (Stephen)
Sattler, Henry Vernon
Saucier, Arthur
Saul, William
Savard, Louis
Scanlan, Francis X.
Schaack, Theodore
Schelfhaut, Philippe
Schmid, Anton
Schmidt (Smith), Charles
Schnabel, (Philip) Joseph
Schoenlau, (Bruno) John
Scholly, Joseph J.
Schonhart, Joseph
Schwalb, (Cajetan) Andrew
Sebrechts, Karel
Shields, John
Shyshkowich, Gregory
Siedlik, Izydor
Sigl, Charles
Simard, Joseph
Smeijers, (François)
Smulders, Aegidius
Stafford, Cletus
Stainforth, Alfred
Sternon, Emile
Stockhausen, (Vitus) Anthony
Stoessel, (Bernardine) George
Stroh, Paul
Strubbe, Edward
Stuhl, Augustine
St. John, (Alexander) Thomas
Thumel, Augustine
Tierney, (James)

Tremblay, (Frederic) Thomas
Trimpel, Peter
Trudel, Alfred
Turner, Joseph
Ullmeyer, (Leonard)
Umana, Salvatore
Urban, Emil
Urben, Henry
Van Geleen, (John)
Van Peteghem, Cyrille
Van de Capellen, Peter
Van den Bemden, Pierre
Van den Bossche, Frans
Van der Beek, (Louis) Aloyse
Van der Sompele, Henri
Vercruysse, (Jerome) Augustine
Verlooy, Edward
Vermeiren, Gustave
Viglianti, Dominic
Vlasak, Clement
Vlassenroot, (Boniface) Camille
Vrijdags, Evarist
Ward, Peter
Wallace, John
Walsh, Eugene (Owen)
Watson, William
Wayrich, William
Weigel, Edward M.
White, William
Wiethorn, (Titus) George
Will, (Leo)
Williams, (Thomas) John
Winters, Arthur
Wissel, Joseph
Wissel, Joseph Raphael
Wynn, Andrew
Zabawa, Kazimierz
Zenkant (Zinkand), (Luke) Joseph
Zimmer, (Chrysostom)
Zinnen, Louis

Note on Sources

The materials for a history of the Redemptorists in English Canada are found mainly in the Archives of the Redemptorist Province of Toronto. These papers, which include newspaper clippings as well as chronicles and personal papers, were supplemented with the files and chronicles preserved in the existing houses or Redemptorist monasteries of Canada. For example, the former home of the provincial government in Toronto, St. Patrick's Rectory, still keeps its own annals and these are especially useful for the history of the Redemptorists in all of English Canada. Correspondence with Rome was not always preserved in Canada, so that files in the Redemptorist General Archives, Rome, are essential reading. For the Redemptorist house of St. Ann's, Montreal, St. Augustine's of Brandon, Manitoba, and of St. Gerard's of Yorkton, Saskatchewan, the papers of the North Brussels (Flemish) Provincial Archives in Belgium were consulted, since these houses were founded by the Belgians. The South Brussels (Walloon) Archives in Tournai, Belgium, were consulted but were unimportant for this study; few Walloons were sent to Canada. For the other houses, the Baltimore Province Archives, in Brooklyn, New York, are important. After the division of the English Canadian Province of Toronto into Toronto for the east and Edmonton for the west in 1961, papers, chronicles, and photographs for the western houses were occasionally sent to the Edmonton Province Archives, most of which are temporarily housed in the Provincial Archives of Alberta, in Edmonton. For information relating to the Ukrainian-language houses that belonged to the Toronto Province, all of the above archives contain some valuable material. Belgian and French-Canadian materials relating to the early years of the English Redemptorists are also held in the archives of the Ste-Anne-de-Beaupré Province. Although diocesan and other religious archives were consulted, few other documents were found and fewer still that showed a different side to the history of the Redemptorists in Canada.

Statistics were newly compiled from the archives for this history, unless otherwise noted. Civil statistics for the period 1867 to 1976 were taken from F.H. Leacy, ed., *Historical Statistics of Canada* (Ottawa 1983) or other Statistics Canada publications.

For many years there was a ban on owning or using photographic equipment, especially on the missions, so that Redemptorists or lay people would not be distracted from the business of saving souls. This leaves us with only a few professionally posed photographs of individuals, groups, and churches. All photographs are from the Toronto Province archives unless otherwise noted.

A selected bibliography of secondary works can be found at the end of the book.

Abbreviations

AGR	Archives of the Redemptorist General Government, Rome
ANALECTA	*Analecta Congregationis Sanctissimi Redemptoris*, Rome: 1922–67
ARCAT	Archives of the Roman Catholic Archives of the Archdiocese of Toronto
ARPB	Archives of the Redemptorist Province of North Belgium, Brussels
ARPE	Archives of the Redemptorist Province of Edmonton
ARPSA	Archives of the Redemptorist Province of Ste-Anne-de-Beaupré
ARPSL	Archives of the Redemptorist Province of St. Louis, Glenview, Illinois
ARPT	Archives of the Redemptorist Province of Toronto
ARPY	Archives of the Redemptorist Province of Yorkton
PAA	Public Archives of Alberta, Edmonton
RABP	Redemptorist Archives of the Baltimore Province, Brooklyn, New York
RR	*Review for Religious*, St. Louis University, Missouri
SH	*Spicilegium Historicum Congregationis Ssmi. Redemptoris*, Collegium S. Alfonis de Urbe, Rome

SM   *Studia Moralia*, Alphonsian Academy, Rome

SOS   General Archives of the Sisters of Service, Toronto

SUPPLEMENTUM   Joseph Wuest, CSsR, *Annales Provinciae Americanae, Supplementum ad I-II-III*, 2 vols., Ilchester, Maryland: 1903–07

WUEST   Joseph Wuest, CSsR, *Annales Congregationis SS. Redemptoris, Provinciae Americanae*, 5 vols. Ilchester, Maryland, and Boston: 1888–1924

Notes

Introduction

1 Hofbauer to Hübl, 6, 7 August 1806, archives of the French secret police in Paris, transcribed in *Monumenta Hofbaueriana, Acta Quae ad Vitam S. Clementis M. Hofbauer Referuntur* ... VI (Torun, Poland 1932), 24–30.

2 Behind the Franciscans, Jesuits, Salesians, Benedictines, the Brothers of the Christian Schools, and the Dominicans, and just ahead of the Marist Brothers, the Oblates of Mary Immaculate, the Society of the Divine Word, the Vincentians, the Spiritans, and the Augustinians.

3 The English translation of "The True Redemptorist" is found in Stanislaus Werguet, *The Model Redemptorist Brother. A Manual of Spiritual Direction and Prayer* (St. Louis, Missouri 1932), 14–43.

4 For a recent critical biography of Alphonsus Liguori, see Frederick Jones, *Alphonsus de Liguori. The Saint of Bourbon Naples 1696–1787* (Dublin 1992). For an overview of Liguori's moral theology, see Théodule Rey-Mermet, *La morale selon St. Alphonse de Liguori* (Paris 1987); for context, see *SM* 25, no.1 (1987) and Louis Vereecke, *De Guillaume d'Ockham à Saint Alphonse de Liguori. Études d'histoire de la théologie morale moderne 1300-1787*: Vol. XII, *Bibliotheca Historica Congregationis SSmi Redemptoris* (Rome 1986).

5 Ignace Bourget, "Circulaire au clergé du diocèse de Montréal," 5 January 1842, *Mandements des évêques de Montréal* I:183-4.

Chapter One: Pioneers in British North America

1 Michael Curley, "The Redemptorist Pioneers in America, 1832-1835," *SH* 4 (1956): 121–55.

2 Joseph Reisach was born 21 January 1808 in Innsbruck, Austria. He completed his memoirs in 1857, in a cramped, corrupt old-fashioned German script. The manuscript is in Reisach's personnel file in RABP and has been transcribed in SUPPLEMENTUM I:278–310.

3 For summaries of this episode, see Eduard Hosp, *Erbe des hl. Klemens Hofbauer. Erlösermissionäre (Redemptoristen) in Österreich 1820-1951* (Vienna 1953), 295-300, and the monthly magazine *Klemens-Blätter. Monatschrift des Volksmissionäre vom Heiligsten Erlöser*, March 1949 to

January 1951. Carl Hoegerl has summarized Hosp's work in "With Francis X. Haetscher, C.SS.R., in Detroit: 1832," *The Province Story. A Redemptorist Historical Review – Baltimore Province* IV, no.1 (19 June 1978): 14–26.

4   Carl Mader, *Die Congregation des Allerheiligsten Erlösers in Österreich. Ein Chronicalbericht über ihre Einführung, Ausbreitung, Wirksamkeit und ihre verstorbenen Mitglieder als kleine Festgabe zur Centenarfeier ihres heiligen Stifters Alphonsus Maria de Liguori* (Vienna 1887), 408. In English, see John M. Lenhart, "Francis Xavier Haetscher, C.SS.R., Indian Missionary and Pioneer Priest (1832-1837)," *Social Justice Review* of 1952: January, 308–11; February, 340–2; March, 366–8; April, 19–22; and May, 49–53.

5   RABP, 324, "Circulare Pl. Revdi P. Provincialis," 26 March 1873, printed in WUEST V, no. 3: 135–49; Joseph Wissel, *The Redemptorist on the American Missions*, 3 vols. (Norwood, Massachusetts 1920), I:3–4.

6   Giuseppe Orlandi, "La missione popolare redentorista in Italia. Dal settecento ai giorni nostri," *SH* 33 (1985): 51–141.

7   ARPT, 577–04, "Redemptorist Missions. Nature, Object and Structure."

8   RABP, 325, "Provincial Regulations for Missions" [1884]. Emphasis in the original.

9   Jansenism is, in the words of John A. Hardon, *Modern Catholic Dictionary* (Garden City, New York 1980), "A system of grace developed by Cornelius Jansenius (1585-1638), … According to Jansenius, man's free will is incapable of any moral goodness … those who receive the grace will be saved; they are the predestined. All others will be lost … The later developments of Jansenism … [produced belief in] God's selective salvation … and moral rigorism, denying God's mercy to all mankind. [This] led to an arbitrary attitude toward the use of the sacraments, notably reducing the frequency of penance and the Eucharist … In 1794, Pope Pius VI condemned a series of eighty-five propositions of the Italian Jansenists."

10   AGR, Belgium, "Vice-province of Canada," Tielen to Mauron, 19 November 1883, about the two extremes of French Jansenism and liberal freemasonry found in Canada; AGR, Baltimore, "Provincialia," Schauer to Mauron, 5 April 1884, about Montreal; Serge Gagnon, *Plaisir d'amour et crainte de dieu. Sexualité et confession au Bas-Canada* (Sainte-Foy 1990), 101.

11   Rey-Mermet, *La morale*, 43; for privileges: George Schober, ed., *Compendium privilegiorum et gratiarum spiritualium quibus ex S. Sedis concessione gaudet Congregatio Ss. Redemptoris*, revised by Jos. Aertnys (Ratisbonae, Romae, Neo Eboraci and Cincinnati 1909); *Compendium Privilegiorum Congregationis SS. Redemptoris* … (Rome 1941).

12   RABP, 325, "Dear Rev. Father: …," (form letter sent to parish priests before a mission) [1886].

13 Ibid., "Provincial Regulations for Missions" [1884].

14 SUPPLEMENTUM I:301–2.

15 ARCAT, petition from the Catholics of Sault Sainte Marie to "Right Rev. Alexander McDonald [MacDonell], Roman Catholic Bishop of Upper Canada," 24 September 1834; ibid., petition from the inhabitants of Sault Sainte Marie to "His Excellency Sir John Colborne, K.B., Lieutenant Governor of the Province of Upper Canada," 12 January 1835.

16 Saenderl to Passerat, 26 June 1833, in WUEST I:246, translated by Edward Day, "The Beginnings of the Redemptorists in the United States: 1832–1840" (Mémoire de Licencié en Sciences Historiques, Université Catholique de Louvain 1958).

17 L. Kenning, "E Commentariis," in SUPPLEMENTUM I:314–16, translated by Day.

18 Reisach in ibid., 303–5.

19 *Minutes of the Annual Conference of the Wesleyan-Methodist Church in Canada, from 1824 to 1845, inclusive; ...* (Toronto 1846).

20 American Baptist Archives Center, Valley Forge, Pennsylvania, Abel Bingham, Sault Sainte Marie, to Lucius Bolles, Baptist Missionary Board, Boston, 27 January 1835.

21 *The Fifth Annual Report of the Society, For Converting & Civilizing the Indians, and Propagating the Gospel, Among Destitute Settlers In Upper Canada; For the Year Ending October 1835* (Toronto 1836), 51.

22 Rese to Leopoldine Foundation, 21 May 1835, in John F. Byrne, *The Redemptorist Centenaries* (Philadelphia 1932), 49.

23 Synod of the [Anglican] Diocese of Algoma Archives, Report of Capt. Thomas G. Anderson, July 1835.

24 Thomas W. Mullaney, *Four-Score Years: A Contribution to the History of the Catholic Germans in Rochester* (Rochester 1916), 23.

25 For a picture of daily life, see *Codex Regularum et Constitutionum Congregationis Ss. Redemptoris Necnon Statutorum A Capitulis Generalibus Annis 1764, 1855, 1894 Editorum* (Rome 1896).

26 RABP, "Reisach," "Tages-Ordnung, der Exercitien und Recolections Tagen der [Lay?] Brüder der Congregation des Allerheiligsten Erlösers."

27 Werguet, *The Model Redemptorist Brother*, 4–18.

28 Stanley Nadel, *Little Germany. Ethnicity, Religion, and Class in New York City, 1845–80* (Urbana, Illinois 1990), 17–19; Heinz Lehmann, *The German Canadians 1750–1937. Immigration, Settlement and Culture*, tr., ed., and intro. by Gerhard P. Bassler (St. John's, Newfoundland 1986).

29 See Michael Curley, *The Provincial Story. A History of the Baltimore Province of the Congregation of the Most Holy Redeemer* (New York 1963), 39–55, 68–70, for reorientation to the German immigrants; for the German-Irish nationalisms among American Redemptorists, see AGR,

Baltimore, "Van de Braak," Adrian Van de Braak to Mauron, 2 August 1859; Ernst Ant. Reiter in *Schematismus der katholischen deutschen Geistlichkeit in den Ver. Staaten Nord-Amerika's; Statistik aller deutschen Missions-Pfarreien, Stationen und Schulen, und Wegweiser für katholische deutsche Einwanderer. Mit einer kirchlichen Karte der Ver. Staaten* (New York, Cincinnati, and Regensburg 1869) labels all of the Redemptorists as German, whether they were born in Germany, Ireland, or the United States.

30 Curley, *Provincial Story*, 343, n110, and WUEST, I:179, 369–70; Archbishop Samuel Eccleston of Baltimore objected to a newspaper article Saenderl was erroneously accused of writing.

31 ARCAT, LB01.104, Czvitkovicz to Bishop Power, 20 February 1844; LB01.105, Power to Saenderl, 28 February 1844, granting faculties in the townships of Wilmot, Waterloo, and for Germans and Ojibwa throughout the diocese; LB02.250, Power to [Czvitkovicz], 18 August 1845; for Power's decision about the printing press, see LB02.252, Power to Saenderl, 26 August 1845; for property, LB02.158, Power to Saenderl, 3 May 1844.

32 AGR, Baltimore, "Index Congregatorum Provincia Americanae, qui ab initio i.e. ab anno 1832 ad Mensem Majum usque anno 1855 dispensati vel expulsi fuere"; WUEST, I:179; for Saenderl's side of the story, see ibid., 369-70 and SUPPLEMENTUM II:95-7.

33 John M. Lenhart, "Rev. Simon Saenderl, C.Ss.R., Indian Missionary," *Social Justice Review:* July-August 1941, 130–2; September, 166–8; October, 206–7; November, 242–4; December, 278–80; January 1942, 314–16; February, 350–3; and March, 386–8; Theobald Spetz, *The Catholic Church in Waterloo County* (Toronto 1916), 17–8, 56, 76, 97, 258; John H. Gilchrist, "The History of Puslinch Lake and the Big Island" (Archives 31, Wall County Historical Restoration Society 1936), typescript.

34 Day, "Beginnings of the Redemptorists," 101.

35 [Joseph Wuest], *Conspectus laborum apostolicorum Congregationis SS. Redemptoris in America septentrionali. Ab anno 1840 usque ad annum 1890* (Ilchester 1893); RABP, 528, "Circa Ministerium PP. Nostrorum anno 1844 ad annum 1856 in Buffalo"; WUEST I:173–4, 191; II:86; Michael Curley, *Bishop John Neumann, C.Ss.R. Fourth Bishop of Philadelphia* (Philadelphia 1952); Alfred Rush, "The American Indians and the German Immigrants in the Missionary Plans and Work of St. John Neumann, 1832–1840," *SH* 25 (1977): 118–29.

36 WUEST II:204, 460–2, III, part 1:334–7; AGR, Baltimore, "Labores apostolici, 1832–1868," "Elenchus Laborum Apostolicorum in Prov. Americana," 108.

37 WUEST III, part 1:334–7; ARCAT, CTA01.07, Heilig to Charbonnel; CTA01.08, Ruland to Charbonnel, 19 November 1853; Byrne, *The Redemptorist*

Centenaries, 198–212; for a chronology of religious in Toronto, see William O'Brien, ed., *Walking the Less Travelled Road. A History of the Religious Communities within the Archdiocese of Toronto 1841–1991* (Toronto 1993), 201.

38   RABP, 322, Cazeau to Ruland, 11 June 1856; [Baillargeon] to Ruland, 28 August 1856.

39   Joseph G. Daly, *Conflict in Paradise. Beginnings of the Redemptorist Mission to the Virgin Islands, 1855–1860* (n.p. 1972), 11; Curley, *The Provincial Story*, 130; for a modern biography, see David J. O'Brien, *Isaac Hecker: An American Catholic* (New York and Mahwah, New Jersey 1992).

40   WUEST III, part 1:378; part 2:139; Lorenz Leitgeb and Karl Tauscher, *Lebensbilder der vom Jahre 1887 bis 1914 verstorbenen Redemptoristen der Österreichischen Provinz* (Vienna 1924), 118–20.

41   F[rançois] Dumortier, *Le Révérendissime Père Nicolas Mauron. Supérieur Général de la Congrégation du Très-Saint Rédempteur (1818–1893) Notice Biographique* (Paris 1901); Maurice de Meulemeester, *Outline History of the Redemptorists* (Louvain 1956); Curley, *The Provincial Story*, 170, 176–7.

42   ARCAT, Helmpraecht to Lynch, 3 and 11 July 1866; Lynch to Powley, 9 September 1871; WUEST V, part 2:175; for an official description of the mission, see AGR, Baltimore, "Provincialia," Helmpraecht to Mauron, 15 February 1866, and WUEST V, part 1:88–9, 169–73.

43   RABP, 325, Lubienski to Wuest, 30 December 1884. Lubienski saw little difference between Austrian and American missions and wanted to purchase Wissel's volumes for use in Galicia; ARPT, [Scrapbook of letters from the Baltimore Provincial sent to St. Patrick's, Quebec City, 1880–1914], Schauer circular, 15 April 1887, recommends Wissel's *The Redemptorist on the American Missions*.

Chapter Two: The First Foundations in Canada

1   ARPT, Annals of St. Patrick's, Quebec, Fr. Pierre-Télesphore Sax to Helmpraecht, 22 April 1873; AGR, Baltimore, "Provincialia," Helmpraecht to Mauron, 5 May 1873.

2   Samuel Boland, "The Redemptorists and the Parish Ministry," *SH* 34 (1986): 3–30.

3   AGR, Baltimore, "Provincialia," Mauron to Helmpraecht, 6 June 1873.

4   Ibid., Mauron to Helmpraecht, 11, 25 October, 4 November 1873.

5   RABP, 595.3, [Taschereau] to Helmpraecht, 10 November 1873; AGR, Baltimore, "Provincialia," Helmpraecht to Mauron, 13 March 1874.

6   The visiting missionaries were Joseph Henning, Nicholas Jaeckel, Xavier Schnuettgen, Timothy Enright, and Theodore Lamy; see AGR, Baltimore, Provincialia, Helmpraecht to Mauron, 5 October 1874, stating that the

mission would be for the trustees and that the "Irish" personnel were only temporary.

7   WUEST V, part 3:456–7.

8   RABP, 595.3, Burke to Helmpraecht, 13 January 1875.

9   ARPT, Annals of St. Patrick's, Quebec, 5–9 February 1875.

10   RABP, 595.3, Henning to Schauer, 17 January 1878.

11   ARPT, Annals of St. Patrick's, Quebec, 21 October 1877: Purgatorian Society; for Calixa Lavallée: April 1879; RABP, 595.3, Burke to Schauer, 19 January and 17 June 1885; "St. Patrick's National and Beneficial Union of Quebec." ARPT, 501-09, "St. Patrick Old Boy's Association ... Quebec ... Bulletin XXXV. May, 1971"; [Scrapbook of letters from the Baltimore Provincial sent to St. Patrick's, Quebec City, 1880–1914], 24 July 1880, and "[Canonical Visitation Book of St. Patrick's, Quebec, 1875–1966]," 7 October 1885.

12   For the attempt to attract men, see ARPT, [Scrapbook of letters from the Baltimore Provincial sent to St. Patrick's, Quebec City, 1880–1914], 22 May 1904. For a discussion of gender roles within Christian families, see Colleen McDannell, *The Christian Home in Victorian America, 1840–1900* (Bloomington 1986), 136–49; Brian P. Clarke, *Piety and Nationalism: Lay Volunteer Associations and the Creation of an Irish-Catholic Community in Toronto, 1850–1895* (Montreal and Kingston 1993), 62–96.

13   ARPT, Annals of St. Patrick's, Quebec, 9 January and 5 March 1876.

14   Redemptorists tried to avoid nationalisms of every kind: see AGR, Baltimore, "Relatione 1878," Schauer, "Visitationsbericht über Paters und Brüder ad. St. Patricium, Quebec"; ibid., "Provincialia," Helmpraecht to Mauron, 8 October 1876; Schauer to Consultor General Michael Ulrich, 22 May 1883; RABP, 325, Reuss to Schauer, 3 July 1883. Bernard Vigod, *Quebec Before Duplessis. The Political Career of Louis-Alexandre Taschereau* (Montreal and Kingston 1986), 45–6 shows how St. Patrick's parish became a Liberal refuge even for French Canadians.

15   WUEST V, part 3:323; AGR, Baltimore, "Provincialia," Helmpraecht to Mauron, 20 August 1875, and "Ad rei memoriam," by Mauron, 21 September 1875.

16   Peter Geiermann, *Annals of the Saint Louis Province*, 3 vols., (St. Louis 1924), and RABP, 245, "Provincia Baltimorensis anno 1897 Pars II" chronicle the many devotions and missions in New Westminister, Vancouver, and Victoria, British Columbia, the Windsor and London areas of Ontario, the western areas of Ontario near the Manitoba border, and in Winnipeg, Manitoba.

17   ARPSL, Girardey to Magnier, 26 November 1897; RABP, 326, Magnier to Litz, 11 December 1897; Schwarz to Litz, 8 January 1898; AGR, Baltimore, "Provincialia," Litz to Raus, 16 January 1898; Vincent J.

McNally, "Church-State Relations and American Influence in British Columbia Before Confederation," *Journal of Church and State* 34, no. 1 (Winter 1992): 93–110.

18 AGR, Baltimore, Provincialia, Mauron to Schauer, 25 October 1878; Schauer to Mauron, 20 April and 5 September 1878.

19 They were: the Alsatian, Joseph Clauss [often spelled Klauss]; the Luxembourger, Louis Zinnen, exiled by the Kulturkampf in 1874; the Belgian Louis Dold; Brother Joachim Kutter from Frohnhofen, Württemberg; the Bavarian Brother Simon Ernst; and the Prussian Frederick Brandstaetter, who arrived later.

20 AGR, Baltimore, "Provincialia," Clauss to Mauron, 5 March 1879.

21 Jean-Pierre Asselin, *Les Rédemptoristes au Canada. Implantation à Sainte-Anne-de-Beaupré 1878-1911* (Montréal 1981); Armand Boni, *Pioniers in Canada, Belgische Redemptoristen in de provincies Quebec, Manitoba en Saskatchewan* (Brussel 1945); Maurice De Meulemeester, *La Province Belge de la Congrégation du T.-S. Rédempteur 1841–1941* (Louvain 1941).

22 ARPT, Annals of St. Patrick's, Quebec, 2 February and December 1880; RABP, 325, Henning to Schauer, 18 November 1880.

23 AGR, Baltimore, "Provincialia," Mauron to Schauer, 28 November and 17 December 1880.

24 Ibid., Schauer to Mauron, 4 March 1881. Schauer uses the word "Kleinigkeitskrämer," which can be translated as fusspot or nitpicker.

25 RABP, 595.5, Henning to Schauer, 27 August 1888; John Ross Robertson, *Landmarks of Toronto*, 6 vols. (Toronto 1894–1914), 4:337, states that the church and property were free of debt when Father Laurent left.

26 Karl Schindler, *To Serve God's People* (Toronto c. 1982) summarizes the Annals; ARPT, 210, Lynch to Schauer, 3 January [1881]; Grimm, born 1835 in Rollbach, Bavaria; Hayden, born 1846 in Craiguenamanagh, Ireland, spent his entire priesthood in Canada; McInerney, born 1843 in New York City; Miller (Mueller), born 1843 in New York City; Brother Alexander O'Neill was born 1842 in Fort Edward, Quebec, was the first Canadian brother to persevere until death, and was also stationed in Saint John, New Brunswick and Portland, Oregon; Krein, born 1849 in Baltimore.

27 RABP, 595.5, Miller to Schauer, 11 May 1881; ARPT, Annals of St. Patrick's, Toronto: [Miller] "Toronto is a city of Apostates and Infidels," December 1880.

28 AGR, Baltimore, "Provincialia," Schauer to Mauron, 19 June 1881.

29 RABP, Annals 1882, "Circa Missiones in Nova Scotia et Terra Nova." The Halifax missionaries were Joseph Wissel, Jacob Keitz, Matthew Bohn, Augustine J. McInerney, Joseph Kautz, and Sebastian Breihof, while the Newfoundland missionaries were Wissel, McInerney, Peter Bausch, Joseph Kautz, and Benedict Kolb.

30   Elinor Senior, "The Origin and Political Activities of the Orange Order in Newfoundland 1863–1890" (M.A. thesis, Memorial University of Newfoundland 1960), 150.

31   William G. Licking, *Reminiscences of the Redemptorist Fathers Rev. John Beil, Rev. Patrick M'Givern, Rev. John O'Brien, Rev. Leopold Petsch* (Ilchester, Maryland 1891), 126.

32   ARCAT, A92, "General Correspondence 1880–1920," Wissel to "Most Rev'd Father!" n.d., about Saint John.

33   Michael Oates, formerly of Quebec City, was superior and was accompanied by Henry Urben, born 1848 in Loretto, Pennsylvania, while Brother Alexander (William O'Neill), also formerly at Quebec, became the first brother officially stationed in Saint John. Father John Beil, born in Baltimore in 1855, soon joined them.

34   AGR, Baltimore, "Provincialia," 25 March 1884.

35   Ibid., Schauer to Ulrich, 4 August 1884; Curley, *The Provincial Story*, 187, wrongly stated that it was on Schauer's initiative.

36   ARPT, Brandon Annals, introduction; AGR, Belgium, "Vice-province of Canada," Catulle to Mauron, 16 May 1892. Catulle was asked by the Belgian emigration society of the Archangel Gabriel to find them a settlement in Canada's Northwest.

37   ARPT, "Elenchus SS. Reliquiarum Congregationis Sanctissimi Redemptoris quae en Ecclesia S. Annae Marianopoli venerentur": with over seven hundred relics and one hundred reliquaries, it was one of the more important collections in Canada.

38   ARPT, Scrapbook of St. Ann's, Montreal, newspaper clipping of the *Post*, 11 November 1885. Since the first Redemptorists in Ireland and St. Patrick himself were not Irish, Strubbe had a point. Strubbe, born in Bruges in 1848, ordained in 1873, professed in 1883, spent almost eighteen years in the Montreal parish. He raised the Young Men's Association to great heights of activity and supported Irish drama. He died in 1905.

39   RABP, 595.4, Schauer to Wuest, 5 August 1884.

40   ARPT, [Scrapbook of letters from the Baltimore Provincial sent to St. Patrick's, Quebec City, 1880–1914], 15 April 1887.

41   Terence Moran, "Popular Devotion and the Congregation of the Most Holy Redeemer," *Readings in Redemptorist Spirituality*, 4 (Rome 1991): 126-37.

42   RABP, 595.3, Henning to Schauer, 17 January 1878. A studendate (sometimes spelled studentate) is the name used by Redemptorists to designate the major seminary and could be any house for students, generally in vows, in philosophy or theology.

Chapter Three: The First Vice-Province of Toronto

1   RABP, 325, Trimpel at Cumberland County, Nova Scotia, to Schauer, 25 November 1885.

2 Sharp, *Reapers of the Harvest*, 230, makes the point about the mission decline, as does ARPB, "Godts, Willem," Godts to his brother, François[-Xavier], 17 July [*c*. 1894].

3 RABP, 595.5, Miller to Schauer, 29 December 1886; ibid., 325, Burke to Schauer, 18 April 1887.

4 Monique Rivet, "Les Irlandais à Québec 1870–1968" (M.A. thesis, Laval University 1969), 64.

5 ARPB, "Catulle, Jan," Catulle to "Rev. Mother," 13 July [1884], about rivalry; RABP, 325, Currier to Schauer, 11 October 1883; AGR, Belgium, Ulrich to [Provincial] Dubois, 27 [?] February 1893, about the rumours amongst the Americans; Dubois to [Ulrich?], 1 March 1893.

6 ARPT, "PL.RR.PP. Provincialis et Visitatoris permanentis. Documenta [Letters from the Belgian Provincial and the Canadian Visitor to St. Ann's, Montreal, 1885–1912]," 25 May 1891; ARPB, "Montreal," Van Aertselaer to Hoyois, 30 October 1897; RABP, 325, Ulrich to Schauer, 26 August 1884; AGR, Belgium, "Rapport sur la Province Belge en 1892," compared the English to the French Canadian.

7 AGR, Belgium, Kockerols to Mauron, 22 November 1886, about an individual Redemptorist to be sent to Canada.

8 Ibid., Van Aertselaer to Dubois, 16 May 1896; ARPB, "Montreal," "Notes Sur l'établissement des Rédemptoristes Belges au CANADA" (n.a., n.d., *c*. 1901?); ARPT, "[Letters from the Belgian Provincial and the Canadian Visitor to St. Ann's, Montreal, 1885-1912]," 3 October 1892.

9 ARPB, "Noviciaat Choristen," Catulle to Kockerols, 24 June 1889; AGR, "Rapport sur le Studendat de Beauplateau. Année scolaire 1893–1894"; ARPT, 145–06, 5 March 1951, records appreciations of McPhail as "the Apostle of the Ottawa Valley."

10 ARPB, "Noviciaat Choristen," Kockerols to [?], 29 March 1889; AGR, Belgium, "Rapport sur le Studendat de Beauplateau. Année scolaire 1893-1894."

11 AGR, Belgium, "Vice-province of Canada," C. Leclerc to Raus, 2 October 1897.

12 RABP, 326, Mauron to Litz, 26 April 1893; AGR, Belgium, "Vice-province of Canada," Mauron circular, 26 April 1893.

13 AGR, Belgium, "Vice-province of Canada," Guillot to [?], 14 November 1897.

14 Ibid., Catulle to [Dubois], 10 July 1895.

15 ARPB, "Montreal," Raus to Van Aertselaer, 30 July 1895.

16 AGR, Baltimore, "Provincialia," Litz to Schwarz, 6 August 1895; ARPB, "Canada – Yorkton," 1894; "Montreal," Dubois to Van Aertselaer, 25 July 1895.

17 The number of Belgians working in Canada at any time can be gleaned

from Alphonse-Marie Parent, "Membres de la Province de Ste-Anne depuis ses premiers débuts" (Ste-Anne-de-Beaupré 1971), while Asselin, *Les Rédemptoristes au Canada*, 103–4, summarizes the French-Canadian numbers.

18 RABP, 326, Litz to Dusold, Easter 1894. Emphasis in the original.

19 AGR, Belgium, Dubois to Van Aertselaer, with a note appended by Raus, 22 November 1897; also ibid., "Vice-province of Canada," Dubois to [Strybol], 1906 October 16. The monastery was closed in 1917, reopened in 1924 and closed again in 1927. The land on the corner of Notre Dame and Nicolet was bought in 1928 and the buildings were torn down by the Montreal Harbour Commission.

20 Archives of the Redemptorist Province of London: John Bennett, born 16 February 1852 at St. John's, Newfoundland, professed 1872 at Bishop Eton, Liverpool, ordained 1877, had been rector in Perth, Scotland, before being named provincial for 1890–94. On his return to England, he was again named provincial for 1898–1904 and 1921–24. In 1913 Bennett left England for Canada, but returned after giving some missions and retreats, because he found the climate too severe. He died 13 December 1938. A short biography is in "A Venerable and Brilliant Nfldr. Thought He Would Not Live to be Ordained," in the St. John's, *Daily News*, 21 February 1938.

21 AGR, Baltimore, "Visitation," 9 March 1897, consists of Magnier's Latin summary of Bennett's notes, which could not be found for this study.

22 ARPSL, Girardey to Magnier, 27 August 1897.

23 AGR, Baltimore, "Visitation," Mullane to Raus, 2 September 1897.

24 ARPSL, Girardey to Raus, 15 January 1898; ibid., Provincial D. Mullane, Letters to and from Rome 1898, 11 January 1898.

25 AGR, Baltimore, "Dodsworth," Dodsworth to [Magnier], 30 October 1897; ibid., "Provincialia," Litz to Schwarz, 13 January 1898.

26 Ibid., "Visitation," Schwarz to Raus, 26 June 1897; RABP, 327, Schwarz to [Loewekamp], 1 June 1898: "... all this talk about this absorbtion [*sic*] of the American houses by the Belgians is *absolutely false* ... One of the very reasons why a Vice Province was started was to prevent the Belgians from *absorbing our houses & fathers* in Canada."

27 RABP, 327, Diary, n.d.: consultors were F.X. Miller and Peter Ward; Albert Stern was rector in Buffalo, Ward rector in Toronto, Philip Rossbach in Rochester, Joseph Henning in Quebec, Michael Corduke in Saint John, Francis Klauder in Detroit, and Patrick Barrett in Grand Rapids. They had all worked in Canada before.

28 Ibid., "The creation of a vice-province is not favorably received by many. That Detroit & Grand Rapids should be detached from West & put to Vice-province is regarded by some as a subterfuge to supply Fathers to west – & optimism says they will be returned." See also Luecking to

Dusold, 2 June 1898; Luecking to Schauer, 20 April 1898; Litz to Schauer, 18 April 1898; and Schwarz to Litz, 19 April 1898.

29   AGR, Baltimore, "Provincialia," Loewekamp to Raus, 28 December 1898; Miller to Raus and Ward to Raus, 1 January 1899.

30   ARPB, "Montreal," Catulle to Van Aertselaer, 14 May 1896; ARPT, 727-01 and 02: the foundation was established on August 15 1898, but the parish had been established in 1893 shortly after the CPR passed through the town. Brandon comprised the town and outmissions to Souris, Monteith, Fairfax, and Carroll to the south, Rapid City, Minnedosa, and Clan William to the North, Alexander to the west, Carberry, Melbourne, Douglas, and Hun's Valley to the east.

31   ARPT, Annals of St. Patrick's, Toronto, 21 November 1898 and 7 March 1900.

32   AGR, Baltimore, "Provincialia," J.H. L[oewekamp] to Schwarz, 24 September 1898, for the ban on building; Frank to Raus, 28 December 1898.

33   RABP, 327, Schwarz to Loewekamp, 18 January 1899; Luecking to Loewekamp, 28 September 1900.

34   ARPSL, Mullane to Schwarz, 16 March 1899, about the Rocky Mountain Vice-province; Mullane to Schwarz, 29 April and 15 July 1899, about visits and rumours in Detroit and Grand Rapids.

35   AGR, Baltimore, "Provincialia," Loewekamp to Schwarz, 19 December 1898; Loewekamp to [Schwarz], 19 December 1899; Luecking to Schwarz, 4 April 1900; Luecking to Raus, 8 February 1901; RABP, 327, Luecking to Loewekamp, 18 October 1899; [Henning?] memorandum, "Reasons why the Houses of the Balt. Province in Canada should not be annexed to the Canadian Province," c. 1899; ARPT, Annals of St. Patrick, Toronto, 14 and 19 September 1901.

36   RABP, 327, Luecking to Loewekamp, 29 March 1900; ARPT, 210, Mullane to Lemieux, 10 September 1901.

37   Schauer was the chronicler in Buffalo and switched back to German after the vice-province collapsed. The Rochester chronicler did not bother to note the collapse. The Toronto chronicler welcomed the news in Gaelic, "Slaupt gy wel!" on 18 May 1901.

38   Curley, *The Provincial Story*, 256: "[Luecking] also promoted ... the initiation of the Baltimore Province into the foreign mission field."

Chapter Four: The Second Vice-Province of Toronto

1   ARPB, "Montreal," "Relation sur les juvénistes qui pourraient aller au noviciat," recommended holding back Thomas Molloy and Donald MacDougal; "Rapport sur le Noviciat de l'année 1904–1905 à Montréal, Canada," recommended holding back Peter O'Hare. The students who were professed were Donald MacDougal, Arthur Winters, Peter O'Hare,

and Gerald Murray, who persevered in part due to McPhail's efforts.

2   ARPB, "Montreal," McPhail to [Van de Steene], 22 March 1909, which includes a list; Baltimore: Sinon Grogan, Stephen Connolly, Peter Costello, John Kane, Charles Kelz, Martin Maloney, Edward Scully, James Woods, William Hogan, James McCandlish, George Mylett, and John Hanley; St. Louis: Robertson [George Robinson], Dougal McDonald [McPhail's nephew], John McGinn, John Fitzgerald, Timothy Kenny, Edward Molloy, Edward Power, Thomas Cooney, and Thomas Caron; Canada: Edmund Flynn, George Daly, Daniel Holland, Edward Walsh, John McPhail, and Donald MacDougal. Hanley was not born in Canada, although he worked several years in Quebec City and in the first Vice-province of Toronto. McGinn and Molloy's parents lived in the United States.

3   AGR, Belgium, "McPhail, John," McPhail to [Schwarz], 18 February and 23 March 1905.

4   For Daly's methods, see ARPSA, P-Toronto, vol. 2, file 14, "corr. George Daly," Daly to [L.-] Philippe [Lévesque], n.d.

5   AGR, Belgium, "Schwarz, Josephus," Schwarz to Daly, 28 November 1902.

6   ARPSA, F[erdinand] Bourret, "Le R.P. Tim O'Sullivan, C.Ss.R.," 18 December 1960.

7   PAA, 79.187, R78/1, Godts to Mgr [Langevin?], [21] April 1900 (copy of original in Winnipeg Archdiocesan Archives).

8   Ibid., Van Aertselaer to Godts, 24 June 1900; AGR, Belgium, "Vice-province of Canada," Lemieux to [Van Aertselaer], 5 March 1901; Apostolic Delegate Falconio and Archbishop Langevin of St. Boniface to Raus, 21 February 1901; ARPT, 210, Langevin to Godts, 15 July 1903; actually, just after the Belgian Redemptorists took over in 1898, Langevin requested another foundation, this time among the rapidly growing population of Ukrainians; see ARPB, "Catulle, Jan," Langevin to Van Aertselaer, 18 April 1899.

9   ARPB, "Delaere," "Notes données par l'ex P. Decamps."

10 ARPB, "Canada – Yorkton," Delaere to [Van de Steene], 23 February, 17 March, 12 October 1911; Decamps to [Van de Steene], 30 June 1911.

11 AGR, Belgium, "Vice-province of Canada," Van de Steene, "Rapport sur la visite extra-ordinaire du Canada," 20 June to 27 August 1908; ARPB, "Montreal," McPhail to [Van de Steene], 18 May 1909.

12 ARPT, 212, "Annals of the Vice-Province of Toronto, Ontario, Canada" [by Stephen Connolly].

13 ARPT, 210, Daly, "Memoir. The Origins of the Toronto Province" (21 November 1943). The students were Timothy Murphy and Francis Kearney.

14 AGR, Baltimore, "Provincialia," Luecking to P. Murray, 31 July 1909; ibid.,

Toronto, "Provincialia," Lemieux to P. Murray, 13 May 1912; Lemieux and consultors to P. Murray, 31 May 1912.

15 RABP, 136.4, Speidel, "Plan for Vice-Province of Toronto: 1912."

16 AGR, Baltimore, "Visitation," Schauer to [Raus], 2 October 1894, 70–1.

17 ARPT, Daly, "Memoir," 17: the Christian Brothers (1914), the Oblates (1926), and the Holy Cross Fathers (1943) followed the same route, Daly stated, and the Jesuits divided in 1924 along geographic but, in reality, along linguistic lines. The newspaper article can be found in the Saint John *New Freeman*, 13 July 1912.

18 Robert Choquette, *Language and Religion. A History of English-French Conflict in Ontario* (Ottawa 1975), 117–38. For evidence of McPhail's attitude to bilingual schools, see RABP, 595.5, mission report of 24–31 August 1913.

19 RABP, 329, Schneider to Dooper, 9 October 1912; AGR, Baltimore, "Provincialia," petition of 23 October 1912 and reply of 6 November 1912.

20 ARPT, 212, "Annals of the Vice-Province of Toronto, Ontario, Canada," 4. The four boys were Leo. O'Leary, Joseph O'Donnell, Ambrose O'Donnell, and Wilfrid O'Donnell. David O'Donnell, Joseph's older brother, also became a Redemptorist priest.

21 Ibid., [Connolly?] to P. Murray, *c.* 1913; AGR, Toronto, "Provincialia," Lemieux to P. Murray, 17 June 1912; ARPB, "Yorkton," Lemieux to Van de Steene, 25 September 1911; AGR, Baltimore, "Provincialia," Schneider to P. Murray, 26 February 1914 [10, verso].

22 ARPT, "Chronicum Missionum Montreal 1912–1931," 1913; RABP, 595.5, Mission reports, e.g., of St. Patrick's parish, Cathedral chapel, St. John's, Newfoundland.

23 ARPT, Annals of St. Patrick's, Toronto, 15 December 1899 and 20 October 1900.

24 ARCAT, Luigi Pautasso, "Archbishop Fergus P. McEvay and the Betterment of Toronto Italians"; John Zucchi, "Church and Clergy, and the Religious Life of Toronto's Italian Immigrants, 1900–1940," *Canadian Catholic Historical Association Study Sessions* 50 (1983): 533-48.

25 ARPB, "Canada – Yorkton," Delaere to "Très Révérend et Cher Père Recteur," 4 September 1912.

26 AGR, Belgium, "Lemieux, Alphonse," Lemieux to P. Murray, 27 and 29 September 1912, 24 and 25 January, 23 February, 3 March 1913; ibid., "Budka," Budka to P. Murray, 20 February, 18 March 1913; ibid., Toronto, "Provincialia," Van de Steene to P. Murray, 19 and 24 October 1912; also very useful is Andrii Krawchuk, "Between a Rock and a Hard Place: Francophone Missionaries among Ukrainian Catholics," *Canada's Ukrainians, Negotiating an Identity*, Lubomyr Luciuk and Stella Hryniuk, eds. (Toronto 1991), 206–17.

27   RABP 329, Brick to Schneider, 5 November 1912, quoting Speidel: "You must do all you can to hinder those Belgian Fathers to start another Vice-Province out there; this will close the door for you. I'll do what I can here."; ibid., G. Murray and P. Leonard to Schneider, "Report on the French Mission Question," [8 September 1917]; ARPSA, P-1, Lemieux, 8 "Correspondence et documents," 15 June 1917.

28   RABP, 329, "Conventio circa Antillas, Canadam et Galiciam." The only Belgian to join the Toronto Vice-province was Joseph Jacqmin, also known as Jackman.

29   AGR, Belgium, "Visitatio canonica extraordinaria anno 1901"; RABP, 596.1, Duke to Schneider, 4 February 1914: "St. Augustine's is an English, not a Polish parish. It is true, the Poles outnumber the English speaking people"; Growchowski to Schneider, 10 February 1915, about Brandon's decline; ARPT, 721–03, Derling to Brick about Yorkton, 14 October 1913.

30   RABP, 329, [Speidel] to [Schneider], 24 August 1912; P. Murray to Schneider, 27 January 1914.

31   AGR, Toronto, "Provincialia," Connolly to P. Murray, 6 April 1912; McPhail to P. Murray, 13 April 1913; ARPT, Annals of St. Patrick's, Toronto, 20 September 1912.

32   AGR, Toronto, "Provincialia," Daly to Consultor General Hallet [*sic* for Othmar Allet], 20 September 1913; Connolly to P. Murray, 10 August 1913; ARPT, 571-01: the actual cost in 1913 was $3234.31 for seven minor seminarians, which was more than double the cost in 1912 ($1,400) for the minor seminary at St. Ann's. By 1914 there were twenty-one Canadians in North East, allowing economies of scale and the cost was $4,947.45.

33   RABP, 329, F. Sp[eidel] to [Schneider], 16 October 1912.

34   AGR, Baltimore, "Provincialia," Schneider to P. Murray, 25 May and 5 June 1914.

35   PAA, 79.187, R79/1, Schneider to Duke, 30 December 1913, 24 January 1914; RABP, 595.5, Brick to [Schneider], 2 January 1914; "Consultationes Provincialis 1909–1921," 24 January 1914; ibid., 136.4, Dooper, "Re: Canadian Questions."

36   ARPT, 712–01, Elmwood typescript annals, 11.

37   RABP, 329, P. Murray to Schneider, 9 February, 21 March, and 21 April 1914.

38   AGR, Baltimore, "Provincialia," Baltimore to P. Murray, 29 April 1914.

39   Ibid., Baltimore's reasons for Quebec basement church on Grande Allée to P. Murray, 30 April and 1 May 1914.

40   Ibid., Schneider to P. Murray, 31 May 1914.

41   See, for example, ARPT, 595.5, Schneider to Brick, 2 April 1914; ibid., 730-01, Connolly to Brick, 5 April 1914.

Chapter Five: The Formation of the Toronto Province

1 ARPT, 300-04, Walsh to Mulhall [?], 17 November 1919, about German-born Redemptorists; RABP, 329, Knell to Schneider, 16 February 1916, 22 June 1917, about student difficulties in border crossing; ARPT, 210, Mulhall to Walsh, 23 December 1917, about letters being opened; ibid., Brandon Annals, 22 November 1917; RABP, 329, Beierschmidt to Schneider, 7 September 1918, about a Canadian student being detained at the border "and locked up for a few hours until a higher official was satisfied with his statement."

2 RABP, "Consultationes Provincialis 1909–1921," 29 July 1915.

3 ARPT, "Provincial Consultations 1915–1942"; useful insight into Grogan's education in the Baltimore Province can be had in Paul T. Stroh, *Ilchester Memories: 1868–1957. The Golden Jubilee of the Redemptorist Novitiate at Ilchester, Maryland, 1907–1957* (St. Mary's College, Ilchester, Maryland 1957), where he as well as other Canadians appear in text and photographs.

4 *ANALECTA* (1923), 113–17, contains the most complete biographical notice.

5 ARPT, Letterpress, Mulhall to Woods, 3 March 1916.

6 Ibid., 210, [Mulhall] to Kenzel, [?] 1917.

7 "Catholic Priests Deny Charge of Disloyal Acts," *Winnipeg Telegram*, 25 September 1917; Mark G. McGowan, "Toronto's English-Speaking Catholics, Immigration, and the Making of a Canadian Catholic Identity, 1900–30," in Terrence Murphy and Gerald Stortz, eds., *Creed and Culture. The Place of English-Speaking Catholics in Canadian Society, 1750–1930* (Montreal and Kingston 1993), 204–45.

8 ARPT, 300-02, Mulhall to [Speidel], 17 December 1917; RABP, "Consultationes Provincialis 1909–1921," 17 December 1917; ibid., 8 June 1917: "A remonstrance couched in respectful language was made to the Archbps and Bps of Canada who had resolved not to allow our Fathers to give missions in Canada." ARPT, 212, Schneider to Mulhall, 25 June 1917; Letterpress, Mulhall to Schneider, 1 January 1918.

9 ARPT, 300-02, [Mulhall] to [Speidel], 26 February 1918; [Speidel] to Mulhall, 8 April 1918: "Daly is a spoiled child; he should learn to obey and to keep the rule."

10 Ibid., "Provincial Consultations 1915–1942," 16 October, 7 November 1916, and 16 August 1917; ibid., 300-02, Speidel to Mulhall, 16 August 1917.

11 RABP, "Consultationes Provincialis 1909–1921," 11 July 1916; 14 April 1917: "Quebec is too damp and cold to be suited for a novitiate; ... St. John, N.B. would be ample for a novitiate (or E. Kildonan); that Quebec would not be a mission house in 100 years."

12 ARPT, Annals of St. Patrick's, Toronto.

13 Ibid., 300-02, [Speidel] to Mulhall, 9 January 1917, 14 November 1917.

14 AGR, Toronto, "Provincialia," [Mulhall] to P. Murray, 14 January 1919; ARPT, Annals of St. Patrick's, Toronto, 16 May 1919; ibid., 501-05, Costello to Mulhall, 20 May 1919; ibid., 301-02, Coughlan circular, 23 November 1920, about total collected.

15 RABP, "Consultationes Provincialis 1909–1921," 15 November 1918; ARPT, 571-01, Beierschmidt to Mulhall, 7 July 1918; "Provincial Consultations 1915–1942," 16 July 1918.

16 ARPT, 300-04, Weigel to Mulhall, 24 February 1920; AGR, Baltimore, "Provincialia," Weigel to P. Murray, 22 April 1920. Edward Weigel had been in Canada as a missionary in the Maritimes and as rector from 1893 to 1898 of St. Peter in Saint John.

17 ARPT, 551-01, [Anthony McBriarty], "Brockville," 4.

18 AGR, Toronto, "Provincialia," "Relatio de Visitatione canonicis habitis in Provincia Torontina [16 July 1922]," 17; ARPT, "Provincial Consultations 1915–1942," 14 January 1922, about the decision to allow advanced students to teach the lower classes.

19 ARPT, 300-04, Mulhall to Walsh, 10 July 1920, announcing "consumption"; AGR, Toronto, "Provincialia," Mulhall to P. Murray, 29 September 1920; P. Murray to Mulhall, 28 October 1920; Annals St. Patrick's, Toronto, 4 November 1920, document arrived appointing Coughlan, who took oath of office on 8 November.

20 ARPT, 305, D. Ehman, "My diary [May 1922–1923]"; J. Owens to author, 13 January 1994.

21 AGR, Toronto, "Provincialia," "Relatio de Visitationibus Canonicis habitis in Provincia Torontina [16 July 1922]," 14.

22 ARPT, 569-01, Hill to Daly, 4 December 1943; ibid., "Annals of the Class of '23"; see, for example, 23 January 1921: "The smaller juniors had their choice of a spanking or retreat and many of them chose the former as the lesser of the two evils."

23 The Woodstock Baptist College, originally founded in 1857 as the Canadian Literary Institute, reopened its doors in 1860 and was renamed Woodstock College in 1883. It had offered university-level courses, but with the creation of Toronto Baptist College (later McMaster University, Hamilton), it became a Baptist boys' preparatory school and eventually closed its doors in 1926. When the Redemptorists approached McMaster University to purchase Woodstock, the building was being leased to an Anglican boy's preparatory school.

24 ARPT, 571-05, Coughlan to Kennedy, 14 February 1926. *The Review* ran from 1926 to 1941.

25 Ibid., 148-02, Thomas to Weir, 23 April 1973, refers to "the proverbial pile around Winnipeg, where the confreres supposedly used to throw them out

the train windows on their way to the West."

26 AGR, Baltimore, "Coughlan, Arthurus," Coughlan, "Advantages of a Special Italian CSSR House," 6 August 1926.

27 SOS, Coughlan to Donnelly, 12 March 1921; Coughlan to Daly, 9 August 1924; Coughlan to Donnelly, 11 May 1942; AGR, Toronto, "Provincialia," Coughlan to P. Murray, 13 January 1922.

28 SOS, [Coughlan] to Daly, 29 September 1921, and 17 May 1922; ARPT, unfiled, Coughlan to Daly, 2 May 1922.

29 George Daly, *Sisters of Service. A Great Catholic and National Endeavour* (Toronto n.d.), 6.

30 O'Brien, ed., *Walking the Less Travelled Road*, 158–160; for statistics, see ARPT, 140-10, and *Service in Hope, 1922–1972* (Toronto 1972).

31 ARPT, 300-01, P. Murray to Coughlan, 7 November 1922; PAA, 79.187, R57/60, [Daniel Ehman], "Vancouver Tape 1. Cog[hlan]"; R57/64, [idem], *Golden Years 1923–1973. Golden Jubilee. Parish of Our Lady of Perpetual Help, Vancouver B.C.* (n.p. n.d.).

32 AGR, Toronto, "Provincialia," Coughlan to P. Murray, 16 July 1922, 30; ibid., "Brandon," Coughlan to P. Murray, 23 October 1923; ARPT, 800 "Winnipeg," Sinnott to Coughlan, 7 September 1923; Brandon was given up 20 August 1924; P.J. O'Sullivan, *By Steps, Not Leaps. St. Augustine of Canterbury Parish. Brandon, Manitoba. 1881-1981* (n.p. 1981).

33 PAA, 88.508, Edward Kennedy, "The Redemptorists in Western Canada. A Brief Historical Overview," ed. David Louch, (Edmonton 1987), 4: "Ordained from these years in Regina were: Daniel Ehman, Gabriel Ehman, Joseph Boyle, Edward Boyle, Fred Lane, Wallace Malone, Edward McDonald, Frank Malone, John Martin and Oscar Dietz"; Dietz was born, however, in Vancouver. C. Kramer was born in Regina, as was L. Wojciechowski who joined from the diocese in 1923, and P. Collison, although born in the United States, joined the Redemptorists through Regina.

34 AGR, Toronto, "Status Realis," 1923, 1925, 1926 and 1927 reports; Coughlan, "Details of loan and mortgage of St. Patrick's, Toronto for Edmonton and Vancouver foundations," 23 October 1923; ARPT, 266, "Memorandum Re:– Financial Condition of the Toronto Province, The Congregation of the Most Holy Redeemer, Dated January 25th, 1945."

35 AGR, Toronto, "Provincialia," P. Murray to "Very Reverend Fathers and Dear Brothers of the Toronto Province of the Congregation of the Most Holy Redeemer," 2 October 1923, to be read on retreat days.

36 Ibid., Coughlan to Speidel, 23 April 1924.

37 ARPT, 301-01, [Speidel] to Coughlan, 3 April 1924: "Fr. Daly will always be considered as the power behind the throne, which will eventually work out bad for you and your subjects. Therefore Fr. General would like to see him removed from Toronto and sent to the West."

38 John Kane, born Quebec City, 1877, ordained 1904, was forty-nine years old; John Barry, born Rat Portage, North-West Territories (later named Kenora, Ontario), 1880, ordained 1907, was forty-seven.

39 ARPSA, P-Toronto, Vol.2, file 1, Mylett to Lévesque, 1 October 1932, humorously describing McPhail's version of English-Canadian Redemptorist history.

Chapter Six: Moving from East to West

1 ARPSA, "Gerald Murray"; AGR, Toronto, "Provincialia," Coughlan to Speidel, 2 April 1927; G. Murray to P. Murray, 3 April 1927; a short biography is available in *ANALECTA* (1951), 103-5; Kelz's reputation and the canoe imagery were recorded by the students in their private annals: see ARPT, "Annals of the Class of '23."

2 *ANALECTA* (1937), 66; for Kramer's work, see ARPT, 726-01, Kramer to Fuller, 27 April 1942.

3 Coughlan had given Henry McGuire the permission to start the *Patrician*. No copies of the magazine have been found to date, but the title is reminiscent of the Patrician Publishing Co. of Boston and Quebec City which produced *Oatcakes and Sulphur* and which may have been a pseudonym for the Redemptorist Fathers' Boston printing press. There may have been only one issue since the costs were prohibitive and Provincial Murray forbade further publication.

4 Greenall's biography is in *ANALECTA* (1948), 250–2; Augustine G. Bennett, "Poems or Perhaps Just Rhymes," ed. J.N. Bennett, CSsR (Toronto 1986), 68p.; an example of a poem used in the devotions is the well-known "Redemptorist Rosary," by the Belgian Brother Idesbald (Louis Monstrey), who spent thirty-eight years working for the Ukrainians and died in Yorkton in 1934.

5 AGR, Toronto, "Provincialia," G. Murray to P. Murray, 10 November 1928; ARPT, "Charlottetown Annals 1929/54."

6 AGR, Toronto, "Provincialia," G. Murray to P. Murray, 9 September 1928; *At the Foot of the Hill. Commemorating the 50th Anniversary of Our Lady of Perpetual Help Parish* (Calgary [1975?]).

7 AGR, Toronto, "Provincialia," P. Murray to G. Murray, 4 December 1928.

8 ARPB, "Yorkton," 3 March 1919. Daly's arguments in favour of assimilation were also sent to the Ukrainian Redemptorists: see Emilien Tremblay, *Le Père Delaere et l'église ukrainienne du Canada* (Ottawa 1960), 283–4; these same arguments appeared in the *Northwest Review* beginning 7 February 1920, under the alias of "Miles Christi," one of Daly's usual pen names, and then in Daly's book *Catholic Problems in Western Canada* (Toronto 1921).

9 Documentation for this episode is rare. Delaere may have been named visitor, a delegate of the Belgian provincial. Both terms, visitor and vice-

provincial, were used interchangeably, but each had a separate status. A visitor often was named for a provincial who could not visit the houses. He reported to the provincial who still made the decisions. A vice-provincial, although also a delegate of the provincial, had decision-making and financial powers. Sometimes, a vice-provincial would also be named a visitor and would make the canonical visitation of the religious houses on behalf of the provincial.

10   Roman Chomiak, "The Yorkton CSSR Province: A Historical Review," translated by George Perejda; ARPB, "Delaere," "Visite Canonique à Yorkton 27 Sept. au 2 Octobre 1926," 14 October 1926, describing the need for more men.

11   ARPB, "Yorkton," Van den Bossche papers, Daly to [Van de Steene], 21 July 1922; AGR, Toronto, "Daly," Daly to P. Murray, 20 June 1926; SOS, Coughlan to Daly, 13 [J?] 1928.

12   ARPB, "Yorkton," "Transfert de la vice-province Ruthène du Canada à la province de Toronto," Kinzinger to [Desmyter], 3 August 1928; PAA, 88-508, Daly to G. Murray, 18 August 1928.

13   PAA, 88.508, Walsh to G. Murray, 27 July and 16 August 1928, 20 March and 8 May 1929; Delaere to G. Murray, 29 April 1929; ARPB, "Delaere," "Notes données par l'ex P. Decamps," about Walsh's personality conflicts with Achille Delaere; for Barron, see AGR, Toronto, "Visitation," report of 25 August 1929.

14   PAA, 88-508, Lemieux to G. Murray, 18 October 1929; Delaere to G. Murray, 30 October 1929; Costello to Bishop Basil Ladyka, 21 October 1930.

15   ARPY, Delforge Papers, Kinzinger to Delforge, 14 December 1930.

16   ARPT, 754-03, Cantwell to Barron, 1930 March 11, about the loss to the Toronto Province; ibid., 302, P. Murray to G. Murray, 18 March 1930; "Provincial Consultations 1915–1942," 1930 October 13, about loan of George Coffin; ibid., 303-03, Murray to Costello, 9 April 1932, about loan of John Barry; for information about Murray's episcopal career, see D[uncan] F. Robertson, *The Sword of Saint Paul. A History of the Diocese of Saskatoon 1933–1983* (Saskatoon 1982), 25–33.

17   ARPT, 303-03, Costello to Hauser, 23 February 1931: "I am trying to establish uniformity in our Province and as far as possible conform to the practices of the Baltimore Province."

18   Ibid., Costello to McEnniry, 2 May 1931.

19   AGR, Toronto, "Provincialia," Costello to McEnniry, 4 December 1930.

20   ARPT, 303-01, McEnniry to Costello, 9 March 1931.

21   AGR, Toronto, "Provincialia," G. Murray to P. Murray, 2 July 1929; ARPT, 302-02, P[eter] O'Hare to G. Murray, 31 October [1928]; ibid., 553-01, Hogan to G. Murray, 17 April 1929.

22   AGR, Toronto, "Visitation," 1936.

23 Margaret Sanche, *Heartwood. A History of St. Thomas More College and Newman Centre at the University of Saskatchewan* (Muenster, Saskatchewan 1986), 17–18, 58–9.

24 ARPT, 573-02, Fuller to Costello, 10 January 1935.

25 AGR, Toronto, "Provincialia," Costello to McEnniry, 2 March 1936; Daly's activities on behalf of the Redemptorists contradict Costello's low assessment of Daly's work for the Toronto Province: for Edmonton, for example, see ARPT, 713-03, Archbishop H.J. O'Leary to G. Murray, 17 December 1928.

26 AGR, Toronto, "Visitation," 1934; ibid., "Provincialia," [McEnniry] to "Father Master" [of Novices, Fuller], 4 December 1935 and 3 April 1936, about Daly as provincial or as consultor, and Fuller's reply, 25 April.

27 PAA, 79.187, R53/37, Dawson Creek Annals, 1 December 1936; *What One Brother Can Do! Brother Thomas C.Ss.R. 1883–1955* (Toronto 1958) describes Brother Thomas Labelle's work in both the Beaupré and Toronto provinces.

28 ARPT, 720-01, for files on Conway.

29 Anthony McBriarty, "The History of the Redemptorists in Western Canada," *The Canadian Catholic Historical Association. Report 1946-1947*, 91–2; Douglas Pankhurst, "A Survey of the Apostolate of the Redemptorist Fathers and Brothers in Nelson, B.C. 1937–1987" (typescript presented to the Faculty of Canon Law, Saint Paul University, Ottawa 1989).

30 AGR, Toronto, "Status Realis," McEnniry to Muldoon, 26 January 1936.

31 ARPT, 266, "Memorandum Re:-Financial Condition of the Toronto Province The Congregation of the Most Holy Redeemer Dated January 25th, 1945," 11.

32 Ibid., 716-05, McGuigan to Hill, 21 August 1931; McGuigan to [Costello], 28 October 1933.

33 AGR, Toronto, "Visitation," 1936; ARPT, 715-01, Daly to [Fuller], 7 October 1937; ibid., 304-01, [Fuller] to McEnniry, 15 November 1937, about Fuller as bishop.

34 ARPT, Annals of St. Patrick's, Toronto, 6 November 1939; one Polish refugee, Bruno Switalski, spent the war with the Toronto Province, teaching in Woodstock.

35 Ibid., 140-8, "Pallottines," letters of the apostolic delegate to Fuller.

36 Ibid., 304-01, P. Murray to Fuller, 20 and 24 July 1945; McEnniry to Fuller, 5 April 1945.

37 PAA, 79.187, Box 49, R.182/52, "Daniel Ehman, C.Ss.R., Historical …"

38 ARPT, 551-10, Douglas Pankhurst, "Students Attending St. Mary's – 1920–1941," [1947].

Chapter Seven: "This Spirit of the World"

1 ARPT, Gerard Hartley, "Research Report on WWII Redemptorist Chaplains. NAC Canadian Chaplains Service (CCS)," 1 June 1994.

2 Ibid., 990, "Data Re Chaplains 1939–1945," 6 January 1951; Moreau to Fuller, 28 November 1942, about the advantages of the war. The *Yank Club* newsletter was renamed the Perpetual Help Mission Club.

3 Ibid., 304-02, Antoniutti to Fuller, 6 November 1941; ibid., 990, A. Charest, Assistant Principal Chaplain (RC), to Fuller, 15 July 1942; C.L. Nelligan, Bishop of Pembroke, circular letter, 31 August 1942.

4 Ibid., 990, Ryan to Fuller, 3 January 1943.

5 Ibid., Ryan to Fuller, 5 November 1943.

6 Ibid., 400 "Coghlan," Coghlan to [Fuller], 29 January 1945, about Ryan.

7 AGR, Toronto, "Provincialia," P. Gallery to P. Murray, 14 June 1945; ibid., "Visitation," Molloy to P. Murray, 12 June 1945.

8 [J.J. Galvin], *The Redemptoristines* (Esopus, New York 1958); Théberge, *Des Rassembleurs d'hommes,* 237-8.

9 ARPT, 145-6, Fuller to Sister Mary Paul, OSsR, 9 December 1946, and memorandum by McBriarty; members were Mother Mary Paul Eagle, Vicar Mary Celeste Bucknall, Sister Mary Veronica O'Rourke, and Lay Sister Mary Joseph O'Grady; see *ANALECTA* (1948), 239 for the enclosure.

10 [Sister Mary Alphonsus (Selma Bartlett), OSsR], "History of the Fort Erie Community of Redemptoristines" (*c.* 1993); ARPT, 145–6, 2 September 1947 for Fuller's statement.

11 ARPT, 304-01, [Fuller] to Buijs, 13 July 1947; ibid., 304-07, G. Ehman to Fuller, 25 July 1947; ibid., 305-08, G. Ehman to D. Ehman, 11 August 1947.

12 Daniel Ehman, ed., *The Joseph Ehmann Family Tree 1823-1968* (n.p. 1968); ARPT, 504-11, "The Christian Family Spokes' Club" [1933-34]. He was transferred to Toronto from January to May 1933 to replace Father Paul Stroh temporarily while Father Stroh recovered from the exhaustion brought on from organizing the growing German Catholic community in Toronto; see also ARPT, Annals of St. Patrick's, Toronto, clipping: "Father Ehman's Mission Shatters all Previous Records," April 1946.

13 ARPT, 508-01, "Protokoll des Erzbischofs von Toronto an die Deutschekatholiken [*sic*] in Toronto," 24 September 1936.

14 Ibid., 508-01, Fuller, "Agreement re Property at Elgin Mills, Ont., One Mile North of Richmond Hill, Ont.," *c.* 1945.

15 Ibid., 170, "Shrines of Our Mother of Perpetual Help already established according to diocese," 1 November 1950.

16 National Archives of Canada, RG24, vol. 15, p. 629, War Diary, February

1943, and [M. Meehan], "Radio and Television Apostolate," in Schindler, *To Serve God's People*, 180–1.

17 AGR, Toronto, "Provincialia," McEnniry to Fuller, 29 October 1941, sending enthusiastic permission for "the negro apostolate."

18 ARPT, 304-10, [Fuller] to Hermans, 9 July 1947, announcing decision and passing on Daly's greetings; ibid., [J. Dwyer], "West Indian Mission," n.d.

19 Ibid., 148-01, Antoniutti to Fuller, 14 December 1946; Fuller to Antoniutti, 18 December 1946.

20 See Samuel Boland, "The Redemptorists in the Foreign Mission Field," *SH* 32 (1984): 130.

21 ARPT, 148-02, Girse to [Fuller], 5 July 1947; Fuller to Taguchi, 16 July 1947.

22 Ibid., 148-01, Taguchi to Fuller, 27 August 1947; AGR, Toronto, "Maizuru," "Information concerning the Religious and Civil Conditions of the Tango and Tamba Districts," *c.* 1947.

23 R. Connaughton, F. Cunerty Jr., J. Glavine, F. Keogh, D. O'Rourke, R. MacDonald, and B. Hutchison were the later missionaries. T. Doyle, G. McNulty, and A. Sullivan were briefly in Japan as students.

24 ARPT 148-01, Fuller to Ehman, 27 July 1948; [Ehman] to Girse, 17 March 1948; ibid., 148-02, Taguchi to Ehman, 25 August 1951.

25 Ibid., 148-01, Taguchi to Ehman, 2 January 1948: "Even though the Fathers would be taking over existing Parishes, their [...] work for years to come will be missionary work, and there will be just a minimum opportunity for Spiritual Exercises, Retreats, Missions and so forth."

26 AGR, Toronto, "Maizuru," "Canonical Visit to the Japanese Missions of the Toronto Province (June 10th to July 14th, 1952)," 16; ARPT, 148-02, Ehman to Fuller, 2 January 1951; ibid., 148-25, [Fuller] to Buijs, 9 February 1951.

27 AGR, Toronto, "Provincialia," D. Ehman to Buijs, 12 March 1950; Keogh to Buijs, 12 March 1950; ARPT, 510-01, Buijs to Ehman, 2 April 1950.

28 ARPT, 305-02, D. Ehman to Keogh, 18 February 1948.

29 Ibid., D. Ehman to Keogh, 1 March 1949.

30 Ibid., 568-04, Lambert to Ehman, 23 December 1950; ibid., "[Provincial Consultations 1942–1962]," 4 August 1951; AGR, Toronto, "Provincialia," Ehman to Buijs, 6 August 1951.

31 AGR, Toronto, "Provincialia," Fuller to McEnniry, 9 January 1940; D. Ehman to Buijs, 26 April 1950; ARPT, 305-01, D. Ehman to Buijs, 19 May 1950.

32 ARPT, 305-01, Buijs to D. Ehman, 1 July 1951.

33 Ibid., 197, Visitation Report 1937, 25; ibid., 306-15, Ryan to C.F. Sullivan, 11 May 1957.

34 Ibid., 762, [Ryan] to Provincial Wilfrid Hughes, 7 June 1956.

35   Ibid., 400 "Pittman," Pittman to [D. Ehman], 26 July 1950; D. Ehman to [Pittman], 28 July 1950; John S.R. Gosse, ed., *Whitbourne. Newfoundland's First Inland Town. Journey Back in Time ... 1884–1984* (Whitbourne 1985).

36   Ibid., 575-08, Harrington to Muldoon, 14 January 1944; Woodstock Annals, 27 October–30 November 1936.

37   Ibid., 161-05, "Father General's Visit. His Addresses. Woodstock. August 1951."

38   Ibid., unfiled, D'Arcy Egan, "Report of Meeting Held at St. Alphonsus Seminary Woodstock, Ontario, May 27, 1953" in Ryan, "The Windsor Project," 20–2.

39   Ibid., 505-03, Ryan to Archbishop P.J. Skinner of St. John's, Newfoundland, 30 June 1956.

Chapter Eight: The Years of the Second Vatican Council

1   *Acta Apostolica Sedis* 43 (1951): 34. Accommodation to modern needs is a hallmark of Pius XII's papacy although it became part of John XXIII's reputation instead, because John called an ecumenical council into being; see Peter Hebblethwaite, *John XXIII. Pope of the Council* (London 1985).

2   ARPT, 400 "Meyer," [Ryan] to Provincial Wilfrid Hughes, Clapham, England, 7 February 1956; ibid., 306-7, Grangell to Ryan, 9 April 1956.

3   Gaudreau's style of leadership can be seen in ibid., 306-01, Gaudreau to Ryan, 20 April 1959; for Ryan, see ibid., 568-05, anonymous, 9 December 1955; ibid., 620-08.

4   Ibid., 306-01, "Summary. Ryan's Visitation Report of 1959."

5   R. Gallagher, "The Systematization of Alphonsus' Moral Theology Through the Manuals. The Story of transformation, abandonment and rejection as evidenced in the treatment of the *habituati et recidivi*," *SM* 25 (1987): 276.

6   Leo Scheffczyk, "Main Lines of the Development of Theology between the First World War and the Second Vatican Council," in *History of the Church*, Hubert Jedin, ed., 10 vols. (New York 1981), 10: 272–7.

7   Bernhard Haering, "Moral Theology and the Apostolic Formation of the Priest," in James Keller and Richard Armstrong, eds., *Apostolic Renewal in the Seminary In the Light of Vatican Council II* (New York 1965), 184. Haering's "core concept" is in his autobiography, *My Witness for the Church* (New York and Mahwah, New Jersey 1992), 24.

8   For Gaudreau's views on unreasonable obedience, see ARPT, 308-04, Gaudreau to Lockwood, 13 January 1965.

9   Ibid., Annals of the Students of Holy Redeemer College, Windsor, 27 August, 20 September, 6 October 1963. The vernacular was used until the bishop of the diocese repeated the Church's law on the use of Latin by

diocesan clergy. The dialogue mass, where the people gave the Latin responses of the altar server, had been approved in 1922 but had rarely been celebrated until the Second Vatican Council.

10   Ibid., 513-18, D'Arcy Egan, "Critical Situation," 7.

11   PAA, 79.189, Box 2, R26/8, "Outgoing correspondence and circular letters from Prov ... J.A. Ryan and V.P. Sup. B. Johnson 1956–1959," April 1960.

12   Ibid., 79.187, Box 4, R.29/12, Demerah, "Minutes of the Discussions following Papers Read at the Mission Conference held at St. Mary's College, Brockville, June 23-25 1961 and Resolutions voted upon at the same Conference"; for an overview of the Congregation, see John J. Ruef, *Redemptorist Parish Missions 1945–1976. Survey Number Three* (Rome 1979).

13   ARPE, Liguori House, G. Ehman to Grangell, 10 February 1957.

14   Ryan quashed such murmurings by writing G. Ehman that "I cannot help thinking that all would not be of the mind 'the west only for the west' (and 'the east for the east, for the west, for Japan'!)": see ARPT, 306-04, 2 January 1957.

15   Ibid., 306-14, [G. Ehman?], "Proposed Plan for Personnel in the Event That the Vice-Prov. of Edmonton is erected 'into a Full-Fledged Province'," [12 July 1957].

16   ARPE, G. Ehman to R. Miller, 31 May 1961 [copy].

17   ARPT, 306-01, Ryan to Gaudreau, 27 February 1959; Ryan memo, 3 March 1961, about meeting with Gaudreau to discuss Edmonton's status; ibid., 700-04, notes of conversation between R. Miller and Ryan, 21 April 1960.

18   Ibid., 148-03, "Report of Visitation of the Maizuru Mission ...," June 24-September 8, 1958 ...": eleven fathers, two of whom were on missions and two others in studies, and five brothers cared for fourteen places. All of them were in the Kyoto diocese except for a recent foundation in Suita in the Osaka diocese. When Patrick Hennessey replaced the seemingly perpetual superior, Fuller, Hennessey instituted a renewed emphasis on cooperation and missions to non-Catholics.

19   Ibid., 148-25, Gaudreau circular to Toronto, 16 October 1955; ibid., 306-14, Ryan to G. Ehman, 17 April 1957; ibid., 195, "Report on Opinion Survey of Toronto Redemptorist Brothers conducted by Canadian Surveys Limited."

20   Ibid., 307-01, O'Reilly to Gaudreau, 12 December 1963.

21   Ibid., 505-03, Archbishop P.J. Skinner of St. John's to Ryan, 14 May 1955 and 17 February 1956; "Over Fifty Thousand Attend Exercises of Archdiocesan Missions," in *The Monitor. Newfoundland's Catholic Journal*, July/August 1957.

22   Bishop Carter's parents lived in St. Patrick's parish, Quebec City, before moving to Montreal; ARPT, 307-08, Carter to O'Reilly, 21

October 1963, about Demerah; O'Reilly to Boyce, 11 November 1963, about the General Mission; Carter to O'Reilly, 26 November 1963.

23 Author's interview with William Murphy, 16 August 1991; ARPT, 307-01, Gaudreau to O'Reilly, 5 June 1964; ibid., 307-08, O'Reilly to J. James, 25 June 1964.

24 ARPT, "[Provincial Consultations 1963-1966]," 1 July 1964; ibid., Gaudreau to Lockwood, 7 November 1965.

25 Ibid., 754-03, [Ryan] to T.W. Coyle, Oconomowoc, 9 August 1956; ibid., 513-18, "Meeting with Faculty HRC January 21, 1960."

26 Murphy revealed his authorship of the Xavier Rynne articles and books in the Redemptorist historians' meeting of 1987 in Esopus, New York. The *New York Review of Books* (12 August 1993), also identified Xavier Rynne as Murphy. Amongst Redemptorists it was common knowledge that Murphy's mother's maiden name was Rynne.

27 ARPT, 513-18, Egan, "Critical Situation," 2.

28 Ibid., 306-01, "General Observations on the 1959 Visitation," section: "*A Serious Problem relative to the spiritual life and charity of the Province?*"

29 Cornelius J. McElligott, *The Crown of Life. A Study of Perseverance* (St. Louis, Missouri 1963). When McElligott tried to prepare an article for publication summarizing his findings, Ryan vetoed it; see ARPT, 400 "Ryan," 21 November 1965.

30 ARPT, 308-04, Lockwood to Gaudreau, 10 July 1964, about Grant's removal.

31 Interview with Edward Boyce, 27 August 1991; further evidence of telephone tapping is in ARPT, 308-04, [Lockwood] to Gaudreau, 7 January 1966, and Gaudreau to Lockwood, 17 January 1966. On 16 August 1991 William Murphy stated that Lockwood objected to such means when he found out that they were being used to form professors' recommendations for or against candidates. This angered the professors and Murphy who argued that such measures were necessary to find out about unworthy candidates. Gaudreau objected to the methods, but if tapes were available, they were to be sent to Rome, since Gaudreau had final authority in recommending individuals for ordination.

32 ARPT, 308-04, Lockwood to Gaudreau, 21 September 1964; ibid., 620-02, R. Macdonald, "The Psychology of a Redemptorist Mission."

33 "RC priests, brothers leaving their vocations," *Windsor Star*, 7 May 1965.

34 ARPT, 308-14, Lockwood to Gaudreau, 17 April 1964; interview with Boyce, 27 August 1991; ibid., 400 "Boyce, Edward," Boyce to Lockwood, 24 June and 1 July 1965.

35 Ibid., "Brief Signers," with notes on which had recently died or left the Congregation (*c.* 1970). Amongst Edward Kennedy's private papers is a prior draft of the brief.

36   Ibid., 800B "Brief," "Jottings," by [Harrington?]; and an untitled three-page more emotional commentary in W.D. Murphy's style.

37   Ibid., 308-04, Lockwood, Harrington, and Murphy to Gaudreau, 22 August 1965: problems "aggravated by the sniping and exaggerated criticisms of the Edmonton Provincial Superior"; ibid., 148-39, Weir to Campbell, 24 January 1965, about Toronto's silences.

38   ARPE, Liguori House, Johnson to O'Reilly, 21 June 1965.

39   Ibid., Johnson to [Georges Boisjoli], 19 July 1965; for dispersal, see PAA, 79.187, Box 3, R26/14, Johnson to L. Feehan, 22 June and 6 July 1965.

40   ARPT, 400 (Harrington), Harrington to Lockwood, 3 May 1965. Knowing that a visitation would take place, Johnson told several students that "help is on the way." See PAA, 79.187, Box 3, R26/14, Circular Letters Johnson 1963-5, Johnson to "Dear Frater," 19 May 1965.

41   ARPT, 754-03, Lockwood to Schmitt, 8 November 1965; ibid., unfiled, Gaudreau to Lockwood and Gaudreau to Boyce, 7 November 1965.

42   Ibid., 754-03, Schmitt to Lockwood, 29 November 1965.

43   John Grindel and Sean Peters, "Religious-Life Issues in a Time of Transition," *RR* 51 (1992): 269. A study of the Redemptorist personnel files reveals that the immediate reasons for leaving almost divided equally into problems with poverty, chastity, and obedience. A slightly higher percentage of brothers had problems with poverty; several left to take care of family members. Some priests had problems with the new definitions of priesthood and once that was in question, the commitment to Redemptorist priesthood weakened. In general, a crisis in one area led to crises in all and then the decision to leave.

Chapter 9: "The New Breed"

1   ARPT, 754-03, [Lockwood] to Schmitt, 20 November 1965. Experimentation was officially granted to all provincials seven months later. Toronto was the test case.

2   Ibid., 620-06, Ryan, "Personnel of the Toronto Province C.SS.R. According to occupation," January 1966.

3   Ibid., 308-01, [Lockwood?] to F. Jones, 27 February 1966, about the "Brief gang"; ibid., 280-02, W.D. Murphy, "Comments on 'Report of Meeting III – Keswick, April 23-24, 1966' Issued by the Commission on Clerical Formation."

4   *Perfectae caritatis* translated in *RR* 26 (1967): 391–403, section 3. For an overview, see Elizabeth McDonough, "Conciliar and Postconciliar Documents on Consecrated Life," *RR* 52 (1993): 780–6.

5   ARPT, 180-06, Lockwood, "The Purpose of the Congregation," 22 March 1967, which also argued for recognition of St. Clement Hofbauer as the second founder of the Redemptorist Congregation.

6   Ibid., 285, Boyce and J. Madigan, "Redemptorist Survey for Renewal ... 1967. Province of Toronto, Vice-Province of Japan."

7   Ken Caunce, "Bouquets, brickbats for General Mission," *Windsor Star* in the ms Annals of St. Alphonsus, Windsor, p. 165, May 1967.

8   ARPT, 148-02, Lockwood to Amaral, "Memorandum re Toronto Province," 12 November 1967; ibid., 513-18, [Lockwood] to Scanlan, 22 October 1967, about the General Chapter's acceptance of proposal to experiment with election of provincials. Interestingly, Gaudreau stated he had been thinking of resigning since 1965, the same year that saw the Windsor seminary dispersed.

9   Ibid., 309-02, circular, 7 February 1968.

10   E.g., ibid., 575-01, "The World in which We Live," 12 February 1969; ibid., 309-02, circular, 3 July 1969.

11   Ibid., 280-02, Maloney, "Report – Pastoral Priorities Study – Toronto Province," 15 November 1982.

12   B. [*sic*] Boyce, "A Sociological Appraisal of the New Trends," *New Trends in Religious Life. Donum Dei Series* 14 (1969): 135 cited in John M. Lozano, "Trends in Religious Life Today," *Religious Life at the Crossroads*, David A. Fleming, ed., (New York and Mahwah, New Jersey 1985), 134 n1.

13   ARPT, "Tentative Terms of Reference for the Provincial Council of the Toronto Province, Canada (Consilium Provinciale Amplificatum)," *c.* 1971. Richard Bedard, fifty-one years old, became first consultor and Frank Maloney, forty-eight, second consultor. R. Corriveau, J. Farrell, J. Corkery, and A. Alexander became councillors. See ibid., 308-04, Lockwood to Amaral, 3 February 1968, describing the provincial chapter and election as a replica of the general council.

14   Ibid., "Staff Meetings [Madonna House]," 14 June 1960; Ryan disagreed with D. Ehman's policy of turning the magazine into a purely devotional medium. He insisted that the *Madonna* was to remain a family magazine paying its own way and making money if possible: ibid., 511-05, Ryan to J.N. Bennett, 3 April 1960.

15   Ibid., 309-02, Carter to Boyce, 16 May 1968; Carter to Rev. Edward Gatfield, 21 May 1968; Carter to J.T. Grannan, 29 May 1968: "I feel that you, Fathers Dick and Frank, have had some tendency to over-estimate the value of shock treatment."

16   Ibid., 286-01, "Redemptorist Community 645 Queen St. E. Toronto 8., March 4, 1969"; ibid., 195, "Brothers' Commission," 29 November 1969.

17   Ibid., "Provincial Consultations June 1966–1978," 17 January 1972. During the previous three years, the Redemptorists had rotated their men through Springhill, much to the concern of the archbishop. While short-term commitments fit into the Redemptorists' new policy, they did not build a long-term relationship and the archbishop requested that future

Redemptorist commitments in the archdiocese would guarantee that the men stay at least three years before being replaced. In a Congregation suffering personnel departures, such a promise was impossible. No new project replaced Springhill in the Halifax archdiocese.

18 Ibid., 286-05, Corriveau report on Montreal project, 27-28 April 1968, 4 March 1969; report on Lakeshore Experimental Project, 22 June 1970; Brian McKenna, "Three Young Priests with a mission – to disturb," *Montreal Star*, 12 April 1969.

19 The term, "mission to the disillusioned," comes from ARPT, 311-07, Leonard J. Crowley, auxiliary bishop of Montreal, to Thomas, 15 May 1974.

20 The Redemptorists eventually received almost $550,000 in irregular payments. For the newspaper report, see "St. Mary's. What might have been!" *Catholic Register*, 27 December 1969.

21 ARPT, 286-05, 17 April 1970.

22 Ibid., 950, E. O'Reilly to Council, 2 March 1970. In meeting with the council, O'Reilly stated that the councillors were all "crazy," because, in their reasoning, they could ask every Redemptorist, even Provincial Boyce, to demonstrate commitment by requesting a year's leave of absence. O'Reilly successfully argued on his own behalf that under canon law the council had no right to deprive a permanently-vowed religious of support except after a canonical dismissal. The council could and did ask the temporarily-vowed religious to leave.

23 Ibid., 125, "Meeting of Representative Priests with the Canadian Bishops," 7 April 1970, to discuss celibacy; "RC school rejects new 'crackpot' image," *Windsor Star*, 16 January 1970, reported that: "Charges have been levelled by Roman Catholic religious and lay persons that the Divine Word Centre in London is using its quarters as a 'sounding board for renegade crackpot' priests."

24 PAA, 79.187, R134/1, "Chronicle."

25 ARPT, 286-05, 13 April 1971.

26 Ibid., 26 April 1972. The Notre Dame Sisters had purchased the former Peterborough rectory.

27 Ibid., 286-01, "Minutes of the Meeting of the Provincial Council ... January 3-4, 1972"; "Minutes of Meeting of the Provincial Council — Toronto Province," [31 October–1 November 1973]; ibid., 286-05, Maloney, manuscript notes, 1 February 1972.

28 Ibid., 311-08 and 285, Thomas circular, 13 April 1972.

29 Ibid., 286-05, A.J.T. [Thomas], "Thoughts on the Direction of the Apostolate of the Toronto Province," for the E.P.C. meeting of 5-6 March 1974.

30 Ibid., 285, "Address to the Delegates to the Provincial Chapter," 28 June 1972; "Re: C.SS.R. Missions As We Are Preaching Them 10 Years After

The Opening of the Vatican Council II"; "Presentation on Preaching," 18-20 October 1972.

31 Ibid., 145-06, Sister M. Gerarda, "[History of the OSSR in Canada] August 1947."

32 Ibid., 146, McSherry to "Sister," 1 November 1968; ibid., 145-06, "Our History and the Toronto C.Ss.R. Province."

33 Ibid., 145-01, Pfab to Sister Superior and the Sisters of Keswick, 1 May 1971; ibid. 145-04, K. Johnson to F.V. Allen, auxiliary bishop of Toronto, 2 December 1971.

34 Ibid., 145-01, 8 August 1972. See also ibid., 146-02, Patricia Anne, OSsR, to Amaral, 10 June 1972.

35 Ibid., 145-01, K. Johnson to Dhont, 4 April 1974.

Chapter Ten: "Emerging Stability"

1 ARPT, 285, 17 June 1975.

2 The chapter of 1971 voted that $300,000 be set aside in a trust fund for the sick and needy: see ibid., 285, "Resolutions Passed by the Chapter of 1971."

3 Ibid., 312-01, "Annual Report," 20 June 1980.

4 Ibid., 285, "Address to Delegates – Opening of Provincial Chapter – January 27, 1976," 6.

5 Ibid., "Provincial Chapter. Toronto Province Minutes and Notes. Holy Redeemer College, Windsor, Ontario. February 7-9, 1977."

6 "The Redemptorists, A Study of The Spirit of the Founder, St. Alphonsus M. Liguori and of the Missionary Institute, The Congregation of the Most Holy Redeemer," (n.p. [1977?]).

7 ARPT, 148-02, Marcel Blais to Boyce, 24 February 1968; Boyce, "Impressions About the Maizuru Mission," 30 September 1968; "Meeting of the Fathers and Brothers of the Redemptorist Vice-Province of Maizuru, Japan," 7-8 October 1968.

8 Ibid., 148-30, Campbell to Tanaka, 21 August 1979; ibid., 766, Campbell to Maloney, 26 November 1979.

9 Ibid., 148-32, Horn to Maloney, n.d., received 28 August 1981; ibid., 148-01, Fuller to D. Ehman, 13 October 1947.

10 Ibid., 660, "Report of the Preaching Group re. GEM," 11 January 1980.

11 Ibid., 285, Minutes of the 1982 Provincial Chapters, 8.

12 "Minstrels," *Co-Redemptorist News*, September 1964. R. Nadeau, L. Norman, D. Purschke, P. Curtin, D. Ference, and F. Hrbolich were in the original group.

13 ARPT, 285, "Address to the Delegates – Opening of the Provincial Chapter – April 24, 1982."

14   Ibid., 311-09, memo., W.D. Murphy, September 1972. As chapels were planned in Quebec City's suburbs, the old chapel of Our Lady of Perpetual Help in Diamond Harbour (the Cove) closed in October of 1962. The old church of St. Patrick's on McMahon Street closed in 1966. Neglect and vandalism in 1968, and then a small earthquake and two fires in 1970 destroyed the old church. The land was sold in 1972. A chapel built in the new St. Lawrence College of St. Foy in 1959 became a subsidiary chapel to the new St. Patrick's on Grande Allée in 1964. By 1966 the St. Foy congregation became St. Vincent's parish. Since 1955, the Redemptorists cared for St. Stephen's congregation in Sillery; in 1967, Sillery's St. Stephen's chapel was built.

15   ARPSA, MA-Projets-9, Guy Pilote, "Le projet Saint Patrice," with correspondence between Maloney, Steacy, and Marc-André Boutin.

16   Twelve members out of a total of one hundred and five members living and belonging to the Toronto Province in 1981 were born in the province of Quebec. They were Fathers Gilbert Doyle, D'Arcy Egan, James Farrell, Raymond Fitzgerald, Martin Foley, Gerald Grant, William O'Flaherty, Leo Rolls, Desmond Scanlan, Alphonsus Thomas, Brothers Reginald (William Brytan) and Kevin (Matthew Garvey). These statistics do not include people born elsewhere yet adopting Quebec as home, such as Father William Murphy.

17   ARPT, 285, "Report to the E.P.C. from the Outreach Project Commission," November 1982.

18   PAA, 88.508, E. Kennedy, "The Redemptorists in Western Canada," 14-15.

19   ARPT, 285, "Minutes of the Provincial Chapter of the Toronto Province May 26-30, 1986," Appendix VIII, "Redemptorist Vocations."

20   Josephus Loew, "Ordo Faciendi Professionem CSSR," *SH* 5 (1957): 35-6; Andreas Sampers, "Epistulae 20 S. Alfonsi Ineditae," *SH* 13 (1965): 6-7; idem, "Institutum Oblatorum in Congregatione SS. Redemptoris Rectore Maiore N. Mauron, 1855-1893," *SH* 26 (1978): 75-142.

21   ARPT, 280-01, Ryan to Pankhurst, 22 May 1953.

22   Ibid., 307-06, K. Johnson to O'Reilly, 9 November 1961, asking whether Co-Redemptorists were to become a third order.

23   Ibid., 312-01, Maloney, "Annual Report," 11 February 1981.

24   Ibid., 285, "Analysis Statement on the Clerical Personnel Situation of the Toronto Province," 1978.

Epilogue

1   ARPT, 285, "Minutes of the Provincial Chapter of the Toronto Province May 20-24, 1985," citing Constitution 20.

2   Juan Manuel Lasso de la Vega, CSsR, "To Read the Signs of the Times," *Communicanda* 3 (8 September 1994): 17.

Select Bibliography

Asselin, Jean-Pierre. *Les Rédemptoristes au Canada. Implantation à Sainte-Anne-de-Beaupré 1878-1911*. Montreal: Bellarmin, 1981.

Boland, Samuel J., CSsR. *A Dictionary of the Redemptorists*. Rome: Collegium S. Alfonsi de Urbe, 1987.

Bolduc, Charles, CSsR, François Bouchard, CSsR, Gérard Lebel, CSsR and Gérard Tremblay, CSsR. *La Province Rédemptoriste de Ste-Anne-de-Beaupré. En Marche*. Ste-Anne-de-Beaupré: privately printed, 1993.

Byrne, John F., CSsR. *The Redemptorist Centenaries*. Philadelphia: Dolphin Press, 1932.

Carey, Patrick W. *People, Priests, and Prelates. Ecclesiastical Democracy and the Tensions of Trusteeism*. Notre Dame, Indiana: University of Notre Dame Press, 1987.

Choquette, Robert. *Language and Religion. A History of English-French Conflict in Ontario*. Ottawa: University of Ottawa Press, 1975.

Clarke, Brian P. *Piety and Nationalism: Lay Volunteer Associations and the Creation of an Irish-Catholic Community in Toronto, 1850–1895*. Montreal and Kingston: McGill-Queen's University Press, 1993.

Curley, Michael J., CSsR. *Bishop John Neumann, C.Ss.R. Fourth Bishop of Philadelphia*. Washington: Crusader Press, 1952.

————. *The Provincial Story. A History of the Baltimore Province of the Congregation of the Most Holy Redeemer*. New York: The Redemptorist Fathers, Baltimore Province, 1963.

Daly, George Thomas, CSsR. *Catholic Problems in Western Canada.* Toronto: Macmillan, 1921.

De Meulemeester, Maurice, CSsR. *Bibliographie générale des écrivains Rédemptoristes,* 3 vols. La Haye: Martinus Nijhoff, 1933–39.

————. *La Province Belge de la Congrégation du T.-S. Rédempteur 1841-1941.* Louvain: Saint-Alphonse, 1941.

————. *Outline History of the Redemptorists.* Louvain: Saint-Alphonse, 1956.

Dolan, Jay P. *Catholic Revivalism. The American Experience (1830-1900).* Notre Dame, Indiana: University of Notre Dame Press, 1978.

Fleming, David A., SM, ed. *Religious Life at the Crossroads.* New York and Mahwah, New Jersey: Paulist Press, 1985.

Geiermann, Peter, CSsR. *Annals of the Saint Louis Province.* 3 vols. St. Louis: privately printed, 1924.

Haering, Bernhard, CSsR. *The Law of Christ.* 3 vols. Westminster, MD: Newman Press, 1961–66.

————. *My Witness for the Church.* Translated by Leonard Swidler. New York and Mahwah, New Jersey: Paulist Press, 1992.

Hebblethwaite, Peter. *John XXIII. Pope of the Council.* 1984. Reprint London: Geoffrey Chapman, 1985.

————. *Paul VI: the First Modern Pope.* Mahwah, New Jersey: Paulist Press, 1993.

Hosp, Eduard, CSsR. *Erbe des hl. Klemens Hofbauer. Erlösermissionäre (Redemptoristen) in Österreich 1820–1951.* Vienna: 1953.

Hostie, Raymond, SJ. *Vie et mort des ordres religieux. Approches psychosociologiques.* Paris: Desclée de Brouwe, 1972.

Jones, Frederick M., CSsR. *Alphonsus de Liguori. The Saint of Bourbon Naples 1696–1787.* Dublin: Gill & Macmillan, 1992.

Lehmann, Heinz. *The German Canadians 1750–1937. Immigration, Settlement and Culture.* Translated by Gerhard P. Bassler. St. John's, Newfoundland: Jesperson Press, 1986.

Luciuk, Lubomyr, and Stella Hryniuk, ed. *Canada's Ukrainians: Negotiating an Identity*. Toronto: Ukrainian Canadian Centennial Committee and University of Toronto Press, 1991.

McGowan, Mark, and Brian P. Clarke, ed. *Catholics at the Gathering Place. Historical Essays on the Archdiocese of Toronto, 1841-1991*. Toronto: Dundurn Press, 1993.

Murphy, Terrence and Gerald Stortz, ed. *Creed and Culture. The Place of English-Speaking Catholics in Canadian Society, 1750-1930*. Montreal and Kingston: McGill-Queen's University Press, 1993.

O'Driscoll, Robert and Lorna Reynolds, ed. *The Untold Story: The Irish in Canada*. 2 vols. Toronto: Celtic Arts of Canada, 1988

O'Brien, David J. *Isaac Hecker: An American Catholic*. New York and Mahwah, New Jersey: Paulist Press, 1992.

O'Brien, William, CSB et al., eds. *Walking the Less Travelled Road. A History of the Religious Communities within the Archdiocese of Toronto 1841–1991*. Toronto: Archdiocese of Toronto, 1993.

Pitzer, Sister Mary Agnes. *As Ever, (Rev.) Daniel Ehman, C.SS.R.* Toronto: privately printed, 1978.

Rey-Mermet, Théodule, CSsR. *La morale selon St. Alphonse de Liguori*. Paris: Cerf, 1987.

Ruef, John J., CSsR. *Redemptorist Parish Missions 1945–1976. Survey Number Three*. Rome: Redemptorist General Secretariat for the Apostolate, 1979.

Schindler, Karl J., CSsR. *To Serve God's People. A Hundred Years of the Redemptorists at St. Patrick', the Cradle of the Toronto Province 1881–1981*. Toronto: privately printed, *c.* 1982.

Sharp, John. *Reapers of the Harvest. The Redemptorists in Great Britain and Ireland 1843-1898*. Oscott Series 4. Dublin: Veritas Publications, 1989.

Skinner, T. L[awrence], CSsR. *The Redemptorists in the West*. St. Louis, Missouri: privately printed, 1933.

Stroh, Paul T., CSsR. *Ilchester Memories: 1868-1957. The Golden Jubilee of the Redemptorist Novitiate at Ilchester, Maryland, 1907–1957.* St. Mary's College, Ilchester, Maryland: Redemptorist Fathers, 1957.

Taves, Ann. *The Household of Faith. Roman Catholic Devotions in Mid-Nineteenth-Century America.* Notre Dame, Indiana: University of Notre Dame Press, 1986.

Théberge, Rodrigue, CSsR. *Des rassembleurs d'hommes. La Congrégation du Très-Saint-Rédempteur. Les Rédemptoristes.* Sainte-Anne de Beaupré: Presses de la revue *Sainte Anne de Beaupré,* 1978.

Tremblay, Emilien, CSsR. *Le Père Delaere et l'église ukrainienne du Canada.* Ottawa: privately printed, 1960.

Vereecke, Louis, CSsR. *De Guillaume d'Ockham à Saint Alphonse de Liguori. Études d'histoire de la théologie morale moderne 1300–1787.* Bibliotheca Historica Congregationis SSmi Redemptoris Rome, vol. XII. Rome: Collegium S. Alfonsi de Urbe, 1986.

Voisine, Nive, ed. *Histoire du catholicisme québecois.* 3 vols. in 5 books. Published: vol. 2, books 1 and 2; vol 3, books 1 and 2. Montreal: Boréal, 1984–1991.

Werguet, Stanislaus, CSsR. *The Model Redemptorist Brother. A Manual of Spiritual Direction and Prayer.* Translated and adapted by Rev. Joseph W. Printon, CSsR. St. Louis, Missouri: Redemptorist Fathers, 1932.

Wissel, Joseph, CSsR. *The Redemptorist on the American Missions.* Third edition by Thomas Mullaney, CSsR. 3 vols., Norwood, Massachusetts: privately printed, 1920.

Index

Pointe-aux-Trembles, Quebec: 23
Poland: ix, xvii-xviii, xxvi, 149
Polish Canadians: 25, 89, 92, 131, 136, 152, 156, 184-5, 198
Poll tax: 208
Polygamy: 10-11
Poor, the: xx, 73, 118, 129, 155, 309
Pope, George: 192
Pope: John XXIII, 215, 234; John Paul I, 289; John Paul II, 188, 285, 289; Paul VI, 234, 250; Pius IX, xxiv, 24-5, 28; Pius XI, 159; Pius XII, 189, 215
Port Stanley, Ontario: 25
Portland, New Brunswick. *See* Saint John
Portuguese Canadians: 226
Poverty, vow of: xviii, xx, 19, 208, 287-8
Power, Albert: 300
Power, Charles: 211
Power, Michael: 19, 23
Power, Thomas: 50
Prayer: xx, 5, 15-6, 62, 180, 194, 232, 238, 250, 273
Preaching: xvii, xxi, 2, 15, 23, 68, 293, 306. *See also* Missions
Precious Blood Sisters: 198
Prescott, Ontario: 123-4, 173, 202
Prince Edward Island: 50-1, 145
Prince Rupert, British Columbia: 166, 231
Priorities: 286
Prison apostolate: 259-60. *See also* Collins Bay Penitentiary
Privileges, papal: 7
Propaganda Fide: 42, 193-4
Prost, Joseph: 18
Protestantism: 12-3, 23, 26, 34, 36, 50-1, 87, 118, 162-3, 198, 208; Anglicans, 10, 12-3, 51, 166; conversion, 8, 27, 39, 132; criticism of, 108, 213, 263; Holy Rollers (Hornerites), 124; Methodism, 12-3, 51; Ukrainian Canadians, 146, 149
Providence Villa (Centre), Scarborough: 285
Provinces, Redemptorist: 20-1; cooperation, 274-5
Provincial, office of: 21, 281; Edmonton: 283

Puchheim, Austria: 27
Puerto Rico: 81-2, 113, 164, 171
Purgatorian Society: 38, 49, 155, 165, 226
Purgatory: xxi
Puslinch Island, Ontario: 20

Q

Quebec City: 28, 211; English missions, 205; rectory, 120, 126, 144, 154; St. Brigid's Home, 142; St. Patrick, 32-41, 45, 48, 60, 63-4, 68-71, 77, 140, 144

R

Race relations: 189, 234
Radway district, Alberta: 137
Rahner, Karl: 234
Railway car chapel ministry: 131
Raus, Matthias, 75-9, 88
Reading, spiritual: xx, 16
Reardon, Fred: 302-4
Rebellions: 14, 18
Recollection: 15
Redemptorist Brothers' News: 227
Redemptorist Centre for Growth: 300-1
Redemptorist on the American Missions, The: 4, 59
Redemptorist Rosary: 352 n4
Redemptorist Survey for Renewal: 252
Redemptoristines, x, 180-3, 201, 207, 214, 275-7, 309
Refugees. *See* Chapel Grove
Regina, Saskatchewan: 122; Cathedral, 110, 117-8, 120, 130, 137; Ukrainian-Canadians, 152, 156, 183
Regionalism: 141, 224, 311
Reisach, Joseph: 1, 3, 8-11, 14-18, 21, 24, 27
Relics: 45, 56
Religious communities: x, 18, 160, 307, 309, 338 n37
Renewal: 8, 15, 40, 47-8, 62, 137, 313. *See also* Mission
Renouf, Thomas: 159
Rese, Frederick: 8, 12, 14
Responsibility, personal: 255
Retreats: xx, 15, 137, 145, 168-9, 194

Revelstoke, British Columbia: 167
Revivals: 7. *See also* Missions
Revolutions: xxvii, 20-1, 27
Richmond Hill, Ontario: 185
River Head, Newfoundland: 50
Rivière-des-Prairies, Quebec: 200
Rochester, New York: 18, 21-3, 75, 77
Rocky Mountain Vice-province: 81
Rocmora Nursing Home, Saint John: 285
Roman Province: 21
Romania: 3
Rosary: xx, 5, 16, 36, 194, 206
Roseau Vice-province: 189
Rosedale (Toronto), Ontario: 132
Rossbach, Philip: 344 n27
Ruland, George: 23-5
Rule, the: xx-xxiii, xxvii, 18, 20, 31, 39; 64, 77, 115, 130, 154, 180, 183, 188, 196; Americans, 71, 137-9; Constitutions and statutes: xx, 126, 204, 252, 285, 309; Redemptoristines, 180; revisions, 239, 250-1, 278, 284-5
Russia: xvii
Ryan, Arthur: lecturer, 143-5; military chaplain, 177, 179, 190; radio, 187; provincial, 201-27, 231, 233, 235-6, 241; later life, 240, 248-9
Ryan, Francis: 188
Rynne, Xavier. *See* Murphy, Francis-Xavier

S

S.E.R.V.E.: *See* Summer Endeavor in a Redemptorist Volunteer Experience
Sacraments: 4, 7, 9-10; sacramentals, 8
Sacred Congregation for Oriental Churches: 156
Sacred Congregation for Religious and Secular Institutes: 155, 261
Sacred Congregation for the Propagation of the Faith. *See* Propaganda Fide
Sacred Heart missions, Nelson, British Columbia: 167
Sacred Heart, Williams Lake: 166